Sicut lilium inter spinas sic amica mea inter filias

On The Cover: We use the symbol of the "lily among the thorns" from Song of Solomon 2:2 to represent the Baptist History Series. The Latin, ***Sicut lilium inter spinas sic amica mea inter filias***, translates, "As the lily among thorns, so is my love among the daughters."

THE

HISTORY

OF THE

English Baptists

Vol. I

HANSERD KNOLLYS
1598-1691

THE

HISTORY

OF THE

English Baptists,

FROM THE

REFORMATION

To the Beginning of the

Reign of King GEORGE I.

VOL. I.

CONTAINING

Their HISTORY to the RESTORATION of King CHARLES II.

By THO. CROSBY.

LONDON:

Printed for, and sold by, the EDITOR, either at his House in *Vine-Street, Minories*; or at his House upon *Horse-ly-down, Southwark*,

MDCCXXXVIII.

he Baptist Standard Bearer, Inc.

NUMBER ONE IRON OAKS DRIVE • PARIS, ARKANSAS 72855

Thou hast given a *standard* to them that fear thee;
that it may be displayed because of the truth.
-- *Psalm 60:4*

Reprinted
by

THE BAPTIST STANDARD BEARER, INC.
No. 1 Iron Oaks Drive
Paris, Arkansas 72855
(501) 963-3831

THE WALDENSIAN EMBLEM
lux lucet in tenebris
"The Light Shineth in the Darkness"

ISBN #1-57978-901-3

TO THE
READER.

I AM well aware, that some things contained in this history may awaken prejudice, censure, or displeasure, and occasion objections and offence, both to the treatise and my self. And I know that some have already declared their opinion, that facts which bring no credit to the persons of whom they are related, ought to be buried in oblivion. But such persons seem to me to be very ignorant of the duty of an historian. In answer to whom I shall only observe, that those heretical persons of the denomination of Baptists, on whom the sword of the magistrate fell so heavy, are yet upon record, and not omitted even by so late an author as the reverend Mr. Neal, and so exposed to the view of men from age to age. Therefore I thought t needful, as well as just, to have these things set in a clear open light, to disabuse all those who may have been imposed upon by false or partial and defective history in this matter, and to remove, or prevent, or allay, scandal, or censure, for time to come; and I am apt to think that many readers now and hereafter would have thought me partial, had I not taken notice of them. Neither do I think that it reflects any odium on the English Baptists, that some of their opinion in the point of Baptism, have been charged with heretical notions and heterodox opinions, Name me that body of christians in the world, which may not be equally, if not more, chargeable with the same. And yet I doubt not, God hath many faithful servants in this kingdom, amongst all the denominations of christians, who notwithstanding the imputation of heresy and heterodoxy charged on them by others, will be found among the blessed in the kingdom of glory.

And as it is utterly unreasonable to impute the miscarriages of some, to the rest of that body to which they belong,

belong, until they profeſs and manifeſt their approbation of them; ſo it is much more unreaſonable to impute the miſcarriages *and* bad principles *of perſons long ſince dead, to* thoſe, *who in ſome one point, now believe and act as they did, but own not, nor abet either their* bad principles, *or their* practical enormities.

Now though many, even of the learned, *and ſo late an* author *as Mr.* Neal, *from whom we might have looked for more chriſtian treatment, have made it their buſineſs to repreſent the* Anabaptiſts, *as they are pleaſed in contempt to ſtile them, in* odious colours, *and to write many* bitter things, *even* notorious falſhoods *concerning them, nay,* to faſten *doctrines upon them, which they never approved; yet, as ſhall be ſhewn in the ſequel of this* hiſtory, *no one ſect of chriſtians in this kingdom have merited more the favour and good eſteem of their* governours *and* chriſtian brethren, *by their peaceable carriage and behaviour towards them, than they have done. What* ſect *of chriſtians have ſhewed the like contentedneſs under the deprivations which the* legiſlature *has ſeen needful to lay upon the* Diſſenters *in general, than they? Who have been more content with the liberty allowed them by law than they? But not to be tedious in an epiſtolary way, I ſhall refer the* reader *to the work itſelf, and leave him to judge whether I deſerve to be* reproached *for avoiding partiality.*

He that conſiders the great trouble and pains that muſt attend the reading ſo many voluminous books, *to take in the compaſs of ſo many years included in this* hiſtory; *and the perplexing thoughts and difficulties under which an* author *labours, whoſe principal end is to ſet things in a juſt and fair light, will, if he be candid, eaſily paſs by ſmall faults and little inadvertencies; but if there ſhall appear in the courſe of this* hiſtory *any conſiderable miſtakes, I ſhall hold my ſelf obliged to ſuch* gentlemen, *who ſhall be pleaſed to repreſent them, promiſing to take the firſt opportunity that ſhall preſent, to retract or amend the ſame.*

Tho. Croſby.

THE PREFACE.

WHOEVER writes a Book ſeems by cuſtom obliged to write a *preface* to it; wherein it is expected, he ſhould ſhew the motives which induced him to write the ſame.

'TIS now many years ſince the materials, of which a great part of this treatiſe is formed, came into my hands. Had the ingenious collector of them lived to digeſt them in their proper order, according to his deſign, they would have appeared much more beautiful and correct, than now they do. I might here expatiate in his praiſe, and ſay a great deal of my own knowledge, both as to his induſtry and acquirements: But, as I ſhall hereafter have occaſion to mention him, I omit it here: And ſhall annex to this *preface* the ſeveral opinions of the firſt riſe of the *Baptiſts*, which he deſigned as an introduction to his intended hiſtory of them; being

Mr. Benj. Stinton.

ing the only piece of that work which he had compleated.

I WAS in hopes ſome able hand would have undertaken to compleat what was wanting, in order to finiſh this work. To render the ſame leſs burthenſome to ſuch an undertaker, I employed my ſpare hours, in the beſt manner I could, to digeſt the materials in their proper order, and ſupply the vacancies; till at length, at the requeſt of two worthy *Baptiſt* miniſters, both ſince deceaſed, I communicated them to the Reverend Mr. *Neal*, who had undertaken to write an *Hiſtory of the Puritans*; under which general name, I did apprehend the *Engliſh Baptiſts* might very well be included: And he had them in his hands ſome years.

Mr. Wallin. *Mr.* Arnold.

THE good character of the gentleman, with the importunity of my two friends afore-mentioned concurring (though I muſt confeſs it was with doubting) yet made me yield ſo to do. But I was ſurprized to ſee the ill uſe Mr. *Neal* made of theſe materials; and that the riſe and progreſs of the *Engliſh Baptiſts*, their confeſſion of faith, their character, and their ſufferings, were contained in leſs than five pages of his third volume; and that too with very great partiality, as ſhall hereafter be proved.

AND it is but too well known, concerning *Pædobaptiſt* authors in general, that when they have been neceſſitated to ſpeak in favour of the opinion of the *Baptiſts*, preſently a vail has been drawn over the ſame, either reſpecting their perſons, principles, or morals; ſo that it is not an eaſy thing for ſtrangers to form a right judgment of them; which

which makes an hiſtory of them neceſſary, without any further apology. Yet, conſidering the great variety of opinions and humours that are in this kingdom, and the coarſe treatment even of the moſt celebrated authors, upon the moſt ſublime ſubjects; a man had need have a good ſhare of courage, and a firm aſſurance of the juſtice of his cauſe, that ventures to appear publickly in ſuch a cenſorious age.

THE *Editor* does preſume he is thus ſupported; and declares, That what he has here written is purely deſigned to inform the honeſt and well-meaning Chriſtian, whether *Pædobaptiſt*, or *Baptiſt*; by whom he hopes it may be candidly received, in proportion to the integrity of his intentions.

Mr. *Neal*, in his preface, concludes thus: 'I am ſufficiently aware of the delicacy of 'the affairs treated of in this volume, and of 'the tenderneſs of the ground I go over; 'and, though I have been very careful of 'my temper and language, and have endeavoured to look into the myſterious conduct of the ſeveral parties with all the indifference of a ſpectator, I find it very 'difficult to form an exact judgment of the 'moſt important events, or to ſpeak freely 'without offence; therefore, if any paſſionate or angry writer ſhould appear againſt 'this, or any of the former Volumes, I 'humbly requeſt the reader to pay no regard 'to perſonal reflections, or to inſinuations of 'any ill deſigns againſt the eſtabliſh'd religion, or the publick peace, which are entirely groundleſs.

Hiſtory of the Puritans, Vol. III.

'In historical debates, says he, nothing 'is to be received upon trust, but facts are to 'be examined, and a judgment formed upon 'the authority by which those facts are sup-'ported; by this method we shall arrive at 'truth: And if it shall appear, that, in the 'course of this long history, there are any 'considerable mistakes, the world may be 'assured I will take the first opportunity to 'retract or amend them".

A NOBLE declaration, indeed! But let us now see how consentaneous his representation of the *English Baptists* is thereto, especially, considering what materials he was intrusted with.

He allows there were no less than fifty four congregations of them in *England* in the year 1644. and says:

Vol. III. *p.* 161. 'Their confession [of faith] consisted of 'fifty two articles, and is strictly *Calvini-'stical* in the doctrinal part, and according 'to the independant discipline; it confines 'the subject of baptism to grown Christians, 'and the mode to dipping; it admits of 'gifted lay-preachers, and acknowledges a 'due subjection to the civil magistrate in all 'things lawful".

He proceeds then to their character; which, in my opinion, is one piece of that *tender ground* he was to go over: And how careful he was of his temper and language, let the reader judge. For, says he,

Ib. *p.* 162. 'The advocates of this doctrine were, 'for the most part, of the meanest of the 'people; their preachers were generally 'illiterate, and went about the countries 'making proselytes of all that would sub-

'mit

'mit to their immersion, without a due re-'gard to their acquaintance with the prin-'ciples of religion, or their moral cha-'racters".

WHAT a malicious slander is this! cast upon a whole body of Christians, consisting of fifty four congregations, according to his own acknowledgment! To me it seems unchristian, without ground, a fact unexamined, a judgment formed without any authority produced to support the fact; and consequently the reader left to form his judgment upon Mr. *Neal*'s *ipse dixit*, repugnant to his noble declaration.

But lest this should not be enough, he concludes their character by adding thus:

'The people of this perswasion were more 'exposed to the publick resentments, because 'they would hold communion with none but 'such as had been dipped. All, says he, 'must *pass under this cloud* before they 'could be received into their churches; and 'the same *narrow spirit* prevails too general-'ly amongst them even at this day".

THIS is a home stroke; and reaches the present as well as preceding ages. But I am verily perswaded the present *English Baptists* will not be much affected with his raillery; since our blessed Lord and Saviour himself did not disdain to *pass under this cloud*, as Mr. *Neal* is pleased to phrase it.

DR. *Featly*, writing against the *Baptists* in his day, says: 'He could hardly dip his pen 'in any other liquor, than the juice of gall". And I find Mr. *Neal* has not only read the *Doctor*, because he quotes him two or three times, but learned some of his language too: What of wit he may imagine in ſuch kind of phraſeology, I know not; but ſure I am, *Chriſt's Ordinances* ought to be mentioned with more reverence, by thoſe who profeſs themſelves to be Chriſtians.

THE ingenious Dr. *Wall*, in his elaborate hiſtory of infant baptiſm, ſpeaking of the moſt ancient rites in baptiſm, acknowledges dipping to be ordinarily uſed in baptiſm. For, ſays he:

Vol. II. *p.* 291. 'THEIR general and ordinary way was 'to baptiſe by immerſion, or dipping the 'perſon, whether it were an infant, or grown 'man or woman, into the water. This, 'he adds, is ſo plain and clear, by an infinite 'number of paſſages, that as one cannot but 'pity the weak endeavours of ſuch *Pædobaptiſts*, as would maintain the negative of 'it; ſo alſo we ought to diſown, and ſhew 'a diſlike of the profane ſcoffs which ſome 'people give to the *Engliſh Anti-Pædobaptiſts*, 'merely for their uſe of dipping. 'Tis one 'thing to maintain, that that circumſtance is 'not abſolutely neceſſary to the eſſence of 'baptiſm; and another, to go about to re'preſent it as ridiculous and fooliſh, or as 'ſhameful and indecent; when it was, in all 'probability, the way by which our bleſſed 'Saviour, and for certain was the moſt uſual 'and ordinary way by which the ancient 'Chriſtians, did receive their baptiſm".

AND, ſpeaking of the preſent ſtate of the *Anti-Pædobaptiſts* in *England*, he ſays:

Ib. p. 216. 'THEY, that are now, are as commend'able, as any other ſort of men are, for a 'ſober and grave, quiet and peaceable way 'of living. They profeſs obedience to Ma-

giſtrates:

'gistrates: *And a little further*, They are 'particularly commended for maintaining 'their poor liberally; as also for passing 'censures upon such members of their own 'congregations as live disorderly. This cha-'racter of obedient subjects, is what they 'now own and profess, and what I hope is 'the real sentiment of most of them".

AND I add, it was what they did always own and profess ever since they had a being in this kingdom; and that neither Dr. *Wall*, nor any other, is able to prove the contrary. His silly story about Mr. *Hicks*, I find in his latter edition, is recanted; therefore shall say nothing about it.

BISHOP *Burnet*, speaking of the *English* *Baptists*, gives them this character: *History of his own Time*, p. 702.

'THE *Anabaptists*, says he, were generally men of virtue, and of an universal 'charity".

AND I would here observe, That though in the title page of this book, and throughout the same, I use the term *Baptist*, except in quotations from authors; it is not, as Dr. *Wall* observes, to cast a reproach on our adversaries; but because I think it the most proper term, by which we can be distinguished from other Christians.

INDEED he says: 'As they disown the 'name of *Anabaptists*, or *Rebaptizers*, so 'I have no where given it to them. As on 'the contrary, I do not give them the name 'of *Baptists*, nor of the baptized people; 'for that is to cast a reproach upon their ad-'versaries, as concluding that they are not so. 'Every party, while the matter continues in 'dispute, ought to give and take such names *Dr.* Wall, *p.* 2, 99.

'as caſt no reproach on themſelves, nor their 'opponents, but ſuch as each of them own; 'and ſuch are the names that I uſe."

So that this worthy gentleman has taken upon himſelf to be our godfather, and given us the name of *Anti-Pædobaptiſts:* But, as we are not infants, we have an undoubted right to put in our exceptions.

BESIDES the length of the word, for I do not love hard names, it ſeems to me no proper name; becauſe the people called *Quakers*, from whom we differ in judgment, as well as from the *Pædobaptiſts*, may be included; and therefore I have rejected it. Neither ſhall I think that he has aſſumed to himſelf and party a proper name, till ſprinkling, pouring, or any other way of waſhing beſides dipping, is fairly proved to be baptiſm, either from ſcripture or antiquity.

BUT, to return to Mr. *Neal.* If he would have us to underſtand by his ill-natured phraſe, *narrow Spirit*, that he means, becauſe we will not receive unbaptized perſons to the communion of our churches, therefore we are a people of *narrow Spirits*; then the deſigned reproach, which he would fix on the *Engliſh Baptiſts*, fits all the chriſtian churches in all ages: For it is their declared opinion, That no perſons unbaptized ought to be received to the communion of the chriſtian church, and they practiſe accordingly.

To omit a cloud of witneſſes I might produce, who concur in their teſtimonies, that this *great ordinance of baptiſm*, is not only the ſacrament of *initiation*, but alſo to be continued in the church unto the end of the world, I ſhall

I ſhall only add a few general and comprehending teſtimonies:

1. In the articles of religion, publiſhed by his Majeſty's ſpecial command, *Anno* 1642. we have the judgment of the *church* of *England*, viz.

'Baptism is not only a ſign of profeſ-'ſion, and mark of difference, whereby 'chriſtian men are diſcerned from others that 'be not chriſtned; but it is alſo a ſign of re-'generation, or new birth, whereby, as by 'an inſtrument, they that receive baptiſm 'rightly are grafted into the church; the pro-'miſes of the forgiveneſs of ſin, and of our 'adoption to be the ſons of God by the 'Holy Ghoſt, and viſibly ſigned and ſealed; 'faith is confirmed, and grace increaſed by 'virtue of prayer unto God, *&c.*"

2. The judgment of the *Presbyterians*, ſuitable to which they expreſs themſelves in their larger and ſhorter catechiſms, we find in the confeſſion of faith put forth by the aſſembly of divines, *Anno* 1658.

'Baptism, ſay they, is a ſacrament of 'the *New Teſtament*, ordained by Jeſus 'Chriſt, not only for the ſolemn admiſſion of 'the party baptized into the viſible church, '*but alſo to be unto him a ſign and ſeal of the* '*covenant of grace, of his ingrafting into* '*Chriſt, of regeneration, of remiſſion of ſins,* '*and of his giving up unto God, through* '*Jeſus Chriſt, to walk in newneſs of life:* 'Which ſacrament is by Chriſt's own ap-'pointment to continue in his church until 'the end of the world".

3. The

3. THE judgment of the *Congregational* (commonly called *Independent*) churches, we have in their confeſſion of faith at the *Savoy*; where were many of their Elders in *October* 1658, printed *Anno* 1659.

'BAPTISM, ſay they, *is a ſacrament of 'the New Teſtament, ordained by Jeſus 'Chriſt, to be unto the party baptized, a 'ſign and ſeal of the covenant of grace, of 'his ingrafting into Chriſt, of regeneration, 'of remiſſion of ſins, and of his giving up 'unto God, through Jeſus Chriſt, to walk 'in newneſs of life: Which ordinance is 'by Chriſt's own appointment to be con-'tinued in his church until the end of the 'world*".

4. THE *Engliſh Baptiſts* judgment you have in their confeſſion of faith, *Appendix* N° 2. Art. XXXIX. and N° 3. Art. XXIV.

IT is certainly commendable to keep the ordinances of Chriſt pure, as they were delivered; becauſe it prevents the creeping in of the inventions of men in the worſhip of God. Man is naturally apt to be medling that way, and mixing ſomething of his own with thoſe ſacred inſtitutions which God has with greateſt ſeverity prohibited; having not ſpared any, no not his own people, though what they have done ſeems not to be out of any wicked intentions, but rather out of an ignorant zeal: Of which there are many inſtances in ſcripture.

The Reverend Mr. *Neal* would do well to convince the *Engliſh Baptiſts*, That *ſprinkling* of *infants* is the *baptiſm* which Chriſt in-

2 ſtituted,

ſtituted, and the Apoſtles practiſed. For we grant, that it is praiſe-worthy for the churches of Jeſus Chriſt to preſerve and keep the ordinances of Chriſt, as they have been delivered by Chriſt and his Apoſtles to them. And if, after a full and fair conviction from ſcripture, we remain ſtill obſtinate, a worſe name than that of *narrow Spirits* might be juſtly fixed on us.

I SHALL only reply to Mr. *Neal* in the words of the Reverend Mr. *Jeremiah Burroughs*; who, though a *Pædobaptiſt*, very excellently expreſſes himſelf in his book, intituled, *Goſpel Worſhip, or the right Manner of ſanctifying the Name of God*, p. 8, 9, *&c.* His words are theſe:

'ALL things in God's worſhip muſt have 'a warrant out of God's word, muſt be 'commanded; it is not enough that it is not 'forbidden, and what hurt is there in it? 'but it muſt be commanded ——— When 'we come to *matters of religion*, and the '*worſhip of God*, we muſt either have a '*command*, or ſome-what out of *God's word*, 'by ſome conſequence drawn from ſome '*command*, wherein God manifeſts his will; 'either a *direct command*, or by comparing 'one thing with another, or drawing conſequences *plainly* from the words, we muſt 'have a *warrant* for the *worſhip* of God, *&c.* '——— When any creature is raiſed in a 'religious way above what it hath in it by 'nature, if I have not ſcripture to warrant 'me, I am therein *ſuperſtitious* ——— We 'muſt be all *willing worſhippers*, but not '*will worſhippers*. You ſee how ſevere God 'was to *Nadab* and *Abihu*, for but taking *page* 10.

'*other*

‘ *other fire*, than that which God appointed’
‘ to offer up incenſe, though there was no di-
‘ rect commandment *againſt* it, *&c.*

page 11. ‘ In the matters of *worſhip* God ſtands
‘ upon *little* things; ſuch things as ſeem to
‘ be very ſmall and little to us, yet God
‘ ſtands much upon them in the matter of
‘ worſhip. For there is nothing wherein the
‘ prerogative of God doth more appear than
‘ in worſhip, as princes ſtand much upon
‘ their prerogatives——There are things
‘ in the worſhip of God that are not written
‘ in our *hearts*, that only depend upon the
‘ will of God revealed in his word; which
‘ were no duties except they were revealed
‘ there. And theſe are of ſuch a nature as
‘ we can ſee no reaſon for, but only this, *be-*
‘ *cauſe God will have them*——Though men
‘ would think it a little matter, whether *this*
‘ fire or *that* fire, and will not *this* burn as
‘ well as *that?* but God ſtands upon it —
‘ When *Uzzah* did but touch the ark, when
‘ it was ready to fall, we would think it no
‘ great matter; but one touch of the ark
‘ coſt him his life. There is not a *Minim* in
‘ the *worſhip* of *God*, but *God* ſtands migh-
‘ tily upon it——For a man to gather a
‘ few ſticks on the ſabbath, what great mat-
‘ ter was it? but God ſtands upon it. So
‘ when the men of *Bethſhemeſh* did but look
‘ into the ark, it coſt the lives of fifty thou-
‘ ſand and ſeventy men, *&c.*

page 12. *He further adds*, ‘ That there is no
‘ privileges or dignities of man that can
‘ ſecure them from God's ſtroke; inſtancing
‘ *Nadab* and *Abihu*'s caſe, *Moſes* the man of
‘ God being their uncle, and *Aaron* their fa-
‘ ther,

'ther, men newly consecrated to the priests 'office, renowned men that God put much 'glory upon; yet, if they will venture but 'to offend God in this little thing, his wrath 'breaks out upon them, and kills them pre-'sently, *&c.*"

HE adds much more to the same effect, and offers several reasons by which he judgeth that *Nadab* and *Abihu* were good men; and gives a plain demonstration that they had no wicked design: As,

1. THEY were young men, newly come to their office, and might not understand all things, as if they had had longer experience.

2. IT's observable, for *ver.* 1. 'tis called *strange fire which he commanded not*, that if there be not a command for our practice, nor such a president as the scripture approves of, no human *pretence* can excuse the transgressor from the judgment of God.

Will Mr. *Neal* admit *Roman Catholicks*, who profane the ordinance of the supper, to the communion of his church? We believe in our consciences that sprinkling children is a profanation of the ordinance of baptism, and so consequently reject it; therefore our spirits will appear no narrower than his own. And if, upon a serious review of this passage last quoted, he will endeavour to be careful of his temper, I may hope in the next edition to see it appear in better language.

WITH respect to their sufferings Mr. *Neal* very justly observes, that ministers have a right by preaching to oppose doctrines *; but

* *Such as they believe to be erroneous, I would suppose he means.*

un-

unjuſtifiable at the ſame time to fight them with the ſword of the civil magiſtrate, and ſhut them up in priſon: And then mentions five or ſix, with little more than their names, of whom he had a large account, reſpecting their ſufferings, before him. But they were *Baptiſts*, and ſo not worthy of his notice, unleſs he can add ſomething to degrade them.

page 163. The firſt he mentions is Mr. *Henry Denne*; of whom he only ſays, he was formerly ordained by the biſhop of St. *Davids*, and poſſeſſed of the living of *Pyeton* in *Hertfordſhire*. Then he mentions Mr. *Coppe*; and ſays, he was miniſter in *Warwickſhire*, and ſome time preacher to the garriſon in *Compton Houſe*.

The next he mentions is Mr. *Hanſerd Knollys*; who was, ſays he, 'Several times 'before the committee for preaching *Antinomianiſm*, and *Anti-Pædobaptiſm*; and being forbid to preach in the publick churches, 'he opened a ſeparate meeting in great 'St. *Hellens*; from whence he was quickly 'diſlodged, and his followers diſperſed".

If *Antinomianiſm* be ſuch a brand of infamy, as to put a vail upon the character of ſo good and pious a man as Mr. *Hanſerd Knollys*; how came it to paſs that Dr. *Criſp* had more than a whole page beſtowed on him in encomiums to his praiſe, which I doubt not but he juſtly deſerved? If I may be permitted to anſwer without offence, and incurring the cenſure of an angry writer; it ſhould be, becauſe he was an *Independent Pædobaptiſt*.

IN the next place he says, ‘ Mr. *Andrew* ‘ *Wyke*, in the county of *Suffolk*, was impri- ‘ soned on the same account; and Mr. *Oates* ‘ in *Essex* tried for his life at *Chelmsford* as- ‘ sizes for the murder of *Ann Martin*, be- ‘ cause she died a few days after her immer- ‘ sion of a cold that seized her at that time”.

THIS is so unrighteous a piece of partiality, that no sentence too severe can be passed upon it; because he had before him a full account of that affair; and thereby knew how honourably he was acquitted, notwithstanding the most earnest and pressing endeavours of his *Pædobaptist* Brethren to bring him in guilty, thereby to fix an odium on the practice of immersion.

I WAS at a stand why this gentleman's christian name, *Samuel*, was left out in Mr. *Neal*'s narration; seeing Mr. *Neal* had it before him. And I can assign no other reason for it, unless it were to impose on his readers, that they might take him to be *Titus Oates*, so noted in our histories with a brand of infamy upon him. But I must leave that to his own conscience; and refer my readers to page 236 of this history, where they will find, among others, the same account of these persons mentioned by Mr. *Neal* as communicated to him, and leave them to judge of his partiality in this matter.

To bring up the rear of the *Baptists* sufferings; poor *Laurence Clarkson*, with his recantation at large, is exhibited.

AMONG the thousands of *Baptists* in *England* here is one produced; who, through the severity of the times, and being but an unsteady

ſteady man in his principles, and one that had not been uſed to ſuffer for conſcience ſake, was tempted to make this recantation, finding he could no other way obtain his liberty.

He had been ſix months in priſon, committed by the *Pædobaptiſt* committee of *Suffolk*, for that ſo heinous a crime of baptizing by immerſion; a crime ſo great, that all the interceſſion of his friends, though he had ſeveral, could not procure his releaſe; the committee being fully reſolved not to let ſuch crimes go unpuniſhed: Nay, though an order came down, either from a committee of parliament, or chairman of it, to diſcharge him, yet they refuſed to obey it.

Mr. *Edwards*, who firſt publiſhed this account, did it to expoſe the ſectaries, againſt whom he had an implacable hatred. But, whether the weakneſs of this man under his oppreſſion, or the folly and wickedneſs of his perſecutors, were hereby more expoſed, let the reader judge.

However, the *Pædobaptiſts* gain'd no great honour by a proſelyte made after this manner: For upon his releaſe he turned *ſeeker*; and when the *Baptiſts* expelled him from their ſociety, as a man that had denied the truth to eſcape ſuffering, he writ a ſmall Pamphlet *, wherein he endeavours to excuſe himſelf, by ſaying, That he did not aſſert the baptiſm of believers by immerſion to be an error, but only intended that it was erroneouſly practiſed, there being now no true churches, nor true

* *The Pilgrimage of Saints by Church caſt out; in Chriſt found ſeeking truth.*

admin-

administrators of that ordinance. And it is no wonder, that a person who could make such a vile submission to his worshipful persecutors, should afterwards make such equivocations, to extenuate his crime.

BISHOP *Jewel* signed the popish articles; and archbishop *Cranmer* subscribed a recantation. Here are for Mr. *Neal* two eminent *Pædobaptist* Recanters, for one poor Baptist: And if he has any more such instances, I will endeavour to supply him at the same rate.

Fuller, *Cant.* 16. *Lib.* 8. *p.* 9, 23.

THIS partiality of Mr. *Neal* revived my resolution to compleat this Treatise, in the best manner I could, for a publication; and what is wanting in it of elegancy of phrase, hath been endeavoured to be supplied in the truth of the relation, which is the only commendation of history, and much preferable to that artificial stuff, which may find better access to some ears.

AND therefore to the *English reader* I would now address my self, because in this land were these actions done; and their fore-fathers, with bleeding hearts and distilling eyes, were spectators of, and common sufferers under, the insulting paces of tyrannical, arbitrary power, and unlimited prerogative, and had a cup of blood prepared for them; though, blessed be God, it is otherwise with us.

THIS Essay being the first of the kind, that has been published in this kingdom, it is to be hoped some abler hand in time may improve the same, and a more full account be given of the *English Baptists*.

THE design of the reverend Mr. *Benjamin Stinton*'s History being to give an account of the *English Baptists* only, he thought it might not be improper, and did intend to introduce it with ſome account of the origin of their opinion, and who have been reported to be the authors of it. And ſince there are various accounts given of this matter, ſays he, I ſhall briefly relate the different opinions about it, as well thoſe held by the *Pædobaptiſts*, as thoſe of the *Anti-Pædobaptiſts*, concerning their own original, and then leave the reader to judge which has the greateſt appearance of truth.

THEY are generally condemned as a new *ſect*, whoſe opinion and practice, with relation to baptiſm, was not known in the Chriſtian church till about two hundred years ago. Biſhop *Burnet* ſays, 'At this time [*anno* 1549] 'there were many *Anabaptiſts* in ſeveral parts 'of *England*. They were generally *Germans*, whom the revolutions there had forced 'to change their ſeats. Upon *Luther*'s firſt 'preaching in *Germany*, there aroſe many, 'who building on ſome of his principles, carried things much further than he did. The 'chief foundation he laid down was, that the 'ſcripture was to be the only rule of Chriſtians. Upon this many argued, that the 'myſteries of the Trinity, and Chriſt's incarnation and ſuffering, of the fall of man, 'and the aids of grace, were indeed philoſophical ſubtilties, and only pretended to be 'deduced from ſcripture, as almoſt all opinions of religion were, and therefore they 'rejected them. Among theſe the baptiſm 'of infants was one: They held that to be 'no baptiſm, and ſo were re-baptized. But 'from this; which was moſt taken notice of, 'as

Hiſt. Ref. Part II. p. 110.

'as being a visible thing, they carried all the 'general name of *Anabaptists*.'

MR. *Marshal* says, 'That the first that 'ever made a head against it [infant-bap- 'tism] or a division in the church about it, 'was *Baltazar Pacommitanus* in *Germany*, 'in *Luther*'s time, about the year 1527.' This *Baltazar* is stiled *Baltazar Huebmar Pacimontanus*, Dr. in *Waldshut*, a town near the *Helvetians*. He was a man of great note for learning, and did by his preaching and writing very much promote his opinion. He was burnt at *Viana*, in 1528. for which he is esteemed a martyr by his followers.

Sermon on Infant-baptism, p. 5.

Zuinglius, *in the epistle before his answer to his book on Baptism.*

BUT, says Mr. *Tombs*, *Bellarmine* and *Cochleus* say, that *Erasmus* himself had sowed some seeds of it also. And whoever reads his works, will find several things in them favouring the opinion of the *Anti-Pædobaptists*: As when he saith, in his union of the church, 'It is no where expressed, in the 'apostolical writings, that they baptized 'children;' and again, upon *Rom.* vi. 'Bap- 'tizing of children was not in use in St. *Paul*'s 'time; and that they are not to be con- 'demned, who doubt whether childrens bap- 'tism was ordained by the Apostles.'

Examen. p. 22.

De ratio Conc.

JOHN GERHARD, a *Lutheran* minister, derives the original of this sect from *Carolostadius*, who was conversant with *Luther*, *Melancthon*, and the other reformers, and assisted them in that blessed work. He says, that he is called the father of the *Anabaptists*, by *Erasmus Alberus*.

Tom. 40. *of his Common Places.*

SLEIDAN, who writ the history of the *Anabaptists*, does not go so far, but asserts of him, 'that he praised their opinion.'

OSIANDER affirms, ‘ that he joined ‘ himſelf to them.’

MELANCTHON, who was well acquainted, both with the man and his opinions, ſays of him, ‘ that he endeavoured to promote the goſpel, tho’ in a wrong courſe.’

Com. 1 *epiſt. Cor.* ix. 24.

Page 6.

The ſhort hiſtory of the *Anabaptiſts*, publiſhed in 1647, ſays; ‘ It is hard to ſay, whether *Caroloſtadius*, or one *Nicholas Stork*, ‘ was the firſt founder of baptiſm.’

Hiſt. Anab. Lib. ii. Sect. ii.

Tombe's Examen. p. 22.

ARNOLDUS MESHOVIUS, another hiſtorian of thoſe times, lays it ſtill nearer the door of the firſt reformers; and ſays, ‘ That ‘ the buſineſs of *Anabaptiſm* began at *Wittenburg*, anno Chriſti 1522. *Luther* then lurking in the caſtle of *Wartpurg* in *Thuringia*, ‘ by *Nicholas Pelargus*; and that he had companions at firſt, *Caroloſtadius*, *Philip Melancthon*, and others; and that *Luther* returning from his *Patmos*, as he called it, ‘ baniſhed *Caroloſtadius*, and the reſt, and ‘ only received *Philip Melancthon* into favour ‘ again.’

These paſſages make it probable that this queſtion abount Infant-baptiſm was agitated among the reformers themſelves, and that ſome of them were at firſt for rejecting that practice.

De Rit. Bap. Lib. ii. c. 1.

Wall, Part II. p. 179.

VICECOMES, a learned *Papiſt*, has left upon record, that *Luther*, *Calvin*, and *Beza*, were adverſaries of infant-baptiſm: Though the *Pædobaptiſts* look upon this only as a ſlander caſt upon them.

’Tis certain that *Zuinglius*, that holy and learned reformer, who flouriſhed about the year 1520, was for ſome time againſt it, as he ingenuouſly confeſſes, in theſe words: ‘ When

'When this opinion was every where so 'rashly and without consideration received, 'That all men believed that faith was con-'firmed by signs, we must necessarily expect 'this sad issue, that some would even deny 'baptism to infants; for how should it con-'firm the faith of infants, when it is manifest 'that they as yet have no faith? Wherefore 'I my self, that I may ingenuously confess 'the truth, some years ago, being deceived 'with this error, thought it better that chil-'drens baptism should be delayed, till they 'came to full age: Though (adds he) I never 'broke forth into that immodesty and impor-'tunity, as some now do.'

De Bap. Tom. II. p. 63.

Baxter's Scripture Proofs, p. 291.

If some of the other reformers were at first of this opinion, as his Words imply, yet they might think it impracticable to carry their reformation so far at once, and that it might overthrow what they had already so happily done: And when some of this opinion afterwards had brought a scandal upon the *Protestants*, and occasioned such confusions all over *Germany*, they might be tempted to renounce this opinion, and write with so much zeal and anger, as they did against those who maintained it.

'Tis still more evident, that these first reformers look'd upon sprinkling as a corruption of baptism, and endeavoured to introduce the primitive rite of dipping, as is practised by the *English Baptists*.

LUTHER has, in several places, fully declared his opinion in this matter:

'Baptism, saith he, is a *Greek* word; 'it may be termed a dipping, when we dip 'something in water, that it may be wholly

Duveil *on* *Acts* viii. 38. 'covered with water: And although that 'custom be now altogether abolished among 'the most part, for neither do they dip the 'whole children, but only sprinkle them with 'a little water, they ought altogether never-'theless to be dipt, and presently to be drawn 'out again; for the etymology of the word 'seems to require that.'

In another place he says; 'Washing from 'sins is attributed to baptism; it is truly in-'deed attributed, but the signification is softer 'and slower than that it can express baptism, 'which is rather a sign both of death and re-'surrection. Being moved by this reason, 'I would have those that are to be baptized, 'to be altogether dipt into the water, as the 'word doth sound, and the mystery doth 'signify.'

And that this was the opinion and practice of the chief leaders in the reformation, appears by something remarkable, that happen'd in those times concerning this matter.

JOHANNES BUGENHAGIUS POMERANIUS, who was a companion of *Luther*, and succeeded him in the ministry at *Wittenburg*, a very pious and learned divine, tells us, in a book he published in the *German* tongue, *Anno* 1542,

'That he was desired to be a witness of 'a baptism at *Hamburgh*, in the year 1529. 'That when he had seen the minister only 'sprinkled the infant wrapped in swathling-'clothes on the top of the head, he was 'amazed; because he neither heard nor saw 'any such thing*, nor yet read in any history,

* *Among the Protestants I suppose he meant.*

'except

'except in case of necessity, in bed-rid per-'sons. In a general assembly therefore of all 'the ministers of the word, that was convened, 'he did ask of a certain minister, *John Fritz* 'by name, who was some time minister of '*Lubec*, how the sacrament of baptism was 'administred at *Lubec?* Who for his piety 'and candour did answer gravely, that infants 'were baptized naked at *Lubec*, after the 'same fashion altogether as in *Germany*. 'But from whence and how that peculiar 'manner of baptizing hath crept into *Ham-*'*burgh*, he was ignorant. At length they 'did agree among themselves, that the judg-'ment of *Luther*, and of the divines of *Wit-*'*temburg*, should be demanded about this 'point: Which being done, *Luther* did write 'back to *Hamburgh*, that this sprinkling was 'an abuse, which they ought to remove, 'Thus plunging was restored at *Hamburgh*.'

BUT notwithstanding this, Dr. *Featly* and many others will have it, that *Anabaptism* took its first rise at *Munster*; and that *Nicholas Stork*, *Thomas Muncer*, *John* of *Leyden*, *Mark Stubner*, *Knipperdoling*, *Phiffer*, and such like, were the first teachers of this doctrine, and founders of the sect.

THESE men denied the doctrine of the Trinity, the incarnation of Christ, the authority of magistrates, the lawfulness of taking oaths, and almost all the Christian doctrines; and were guilty of several gross enormities, such as poligamy, rebellion, theft and murder; They seized the city of *Munster*, proclaimed *John* of *Leyden* their king, committed abundance of violence, and caused tumults and rebellions in several places.

THE extravagant doctrines, and seditious practices of these men, are every where charged upon the opposers of infant-baptism, to render them odious, and a dangerous and seditious sect, not fit to be tolerated in any nation, whose principles have so bad a tendency, and whose beginning was so scandalous.

IN return to all which, the *Baptists* alledge in their own defence, that the *Papists* improve this story after the like manner, against the new begun reformation it self, and represent it as the consequence of letting men have the scriptures to read, and the liberty of judging for themselves in matters of religion.

THAT there is great reason to suspect the truth of many things reported of this People, is evident: For in a time of war, and popular tumults, it is not easy to come at a certain knowledge of what is transacted; and if a design miscarries, it is generally censured, how just or good soever it was. The *Roman Catholicks* charge the *Vaudois*, and *Albigeois*, and sometimes the *Lutherans*, with crimes almost as black as they do these *Anabaptists*: And as for the Protestants of those times, they persecuted this sect with so much cruelty, and wrote against them with so much bitterness, that it discredits very much what they say of them, at least makes it probable they took up some reports concerning them upon very slender evidence.

Bayle's Dictionary, Anabaptists.

NEITHER do the histories of those times agree in the accounts they give of them; for some charge them with more crimes, and much greater, than others do; some accuse them with those things which are directly contrary to what is affirmed of them by others; and

and ſome with things ſo incredible, that their adverſaries themſelves look upon them to be but ſlanders.

THEY ſay alſo, that there is no juſt reaſon to lay thoſe wars and tumults in *Germany* at the door of the *Anabaptiſts*; for it is plain, in the hiſtories of thoſe times, that *Papiſts*, as well as *Proteſtants*, and of theſe the *Pædobaptiſts* as well as *Anabaptiſts*, were concerned in them. *Biſhop* **Jewel's** *Defence*, P. I. c. 4.

AND the chief occaſion of their riſing, was the defence of their civil liberties. When they drew up a manifeſto of their demands, in twelve heads, and preſented it to the magiſtrates, who had promiſed to hear their complaints, and do them juſtice, there is but one article, that directly regards religion; which was, that they might have liberty to chuſe the miniſters of their churches, and depoſe them afterwards, if they ſaw occaſion. *Dupin's Ecc. Hiſt.* Cent. 16. Lib. i. p. 79.

THE confuſions at *Munſter*, where the blackeſt part of this tragedy was acted, were begun by a *Pædobaptiſt* miniſter of the *Lutheran* perſuaſion, one *Bernard Rotman*, preacher at the church of St. *Maurice* in that city; and were carried on by him, with ſeveral other *Lutherans*, for ſome time, before any *Anabaptiſt* appeared to have a hand in it. *Spanhemius Hiſt. Anab.* p. 12. *Hook's Apol.* p. 11. *Sleidan.*

AND though *Muncer* and *Phiffer* are ſaid to have denied infant-baptiſm, and to have inſtilled the ſame opinion into others, yet they had not received or profeſſed this principle till ſome time after theſe inſurrections were begun in ſeveral parts of *Germany*. If theſe men were as vile as they are repreſented to be, and guilty of all thoſe crimes of which they are accuſed, this could not have proceeded from their opinion about baptiſm, which

which can have no ſuch tendency: Nor is there any colour of juſtice, in charging thoſe crimes upon other Chriſtians of that denomination, who abhor their erroneous tenets, and behave themſelves after the moſt inoffenſive manner. If all the errors which have been maintained, and all the thefts, murders, adulteries, and rebellions, which have been committed by *Pædobaptiſts*, were to be made the conſequence of that opinion, it would ſoon appear a very bloody and dangerous tenet indeed, and render thoſe who held it much more odious than *Anabaptiſts*.

But that which is more material to our enquiry after the firſt riſe of this ſect is, That theſe men did not advance this tenet concerning baptiſm, as a thing entirely new, but what was taught by others, who rejected the errors and corruptions of the church of *Rome*, as well as themſelves; and affirmed it to have been the opinion of the *Waldenſes* and *Petrobruſians*, who had gone before them.

They did not ſet up themſelves upon this account as the heads and founders of a new ſect, or religion, as enthuſiaſtical perſons are too ready to do, if there be but the leaſt room for it.

Vol. I. Cent. 16. Lib. v. p. 45. *DUPIN*, a perſon well acquainted with eccleſiaſtical hiſtory, calls this the revival of the error.

There were before, and about this time, many people of their opinion concerning baptiſm, who had made a declaration of much better principles, and under better leaders.

Hiſt. Reform. Vol. II. p. 110. Bishop *Burnet* ſays, 'There were two 'ſorts of theſe [*Anabaptiſts*] moſt remark- 'able: The one was of thoſe who only 'thought

'thought that baptiſm ought not to be given 'but to thoſe who were of an age capable of 'inſtruction, and who did earneſtly deſire 'it ——These were called the gentle, or 'moderate *Anabaptiſts*: But others, who car-'ried that name, denied almoſt all the prin-'ciples of the Chriſtian doctrine, and were 'men of fierce and barbarous tempers —— 'Theſe being joined in the common name 'of *Anabaptiſts*, with the other, brought 'them alſo under an ill character.'

MONSEIUR *Bayle*, ſpeaking of the many martyrs that the *Anabaptiſts* boaſt of, and their martyrology, being a large book in *Folio*, ſays:

'COULD it only produce thoſe that were put 'to death for attempts againſt the govern-'ment, its bulky martyrology would make 'but a ridiculous figure. But it is certain, 'that ſeveral *Anabaptiſts*, who ſuffered death 'couragiouſly for their opinions, had never 'any intention of rebelling. Give me leave 'to cite an evidence, which cannot be 'ſuſpected; it is that of a writer, who has 'exerted his whole force in refuting this ſect. 'He obſerves, that its great progreſs was 'owing to three things: The firſt was, That 'its teachers deafned their hearers with num-'berleſs paſſages of ſcripture: The ſecond, 'That they affected a great appearance of 'ſanctity: The third, That their followers 'diſcovered great conſtancy in their ſuffer-'ings and deaths. But he gives not the leaſt 'hint, that the *Anabaptiſt* martyrs ſuffered 'death for taking up arms againſt the ſtate, 'or ſtirring up the people to rebellion.'

Dictionary, Anabaptiſts, *Letter* F, 2d. Edit.

Guy de Bres.

MON-

MONSEIUR *Bayle* being a *Papiſt*, and the author he cites a *Proteſtant*, made this remark upon it:

'OBSERVE by the way, ſays he, that this 'author refutes his adverſaries, juſt as the '*Catholicks* refute the *Proteſtants:* And then 'ſhews how the arguments uſed againſt the 'one, are of equal force againſt the other.'

GEORGE CASSANDER, who lived in thoſe times, had diſputed with the *Anabaptiſts*, and viſited ſome of their miniſters in priſon, does in his epiſtle to the duke of *Gulick* and *Cleve*, give a very good character of them who dwelt in *Belgick* and lower *Germany*, even when ſome others were guilty of ſuch extravagancies at *Munſter* and *Battenburgh*. He ſays,

'That they diſcovered an honeſt and a 'pious mind; and that they erred from the 'faith, through a miſtaken zeal, rather than 'an evil diſpoſition; that they condemned 'the outragious behaviour of their brethren of '*Munſter*; that they taught that the kingdom of Jeſus Chriſt was to be eſtabliſhed 'only by the croſs. They deſerve therefore, 'adds he, to be pitied and inſtructed, rather 'than to be perſecuted.'

Hornbeek's Sum. Con. *p.* 364.

THE learned *Beza* alſo gives a very honourable account of many of them in his epiſtle to the *Gallo-Belgic* churches at *Embden*, and ſays:

'Many of the *Anabaptiſts* are good men, 'ſervants of God, and our moſt dear bre'thren.'

THESE authors had more juſtice than to condemn the innocent with the guilty, and to aſperſe

aſperſe the whole for the errors and diſorders of a ſmall part.

THE great number of *Anabaptiſts* that were about this time in ſeveral parts of *Germany*, and other countries, make it improbable, that theſe frantick men at *Munſter* ſhould be the founders of this ſect, or ſo much as the firſt that revived the queſtion, about childrens baptiſm in thoſe times.

THOSE ſtirs at *Munſter* did not begin till the year 1532. nor did they come to any great height, or any *Anabaptiſts* appear in that city till the year 1533. And yet we find great oppoſition made againſt *Anabaptiſts* before this in ſeveral parts, both by diſputations and writings, and ſome ſevere laws made againſt their opinion. Spanhemius, p. 13.

THEY were oppoſed at *Augsburg* about the year 1516. by *Regius:* In *Saxony* by *Luther*, 1522. In *Thuringia* by *Micerius*, 1525. In *Switzerland*, at *Zurick*, there were three publick diſputations held between *Zuinglius* and the heads of the *Anabaptiſts*, in *Jan. March*, and *Nov.* 1525. *Oecolampadius* alſo diſputed with theſe Hereticks, as he calls them, the ſame year at *Bazil*; and again in the Years 1527, and 1529.

THIS opinion prevailed ſo faſt, that to prevent the growth of it, the magiſtrates of *Zurick* publiſhed a ſolemn edict againſt it in 1525. requiring all. perſons to have their children baptized, and forbidding rebaptization, under the penalty of being fined, baniſhed, or impriſoned. Another was put forth in 1530. making it puniſhable with death.

'IN

Hooke's *Apology*, p. 29.

'In the year 1528. *Hans Shaeffer*, and 'Leonard Freek, for opposing infants baptism, were beheaded at *Schwas* in *Germany*; 'and *Leopald Suyder* at *Augsburg* for the 'same.

'At *Saltzburg* eighteen persons of the 'same faith were burnt; and twenty five at '*Waltsen* the same year.

'Anno 1529. twenty of them were put 'to death in the *Palatinate*; and three hun- 'dred and fifty at *Altze* in *Germany*. The 'men for the most part beheaded, and the 'women drowned.

'Anno 1533. *Hugh Crane*, and *Marga- 'ret* his wife, with two more, were martyred 'at *Harlem*; the woman was drowned; the 'three men were chained to a post, and roast- 'ed by a fire, at a distance, till they died. 'This was the very same year that the rising 'was at *Munster*.

Ib. p. 30.

'Likewise in the Protestant *Cantons* in '*Switzerland*, they were used as hardly, 'about the same time.

'Anno 1526. one *Felix Mentz*, a *Bap- 'tist* minister, was drowned at *Zurich*.

'Anno 1530. two of the baptized bre- 'thren were burnt.

'Anno 1531. six more of the congrega- 'tion of *Baptists* were martyr'd in the same 'place.

'Anno 1533. two persons, *Lodwick Test*, 'and *Catherine Harngen*, were burnt at '*Munster*.'

There is part of a letter, preserved in an author not to be suspected, that was written to *Erasmus*, out of *Bohemia*, dated *October* 10, 1519. in which an account is given of

a

a sect then in being, and which had been in that country for above ninety years, who by the character given of them, appear to be *Anabaptists*; and were not only long before *Stork* and *Muncer*, but also before *Luther* and *Calvin*, who set themselves to oppose the church of *Rome*. The letter describes them thus: 'These men have no other opinion of the 'Pope, cardinals, bishops, and other clergy, 'than as of manifest antichrists. They call 'the Pope sometimes the beast, and some-'times the whore, mentioned in the *Revela-'tions*. Their own bishops and priests they 'themselves do chuse for themselves; igno-'rant and unlearned laymen, that have wife 'and children. They mutually salute one 'another by the name of brother and sister. 'They own no other authority than the scrip-'tures of the Old and New Testament: 'They slight all the Doctors, both ancient 'and modern, and give no regard to their 'doctrine. Their priests, when they cele-'brate the offices of the mass [or commu-'nion] do it without any priestly garments; 'nor do they use any prayer or collects on 'this occasion, but only the Lord's prayer, 'by which they consecrate bread that has been 'leavened. They believe or own little or 'nothing of the sacraments of the church: 'Such as come over to their sect, must every 'one be baptized anew, in mere water. 'They make no blessing of salt, nor of 'water; nor make any use of consecrated oil. 'They believe nothing of divinity in the sa-'crament of the Eucharist, only that the 'consecrated bread and wine do by some 'occult signs represent the death of Christ;

Colomesius's *Collection*, ep. 30.

Wall's *Hist. Bapt.* Part II. p. 200.

'and accordingly, that all that do kneel down 'to it, or worſhip it, are guilty of idolatry. 'That that ſacrament was inſtituted by Chriſt 'to no other purpoſe but to renew the me-'mory of his paſſion, and not to be carried 'about, or held up by the prieſt to be gazed 'on. For that Chriſt himſelf, who is to be 'adored and worſhipped with the honour of '*Latreia*, ſits at the right hand of God, as 'the Chriſtian church confeſſes in the creed. 'Prayers to ſaints, and for the dead, they 'count a vain and ridiculous thing; as like-'wiſe auricular confeſſion and penance, en-'joined by the prieſt for ſins. Eves and 'faſt-days are, they ſay, a mockery, and 'the diſguiſe of hypocrites. They ſay, the 'holy days of the virgin *Mary*, and the 'Apoſtles, and other ſaints, are the inven-'tion of idle people; but yet they keep the '*Lord's-day*, and *Chriſtmas*, and *Eaſter*, and '*Whitſontide*, &c.'

THIS deſcription does almoſt in every thing fit the modern *Anabaptiſts*, eſpecially thoſe in *England*. Their ſaluting one another by the name of brother and ſiſter; their chuſing their own miniſters, and from among the laity; their rejecting all prieſtly garments, and refuſing to kneel at the ſacrament; their ſlighting all authorities but that of the ſcriptures, but eſpecially their baptizing again all that embraced their way, does certainly give the *Baptiſts* a better right than any other Proteſtants, to claim theſe people for their predeceſſors.

'TIS true, ſome zealous *Pædobaptiſts*, who would willingly have none thought ſober and religious, who deny baptiſm to children, have

have insinuated that these *Pyghards*, and followers of *Hus* in *Bohemia*, did not baptize such as came over to them, from any dislike of infant-baptism, but of those ceremonies which the church of *Rome* used in it. And *Ottius* does positively affirm this to be the reason of it.

BUT there is no proof from any authentic histories that those early Protestants, who retained infant-baptism, did any of them, upon their departing from Popery, reject their baptism in that church, and receive a new baptism.

WALDEN, who lived in those times, and writ against the *Hussites* in *Bohemia* above an hundred years before *Ottius*, affirms, 'That some of them maintained this heresy, 'That believers children were not to be baptized; and that baptism was to no purpose 'administred to them.'

Tom. III. Tit. v. c. 53. Marshall *against* Tombs, *page* 65.

WE must therefore look for a more early beginning of this sect and opinion than the insurrection at *Munster*, or the reformation in *Germany*. And we find there are some of the *Pædobaptists*, and those of no small repute, who affirm, that the *Albigenses* were the first who dared positively to declare against infant-baptism, and call the preaching of this opinion, by *Muncer*, *Stork*, &c. only a reviving of that error.

Cassander Dupin. *Cent.* 16. *Lib.* v. *page* 45.

OF this sect there was a great number, in divers parts of *France* and *Bohemia*, above three hundred years before *Luther*'s and *Calvin*'s reformation. They went under different names, either from the places that were fullest of them, or the persons who were their principal leaders: But the name of *Albigenses* and *Waldenses* were the titles most commonly

Fox, *Vol.* I. *p* 299.

given to them; the one from *Albi*, a place ſo called in *Languedoc*, in which were great numbers of them; the other from one *Waldus*, the ſuppoſed founder of that ſect, who was a rich and learned citizen of *Lyons*, and began there to oppoſe the errors and ſuperſtitions of the church of *Rome*, about the year 1160.

THE *Papiſts* impute a great many heinous crimes to theſe people; a method which they generally take with all who have diſſented from their church. And yet *Reinerus*, a zealous oppoſer of them, gives a very honourable account of this ſect.

Danvers, *page* 344.

'THEY are, ſays he, in their manner 'compos'd, and modeſt; no pride in apparel, becauſe they are therein neither coſtly 'nor ſordid. They tranſact their affairs 'without lying, fraud, and ſwearing, being 'moſt upon handicraft trades: Yea, their 'doctors or teachers are *weavers* and *ſhoemakers*, who do not multiply riches, but 'content themſelves with neceſſary things. 'Theſe *Lyoniſts* are very chaſte and temperate, both in meats and drinks; who 'neither haunt taverns, or ſtews: They do 'much curb their paſſions; they are always 'either working, teaching, or learning, &c. 'very frequent in their aſſemblies and worſhips, &c. They are very modeſt and 'preciſe in their words, avoiding ſcurrility, 'detraction, levity, and falſehood.'

THOSE who write againſt the *Baptiſts*, charge them with abundance of hereſies, and monſtrous doctrines; ſo that it is not eaſy with certainty to come at their opinions.

As to the matter of Baptiſm, ſome repreſent thoſe they write againſt, as denying all baptiſm.

baptiſm. Others ſpeak of ſome that allowed baptiſm to the adult, but denied it to infants. Others again accuſe them of no error at all about baptiſm. But there is an expedient found out to reconcile this hiſtorical difference, which both parties agree to, and ſeems to be the truth, *viz.* That there were ſeveral ſects, who went under this general name of *Waldenſes* or *Albigenſes*, like as there are of *Diſſenters* in *England*. That ſome of theſe did deny all baptiſm, and others only the baptiſm of infants. That many of them were of this latter opinion, is affirmed in ſeveral hiſtories of this people, as well ancient as modern. I will for brevity-ſake only mention one, whoſe authority is the rather to be taken, becauſe he was not only a *Pædobaptiſt*, but alſo ſet himſelf with great care to find out the truth of this matter. 'Tis that of *Chaſſanian*, who in his hiſtory of the *Albigeois* ſays:

'SOME writers have affirmed that the *Albigeois* approved not of the baptiſm of infants: Others, that they entirely ſlighted this holy ſacrament, as if it was of no uſe, either to great or ſmall. The ſame has been ſaid of the *Vaudois*; though ſome affirm, that they have always baptized their children. This difference of authors kept me for ſome time in ſuſpenſe, before I could come to be reſolved on which ſide the truth lay. At laſt conſidering what St. *Bernard* ſays of this matter, in his 66th Homily on the ſecond chapter of the *Song of Songs*, and the reaſons he brings to refute this error, and alſo what he wrote *ad Hildefonſum comitem Sancti Ægidii*, I cannot deny that the *Albigeois*, for the greateſt

Stennet *againſt* Ruſſen, *p.* 81.

 'part,

'part, were of that opinion. And that 'which confirms me yet more in the belief 'of it, is, that in the hiſtory of the city of '*Treves*, which I have mentioned before, at 'the end of the fourth chapter, 'tis ſaid, that 'at *Ivoi*, in the dioceſe of *Treves*, there were 'ſome who denied that the ſacrament of bap-'tiſm was available to the ſalvation of in-'fants: And one *Catherine Saube*, who was 'burnt at *Montpelier*, in the year 1417. for 'being of the mind of the *Albigeois*, in not 'believing the traditions of the *Romiſh* church, 'had the ſame thoughts concerning infant-'baptiſm, as 'tis recorded in the regiſter of 'the town-houſe of the ſaid city of *Mont-'pelier*; of which we ſhall ſpeak at the end 'of the fourth book. The truth is, they did 'not reject this ſacrament, or ſay it was uſe-'leſs; but only counted it unneceſſary to in-'fants, becauſe they are not of age to believe, 'or capable of giving evidence of their faith. 'That which induced them, as I ſuppoſe, 'to entertain this opinion, is what our Lord 'ſays: *He that believeth, and is baptized, 'ſhall be ſaved; but he that believeth not, 'ſhall be damned.*'

CASSANDER, who has examined the queſtion about infant-baptiſm with much care, and is ſaid to have writ with more impartiality concerning the *Anabaptiſts* than any other author, makes *Peter de Bruis*, and *Henry*, who lived four hundred years before all this, to be the firſt that taught this opinion, and practiſed according to it. For, ſpeaking of theſe pretended hereticks, he affirms of them; 'That 'they firſt openly condemned infant-baptiſm, 'and ſtiffly aſſerted that baptiſm was fit only

Caſſander's *Infant bapt. Pref.*

'for the adult; which they both verbally 'taught, and really practised in their administration of baptism.'

AND after him, Dr. *Wall* says: 'I take 'this *Peter Bruis*, and *Henry*, to be the first 'Antipædobaptist preachers that ever set up 'a church, or society of men holding that 'opinion against infant-baptism, and re-baptizing such as had been baptized in infancy;' and calls them, in the contents, the two first *Antipædobaptist* preachers in the world. *History of Infant-baptism, Book II. p. 184.*

BUT lest these early reformers should bring any reputation to the *Anabaptists*, he relates several infamous stories and malicious slanders cast upon them by the *Papists*, without any endeavours to clear them: A method that he would hardly have taken with the first leaders of the reformation, either in *England* or *Germany*.

THESE were both *Frenchmen*, and began to propagate their doctrines, and found the sect, who after their names were called *Petrobrusians* and *Henricians*, in *Dauphine*, about the year 1126.

THEY had both of them been in priests orders, and had each of them a place or employment in that office: The former having been a minister of a parish-church, but was turned out: The latter a monk, but had deserted the monastery, upon the change of his principles; for which reason they were called apostates, as well as hereticks.

PETER began first; and after he had for some time published his opinions, and drawn many followers after him, *Henry* became his disciple, and afterwards his successor.

The errors they are said to defend, are digested into six articles.

1. That infants are not to be baptized.

2. That temples or altars ought not to be built; and, if built, to be pulled down again.

3. That crosses are not to be worshipped, but rather broken, or trodden under foot.

4. That the mass is nothing, and ought not to be celebrated.

5. That dead men receive no benefit from the prayers, sacrifices, *&c.* of the living.

6. That it is a mocking of God, to sing prayers in the church.

Their opinion concerning Baptism, is all that needs here to be enquired into.

PETER, abbot of *Clugny*, writ an epistle to three bishops of *France*, against these hereticks and their followers, in the year 1146. the time when they chiefly prevailed. He accuses them of all these tenets, and makes their denying of infant-baptism the first, and expresses it thus.

The first Proposition of the new Hereticks.

Wall's *History of Infant-baptism*, Part II. p. 173.

'They say, Christ sending his disciples 'to preach, says in the gospel, *Go ye out into all the world, and preach the gospel to every creature: He that believeth, and is baptized, shall be saved; but he that believeth not, shall be damned.* From these words 'of our Saviour it is plain that none can be 'saved, unless he believe, and be baptized; 'that is, have both christian faith and bap-

'tism;

'tiſm; for not one of theſe, but both toge-'ther, does ſave: So that infants, tho' they 'be by you baptized, yet ſince by reaſon of 'their age they cannot believe, are not ſaved. 'It is therefore an idle and vain thing, for 'you to waſh perſons with water, at ſuch 'a time when you may indeed cleanſe their 'ſkin from dirt in a human manner, but not 'purge their ſouls from ſin: But we do ſtay 'till the proper time of faith; and when a 'perſon is capable to know his God, and be-'lieve in him, then we do, not as you charge 'us, re-baptize him, but baptize him; for 'he is ſo to be accounted, as not yet baptized, 'who is not waſhed with that baptiſm, by 'which ſins are done away.'

THIS account of their practice does perfectly agree with the *modern Baptiſts:* And the author who relates it, ſays alſo,

'THAT they were reported to renounce 'all the Old Teſtament, and all the New, 'except the four goſpels. But this he ſays 'he was not ſure of; and would not im-'pute it to them, for fear he might ſlander 'them.'

So it appears that he took ſome care in reporting their opinions, and can hardly be ſuppoſed to accuſe them ſo poſitively of that which he only had by hearſay, or at leaſt to make it the firſt article of their hereſy.

A YEAR after this *author* had written againſt them, St. *Bernard*, abbot of *Clareval*, was deſired by the Pope to accompany ſome biſhops, whom he had ſent to ſtop the ſpreading of theſe doctrines, and reduce thoſe who had been led into them. When they came nigh to the territory of the earl of St. *Giles's*,

Bernard writes a letter to the ſaid earl, in whoſe country the aforeſaid *Henry* was at this time harboured; in which he recounts what miſchiefs that heretick, as he calls him, had done.

Wall's *Hiſt. Bapt.* Part II. p. 175.

'The churches, ſays he, are without 'people; the people without prieſts, *&c.* 'God's holy place is accounted profane; the 'ſacraments are eſteemed unholy, *&c.* Men 'die in their ſins; their ſouls carried to that 'terrible judicature, alas! neither reconciled 'by penance, nor ſtrengthned by the holy 'communion. The infants of *Chriſtians* are 'hindred from the life of Chriſt, the grace 'of baptiſm being denied them: Nor are 'they ſuffered to come to their ſalvation, 'tho' our Saviour compaſſionately cries out in 'their behalf, ſaying, *Suffer little children* '*to come to me*, &c.'

The ſame St. *Bernard* publiſhed a little after ſeveral ſermons; in one of which he complains of a ſort of hereticks, who pretended to derive their doctrines from the Apoſtles, ſuppoſed to be theſe *Petrobruſians* and *Henricians*: Concerning whom he ſays,

Sermon in Cant. 66.

'They laugh at us for baptizing infants, for 'our praying for the dead, and for deſiring 'the prayers of the ſaints: They believe no 'fire of purgatory after death, but that the 'ſoul when it departs the body preſently paſſes 'either into reſt or damnation.'

'Tis true, that both theſe authors give them but an ill character, and impute many errors and vile practices to them: But, of theſe, the *Pædobaptiſts* themſelves are willing to clear them.

The truth is, ſays Mr. *Marſhall*, ‘ Theſe two men did, for twenty years together, ſo much ſpread the doctrine of the *Waldenſes*, and ſo plague the biſhops mitres, and the monks bellies, that I wonder not, though they charged any thing upon them, which might make them odious to the people.’ *Infant-bapt.* p. 66.

Their new doctrine did ſtrangely ſpread in a little time; and tho' it began only in *Dauphine*, it ſoon obtained in moſt of the provinces of *France*; and from being buzz'd about in deſarts, and little villages, it began quickly to be owned by great crouds of people, and entertained in populous towns and cities: Which greatly enraged the *popiſh clergy*, and occaſioned a very hot perſecution. *Peter* was in the year 1144 taken in the territory of St. *Giles*, and according to the laws of thoſe times burnt to death. *Henry* eſcaped for ſome time after this, and went on to propagate the ſame doctrines in ſeveral places; but at length he was taken alſo, and delivered in chains to the biſhop of *Oſtia:* But what was done with him is not ſaid, tho' it may eaſily be ſuppoſed; for the men of that character don't uſe to be guilty of letting hereticks eſcape out of their hands.

These perſons lived in the 12th century after Chriſt, and had a great number of followers, who kept themſelves clear of many groſs errors, with which the church of *Rome* was corrupted in that dark time. And yet there were two famous perſons, who lived and attempted a reformation of religion, above an hundred years before theſe; who are alſo accuſed of broaching this doctrine, and found-

ing

ing a ſect that denied the baptiſm of infants: That is, *Bruno* and *Berengarius*; the former was biſhop of *Angers*, and the latter deacon of the ſame church.

BOTH theſe are ſaid to have attempted a reformation of ſome corrupt doctrines and practices of the church of *Rome*, about the year 1035. among which the practice of baptizing infants was one. Of this there are two witneſſes produced, which Dr. *Wall* acknowledges to have great appearance of truth, notwithſtanding his endeavours to render it ſuſpicious.

ONE proof that theſe men were againſt infant-baptiſm, is from a letter written by *Deodwinus*, biſhop of *Leige*, to *Henry* I. king of *France*; in which are theſe words:

Wall's *Hiſt.* c. vii. Part II. p. 159.

'There is a report come out of *France*, and 'which goes thro' all *Germany*, that theſe 'two,' *viz.* *Bruno* and *Berengarius*, 'do 'maintain that the Lord's body [the hoſt] 'is not the body, but a ſhadow and figure 'of the Lord's body. And that they do 'diſannul lawful marriages; and, as far as 'in them lies, overthrow the baptiſm of in'fants.'

THE other proof produced, is from *Guitmund*, who wrote againſt *Berengarius*, towards the latter end of his life. This *author*, after he had taken notice of the afore-mentioned letter, and the opinions therein laid to

Ibid. Part II. p. 160.

their charge, ſays: 'That *Berengarius* finding 'that thoſe two opinions [of marriage, and 'baptiſm] would not be endured, by the 'ears even of the worſt men that were, and 'that there was no pretence in ſcripture to be 'brought for them, betook himſelf wholly

'to

'to uphold the other [*viz.* that againſt tranſubſtantiation] in which he ſeemed to have the teſtimony of our ſenſes on his ſide, and againſt which none of the holy fathers had ſo fully ſpoken, and for which he pick'd up ſome reaſons, and ſome places of ſcripture miſunderſtood.'

THIS ſeems to be agreeable to the method of the firſt *authors* of the preſent reformation in *England* and *Germany*. They ſet out with a deſign to reſcue both the ſacraments from their corruptions and abuſes, as has been proved; yet finding the common people uncapable of receiving ſo great an alteration at once, dropt the buſineſs of baptizing children, and bent their chief endeavours againſt Tranſubſtantiation.

THESE were two famous *champions* for the truth, againſt popiſh errors and ſuperſtitions; eſpecially the latter: And for above an hundred years after, all that ſtood up for the purity of the Chriſtian religion, were called *Berengarians*. And ſo many were his followers, that *Matthew Paris* ſays, he drew all *France*, *Italy*, and *England*, to his opinion.

IF any ſtill doubt, whether there were in this age ſeveral who oppoſed the baptiſm of infants, let them read Dr. *Alix*'s remarks on the ancient church of *Piedmont*, and particularly what he ſays concerning one *Gundulphus*, and his followers in *Italy*; divers of whom were examined by the biſhop of *Cambray* and *Arras*, in the Year 1025. who repreſents them to have given the following Reaſon againſt infant baptiſm, *viz.*

Stennet *against* Ruſſen, *p.* 85.

'BECAUSE to an infant, that neither wills 'nor runs, that knows nothing of faith, is 'ignorant of its own ſalvation and welfare; 'in whom there can be no deſire of regene-'ration, or confeſſion of faith; the will, 'faith, and confeſſion of another man, ſeems 'not in the leaſt to appertain.'

THUS do the moſt learned of the *Pædo-baptiſts* themſelves make the firſt riſe of the *ſect*, they in contempt term *Anabaptiſts*, to be at leaſt five hundred years before the con-fuſions at *Munſter*, where others would fix their origin. Nor do ſome ſtop here; but go ſtill farther back, to find out the authors and founders of this ſect, even to the fourth century. For Mr. *Long*, Prebendary of St. *Peter*'s, *Exon*, ſays:

Hiſtory, Donatiſts, p. 60.

'For, though there were great fewds be-'tween the *Donatiſts*, and others, that ſepa-'rated from them, on the like pretences 'as they ſeparated from the *Catholicks*, as '*Maximinianiſts* and *Luciferians*, who were 'profeſſed *Anabaptiſts*.'

NOW the *Donatiſts* flouriſhed about the year 400. as appears by ſeveral edicts pub-liſhed againſt them about that time: And, though the name of *Anabaptiſt* is given in ſeveral ancient writers to the *Donatiſts*, and *Arians* in general, this was not becauſe they objected againſt the baptiſm of infants; but for their baptizing thoſe again, who had been baptized before by the *Catholicks*, either in infancy, or at age.

BUT now, concerning the *Luciferians*, Mr. *Long* aſſerts:

Ib. *p.* 103.

'THAT they did not only rebaptize the 'adult, that came over to them, but refuſed

'to

'to baptize children, contrary to the practice 'of the Church, as appears, ſays he, by ſe- 'veral diſcourſes of St. *Auguſtin.*'

THESE, by his account, were the moſt moderate of thoſe who ſeparated from the Catholick church in thoſe times: That they were called *Luciferians* from *Lucifer Calaritanus*, biſhop of *Sardinia*, once a zealous defender of the Catholick faith againſt the *Arians*, for which he was baniſhed by them, when they had the Power; and that his ſeparation from the *Catholicks* was occaſioned by their ſhewing too much countenance to the *Arians*, and admitting them upon too eaſy conditions, not only into their communion, but into eccleſiaſtical dignities.

Hiſtory, Donatiſts, *p.* 102.

HE was a man greatly eſteemed and commended on many accounts by the *Catholicks*; great numbers were of his perſwaſion, and followed him, and ſtood independent on the *Donatiſts* congregations, or any of the other factions.

MR. *Philpot* the martyr, in a letter of his to his fellow-ſufferer, who ſcrupled infants baptiſm, finds out another about this time, on whom he fathers the firſt riſe of this opinion.

Ib. *p.* 103.

ONE of his fellow-ſufferers for the Proteſtant religion, being in doubt about the lawfulneſs of infant baptiſm, writ a letter to him about it. In *Philpot*'s anſwer to this, he ſays,

'THAT *Auxentius* one of the *Arians* 'ſect, with his adherents, was one of the firſt 'that denied the baptiſm of children; and 'next after him, *Pelagius* the Heretick, and 'ſome

Caſe of Infant Baptiſm, p. 96.

'ſome other that were in St. *Bernard's* time, 'as it appears by his writings.'

Socrates, *Eccleſi. Hiſt.* Lib. IV. Ch. XXV. *Greek Copy,* Ch. XXX.

THIS *Auxentius* was biſhop of *Milan*, and departed this life in the year 378. being ſucceeded in his biſhoprick by St. *Ambroſe*, who is remarkable for his being elected a biſhop before he was baptized.

OTHERS have followed this opinion; as *Bullinger* *, *George Phillips* †, *Holms* ‖, and the *Athenian Oracle* ‖‖.

Wall's *Hiſt.* Vol. II. Ch. IV. Sect. III.

I SHALL not enquire into the truth of theſe repreſentations: Both the *Donatiſts* and *Arians* are termed *Anabaptiſts* in ſeveral ancient *authors*; but the occaſion of giving them that title is diſputed. However, ſince they were accuſed of groſs hereſies, and the authors of a dreadful ſchiſm in the church, ſome writers againſt the *Baptiſts* are willing enough to repreſent theſe as their predeceſſors.

BUT, if this be doubtful, there is ſtill a more early oppoſer of infant baptiſm produced by others; of which there is ſuch authentic proof, as not to be denied by any; and that is *Tertullian*, who flouriſhed about the year 200, and was very famous in the Chriſtian church, leaving many learned writings behind him.

THIS man is the firſt chriſtian writer, who expreſly mentions ſuch a practice as baptizing of infants, and at the ſame time condemns it, as an unwarrantable and irrational practice.

* Tom. III. Sect. VIII. † *Anſw. to* Lamb. *p.* 137. ‖ *Animad. on* Tom. *p.* 93. ‖‖ Vol. III. *p.* 245.

CHAS-

CHASSANIAN, a learned *Frenchman*, and zealous *Pædobaptiſt*, in his hiſtory of the *Albigeois*, having proved that they rejected the baptiſm of infants, tho' he thinks that they erred in this matter, yet endeavours to excuſe them, by alledging, 'That they were not the firſt who were of this opinion, ſeeing *Tertullian* was for deferring baptiſm, till perſons came to years of diſcretion.' Dr. *Wall*, who in one place calls *Peter Bruis* and *Henry* the two firſt *Antipædobaptiſt* preachers in the world, yet in another place acknowledges there was, in the firſt four hundred years, one *Tertullian*, who adviſed it to be deferred till the age of reaſon; and one *Nazianzen* till three years of age, in caſe of no danger of death. Mr. *John Goodwin* the *Independent*, being engaged in this controverſy, ſays, 'That *Tertullian* ſeems to have been the firſt who perſuaded Chriſtians to delay baptiſm, eſpecially the baptiſm of their children, until afterwards.' Mr. *Stokes* alſo calls *Tertullian* the firſt *Antipædobaptiſt* in the world.

Stennet *againſt* Ruſſen, *p.* 83.

Wall's *Hiſt. Bapt.* Part I. p. 82.

Catabap. p. 74.

Remarks on Dr. Gale, *p.* 53.

BOTH parties in this controverſy cite *Tertullian*'s words, as making for them. The *Pædobaptiſts*, to prove there was ſuch a practice as baptizing infants in the Chriſtian church, as early as *Tertullian*'s time: The *Baptiſts*, to improve what he ſays againſt it; and to ſhew that the firſt writer that makes any mention of ſuch a cuſtom, diſlikes and condemns it. For thus he expreſſeth himſelf:

'THEY whoſe duty it is to adminiſter baptiſm are to know, That it muſt not be given raſhly, *give to every one that asketh thee*, has its proper ſubject, and relates to 'almſ-

Tertull. *de Bapt.* c. 18.

'almſgiving: But the command rather is here 'to be conſidered; *Give not that which is* 'holy to dogs, neither caſt your pearls before 'ſwine; and that, *lay hands ſuddenly on no* 'man, *neither be partaker of other mens* 'faults. Therefore, according to every ones 'condition and diſpoſition, and alſo their age, 'the delaying of baptiſm is more profitable, 'eſpecially in the caſe of little children; 'for what need is there, that the godfathers 'ſhould be brought into danger, becauſe they 'may either fail of their promiſes by death, 'or they may be miſtaken, by a child's pro-'ving of wicked diſpoſition. Our Lord 'ſays, indeed, *forbid them not to come unto* 'me; therefore let them come when they are 'grown up; let them come when they under-'ſtand, when they are inſtructed, whither it 'is that they come; let them be made Chri-'ſtians, when they can know Chriſt: What 'need their guiltleſs age make ſuch haſte to 'the forgiveneſs of ſins? Men will proceed 'more warily in worldly things; and he that 'ſhould not have earthly goods committed to 'him, yet ſhall have heavenly; let them 'know how to deſire this ſalvation, that you 'may appear to have *given to one that* 'asketh.'

Wall's *Hiſt. Bap.* p. 1, 26.

HERE then is a *Baptiſt* as early as the year 200. and if, by that term, we only underſtand an oppoſer of infant baptiſm, he bids very fair for being the firſt; becauſe that ſuppoſes ſuch a practice to be introduced, or at leaſt attempted. We cannot expect, that any ſhould expreſly declare themſelves againſt infants baptiſm before ſuch an opinion was broached, or that any could ſeparate till ſuch a practice

practice was introduced. But, if that term be used to signify such as hold the doctrine, on which infant-baptism is rejected, *viz*. That a personal profession of repentance and faith is necessary from those who are admitted to baptism, this was taught and practised by persons of greater authority than *Tertullian*, and who lived long before his time; as will appear by the next account, which some have given concerning this matter, *viz*.

THAT the baptism of infants was, in the primitive times, left as an indifferent thing; being by some practised, by others omitted.

SOME *Pædobaptists*, of no small reputation, finding themselves so hardly pressed in the business of antiquity, are willing to halve the matter with their Brethren.

I FIND several men of great learning, and diligent searchers into antiquity, to go this way; as *Grotius*, *Daillee*, bishop *Taylor*, and Mr. *Baxter*. What they say to this purpose is worth observing.

GROTIUS, who his adversaries acknowledge, had a vast stock of learning, and was well read in antiquity, says to this purpose in his Annotations on *Matt*. xix. 14. taken partly from *Wall*, and partly from *Poole*.

IT does not appear, that infant-baptism did universally obtain in the primitive times, but was more frequent in *Africa* than any where else. In the councils of the ancients, one shall find no earlier mention of *Pædobaptism* than in the council of *Carthage*.

Wall, par. ii. *p*. 23.

IN *Tertullian*'s time it appears, there was nothing defined concerning the age in which they were to be baptized, that were consecrated

Tertullian *on Baptism*, Ch. xviii.

crated by their parents to Chriſtian diſcipline; becauſe he diſſuades, by ſo many reaſons, the baptizing of infants.

GREGORY NAZIANZEN, ſpeaking of thoſe who die without baptiſm, mentions among the reſt thoſe that were not baptized by reaſon of infancy; and he himſelf, though a biſhop's ſon, and educated a long time under the care of his father, was not baptized till he became a youth, as is related in his life. And *Chryſoſtom*, though according to the true opinion born of Chriſtian parents, and educated by *Miletus* a biſhop, was not baptized till paſt twenty one years of age.

BUT moſt of all, the canon of the ſynod of *Neo Ceſarea*, held in the year 315. is worthy our notice; which determines, that a woman with child may be baptized when ſhe will; for in baptiſm the mother communicates nothing to the child, becauſe, in the profeſſion at baptiſm, every one declares his own reſolution: How much ſoever interpreters draw it to another ſenſe, it is plain, that the doubt concerning baptizing women great with child was for that reaſon; becauſe the child might ſeem to be baptized together with its mother, and a child was not wont to be baptized, but upon its own will and pro-

Com. Cant. Tit. 4. feſſion; and ſo *Balſamon* explains it, that cannot be enlightned or baptized; and alſo *Zonaras*, the child in the womb has then need of baptiſm, when it ſhall be able to deliberate and chooſe; and many of the *Greeks*, ſays *Grotius*, from the beginning to this day, obſerve the cuſtom of detaining the baptiſm of their infants, until they are able to make con-

confeſſion of their own faith; and then concludes, by ſaying, he has not brought this to overthrow the baptiſm of infants, but to ſhew the liberty, antiquity, and difference of the cuſtom.

But notwithſtanding this laſt clauſe, wherein he endeavours to excuſe what he had ſaid, the *Pædobaptiſts* are very angry with him, for what he has publiſhed againſt that practice. One ſays, 'That he was perverted by cardinal *Perron*, who, in his anſwer to King *James*, pleaded the cauſe of the *Anabaptiſts* with all his might.' Another accuſes him with an intention herein to gratify both the *Socinians* and the *Papiſts*. And a third ſays upon this, 'That he was naturally inclined to trim all controverſies in religion that came in his way; and uſing that vaſt ſtock of learning which he had, as princes that would hold the ballance, do their power, to help the weakeſt ſide.'

Rivet's *Apology*.

Marſhal, *Def.* p. 29.

Wall's *Hiſt. Bap.* par. ii. p. 22.

The learned biſhop *Taylor* gives the ſame account, not only when he is repreſenting the arguments of the *Anabaptiſts*, but when he gives his own ſentiments in the caſe. His words are theſe, as quoted by Mr. *Wall*:

'In the firſt age, ſays he, they did, or they did not, according as they pleaſed; for there is no pretence of tradition that the church, in all ages, did baptize all the infants of Chriſtian parents: It is more certain that they did not do it always, than that they did it in the firſt age. St. *Ambroſe*, St. *Jerome*, and St. *Auſtin*, were born of Chriſtian parents; and yet not baptized until the full age of a man, or more.

Diſſwaſive from Popery, par. ii. lib. ii. ſect. iii. p. 117.

Wall's *Hiſt. Bap.* par. ii. p. 24.

AND a little after: 'That it was the 'custom ſo to do in ſome churches, and at 'ſome times, is without all queſtion; but 'that there is a tradition from the *Apoſtles* ſo 'to do, relies on but two witneſſes, *Origen* 'and *Auſtin*; and, the latter having received 'it from the former, it wholly relies on one 'ſingle teſtimony; which is but a pitiful ar'gument to prove a tradition Apoſtolical. 'He is the firſt that ſpoke it; but *Tertullian*, 'that was before him, ſeems to ſpeak againſt 'it; which he would not have done, if it had 'been a tradition apoſtolical.'

RIGALTIUS, another writer who was very converſant with the works of the fathers, gives the ſame account:

Annot. in Cypriani, *Ep.* ad *Fid.*

Wall's *Hiſt. Bap.* par. ii. *p.* 13.

'FROM the age of the *Apoſtles*, ſays he, 'to the time of *Tertullian*, the matter con'tinued *in ambiguo*, doubtful or various; 'and there were ſome, who, on occaſion of 'our Lord's ſaying, *Suffer little children to 'come to me*, though he gave no order to bap'tize them, did baptize even new-born in'fants; and, as if they were tranſacting ſome 'ſecular bargain with God Almighty, brought 'ſponſors and bondſmen to be bound for them, 'that when they were grown up, they ſhould 'not depart from the Chriſtian faith; which 'cuſtom *Tertullian* did not like.'

De Uſu Patrum, *lib.* ii. *ch.* vi.

MONSIEUR *Daille* alſo, who muſt be reckoned amongſt the men of no ſmall learning, was of the ſame opinion. He ſays,

Wall's *Hiſt. Bap.* par. ii. *p.* 25.

'IN ancient times, they often deferred the 'baptizing both of infants, and of other peo'ple, as appears by the hiſtory of the Empe'rours, *Conſtantine* the great, of *Conſtan*'*tius*,

'*tius*, of *Theodosius*, of *Valentinian*, and '*Gratian*, out of St. *Ambrose*; and also by 'the orations and homilies of *Gregory Nazianzen*, and of St. *Basil* on this subject: 'And some of the *Fathers* too have been 'of opinion that it is fit it should be deferred.'

And one would wonder to find, even Mr. *Baxter*, though he had writ so zealously for infant-baptism, and cast such bitter reflections upon those that deny it; yet at length to center in this opinion, and speak more favourably of them.

Baxter's *Life*, book I. *p.* 140.

'And for the *Anabaptists* themselves, says 'he, as I found that most of them were per'sons of zeal in religion, so *many* of them 'were sober, godly people, and differed from 'others but in the point of infant-baptism, 'or at most in the points of predestination, 'and free-will, and perseverance. And I 'found in all antiquity, that though infant'baptism was held lawful by the church, yet 'some, with *Tertullian* and *Nazianzen*, 'thought it most convenient to make no 'haste; and the rest left the time of baptism 'to every ones liberty, and forced none to be 'baptized. Insomuch, as not only *Constan'tine*, *Theodosius*, and such others, as were 'converted at years of discretion, but *Augu'stine*, and many such as were the children of 'Christian parents, one or both, did defer 'their baptism much longer, than I think 'they should have done. So that in the pri'mitive church some were baptized in in'fancy, and some at ripe age, and some a lit'tle before their death; and none were forced, 'but all left free.

Wall's *Hist. Bap.* par. ii. *p.* 26.

AT another time, he ſays, 'In the days 'of *Tertullian*, *Nazianzen* and *Auſtin*, men 'had liberty to be baptized, or to bring their 'children, when, and at what age they pleaſ- 'ed; and none were forced to go againſt 'their conſciences therein.'

THE laſt account we have of this matter is, That in the firſt ages of Chriſtianity, no infants were baptized; but that this practice was brought in, after a certain term of years, without any precedent from *Chriſt*, his *Apoſtles*, or thoſe apoſtolical men that lived next after them. And this is not only the opinion of the *Baptiſts*, but many of the *Pædobaptiſts*, who have ſearched antiquity about this matter, do ingenuouſly confeſs the ſame. Many inſtances might be produced of this; I will only give three or four.

Ib. *p.* 10.

WALAFRIDUS STRABO, who lived about the year 750, is very expreſs in this point: 'It is to be noted, ſays he, That 'in the primitive times, the grace of bap- 'tiſm was wont to be given to thoſe only, 'who were arrived to that maturity of body 'and mind, that they could know and under- 'ſtand what were the benefits of baptiſm, 'what was to be confeſſed and believed; 'and, in a word, what was to be obſerved 'of thoſe that are regenerated in Chriſt. But 'when the diligence about our divine religion 'encreaſed, the Chriſtians underſtanding that 'the original ſin of *Adam* did involve in guilt, 'not only thoſe who had added to it by their 'own wicked works, but thoſe alſo, who ha- 'ving done no wickedneſs themſelves. The 'orthodox *Chriſtians*, I ſay, underſtanding 'this, leſt children ſhould periſh, if they died 'with-

'without the remedy of the grace of regene- Stennet *against* Ruf-
'ration, appointed them to be baptized for sen, *p.* 86.
'the forgiveness of sins.'

LUDOVICUS VIVES, in his notes on *Augustin, de Civitate Dei*, says: 'No 'person was formerly brought to the sacred 'baptistery, till he was of adult age, and 'both understood the meaning of that my-'stical water, and requested once and again 'to be washed in it.'

SUICERUS says the same thing, but is Ib. *p.* 86.
more positive as to the time. 'In the two 'first ages, says he, no person was baptized 'till he was instructed in the faith, and 'inctur'd with the doctrine of Christ, and 'could testify his own faith; because of 'those words of Christ, *He that believeth*, '*and is baptized.* Therefore believing was 'first.'

CURCELLÆUS does not only confess the same, but fixes the time of bringing in infant-baptism. His words are these:

'PÆDOBAPTISM was not known in the Ib. *p.* 87.
'world the two first ages after Christ. In the 'third and fourth it was approved by a few. 'At length in the fifth, and following ages, 'it began to obtain in divers places. And 'therefore we observe this rite indeed as an 'ancient custom, but not as an apostolical 'tradition.'

AND in another place, according to Mr. *Stennet*, he says: 'The custom of baptizing 'infants did not begin before the third age 'after Christ; and there appears not the 'least footstep of it, in the two first cen-'turies.'

I WILL only add to these an *English writer*, whose great learning, and diligent search into antiquity, are well known. I mean the reverend Dr. *Barlow*, afterwards bishop of *Lincoln*.

THIS famous gentleman, before his great preferment in the establish'd church had either bias's'd his opinion, or tempted him to conceal it, frankly acknowledged, That both scripture and antiquity were on the side of the *Baptists*.

Danvers, *Cent.* 4. *p.* 63.

'I BELIEVE and know,' says he, in a letter to Mr. *Tombs*, 'that there is neither 'precept nor example in scripture for Pædo- 'baptism, nor any just evidence for it for 'about two hundred years after Christ. Sure 'I am, that in the primitive times they were '*Catechumeni*, then *illuminati*, or *baptizati*. 'The truth is, I do believe, Pædobaptism, 'how or by whom I know not, came into 'the world in the second century, and in the 'third and fourth began to be practised, tho' 'not generally; and defended, as lawful, 'from the text grosly misunderstood, *John* 'iii. 5. Upon the like gross mistake of '*John* vi. 53. they did, for many centuries, 'both in the *Greek* and *Latin* church, com- 'municate *infants*, and give them the Lord's 'Supper: And I do confess, says he, they 'might do both, as well as either.'

WHEN this letter was published, and improved by the *Baptists*, the advocates for Pædobaptism would not let the bishop rest, till he had either denied the letter, or writ a recantation. At length Mr. *Wills* extorted a letter from him, and leave to publish it. In this the bishop acknowledges his writing as above; but is so far from proving he was mistaken, or had misrepresented the history of those times, that he does not affirm any such thing; only tries to excuse himself, by saying, that he writ it twenty years ago, when he talked more, and understood less; and that whatever objections he had against infant-baptism, he never disturbed the peace of the church, nor declined the practice.

THUS have I traced this matter, till we are brought up to the beginning of Christianity it self: And this last opinion is that wherein the controversy resteth.

I SHALL only add some brief remarks on the account given of the different times assigned by the learned for the first rise of the *Baptists*, and the several persons whom they represent to have been the founders of that sect.

1. THAT the most common opinion concerning the first rise of the *Baptists*, and that which would reflect the greatest odium upon them, has the least appearance of truth in it, and is sufficiently confuted by the *Pædobaptists* themselves: *viz.* That they sprung from those mad and heretical people at *Munster* in *Germany*, a little after the reformation. The most learned of their adversaries, and those that have examined the histories of this people with the greatest care and diligence, make them to be much ancienter, and assign no less than seven other different periods of time for their origin; any one of which being true, will wipe away that scandal.

2. THAT

2. THAT as tradition is generally acknowledged to be the beſt and chief ſupport of infant-baptiſm; ſo even this appears, from their own accounts, to be very precarious and uncertain.

THERE are but two ways, by which they can pretend to juſtify this practice; *viz.* from ſcripture, and from antiquity.

NOW the moſt learned and ingenious of the *Pædobaptiſts* themſelves do confeſs, that there is no expreſs mention of any ſuch thing in ſcripture; and that the arguments from thence are, at moſt, but probable. Their more uſual way therefore is to recur to eccleſiaſtical hiſtory, and the writings of the *Fathers:* But how uncertain and contradictory their accounts are from hence, does ſufficiently appear by this collection.

3. WE may ſee here alſo, that the advocates of infant-baptiſm do themſelves confeſs and prove, that in all ages of Chriſtianity almoſt, there have been ſome who have oppoſed that practice, as an human tradition, and unwarrantable cuſtom.

THE writings of the firſt two hundred years are wholly ſilent about it: The firſt that mentions it, condemns it; and very many of thoſe, who ſtood up afterwards to oppoſe the corruptions and abuſes brought into religion, declared their diſlike of it.

NOW for all this to be granted, and proved too, by the adverſaries of the *Baptiſts*, is no ſmall argument in their favour; and may convince the world, that their ſcruples in this caſe

case are not wholly groundless, nor a mere novelty.

4. In this variety of opinions, and these different accounts from ancient history, those who either want ability or opportunity to search those writings themselves, have most reason to depend on their account, who say, that there are no footsteps of infant-baptism in the first ages of Christianity; and that it appears to have been introduced a considerable time after Christ and his Apostles.

These, I say, supposing them to be men of equal learning and probity with the others, have most reason to be relied on; because it made against their own practice, and what they appeared desirous to support and maintain. Men are too apt to be partial to their own side, and to conceal or let pass any thing that would reflect upon their own practice in religion: He that appears so fair therefore, as to relate what makes against him as well as for him, is freest from suspicion.

Again: Those who appear too angry with them, for making these concessions to the *Baptists*, have not yet been able to confute them, by producing any direction from *Christ* or his *Apostles* to baptize infants, nor one instance of baptizing any such for the first two hundred years. And if it be said, Those who talk thus are but few, in comparison of the great number that oppose them; it is answered, That truth is not always on the side of the greatest number; and that their number is not inconsiderable, when we add to them all the learned among the *Baptists*, and a great number of learned men

in

in the church of *Rome*, who assert the same thing.

Vid. Stennet *against* Russen, *p.* 173.

5. This diversity of opinions among the learned about tradition, and the practice of the Fathers, tends to confirm the *Baptists* in their opinion; That the holy scriptures are to be the only rule of our faith and worship; and that we are to practise nothing, as an institution of Christ, which is not therein contained. Supposing it could be proved, by sufficient evidence, that the churches did immediately after the apostles practise infant-baptism, it would not necessarily follow from thence that it was instituted by Christ, and practised by the Apostles; because the most ancient churches were subject to err, and those christians who lived in the very next age after the Apostles, made several additions, both in doctrine and worship. Their writings may therefore prove fact, but not right: And the grand question would still remain; Whether this practice was derived from *Christ*, and his *Apostles*, or begun by some others after his death?

The writings of the *Fathers* therefore could only furnish them with probable arguments: And we must, after all, refer to scripture for certainty in this, and all other controversies about points of revealed religion. But how defective are they, even in these probable arguments; and how miserably are they divided, in their opinions on this account? It is easy to discern from this collection, that they are much more successful in confuting each other, than in defending themselves: What one calls orthodox, another repreſents as hereſy; and a practice highly applauded by one, is ſeverely cenſured by another. And in eccleſiaſtical hiſtory there is a very great uncertainty, even as to facts.

BUT, in the midſt of theſe confuſions,
we have a ſure word; whereunto we do well 2 Pet. i. 19.
to take heed, as unto a light that ſhineth in
a dark place. To the law therefore, and to Iſa. viii. 20.
the teſtimony; if they ſpeak not according to
this word, it is becauſe there is no light in
them.

THE
CONTENTS.

ERRATA.

PREFACE. Page xiv. line 13. *for* Pyeton *read* Pyrton. p. xix. l. 13. *for* Viana *read* Vienna.

HISTORY. Page 16. line 28. *for* of oil of chrisom, *read* of oil, chrisom, *&c.* p. 56. l. 31. *for* whch *read* which. p. 65. l. 22. *for* peo- *read* people. p. 249. l. 5. *for* much *read* many. p. 325. l. 14. *for* his *read* this. p. 328. l. 31. *for* again *read* against. p. 344. l. 32. *for* defence it *read* defence of it.

THE

HISTORY

OF THE

English Baptists

Vol. I

THE HISTORY OF THE English Baptists.

CHAP. I.

From the time of Wickliff, *to the end of the reign of Q.* Elizabeth.

HOUGH the *English* have, above most nations, been always very zealous of their natural rights and privileges; yet the spirit of persecution has often prevailed in this land, and under the mask of religion, the properties of men have been invaded, liberty of conſcience taken away, and the moſt cruel and barbarous actions committed. And whenever it has been thus, thoſe who were branded with the name of *Anabaptiſts* have been ſure to feel the ſharpeſt part of theſe things.

THE *Martyrology* of the foreign *Anabaptiſts* is a large book in *Folio*; and the account it gives of the number of their martyrs and confeſſors, as well as of the cruelties that were uſed towards them, very much exceeds any thing that has been done in *England*. However, according to their number in this land, and the degree to which perſecution has at any time ariſen, they have always had their full ſhare of it.

Edw. III. An. Dom. 1371.

JOHN WICKLIFF was the firſt perſon of any note, who in *England* oppoſed the corruptions of the pope and his clergy, and who met with any conſiderable ſucceſs in ſo doing. He began this work in the reign of king *Edward* III.

THERE were indeed before him ſeveral who ſhew'd their diſlike of many things in the eſtabliſh'd church, and frequently ſpoke againſt the ſuperſtitious clergy; but theſe were very few, and perſons of no great character, ſuch as did but little towards opening the eyes of the people. But this man having good natural abilities, the benefit of a liberal education, and ſeveral good friends at court to encourage and

and ſupport him, and above all, being extraordinarily qualified and aſſiſted by God, gave the firſt conſiderable check to the errors and ſuperſtition of thoſe times. And though the Reformation was not eſtabliſhed till about 187 years after, yet the firſt ſeeds of it were ſown by him; for which reaſon the beſt hiſtorians of the Reformation in *England*, begin their account from the days of *Wickliff*.

THE famous Martyrogoliſt Mr. *John Fox*, begins the ſecond part of his hiſtory thus: 'Although it be manifeſt and evident 'enough, that there were divers and ſun'dry before *Wickliff*'s time, which have 'wreſtled and labour'd in the ſame cauſe 'and quarrel that our countryman *Wick'liff* hath done, whom the Holy Ghoſt 'hath from time to time raiſed and ſtirred 'up in the church of God, to vanquiſh 'and overthrow the great errors which 'daily did grow and prevail in the world; 'yet notwithſtanding, for ſo much as they 'are not many in number, neither yet very 'famous or notable, we will begin 'the narration of this our hiſtory with '*Wickcliff*, at whoſe time this furious fire 'of perſecution ſeem'd to take its original 'and beginning [a].'

BISHOP *Burnet* alſo begins his account of the Reformation with him, ſaying, 'From

[a] *Book of Martyrs*, firſt edit. p. 85.

'the days of *Wickcliff* there were many 'that disliked most of the received doc- 'trines in several parts of the nation[b].'

Wickliff *a graduate in* Merton *college.*

WE find no mention of him in history till his being a graduate in *Merton* college in *Oxford*[c]; so that no account can be given of his parentage, place of birth, or manner of education. His great abilities soon advanced him to a professorship in the university, and a living, in which he had the cure of souls. When he was convinced, by the word of God, of the idolatry and superstition of the times, and resolved upon a reformation, these two places gave him great advantages for the promoting his design: for by the one he was frequently engaged in disputations with the learned; and by the other, in preaching to the common people. He consider'd with himself, that old customs and principles, that had been long rooted in the minds of the people, could not presently, and all at once, be removed; and therefore resolved to proceed gradually in his design, finding fault first with lesser things, in order to come to the greater; beginning with some logical and metaphysical mistakes, and so proceeding till he came to the doctrine of transubstantiation, and other abuses of the church. He endeavoured to expose the vi-

[b] *History of Reformat.* vol. I. p. 23.

[c] *Fuller's Church Hist.* lib. iv. p. 130.

cious lives and insolent behaviour of the clergy [d]; and especially their assuming the civil power, encroaching upon the prince's prerogative, exacting great sums from the people. This procured him the favour of the court, and particularly the duke of *Lancaster* (the king's son) and the Lord *Piercy*, which proved a great protection to him afterwards, when persecuted by the bishops.

Translates the bible.

'HE translated the bible (says *Burnet* [e]) 'out of *Latin* into *English*, with a long 'preface before it, in which he reflected 'severely on the corruptions of the clergy, 'and condemned the worshipping of saints 'and images, and denied the corporal pre- 'sence of Christ's body in the sacrament, 'and exhorted all people to study the scrip- 'tures. His bible, with this preface, was 'well received by a great many;" and tended greatly to open the eyes of the people, and is the first *English* bible that ever was.

WHAT was done by this famous man, towards removing those corruptions in doctrine and worship which were then in the *English* church, exposed him to the persecution of the *Romish* clergy, who exercised all the rage and power they durst against him.

[d] *Fox*, vol. I. p. 556.

[e] *Hist. Reformat.* vol. I. p. 23.

1376. *Is depriv'd and silenced.* FIRST, he was deprived of his benefice at *Oxford*, and silenced by *Simon Sudbury*, archbishop of *Canterbury*. After this he was summoned to appear before a synod, which sat at St. *Paul*'s church, to answer for his errors before his ordinary; but his two great friends and encouragers, the duke of *Lancaster* and Lord *Piercy*, appearing with him, nothing was done against him at this time.

Ordered by the pope to be prosecuted. AN account of his errors and proceedings being sent to pope *Gregory*, there was quickly a bull sent to *Oxford*, enjoining the university and clergy to apprehend him; and a letter from the pope to the king, requiring his majesty to join with and assist the clergy in prosecuting of him.

THIS gave fresh encouragement to the clergy; who having exhibited certain conclusions against him, cited him to appear again before a convocation of bishops at *Lambeth*, with a full resolution to condemn both him and his errors; but a message came from the court, which put a stop to their proceedings.

SEVERAL other attempts were made against him; but they could not proceed till the duke of *Lancaster* was removed from the king, and then he was condemn'd at *Oxford*: yet he died peaceably in his bed in the year 1385. tho' forty one years after his body was taken up and burnt.

As

As to his opinions, it is very difficult now to have a certain account of them; because they who took ſo much care to burn his bones, did not neglect to deſtroy his books, which of the two were like to do them the moſt hurt. And to do this the more effectually, not only the prelates of *England* and *Bohemia*, but alſo a general council condemned all his books, and commanded them to be burnt; ſtrictly forbidding any perſon to read or conceal any of them, under the penalty of being proceeded againſt as maintainers of hereſy: ſo that in the year 1410, by diligent inquiſition about two hundred of them were gathered together in *Oxford* and *Bohemia*, and committed to the flames. We are now therefore forced to take the account of his opinions from his enemies; and if any credit may be given to their account, he was for carrying the reformation much further than it was in the reign of Q. *Elizabeth*, or ſince. For

His books condemned and burnt.

His opinions.

1. He not only denied the pope's ſupremacy [f], but was againſt any perſon's aſſuming the title and authority of being the *head of the church*; aſſerting, 'That it is 'blaſphemy to call any *head of the church*, 'ſave Chriſt alone.'

Art. 1.

2. He condemned epiſcopacy as being a creature of princes ſetting up. For he

[f] *Fuller à Wald.* p. 131.

Art. 14. asserted, 'That in the time of the apostles 'there were only two orders, *viz. priests* 'and *deacons*; and that a *bishop* doth not 'differ from a *priest*.'

3. HE was for having ministers maintained by the voluntary contributions of the people, and not by tythes settled on

Art. 24. them by law; saying, 'That *tythes* are 'pure alms, and that *pastors* are not to 'exact them by ecclesiastical censures.'

4. HE was not for giving the church a *power to decree rites and ceremonies, and to determine controversies of faith.* For it is

Art. 25, 26. said, 'That he slighted the authority of 'general councils, and affirmed, that wise 'men leave that as impertinent which is 'not plainly expressed in scripture.'

5. HE was also against prescribed forms of prayer, but especially against imposing

Art. 30. of them. For he saith, 'To bind men to 'set and prescript forms of prayers, doth 'derogate from that liberty God hath given 'them.'

Is supposed to have been a Baptist.

I AM inclined to believe Mr. *Wickliff* was a *Baptist*, because some men of great note and learning in the church of *Rome*, have left it upon record, that he denied infant-baptism. *Thomas Waldensis* [g] chargeth him expresly with this opinion; and calls him one of the seven heads that came out of the bottomless pit, for it; saying, 'That

[g] *De Bapt. Sac. Tit.* 5. chap. liii.

'he

'he doth positively assert, That children 'are not to be sacramentally baptized.'

THE same saith *Joseph Vicecomes*[h]: 'As to 'adult baptism, no one ever doubted thereof, 'witness the monuments or writings of all 'the holy fathers and œcumenial coun- 'cils, as well as the scriptures themselves, 'especially the *Acts of the apostles*; but 'as for infants baptism, he tells us, that '*Vincentius Victor*, *Hincmarus* of *Laudun*, 'the *Henrici* & *Apostolici*, *John Wickliff*, '&c. did all of them witness against it in 'their times.'

BESIDES, they charge him with several of those which are called *Anabaptistical* errors; such as the refusing to take an oath[i], and also that opinion, That dominion is founded in grace[k]. Upon these testimonies, some protestant writers have affirmed that *Wickliff* was a *Baptist*, and have put him in the number of those who have born witness against infant-baptism. And had he been a man of a scandalous character, that would have brought reproach upon those of that profession, a less proof would have been sufficient to have ranked him among that sect. Jan Van Bright. Danvers.

BUT in defence of so great and learned a reformer, it is said, that those are only lies and slanders, cast upon him by the *Papists*, *But accounted a slander of the* Papists.

h *De Rit. Bapt.* lib. ii. chap. 1.
i *Art.* 41. *condemned by the* Council of Constance.
k *Fuller*, *Art.* 51.

Papists, his enraged enemies; and that *Vicecomes* has also reckoned *Luther*, *Calvin* and *Beza*, among the adversaries of infant-baptism; which is, say they, a most evident falshood: that if this had been his opinion, the *Council of Constance*, who condemned 45 of his supposed errors, would not have omitted objecting this against him, for in such cases, they commonly over did it: that there is a treatise still extant of *Wickliff*'s, called *Dialogus*, in which he speaks of the baptizing of infants, as being according to Christ's rule; and the parents intention of doing it, as a good intention.

ALL this does indeed render it doubtful whether he was of that opinion. Yet it is to be considered, on the other hand, that the *Papists* were the best capable of giving an account of persons who lived in those times; that though they often cast slanders upon those who opposed their superstitions, it follows not, that all must be false which they said of them. *Fox*, who has related his opinions, has left out one of those condemned in the convocation at
28, 35, *London*, and three of the 45 condemned
and 45. in the *Council of Constance*, as appears by his first edition; which must be concealed for some design, not known. And although when *Wickliff* wrote his *Dialogus*, he held the baptizing of infants; yet it does not hence follow, that he might not afterwards be

be of another mind, and write againſt it in ſome of thoſe two hundred books of his that were burnt; of which, as Mr. *Fuller*[l] ſaith, not a tittle is left.

SEVERAL of the *Romiſh* errors are aſſerted in that book; as purgatory, adoration of angels, the authority of the church, *&c.* which it is plain he afterwards denied. Very few who ſet themſelves to reform religion, ſee all the abuſes in it at firſt; but moſt commonly add new opinions, conſequent to thoſe they at firſt maintained; and ſo an honeſt hiſtorian[m] ſuppoſes *Wickliff* to have done.

THE heretical opinions charged upon *Wickliff* in the latter part of his life, and after his death, are much more numerous than thoſe he was accuſed of at the beginning of his proſecution.

POPE *Gregory* charged him with 18 errors; *Thomas Arundel* archbiſhop of *Canterbury* with 24; the *Council of Conſtance* with 45; *Thomas Waldenſis* computeth 80; *John Luke*, D. D. in *Oxford*, brings up the account to 266; and laſt of all, *John Cocleus* raiſes the number to 303.

Many of Wickliff's *followers were* Baptiſts.

BUT whether he denied infant-baptiſm, or not, it is certain he was the firſt reformer of any note, that ſpread thoſe tenets among the *Engliſh* which tend to overthrow the practice of baptizing infants.

[l] *Church-Hiſtory*, p. 135.
[m] *Fuller*, p. 131.

fants. And if he did not purſue the conſequence of his own doctrines ſo far, yet many of his followers did, and were made *Baptiſts* by it.

HE taught, that no rule or ceremony ought to be received in the church, which is not plainly confirmed by the word of God: and therefore ſaid, 'That wiſe men 'leave that as impertinent, which is not 'plainly expreſſed in ſcripture [n].'

NOW, the following of this rule in reformation, muſt needs tend to the caſting out of infant-baptiſm; the *Pædobaptiſts* themſelves granting, that there is no direction for ſuch a practice in the word, nor one example of it, as will be hereafter ſhewn.

BISHOP *Burnet* obſerves [o], it was the purſuing this principle, that gave riſe to the *Anabaptiſts* in *Germany*; *Luther* having laid it down as a foundation, that the Scripture was to be the only rule of Chriſtians; that many building upon this, carried things further than he did, and denied divers things which he held, and amongſt the reſt the baptiſm of infants.

ANOTHER Tenet of *Wickliff*'s was this [p]: 'That thoſe are fools and preſumptuous, 'which affirm ſuch infants not to be 'ſaved, which die without baptiſm, and

n *Fuller*, p. 132.
o *Hiſt. Ref.* vol. II. p. 110.
p *Fuller*, p. 133.

he

'he denied, that all ſins are aboliſhed in 'baptiſm'.

NOW, it was the opinion that baptiſm waſhed away original ſin, and by a ſecret virtue regenerated the perſon, and that the infant dying without it, was in danger of damnation, that began and eſtabliſhed this practice; therefore this foundation being removed, that practice falls of courſe.

NAY further, it is affirmed to be a doctrine of *Wickliff's*, [q] 'That baptiſm doth 'not confer, but only ſignify grace, which 'was given before.'

AND in his *Dialogus*, although that was written while he retained divers popiſh errors, he aſſerts, [r] 'That children may 'be ſaved without Baptiſm; and that the 'baptiſm of water profiteth not, without 'the baptiſm of the Spirit.' Which ſhews, that even then he was inclinable to the opinion of the *Baptiſts*; and makes it very probable, that when he afterwards threw off many of the errors mentioned in that book, he did alſo reject the baptiſm of infants, as it is charged upon him by his adverſaries.

AMONGST the followers of this great man, both in *Bohemia* and *England*, we find many *Baptiſts*. The Reformation, which began ſo early in *Bohemia*, and

[q] *Fuller* à *Wald. Art.* 35.
[r] *Trialogus*, lib. iv. chap. 11. à *Baxter.*

ſpread

ſpread ſo quickly through moſt parts of *Germany*, was in a great meaſure owing to our *Wickliff*.

SOME have thought that he fled into thoſe parts to eſcape the rage of the *Engliſh* clergy for ſome time, and then returned again, and ſo had propagated his principles ſecretly there. But the account Mr. *Fox* gives [f] us ſeems the moſt probable; which is, that a certain young gentleman of *Bohemia* happening to be at *Oxford*, upon his returning back to the univerſity of *Prague*, took with him ſeveral of *Wickliff*'s books, and communicated them to Mr. *John Hus*, a publick preacher there; and *Hus*, who was a man of great learning, a fruitful wit, and of extraordinary piety, by reading theſe books imbibed the ſame ſentiments of religion which *Wickliff* had, and openly defended both *Wickliff* and his doctrines; and ſo became the firſt reformer there, and founder of that ſect which were called by ſome *Pyghards*, and by others *Huſſites*.

NOW concerning this people, and their ſentiments of religion, we have a very particular account in a letter written to *Eraſmus* out of *Bohemia*, by *Johannes Slechta Coſtelecius*, dated *October* 10, 1519. which makes the riſe of that ſect to be

[f] *Martyrol.* vol. i. p. 606.

above 97 years before that inſurrection at *Munſter*; which ſome would make the firſt riſe of the *Baptiſts*, and many years before *Luther* and *Calvin*.

IN the account he gives of them, he ſays, they mutually ſalute one another by the name of *Brother* and *Siſter*; they own no other authority than the ſcriptures of the Old and New Teſtament; they believe or own little or nothing of the ſacraments of the church; ſuch as come over to their ſect, muſt every one be baptized anew in mere water, *&c.*

Vide *Preface.*

NOW though the account in this letter agrees almoſt in every thing, with the opinions and practice of the *Engliſh Baptiſts*; yet the advocates of infant-baptiſm would fain perſuade us to the contrary, by ſuggeſting that they did not re-baptize thoſe that embraced their opinion, as judging baptiſm in infancy invalid; but judging all baptiſm received in the corrupt way of the church of *Rome* to be ſo. And in confirmation of this, Dr. *Wall* cites *Ottius*[t], who affirms this to be the Reaſon of it.

BUT when the *Pædobaptiſts* argue after this manner, they don't conſider that they hereby caſt the ſame odium upon the proteſtant religion in general, which they have ſo often endeavoured to fix upon the

[t] *Hiſt. Anabapt. anno* 1521.

Baptiſts

Baptists only; *viz.* That they can have no right administrator of baptism amongst them, and consequently no true baptism. For as bishop *Burnet* observes[x], at the beginning of the Reformation, all had been baptized in the corrupt way of the church of *Rome.* If that baptism was nothing, then there was none truly baptized in being. Now it did not seem reasonable, that men who were not baptized themselves, should go and baptize others; and therefore the first heads of the Reformation, not being rightly baptized themselves, seemed not to act with any authority, when they went to baptize others.

IF, on the other hand, they affirm, that the baptism received in the church of *Rome* is valid; then these people must be real *Anabaptists,* who baptized every one anew that came over to their sect.

NOR do we find any that believed infant-baptism to be lawful, who upon departing from the church of *Rome,* did look upon the baptism they had there received as invalid, and so received a new baptism upon their becoming Protestants. They all abhorred indeed the superstitious use of oil of chrisom; yet seeing there was in that baptism the element of water applied, the right words of institution used, and both these administred, as they thought, to a proper subject, they judged it had the es-

[x] Vol. II. p. 113.

sentials

ſentials of a true baptiſm, and accordingly contented themſelves with it.

'TIS therefore moſt reaſonable to conclude, that thoſe perſons were *Baptiſts*, and upon that account baptized thoſe that came over to their ſect, who profeſſed the true faith, and deſired to be baptized into it.

AS for *Ottius*, it is no wonder he aſſerts the contrary. For he writ with a great deal of warmth to expoſe the mad *Anabaptiſts*, who had made ſuch confuſion in *Germany*, and therefore would not allow any ſober and religious people to be of their opinion in any thing. But *Waldenſis*, who lived above an hundred years before *Ottius*, and writ againſt the *Wickliffites* and *Huſſites*, affirms, that ſome of them maintained this Hereſy, [a] 'That 'believers children were not to be baptized, and that baptiſm was to no purpoſe adminiſtred to them.'

BUT to return to *England*: Let us ſee how the doctrines of *Wickliff* prevailed there, and what was taught and practiſed, in the point of baptiſm, by his *Engliſh* diſciples.

AS in *Bohemia* the followers of *Wickliff* went under the name of *Waldenſes*, *Pyghards*, and *Huſſites*; ſo in *England* they were many years called *Lollards*. Wickliff's *followers called* Lollards.

[a] Walden. *Tom.* III. *Tit.* v. *c.* 53. Marſhall, *p.* 65.

UNDER this name were the ſeveral ſtatutes made againſt them; their ſuppoſed hereſies were condemned under the name of *Lollardy*, and the priſon in *London*, to which they were ſent, was called the *Lollards Tower*. Some think they derived this name from *Walter Lollard*, one of the *Waldenſian* preachers in *Germany*, who came into *England* about the year 1315. and propagated ſeveral opinions, agreeing with thoſe afterwards maintained by *Wickliff*. Others ſuppoſe they were ſo called from the *Latin* word *lolium*, which ſignifies *tares*, or hurtful weeds among the corn, and ſo were termed *Lollards*, *quaſi lolia, in ara Domini*.

THE firſt followers of *Wickliff* according to Dr. *Burnet* [b], were generally illiterate and ignorant men, who were led into his opinions, rather by the impreſſions which common ſenſe and plain reaſon made upon them, than by any deep ſpeculations or ſtudy. ‘ There were, ſays he, ‘ ſome few *Clerks* joined to them, but ‘ they formed not themſelves into any body ‘ or aſſociation, and were ſcattered over ‘ the kingdom, holding theſe opinions † ‘ in private, without making any publick ‘ profeſſion of them. Generally they were ‘ known by their diſparaging the ſuperſtiti- ‘ ous *Clergy*, whoſe corruptions were then ſo no-

† *Againſt worſhipping ſaints and images, and the corporal preſence.*

[b] *Hiſt. Ref. vol.* I. *p.* 23.

'notorious, and their cruelty ſo enraged, 'that no wonder the people were deeply 'prejudiced againſt them.'

IN the 5th year of *Richard* II. (at which time *Wickliff* himſelf was alive) a bill for the ſuppreſſing of hereticks paſſed in the houſe of Lords, and was aſſented to by the King, and publiſhed for an act of Parliament, though the bill was never ſent to the houſe of Commons. By this pretended law, ſays *Burnet*, 'it appears, that *Wickliff*'s followers were then very numerous; 'that they had a certain habit, and did 'preach in many places, both in churches, 'church-yards, and markets, without licence from the ordinary; and did preach 'ſeveral doctrines, both againſt the faith 'and the laws of the land, as had been 'proved before the Archbiſhop of *Canterbury*, the other biſhops, prelates, doctors 'of divinity, and of the civil and canon 'law, and others of the clergy; that they 'would not ſubmit to the admonitions, nor 'cenſures of the church, but by their ſubtil 'ingenious words, did draw the people to 'follow them and defend them by a ſtrong 'hand, and in great routs. Therefore it was 'ordained, that upon the biſhops certifying 'into the chancery the names of ſuch 'preachers and their abettors, the chancellour ſhould iſſue forth commiſſions to

Rich. II. An. Dom. 1382. *A bill paſſed the Lords, and ſigned by the King, to ſuppreſs hereticks.*

[c] *Hiſt. Reform.* vol. I. p. 25.

'the ſheriffs, and other the king's mini-
'ſters, to hold them in arreſt and ſtrong
'priſon, till they ſhould juſtify them
'according to the law and reaſon of holy
'church.'

Diſowned and condemned by the commons. THE *popiſh* party made uſe of this pious fraud; and though the next parliament diſowned and condemned that pretended law, yet they found means to get this new act ſuppreſſed, and went on to proſecute the *Lollards* with all the fierceneſs and ſeverity the former law would permit; and ſeveral of their moſt noted preachers were apprehended, impriſoned and harraſſed, by vexatious ſuits in the eccleſiaſtical courts, for as yet there was no law that reached to life.

Henry IV. An. Dom. 1400. *A law made for burning hereticks.* BUT when the crown was uſurped by *Henry* IV. in gratitude to the *clergy*, who aſſiſted him in coming to it, he granted them a law, to their hearts content, for the burning of *hereticks*; which paſſed both houſes in the ſecond year of his reign. And to the *eternal infamy of the* romiſh *clergy*, who procured this bloody law, upon the authority of which ſo much cruelty was afterwards acted, it was entred in the rolls, *Petitio Cleri contra hæreticos* [d].

Will. Sawtre *burnt.* THE firſt who was put to this cruel death in *England*, merely for religion, was *William Sawtre*, who was burnt in *London*,

[d] *Fox*, vol. I. p. 773.

don, An. Dom. 1400. He had been ſome-time miniſter of the pariſh of St. *Margaret*, in the town of *Lynn*; but having entertained the opinions of the *Lollards*, was firſt convicted of hereſy by the biſhop of *Norwich*, and afterwards brought to make a publick recantation of the ſame, and ſo eſcaped for that time: but coming to *London*, and retaining ſtill a zeal for the true religion, he petitioned the parliament that he might be heard in ſome matters relating to religion, which he believed would be for the benefit of the whole kingdom.

THE *clergy* ſuſpecting his deſign, which muſt have been to get the eſtabliſhed religion reformed, or a toleration for ſuch as diſſented, got the matter to be referred wholly to them in convocation; who ſoon condemned him as an obſtinate heretick, and procured a decree from the king for his burning.

[e] THIS *Proto-Martyr* of the *Engliſh* nation is thought by ſome to have been a *Baptiſt*; becauſe the *Lollards*, who lived in the dioceſe of *Norwich*, where this man firſt received and profeſſed his notions, were generally of that opinion [f]: and Mr. *Fox*, in relating the errors of which he was accuſed by the *Papiſts*, uſes the ſame partiality that he had done before in *Wickliff*'s caſe; for of the ten errors of which

[e] *Hook*'s *Apology, Preface.*
[f] *Martyrol.* vol. I. p. 673.

he was convicted by the biſhop of *Norwich*, he conceals the two laſt, as may be ſeen in the ſcroll and recantation.

FOX was doubtleſs ſo honeſt an hiſtorian, as not to record any thing he knew to be falſe; yet it is plain, by theſe and ſeveral other inſtances, he endeavoured to conceal many things that would make againſt the religion eſtabliſhed in his time, or that he thought would be a diſparagement to his *martyrs*.

Wickliff's *followers terrified.*

THE cruel and ignominious death of this good man ſtruck a great terror into the reſt of *Wickliff*'s followers, and made them more cautious how they divulged their opinions for the future; yet ſuch was the craft and diligence of the *clergy*, that they found out means to diſcover many of them, and by virtue of the ſtatute *ex officio*, which they had now obtained, perſecuted them with great cruelty, ſo that the priſons were full of them, many were forced to abjure, and thoſe that refuſed were uſed without mercy [g].

AND as this perſecution began in the dioceſe of *Norwich*, ſo it was carried on with the greateſt heat and violence.

MR. FOX gives an account of an hundred and twenty, who were hereupon accuſed, and committed to priſon for *Lollardy* in about three years time; that is,

[g] *Fuller*, p. 164.

from

from the year 1428, to 1431[h]. Of theſe, ſome through fear either denied or abjured their opinions; others ſuffered cruel penance, and others were burnt alive: as Father *Abraham*, *William White*, *John Wadden*, and others.

Three Lollards burnt

As to the opinions that were held by theſe *Lollards*, or diſciples of *Wickliff*, in *England*, 'tis agreed by all, that they denied the pope's ſupremacy, the worſhipping of images, praying for the dead, and the like popiſh doctrines. Whether they rejected the baptiſm of infants or not, has been doubted by ſome; but that they generally did ſo, is more than probable, from what is left upon record concerning them.

For the better diſcovering who were *Lollards*, there were certain articles drawn up, upon which the *Inquiſitors* were to examine thoſe who were ſuſpected, and if they ſaw need, oblige them to abjure. Among theſe the 12th article was, [i] 'That 'the infant, though he die unbaptized, ſhall 'be ſaved.'

Waldensis, who wrote againſt the *Wickliffites* and *Huſſites*, about the year 1410. affirms, That *Wickliff*'s followers in *Scotland*, and ſome in the biſhop of *Norwich*'s dioceſe did hold[k], That the children

[h] *Fuller*, vol. I. p. 867, *&c.*

[i] *Fox*, vol. I. p. 687.

[k] *Marſhal def. Inf. Bapt.* p. 65.

of believers are not to be ſacramentally baptized; and that they judged it unprofitable to give children eccleſiaſtical baptiſm, [l] ſaying they were ſufficiently clean and holy, becauſe they were born of holy and chriſtian parents.

THE *Dutch* martyrology gives an account of Sir *L. Clifford*, who had formerly been a *Lollard*, but had departed from their opinions, who informed the archbiſhop of *Canterbury*, that the *Lollards* would not baptize their new-born children. And our *Engliſh* martyrologiſt tells us, [m] That the *Lollards* were accuſed of holding theſe errors concerning baptiſm, *viz.* 'That the ſacrament of baptiſm, uſed 'in the church by water, is but a light 'matter, and of ſmall effect; that chriſtian 'people be ſufficiently baptized in the blood 'of Chriſt, and need no water; and that 'infants be ſufficiently baptized, if their 'parents be baptized before them.'

FOX indeed endeavours to excuſe them in theſe things; and ſuppoſes they were only ſlanders caſt upon them by their perſecutors.

IT is certain they did not deny water-baptiſm itſelf, as theſe accuſations ſuppoſe; but becauſe they denied that baptiſm waſhed away ſin, and conferred grace, they

[l] *Baptiſts Anſwer to Wills*, p. 7.
[m] *Fox*, vol. I. p. 868.

charge

charge them with ſaying, that it was a light matter, and of ſmall effect: Becauſe they held, it was the blood of Chriſt that ſaved us, and not water, they accuſe them of this error, that chriſtian people be ſufficiently baptized in the blood of Chriſt, and need no water; and becauſe they rejected the baptizing of infants, as a needleſs ceremony, they condemn them as ſuch that affirmed, that infants be ſufficiently baptized, if their parents were baptized before them.

THE perſecution of the *Lollards* rather encreaſing their number than diminiſhing them, I ſhall not take notice of the particular ſufferers in ſucceſſion; but proceed to the reign of *Henry*, VIII. where I find their principles about baptiſm more fairly ſtated. Hen. VIII An. Dom. 1511.

BISHOP BURNET ſays[n], 'That in the 'reign of K. *Henry* VIII. on the 2d day of '*May*, in the year 1511, ſix men and 'four women, moſt of them being of '*Tenderden*, appeared before Archbiſhop '*Warham*, in his manour of *Knoll*, and 'abjured the following errors:

'1. THAT in the ſacrament of the 'altar is not the body of Chriſt, but ma'terial bread: 2. That the ſacraments of 'baptiſm and confirmation are not neceſſa-

[n] *Hiſt. Reform.* vol. I. p. 27.

'ry,

'ry, nor profitable for mens ſouls: 3. That 'confeſſion of ſins ought not to be made 'to a prieſt: 4. That there is no more 'power given by God to a prieſt than to 'a layman: 5. That the ſolemnization of 'matrimony is not profitable nor neceſſa-'ry, for the well of a man's ſoul: 6. 'That the ſacrament of extreme unction is 'not profitable nor neceſſary for a man's 'ſoul: 7. That pilgrimages to holy and 'devout places be not profitable, neither 'meritorious for man's ſoul: 8. That 'images of ſaints be not to be worſhipped: '9. That a man ſhould pray to no ſaint, 'but only to God: 10. That holy 'water, and holy bread, be not the better 'after the benediction made by the prieſt, 'than before. And as they abjured theſe 'opinions, ſo they were made to ſwear, 'that they would diſcover all whom they 'knew to hold theſe errors, or who were 'ſuſpected of them, or that did keep any 'private conventicles; or were fautors, or 'comforters of them that publiſhed ſuch 'doctrines. Two other men of *Tenderden* 'did that day in the afternoon abjure moſt 'of theſe opinions. The court ſat again 'the fifth of *May*, and the archbiſhop 'enjoined them penance, to wear the 'badge of a faggot in flames on their clothes 'during their lives, or till they were diſ-'penſed with for it; and that in the pro-'ceſſion, both at the cathedral of *Canter-*

'*bury*,

'*bury*, and at their own pariſh-churches, 'they ſhould carry a faggot on their ſhould- 'ers, which was looked on as a publick 'confeſſion that they deſerved burning. 'The ſame day another of *Tenderden* ab- 'jured the ſame doctrines. On the 15th 'of *May* the court ſat at *Lambeth*, where 'four men and one woman abjured. On 'the 19th, four men more abjured. On 'the 3d of *June*, a man and a woman 'abjured; another woman the 26th of '*July*; another man the 29th of *July*; 'two women on the 2d of *Auguſt*; a 'man on the 3d, and a woman on the '8th of *Auguſt*; three men on the 16th 'of *Auguſt*; and three men and a woman 'on the 3d of *September*. In theſe ab- 'jurations, ſome were put to abjure 'more, ſome fewer of the former doc- 'trines: and in ſome of their abjurations, 'two articles more were added. Firſt, 'that the images of the crucifix of our 'lady and other ſaints, ought not to be 'worſhipped, becauſe they were made 'with mens hands, and were but ſtocks 'and ſtones. Second, that money and 'labours ſpent in pilgrimages were all in 'vain. All theſe perſons (whether they were 'unjuſtly accuſed, or were overcome with 'fear, or had but crude conceptions of 'thoſe opinions, and ſo eaſily frighted 'out of them) abjured, and performed the 'penance that was enjoined them. O-

'thers

'thers met with harder meaſure; for on 'the 29th of *April*, in the ſame year 1511. 'one *William Carder* of *Tenderden*, being 'indicted on the former articles, he de-'nied them all but one: *That he had 'ſaid, it was enough to pray to Almighty 'God alone, and therefore we needed not to 'pray to ſaints for any mediation*; upon 'which witneſſes were brought againſt 'him, who were all ſuch as were then 'priſoners, but intended to abjure, and 'were now made uſe of to convict o-'thers. They ſwore, that he had taught 'them theſe opinions. When their de-'poſitions were publiſhed, he ſaid he did 'repent, if he had ſaid any thing againſt the 'faith, and the ſacraments, but he did 'not remember that he had ſaid any ſuch 'thing. Sentence was given upon him 'as an obſtinate heretick, and he was 'delivered up to the ſecular power. On 'the ſame day a woman, *Agnes Grevil*, 'was indicted upon the ſame articles. 'She pleaded *not guilty*; but by a ſtrange 'kind of proceeding, her huſband and 'her two ſons were brought in witneſſes 'againſt her. Her huſband depoſed, that 'in the end of the reign of K. *Edw.* IV. 'one *John Ive* had perſuaded her into 'theſe opinions, in which ſhe had per-'ſiſted ever ſince. Her ſons alſo depoſed, 'that ſhe had been ſtill infuſing theſe 'doctrines into them. One *Robert Har-*

'*riſon*

'*riſon* was alſo indicted, and pleading 'not guilty, witneſſes did prove the ar-'ticles againſt him; and on the 2d of '*May*, ſentence was given againſt theſe 'two, as obſtinate hereticks; and the ſame 'day the archbiſhop ſigned the writs for 'certifying theſe ſentences into the chancery, 'which conclude in theſe words: *Our 'holy mother the church, having nothing 'further that ſhe can do in this matter, 'we leave the forementioned hereticks, and 'every one of them, to your royal highneſs, 'and to your ſecular council.*

'AND on the 8th of *May*, *John Brown* 'and *Edward Walker*, being alſo indicted of 'hereſy, on the former points, they both 'pleaded *not guilty*; but the witneſſes 'depoſing againſt them, they were judged 'obſtinate hereticks, and the former a 'relapſe, for he had abjured before cardi-'nal *Morton*, and on the 19th of *May* 'ſentence was given. When or how the 'ſentences were executed, I cannot find: 'ſure I am, there are no pardons upon 'record for any of them; and it was the 'courſe of the law, either to ſend a pardon, 'or iſſue out the writ for burning them. '*Fox* mentions none of theſe proceedings; 'only he tells, that *John Brown* was ta-'ken for ſome words ſaid in diſcourſe 'with a prieſt, about the ſaying of maſſes 'for redeeming of ſouls out of purgatory; 'upon which he was committed for ſuſ-

'picion

'picion of heresy. But *Fox* seems to have 'been misinformed about the time of his 'burning, which he says was *An. Dom.* '1517; for they would not have kept a 'condemn'd heretick six years out of the fire. 'I never find them guilty of any such cle-'mency.' Thus far Bp. *Burnet.*

IT may very well be supposed, that most of the aforementioned persons were opposers of infant-baptism; else why were they obliged to abjure the opinion of baptism, as being neither necessary nor profitable? But if it be said, that these ten articles were esteemed heretical opinions and errors by the church in that day, therefore if they found any person guilty of one, they obliged them to abjure the whole; then I say, it is evident there were opposers of infant-baptism at that time, and that the rise of the *Baptists* is not of such late date as some would have it.

An. Dom. 1528. *A parliament call'd*

THE king becoming sensible of his error, in being wholly ruled by the *Clergy*, call'd his high court of *Parliament* in the year 1528[m]. The *Commons* complained sharply of their grievances against the *Clergy*[n]; especially in six things, the third of which was, that spiritual men became *farmers* of great granges and farms, to the prejudice of *husbandmen* and *grangers*[o].

m *Baker's Chron.* p. 296.
n *Mart. Hist. kings of* England, p. 382.
o *Hist.* Engl. *in Q.* Eliz. p. 1186.

THE

THE fourth was, becauſe many *abbots*, *priors*, and other ſpiritual men, kept tan-houſes, and ſold wool, cloth, and other wares, as temporal merchants.

I mention this, to ſhew that the *clergy* of the church of *Rome* have been employed in mechanick exerciſes; and I ſhall have occaſion hereafter to make it appear that this has been the caſe of thoſe of the other denominations among proteſtants, as well as the *Baptiſts*; though they have all join'd in warm reflections on them on this account, as if they only were chargeable with this practice.

BUT to proceed, though we find not in hiſtory among the *martyrs*, many who are taken notice of as oppoſers of *infant-baptiſm*, the *hiſtorians* themſelves being *Pædobaptiſts*; yet there is ground ſufficient to believe, that many of them were *Baptiſts*.

JAMES BAINHAM, *Knt.* [p] who was An. Dom.
burnt in *Smithfield*, *Apr.* 30, 1532. ſeems 1532.
by what he ſaid upon his examination before the biſhop of *London*, *Dec.* 15, 1531. to have been an oppoſer of infant-baptiſm.

IN the year 1533. Mr. *John Frith* [q], An. Dom.
who was burnt in *Smithfield*, wrote a ſhort 1533.
tract, which he called *a Declaration of*

[p] *Fox*, vol. II. p. 298.

[q] *Wall. Hiſt. Bap.* Vol. II. p. 207.

Bap-

Baptism. 'Tis published with his other works, *Lond.* 1573.

Ten Anabaptists put to death. KING *Henry* having renounced the pope, and married *Anne* of *Bulloign,* she being a special favourer of the gospel, no great persecution nor abjuration was in the church of *England* during her time; saving, that ten *Anabaptists,* which the registers of *London* make mention of, were put to death in

An. Dom. 1535. sundry places of the realm, *An. Dom.* 1535. Other ten saved themselves by recantation.

Note again, that two more, albeit the definite sentence was read, yet notwithstanding were pardoned by the king, which was contrary to the pope's law [r].

ABOUT this time was *Thomas Cranmer* archbishop of *Canterbury* very busy in projecting the most effectual means for promoting a reformation in doctrine [s]. He moved in Convocation, that they should petition the king for leave to make a translation of the bible; but *Stephen Gardiner,* bishop of *Winchester,* and all his party opposed it, both in Convocation and in secret with the king.

IT was said, that all the heresies and extravagant opinions which were in *Germany,* and from thence brought over into *England,* sprang from the free use of the Scriptures. And whereas in *May,* 1535.

[r] *Fox,* vol. II. p. 325.

[s] *Burnet's Hist. Ref.* vol. I. lib. 3. p. 195.

nine-

nineteen *Hollanders* were accuſed of ſome hereticical opinions, denying Chriſt to be both God and Man, or that he took fleſh and blood of the Virgin *Mary*, or that the ſacraments had any effect upon thoſe that received them. In which opinions fourteen of them remained obſtinate, and were burnt by pairs in ſeveral places. It was pretended, that all theſe drew their damnable errors from the indiſcreet uſe of the Scriptures. Theſe, or however ſome of them, are ſuppoſed to be *Anabaptiſts*, becauſe *Fuller* mentions ſome under that name who ſuffered that year.

Fourteen Hollanders burnt by pairs in ſeveral places.

THE proceedings of the convocation, and the articles of religion therein agreed upon, and publiſhed with the king's authority in 1536. ſhew, that the opinion of the *Baptiſts* was then increaſing in *England*.

An. Dom. 1536.

THIS convocation ſat down in *June*, and after ſome affairs relating to the king's divorce were debated, the lower houſe ſent to the upper houſe, a collection of many opinions that were then in the realm. There are ſixty ſeven ſet down, and are the tenets of the old *Lollards*, new *Reformers*, and *Anabaptiſts*; and after much conſultation and debating, certain articles were agreed upon, and publiſhed with the king's authority.

BY these articles, which are expressed at large by *Fuller* and *Burnet*, it may be seen what sort of men the whole body of the *clergy* condemned as hereticks in those days.

BUT it will be sufficient here to insert only those concerning baptism.

AS touching the holy sacrament of baptism, say they, 'We will that all bi- 'shops and preachers shall instruct and teach 'our people committed by us unto their 'spiritual charge, that they ought and 'must of necessity believe certainly all 'those things which have been always by 'the whole consent of the church ap- 'proved, received and used, in the sacra- 'ment of baptism. That is to say,

'I. That the sacrament of baptism was 'instituted and ordained in the New Testa- 'ment by our Saviour Jesus Christ, as a 'thing necessary for the attaining of everlast- 'ing life; according to the saying of Christ, '*nisi quis renatus fuerit ex aqua & Spi- 'ritu Sancto, non potest intrare in regnum 'cœlorum.*

'*Item*, THAT it is offered unto all 'men, as well infants as such as have the 'use of reason, that by baptism they shall 'have the remission of sins, and the grace 'and favour of God; according to the 'saying of St. *John*, *Qui crediderit & bapti- 'zatus fuerit, salvus erit.*

'*Item*, THAT the promise of grace and 'everlasting life, which promise is ad- joined

‘ joined unto the ſacrament of baptiſm, ‘ pertaineth not only unto ſuch as have ‘ the uſe of reaſon, but alſo to infants, ‘ innocents and children; and that they ‘ ought therefore, and muſt needs be bap- ‘ tized: And that by the ſacrament of ‘ baptiſm, they do alſo obtain remiſſion of ‘ their ſins, the grace and favour of God, ‘ and be made thereby the very ſons and ‘ children of God; inſomuch as infants ‘ and children, dying in their infancy, ſhall ‘ undoubtedly be ſaved thereby, or elſe ‘ not.

‘ *Item*, THAT infants muſt needs be ‘ chriſtened, becauſe they be born in ori- ‘ ginal ſin, which ſin muſt needs be re- ‘ mitted; which cannot be done but by ‘ the ſacrament of baptiſm, whereby they ‘ receive the Holy Ghoſt, which exer- ‘ ciſeth his grace and efficacy in them, ‘ and cleanſeth and purgeth them from ‘ ſin, by his moſt ſecret virtue and ope- ‘ ration.

‘ *Item*, THAT children or men once ‘ baptized, can, nor ought ever to be ‘ baptized again.

‘ *Item*, THAT they ought to repute ‘ and take all the *Anabaptiſts*, and the ‘ *Pelagians* opinions, contrary to the pre- ‘ miſes, and every other man's opinions ‘ agreeable to the ſaid *Anabaptiſts*, or the ‘ *Pelagians* opinions in this behalf, for de-

 ‘ teſtable

‘ teſtable hereſies, and utterly to be con-
‘ demned.

‘ *Item*, THAT men or children having ‘ the uſe of reaſon, willing and deſiring to ‘ be baptized, ſhall by the virtue of that holy ‘ ſacrament, obtain the grace of the remiſſion ‘ of all their ſins, if they ſhall come there- ‘ unto perfectly and truly repentant and ‘ contrite, of all their ſins before com- ‘ mitted, and alſo perfectly and conſtantly ‘ confeſſing and believing, all the articles ‘ of our faith, according as it was men- ‘ tioned in the articles before; or elſe not. ‘ And finally, if they ſhall alſo have firm ‘ credence and truſt in the promiſe of God, ‘ adjoined to the ſaid ſacrament; that is ‘ to ſay, that in and by this ſacrament ‘ which they ſhall receive, God the Father ‘ giveth unto them, for his ſon Jeſus Chriſt's ‘ ſake, remiſſion of all their ſins, and the ‘ grace of the Holy Ghoſt, whereby they ‘ be newly regenerated, and made the ‘ very children of God, according to the ‘ ſaying of Chriſt and his apoſtle St. *Pe-* ‘ *ter*, *Pænitentiam agite*, & *baptizetur* ‘ *unuſquiſque veſtrum*, *in nomine Jeſu* ‘ *Chriſti*, *in remiſſionem peccatorum*, & ‘ *accipiotis donum Spiritûs Sancti*; and ac- ‘ cording alſo to the ſaying of St. *Paul*, ‘ *ad Titum*. 3. *Non ex operibus juſtitiæ quæ* ‘ *fecimus nos*, *ſed ſecundum ſuam miſericor-* ‘ *diam*, *ſalvos nos fecit*, *per lavacrum regene-* ‘ *rationis*

'*rationis & renovationis Spiritûs Sancti, 'quem effudit in nos opulentèr per Jesum 'Christum servatorem nostrum, ut justifi-'cati illius gratia heredes efficiamur, juxtà 'spem vitæ eternæ.*'

Dr. WALL would insinuate, that there were no *Baptists* in *England* at this time; but that the King and Convocation, hearing of some in *Germany*, made and published these articles only by way of prevention, lest such opinions should be brought over hither. But is it probable they would have made so much stir about opinions that were not among them? Besides, the preface put to the articles in the King's name, does plainly contradict this insinuation; for therein it is said by the King: 'We being of late, to our great 'regret, credibly advertised of such diver-'sity in opinions, as have grown and 'sprongen in this our realm, as well con-'cerning certain articles necessary to our 'salvation, as also touching certain other 'honest and commendable ceremonies, 'rites; and usages, now a long time used 'and accustomed in our churches, have 'caused our *Bishops*, and other the most 'discreet and best learned men of our *Clergy* 'of this our whole realm, to be assembled in 'our Convocation, for the full debatement 'and quiet determination of the same.'

AFTER these articles of religion were published, Bp. *Burnet* tells us[a]: 'That 'those that desired reformation were glad 'to see so great a step once made, and did 'not doubt but this would make way for 'further changes. They rejoiced to see 'the Scriptures and the antient Creeds 'made the standards of the faith, without 'mentioning tradition, or the decrees of 'the church.'

BUT what little cause the *Baptists* had to rejoice with them, will appear by what follows:

An. Dom. 1538. FOR in *October* 1538. 'There was a 'commission, says *Burnet*[b], sent to *Cranmer*, *Stokesly*, *Sampson*, and some others, 'to enquire after *Anabaptists*, to proceed 'against them, to restore the penitent, 'to burn their books, and to deliver the obstinate to the secular arm; 'but I have not, says the bishop, seen 'what proceedings there were upon this.'

A proclamation issued against Anabaptists. On the 16th of *November*, the King put forth a proclamation, in which he condemns all the books of the *Anabaptists* and *Sacramentarians*, and appoints those to be punished who vented them; and in *December* following he sent a letter to all the *Justices* in *England*, in which, after many other things, they are earnestly pressed to take care, that all the injunctions, laws

[a] *Hist. Ref.* vol. I. lib. iii. p. 218.
[b] *Ib.* vol. III. lib. iii. p. 159.

and

and proclamations, againſt *Sacramentarians* and *Anabaptiſts*, be duly executed. Which letter may be ſeen at large in *Burnet.*

[c] IN this year alſo there was an act of grace paſſed; in which, beſides other particular exceptions, all *Anabaptiſts* and *Sacramentaries* were excepted, and all thoſe that affirmed, there was a fate upon men, by which the day of their death was unalterably determined.

An act of grace paſſed. Anabaptiſts *are excepted.*

MR. FULLER tells us[d], 'That in this 'year a match being made by the lord '*Cromwell*'s contrivance between King '*Henry* and the lady *Anne* of *Cleve*, *Dutchmen* flocked faſter than formerly into '*England*, and ſoon after began to broach 'their ſtrange opinions, being branded with 'the general name of *Anabaptiſts.* Theſe '*Anabaptiſts*, he adds, for the main are 'but *Donatiſts* new dipt; and this year 'their name firſt appears in our *Engliſh* 'chronicles. I read, ſays he[e], that four *Anabaptiſts*, three men and one woman, 'all *Dutch*, bare faggots at *Paul*'s croſs; 'and three days after, a man and a woman 'of their *ſect* were burnt in *Smithfield*.'

Two Anabaptiſts *burnt in Smithfield.*

THIS, Mr. *Fuller* calls[f] the beginning of the *Anabaptiſts* in *England*; but he is

Fuller'*s account confuted.*

[c] *Hiſtory of Reformat.* vol. III. lib. iii. col. N°. 63.
[d] *Church Hiſt.* lib. iv. p. 229.
[e] *Stow's chron.* p. 576.
[f] *Index, letter* A.

very much miſtaken in his account, both as to their beginning, and the firſt appearance of their name in the *Engliſh* chronicle, as is plain from what has been ſaid before; but however an epitome thereof may not be improper in this place.

[g] IN the articles of religion, ſet forth by the King and Convocation, *An. Dom.* 1536. the ſect of the *Anabaptiſts* are mention'd and condemn'd; and their opinion, that infants are not to be baptized, is particularly oppoſed and cenſured as a deteſtable hereſy.

[h] THE regiſters of *London* mention certain *Dutchmen* counted for *Anabaptiſts*, ten whereof were put to death *Anno Dom.* 1535. other ten repented and were ſaved.

[i] Bp. BURNET ſays, That in *May* 1535. nineteen *Hollanders* were accuſed of ſome heretical opinions; among which this, denying, 'That the ſacraments had any effect on thoſe that received them: Fourteen of them remained obſtinate, and were burnt by pairs in ſeveral places.'

NOW both theſe were three years before *Fuller* begins his account of the foreign *Anabaptiſts* that came into *England*. But beſides this, we have mentioned inſtances of much longer ſtanding, as that of *Waldenſis*, which ſaith, that the *Lollards*,

[g] *Fuller*, p. 217.
[h] *Fox*, vol. II. p. 325.
[i] *Hiſt. Ref.* vol. I. lib. iii. p. 195.

who

who were *Wickliff*'s followers in *Scotland*, and ſome in the biſhop of *Norwich*'s dioceſe, did hold, that the children of *Believers* are not to be ſacramentally baptized, and that they judged it unprofitable to give children eccleſiaſtical baptiſm; ſaying, that they were ſufficiently clean and holy, becauſe they were born of holy and chriſtian parents. Agreeable to this, is the account which Mr. *Fox* gives of ſome faithful chriſtians, who were burnt at *Norwich* about the year 1428. For he ſays, though he endeavours to excuſe them therein, that they ſay, that infants be ſufficiently baptized, if their parents be baptized before them; that chriſtian people be ſufficiently baptized in the blood of Chriſt, and need no water; that the ſacrament of baptiſm uſed in the church by water, is but a light matter, and of ſmall effect.

THERE were about 120 of this opinion; three whereof were burnt alive. Theſe were martyrs of the *Anabaptiſts* opinion in *England*, above an hundred years before Mr. *Fuller*'s date of their beginning.

BUT to return to the perſecution of the *Baptiſts*. We find in Mr. *Fox* certain injunctions, given out in the 30th year of the reign of King *Henry* VIII. on the 6th of *Nov. An. Dom.* 1539. the fourth whereof was this: [k] 'That thoſe that be in any

An. Dom. 1539.

[k] *Fox*, vol. II. p. 440.

' errors,

'errors, as *Sacramentaries*, *Anabaptists*, 'or any other that sell books having such 'opinions in them, being once known, 'both the books and such persons shall be 'detected, and disclosed immediately unto 'the king's majesty, or one of his privy 'council, to the intent to have it punish-'ed without favour, even with the ex-'tremity of the law.'

BY this injunction it appears, that there were some in those days, who were for reforming the Sacrament of the supper from the abuses of the church of *Rome*; that the former were then called *Sacramentarians*, the latter *Anabaptists*.

Thirty one Anabaptists banished and put to death.

[l] IN this year sixteen men and fifteen women were banished, for opposing infant-baptism; who going to *Delf* in *Holland*, were there pursued and prosecuted before the magistrates for *Anabaptists*, and put to death for the same; the men beheaded, and the women drowned. Mr. *Barnes*, who was burnt in *Smithfield*, *Anno Dom.*
An. Dom. 1540. 1540. in his speech to the people at the stake, clearing himself from being an *Anabaptist*, of which he was accused, says, '[m] Which 'sect (meaning the *Anabaptists*) I detest 'and abhor; and in this place there hath 'been burned some of them, whom I never 'favoured, neither maintained.'

[l] *Dutch martyr*. lib. ii. p. 123.
[m] *Fox*, p. 610.

GREATLY

GREATLY did the *clergy* oppose one another at this time, even to the disturbance of the peace of the king himself; as appears by his speech to the parliament, *Decemb.* 24, 1545. where recommending love and unity to his subjects, he saith, '[n] St. *Paul* saith, 'to the *Corinthans*, in the 13th chapter, '*Charity is gentle*, *charity is not envious*, '*charity is not proud*, and so forth, in the 'said chapter. Behold then what love and 'charity is amongst you, when the one 'calleth the other *Heretick* and *Anabaptist*, and he calleth him again *Papist*, *Hypocrite*, and *Pharisee*: Be these tokens 'of charity among you? I see, and hear 'daily, that you of the *clergy* preach one 'against another, teach one contrary to 'another, inveigh one against another, 'without charity, or discretion; some be 'too stiff in their old *Mumpsimus*, others be 'too busy and curious in their new *Sumpsimus*.'

An. Dom. 1545.

THIS part of the King's speech intimates to us, that when the reformation began under his reign, there were many of his subjects went under the name of *Anabaptists*.

YET after all, the *popish clergy* prevailed with the King, and obtained a proclamation for the suppressing and abolishing of such *English* books as might help to explain the Scripture; such as the books of

An. Dom. 1547. *A proclamation against the books of* Wickliff, Frith, *&c.*

[n] *Fox*, vol II. p. 571.

Wick-

Wickliff, *Frith*, *Tindal*, *Barnes*, &c. but within four months after this proclamation was iſſued out, the king died, and providence thereby diſappointed them, by bringing his ſon *Edward* VI. to the throne; who reſtored the holy Scriptures in the mother tongue, aboliſhed the maſſes, and received home ſuch as were baniſhed.

Edw. VI.

HE was but nine years of age; yet proved a moſt happy patron to the goſpel.

Carolus's *requeſt denied by the King.*

° CAROLUS, the Emperor made requeſt to him and his council, to permit lady *Mary* to have *Maſs* in her houſe, without prejudice of the law. Whereunto the King being required by the council to give his conſent, would in no caſe yield to it, notwithſtanding they laid before him what danger might enſue to him by breach of amity with the Emperor. And they being more urgent upon him, the king ſeeing their importunate ſuit, in the end his tender heart burſting out into bitter weeping and ſobbing, deſired them to be content: and ſo refuſed to yield unto the Emperor's requeſt in that behalf.

IN the ſecond year of his reign, the new Liturgy, firſt agreed upon by the *Clergy*, was confirmed by parliament; wherein P Biſhop *Burnet* tells us, they give the following direction about baptiſm.

° *Fox*, vol. II. p. 653.
P *Hiſt. Reform.* vol. II. lib. i. p. 77.

IN

'IN baptiſm, ſays he, there was, beſides 'the forms which we ſtill retain, a croſs 'at firſt made on the child's forehead and 'breaſt with an adjuration of the devil 'to go out of him, and come at him no 'more. Then the prieſt was to take the 'child by the right hand, and to place 'him within the font. There he was to 'be dipt thrice; once on the right ſide, 'once on the left, and once on the breaſt, 'which was to be diſcreetly done. But 'if the child were weak, it was ſufficient 'to ſprinkle water on his face. Then was 'the prieſt to put a white veſtment or 'chriſome on him, for a token of inno-'cence, and to anoint him on the head, 'with a prayer for the unction of the holy 'Ghoſt.' *Baptiſm according to the new liturgy.*

[q] IN his reflections upon this part of the book, when he is pleading for the firſt reformers continuing the uſe of the croſs in baptiſm, he tells us, they did not uſe it, as thinking there was that virtue followed the uſe of it which the *Papiſts* thought: 'For in baptiſm, ſays he, as 'they [the *Papiſts*] uſed the ſign of the 'croſs, they add an adjuration to the *evil* '*ſpirit not to violate it*, and in the making 'it, ſaid, *Receive the ſign of the croſs, both* '*in thy forehead and in thy heart, and* '*take the faith of the heavenly precepts*, '&c.'

[q] *Hiſt. Reform.* vol. II. lib. i. p 80.

Fox

[r] FOX says, 'during the whole time 'of the six years of this king, much tran- 'quility, and as it were a breathing time, 'was granted to the whole church of *Eng- 'land*; so that the rage of persecution 'ceasing, and the sword taken out of the 'adversaries hand, there was now no 'danger to the godly, unless it were only 'by wealth and prosperity, which many 'times bringeth more damage, in corrupt- 'ing mens minds, than any time of perse- 'cution or affliction.

'BRIEFLY, during all this time, 'neither in *Smithfield*, nor any other 'quarter of this realm, any was heard to 'suffer for any matter of religion, either '*Papist* or *Protestant*, either for one opinion 'or the other, except only two; one an '*English* woman, called *Joan* of *Kent*; and 'the other a *Dutchman*, named *George*, who 'died for certain articles, strange and dis- 'sonant from the assertion of the church, 'which here I omit to speak of, for causes 'reasonable.'

An. Dom. 1549. THESE two having denied infant-baptism, and being the only persons who suffered for their sentiments in religion in this reign, I shall give that account of them and their sufferings which I find in Bishop *Burnet* [s].

[r] *Acts and Mon.* p. 685. *first Edit.*

[s] *Hist. Reform.* vol. II. part ii. p. 110, *&c.*

AT

'AT this time, ſays the Biſhop, there were An. Dom. 1547.
'many *Anabaptiſts* in ſeveral parts of *England*; they were generally *Germans*, whom 'the revolutions there had forced to change 'their ſeats. Upon *Luther*'s firſt preaching in *Germany*, there aroſe many, who 'building on ſome of his principles, carried things much further than he did. 'The chief foundation he laid down was, 'that the Scripture was to be the only 'rule of chriſtians. Upon this many argued, that the myſteries of the Trinity, 'and Chriſt's Incarnation and Sufferings, 'of the Fall of Man, and the aids of Grace, 'were indeed philoſophical ſubtilities, and 'only pretended to be deduc'd from Scripture, 'as almoſt all opinions of religion were, 'and therefore they rejected them. Amongſt theſe the baptiſm of infants was 'one. They held that to be no baptiſm, 'and ſo were re-baptized. But from this, 'which was moſt taken notice of, as being a viſible thing, they carried all the 'general name of *Anabaptiſts*.

'ON the 12th of *April* there was 'a complaint brought to the council, that 'with the ſtrangers that were come into '*England*, ſome of that perſuaſion had 'come over, and were diſſeminating their 'errors, and making *proſelytes*: So a commiſſion was ordered for the archbiſhop of '*Canterbury*, the biſhops of *Ely*, *Worceſter* '*er*, *Westminster*, *Chichester*, *Lincoln*, and '*Rochester*; Sir *William Petre*, Sir *Thomas* '*Smith*, Dr. *Cox*, Dr. *May*, and some others, 'three of them being a *quorum*; to examine, 'and search after all *Anabaptists*, *Hereticks*, 'or contemners of the Common-prayer. 'They were to endeavour to reclaim them, 'to enjoin them penance, and give them 'absolution; or, if they were obstinate, to 'excommunicate and imprison them, and 'to deliver them over to the secular pow- 'er, to be further proceeded against. Some 'tradesmen in *London* were brought before 'these *commissioners* in *May*, and were 'persuaded to abjure their former opinions.' *I shall only mention the last of them; which was*, that the baptism of infants was not profitable.

'ONE of those who thus abjured, 'was commanded to carry a faggot next '*Sunday* at St. *Paul*'s, where there should 'be a sermon, setting forth his heresy. 'But there was another of these extreme 'obstinate, *Joan Bocher*, commonly cal- 'led *Joan* of *Kent*. She denied that Christ 'was truly incarnate of the virgin, whose 'flesh being sinful, he could take none 'of it; but the Word, by the consent of the 'inward man in the virgin, took flesh of 'her; these were her words. They took 'much pains about her, and had many 'conferences with her; but she was so 'ex-

Joan Bocher, *called* Joan *of* Kent.

'extravagantly conceited of her own notions, 'that ſhe rejected all they ſaid with ſcorn. 'Whereupon ſhe was adjudged an obſti- 'nate heretick, and ſo left to the ſecular 'power. This being returned to the coun- 'cil, the good King was moved to ſign 'a warrant for burning her, but could not 'be prevailed on to do it. He thought it a 'piece of cruelty, too like that which 'they had condemned in *Papiſts*, to 'burn any for their conſciences; and in a 'long diſcourſe he had with Sir *John* '*Cheek*, he ſeemed much confirmed in 'that opinion.

'CRANMER was imployed to perſuade 'him to ſign the warrant. He argued 'from the law of *Moſes*, by which *blaſ-* '*phemers* were to be ſtoned. He told the 'King, he made a great difference be- 'tween errors in other points of divinity, 'and thoſe which were directly againſt 'the apoſtles *Creed*; that theſe were im- 'pieties againſt God, which a prince, as 'being God's deputy, ought to puniſh, as 'the King's deputies were obliged to puniſh 'offences againſt the King's perſon.

'THESE reaſons did rather ſilence than 'ſatisfy the young King; who ſtill thought 'it a hard thing, as in truth it was, to pro- 'ceed ſo ſeverely in ſuch caſes; ſo he ſet his 'hand to the warrant with tears in his eyes, 'ſaying to *Cranmer*, that if he did wrong 'ſince it was in ſubmiſſion to his autho-

'rity, he ſhould anſwer for it to God. 'This ſtruck the archbiſhop with much 'horror, ſo that he was very unwilling 'to have the ſentence executed; and both 'he and *Ridley* took the woman then in 'cuſtody to their houſes, to ſee if they 'could perſuade her: But ſhe continued 'by jeers and other inſolencies to carry 'herſelf ſo contemptuouſly, that at laſt the 'ſentence was executed on her the 2d of '*May* next year; biſhop *Scorey* preaching 'at her burning. She carried herſelf then 'as ſhe had done in the former parts of 'her proceſs, very undecently, and in the 'end was burnt.'

An. Dom. 1550. [t] IN the year 1550. about the end of *December*, the ſame author aſſures us, that after many cavils in the ſtate, an act paſſed for the king's general pardon; wherein the *Anabaptiſts* are excepted. 'Laſt of all, ſays the Biſhop, [that is, of the acts made by this parliament] 'came the king's 'general pardon; out of which thoſe in 'the tower or other priſons, on the account 'of the ſtate, as alſo all *Anabaptiſts*, were 'excepted.'

THIS exception does plainly intimate, that there were at this time ſome of this opinion kept in the *priſons*, tho' they were not charged with any crimes againſt the ſtate, but for the principles of religion; and

[t] *Hiſt. Reform.* vol. II. lib. i. p. 143.

that

that there was ſo much of the *popiſh* ſpirit of perſecution remaining among thoſe *Reformers*, as to exclude *Anabaptiſts* from the benefit of the king's pardon.

IN the ſame year a viſitation was made of the dioceſe of *London*, by *Ridley*, their new biſhop. Among the other articles which he put to the inferior *Clergy*, this was one; '[u] Whether any *Anabaptiſts*, or 'others, uſed private conventicles, with 'different opinions and forms from thoſe 'eſtabliſhed;' and with other queſtions about *baptiſm* and marriages. *Burnet* ſays theſe articles are in biſhop *Sparrow*'s collection.

The Common-prayer book reviewed.

'[x] ABOUT the end of this year, or the 'beginning of the next, there was a review 'made of the Common-prayer book. Several 'things had been continued in it, either 'to draw in ſome of the *Biſhops*, who 'by ſuch yielding might be prevailed on 'to concur in it, or in compliance with 'the people, who were fond of their old 'ſuperſtitions. So now a review of it 'was ſet about.' *Martin Bucer* [whoſe opinion was highly eſteemed both by the king, and *Cranmer* the archbiſhop, and who had a great hand in all the changes that were made in religion in thoſe times in *England*] 'was conſulted in it, and '*Aleſſe* the *Scotch* divine tranſlated it into

x *Hiſt. Ref.* 158.
u *Ib.* p. 155

'*Latin* for his uſe,' [and with it was ſent over into *Germany*] 'upon which *Bucer* 'writ his opinion, which he finiſhed the 'fifth of *January* the year following.'

Bucer's *opinion thereon.*

IN this he adviſed to a further reformation in many things. 'He wiſhed that 'there was a ſtrict diſcipline to exclude 'ſcandalous livers from the ſacrament.'

'HE wiſhed that the old habits might 'be laid aſide, ſince ſome uſed them ſu'perſtitiouſly, and others contended much 'about them. He did not like the half 'office of communion, or ſecond ſervice to 'be ſaid at the altar, when there was no 'ſacrament. He was offended with the re'quiring the people to receive at leaſt once 'a year, and would have them preſſed to it 'much more frequently. He diſliked that 'the prieſts generally read prayers with 'no devotion, and in ſuch a voice that the 'people underſtood not what they ſaid. 'He would have the ſacrament de'livered into the hands, and not put into 'the mouths of the people, *&c.*'

AS to *Baptiſm*, 'He complained that '*Baptiſm* was generally in houſes, which 'being the receiving infants into the 'church, ought to be done more pub'lickly. The hallowing of the water, the 'chriſme, and the white garment [then 'uſed in baptizing] he cenſured as being 'too ſcenical. He excepted to the exor'ciſing the devil, and would have it turn-

'ed

'ed to a prayer to God; that authoritative way of saying *I adjure*, not being so decent. He thought the godfathers answering in the child's name, not so well as to answer in their own, that they should take care in these things all they could.'

SOME of these things which he excepted to, were corrected afterwards, but others were kept, and are to this day; though the same things are still objected against by most of the *Nonconformists*, and are one great occasion of their dissenting from the established church.

HAVING thus cast out many of those corruptions that were formerly in their worship, and got most of the sees filled with such *Bishops* as were for the Reformation, they set about the purging out those corruptions that were doctrinal; and most of the year following was spent in preparing articles which should contain the doctrines of the church of *England*. These were generally said to be framed by *Cranmer* and *Ridley*. They were agreed upon by the *bishops*, and other learned men, in the Convocation held at *London* in the year 1552. and consisted of forty two articles. As there were three articles more than there are at present, so they exprest several things different from what they are now. All that is proper to be taken notice of here is the eighth, which is concerning original

nal ſin. The *Anabaptiſts* are particularly meant, as affirming, that it conſiſts in the following of *Adam*; for thus it begins.

'ORIGINAL ſin ſtandeth not in the 'following of *Adam*, as the *Pelagians* do 'vainly talk, and at this day is affirmed 'by ſome *Anabaptiſts*; but it is the fault 'and corruption of every man, *&c.*'

'TIS probable ſome of thoſe who oppoſed infants-baptiſm in thoſe times, had embraced the opinions of the *Pelagians* about or iginal ſin. But the *Pædobaptiſts* did generally charge them with this opinion, becauſe they held that *infants* dying without actual ſin, were not damned; and that they need no baptiſm to waſh away original ſin, but were ſaved without it. However, ten years after, when the articles were again reviewed and corrected in many things, they thought it proper to leave this clauſe out, and only charged this hereſy upon the *Pelagians*. The 28th article concerning Baptiſm was the ſame that now it is, except the laſt clauſe, which relates to infant-baptiſm, which they laid down in theſe words: 'The 'cuſtom of the Church for baptizing young 'children, is both to be commended, and 'by all means to be retained in the 'church.'

IT ſeems by this, that the firſt *Reformers* did not found the practice of infants

fants-baptiſm upon ſcripture; but took it only as a commendable cuſtom, that had been uſed in the chriſtian church, and therefore ought to be retained. This new alteration made in the Common-prayer and articles of faith, cauſed the *Papiſts* to ſay, ‘ [x] That the Reformation was like to change ‘ as often as the faſhion did, ſince they ‘ ſeemed never to be at a point in any thing, ‘ but new models were thus continually fra- ‘ ming; to which it was anſwered, that it ‘ was no wonder that the corruptions ‘ which they had been introducing for ‘ above a thouſand years were not all diſ- ‘ covered or thrown out at once.’

THE length of time taken up in altering the Common-prayer and articles, obliges me to place the following ſtory ſomewhat out of courſe.

TWO years after the burning of *Joan* of *Kent*, ſays Biſhop *Burnet*, ‘ [y] One *George* ‘ *Van Pare*, a *Dutchman*, being accuſed for ‘ ſaying, that God the Father was only ‘ God, and that Chriſt was not very God; ‘ he was dealt with long to abjure, but ‘ would not. So on the 6th of *April*, 1551. ‘ he was condemned in the ſame man- ‘ ner that *Joan* of *Kent* was, and on the ‘ 25th of *April* was burnt in *Smithfield*. ‘ He ſuffered with great conſtancy of ‘ mind,

Geo. Van Pare *burnt*

An. Dom. 1551.

[x] *Burnet*'s *Hiſt. Ref.* vol. II. lib. i. p. 190.
[y] *Hiſt. Reform.* vol. II. lib. i. p. 112.

'mind, and kiſſed the ſtake and faggots 'that wêre to burn him. Of this *Pare* 'I find a *popiſh* writer ſaying, that he 'was a man of moſt wonderful ſtrict life, 'that he uſed not to eat above once in 'two days, and before he did eat would 'lie ſome time in his devotion proſtrate 'on the ground. All this they made uſe 'of to leſſen the credit of thoſe who had 'ſuffered formerly; for it was ſaid, they 'ſaw now, that men of harmleſs lives might 'be put to death for *Hereſy*, by the con-'feſſion of the *Reformers* themſelves: and 'in all the books publiſhed in Q. *Mary*'s 'days, juſtifying her ſeverity againſt the '*Proteſtants*, theſe inſtances were always 'made uſe of. And no part of *Cranmer*'s 'life expoſed him more than this did: 'It was ſaid, he had conſented, both to '*Lambert*'s and *Ann Aſkew*'s death in the 'former reign; who both ſuffered for *o-'pinions* which he himſelf held now, 'and he had now procured the death of 'theſe two perſons; and when he was 'brought to ſuffer himſelf, it was called 'a juſt retaliation on him. One thing 'was certain, that what he did in this 'matter flowed from no cruelty of temper 'in him, no man being farther from that 'black diſpoſition of mind; but it was 'truly the effect of thoſe principles by whch 'he governed himſelf.'

THEN *Burnet* goes on to give an account of the moderate *Anabaptiſts*, and ſays, '[z] For the other ſort of *Anabaptiſts*, ' who only denied infants baptiſm, I find ' no ſeverities uſed to them, but ſeveral ' books were written againſt them, to ' which they wrote ſome anſwers. It ' was ſaid, that Chriſt allowed little child- ' ren to be brought to him, and ſaid, *of* ' *ſuch was the kingdom of heaven*; and ' bleſſed them. Now if they were capable ' of the kingdom of *heaven*, they muſt ' be regenerated; for Chriſt ſaid, none but ' ſuch as *are born of water and of the Spirit* ' could enter into it. St. *Paul* had alſo ' called the children of believing parents ' *holy*, which ſeemed to relate to ſuch a ' conſecration of them as was made in ' baptiſm; and *baptiſm* being the ſeal of ' *chriſtians* in the room of *circumciſion* ' among the *Jews*, it was thought the one ' was as applicable to the children, as the ' other. And one thing was obſerved, that ' the whole world in that age, having ' been baptized in their infancy, if that ' baptiſm was nothing, then there were ' none truly baptized in being; but all ' were in the ſtate of mere nature. Now ' it did not ſeem reaſonable, that men ' who were not baptized themſelves, ſhould ' go and baptize others, and therefore the

[z] *Hiſt. Reform.* vol. II. p. 112.

' firſt

'first heads of that *sect* not being rightly 'baptized themselves, seemed not to act 'with any authority when they went to 'baptize others. The practice of the 'church so early begun, and continued 'without dispute so many ages, was at least 'a certain confirmation of a thing which 'had (to speak moderately) so good founda- 'tions in scripture for the lawfulness, tho' 'not any peremptory, but only probable 'proofs for the practice of it.'

An. Dom. 1552.

A motion to reform the Clergy.

THE same author informs us: '[a] That in 'the year 1552. a proposal was made for 'the correcting the great disorders of '*Clergymen*, which were occasioned by the 'extreme misery and poverty to which 'they were reduced. That some motions 'were made about it in parliament; but 'they took not effect: So one writ a 'book concerning it, which he dedicated 'to the lord *Chancellour*, then the bishop 'of *Ely*. He shewed, that without re- 'wards or encouragements, few would 'apply themselves to the pastoral function; 'and that those in it, if they could not 'subsist by it, must turn to other employ- 'ments; so that at that time, says he, 'many *Clergymen* were *Carpenters* and '*Taylors*, and some kept *Alehouses*.'

I mention this, because it is often cast upon the *Dissenters*, and particularly those

[a] *Hist. Ref.* part II. lib. i. p. 202.

called

called *Anabaptists*, that they encourage *Tradesmen* and *Mechanicks*. Now it is plain from their articles, they are for maintaining of *Ministers*, that they may be entirely bent to their sacred office; but if, in case of necessity, they are obliged to follow trades, for the maintenance of themselves and families, it is no more than what the *Clergy*, both *Papists* and *Protestants*, have done, till they could get sufficient allowance by law to free them from it.

BUT to return; these sad instances of persecution practised by the *Protestants* in this king's reign against the *Anabaptists*, are in *Fox*'s *Latin* book of martyrs, but left out in his *English*, out of a tender regard, as is supposed, to the reputation of the *martyrs* in Queen *Mary*'s Days.

[b] THE same is translated by Mr. *Peirce*. It being short, I will oblige the reader therewith, and with Mr. *Peirce*'s remarks upon it.

Peirce's *account and remarks on the burning of* Joan *of* Kent *and* Pare.

'IN king *Edward*'s reign some were put 'to death for heresy. One *Joan Bocher*, 'or *Joan* of *Kent*. Mr. *Strype* tells us, 'her heresy was, That she believed the 'Word was made flesh in the Virgin's belly, 'but not that he took flesh of the Virgin. 'Now, says Mr. *Fox*, when the *Protestant* '*Bishops* had resolved to put her to death, 'a friend of Mr. *John Rogers*, the divi-

[b] *Answ. to* Nichols, p. 33.

'nity-

'nity-reader in St. *Paul*'s church, came 'to him, earneſtly deſiring him to uſe his 'intereſt with the archbiſhop, that the poor 'woman's life might be ſpared, and other 'means uſed to prevent the ſpreading of 'her opinions, which might be done in 'time: urging too, that though while ſhe 'lived, ſhe infected few with her opi-'nions, yet ſhe might bring many to think 'well of it, by ſuffering death for it. He 'pleaded therefore that it was better ſhe 'ſhould be kept in ſome priſon, without an 'opportunity of propagating her notion a-'mong weak people, and ſo ſhe would 'do no harm to others, and might live to 'repent herſelf. *Rogers* on the other hand 'pleaded, ſhe ought to be put to death. 'Well then, ſays his *Friend*, if you are re-'ſolved to put an end to her life together 'with her opinion, chuſe ſome other kind 'of death, more agreeable to the gentle-'neſs and mercy preſcribed in the goſpel; 'there being no need, that ſuch torment-'ing deaths ſhould be taken up, in imita-'tion of the *Papiſts*. *Rogers* anſwered, that '*Burning Alive* was no cruel death, but 'eaſy enough. His *Friend* then hearing 'theſe words, which expreſſed ſo little re-'gard to poor creatures ſufferings, anſwer-'ed him with great vehemence, and ſtri-'king *Rogers*'s hand, which before he held 'faſt, ſaid to him, *Well, perhaps, it may* '*ſo happen, that you yourſelves ſhall have*

'*your*

' *your hands full of this mild burning.* ' And ſo it came to paſs; and *Rogers* was ' the firſt man who was burnt in Queen ' *Mary*'s time.

' THIS *Rogers*, ſays Mr. *Pierce*, was a ' *Nonconformiſt*, and a very excellent man, ' (and died nobly in the cauſe of Chriſt; ' but this *barbarity* of his deſerves to be ' expoſed: and the rather, becauſe God in ' his providence ſeems to have ſhewn his ' great diſpleaſure againſt it. I am apt to ' think *Rogers*'s friend was no other than ' *Fox* himſelf. As to the other inſtance, ' Mr. *Strype* tells us, that in the year 1552, ' *Sept*. 27. a letter was ſent to the arch- ' biſhop, to examine a *ſect* newly ſprung ' up in *Kent*. He ſays, it appears not what ' this *ſect* was; he ſuppoſes they might be ' the *Family of love*, or *David George*'s ' *ſect*; but theſe conjectures of his have ' no good foundation. I am perſuaded ' this *ſect* was no other than ſome good ' honeſt *Diſſenters*, who having been grie- ' ved to ſee ſo much of *Popery* ſtill retained, ' attempted a further Reformation them- ' ſelves, which would be a very diſpleaſing ' thing to our *biſhops*, who expect all men ' ſhould wait their leiſure. Now this I ' ground upon a Story which Mr. *Fox* ' immediately ſubjoins to what I juſt now ' mentioned from him.

' MUCH ſuch another inſtance is report- ' ed concerning *Humphry Middleton* (who ' was

'was afterwards burnt in Queen *Mary*'s 'days.) That when he, with ſome others, 'had been kept priſoners in the laſt year 'of King *Edward*, by the archbiſhop, and 'had been dreadfully teazed by him, 'and the reſt in commiſſion with him, 'were now juſt upon being condemned 'in open court, he ſaid unto him, *Well, 'reverend Sir, paſs what ſentence you think 'fit upon us: but that you may not ſay you 'was not fore-warned, I teſtify that your 'own turn will be next.* And according-'ly it came to paſs; for a little while after 'King *Edward* died, upon which they 'were ſet at liberty, and the *biſhops* caſt 'in priſon. This *Middleton* was afterwards, 'in Queen *Mary*'s days, burnt at *Canter-'bury*; ſo that the *commiſſion* which Mr. '*Strype* mentions, agrees in time and place 'with this ſtory.' Thus far Mr. *Pierce*.

MR. *Hugh Latimer*, in his Lent-Sermons preach'd before King *Edward* VI. ſays [e],

'THE *Anabaptiſts*, that were burnt here 'in divers towns in *England*, as I heard 'of credible men, I ſaw them not myſelf, 'went to their death even intrepid, as ye 'will ſay, without any fear in the world, 'chearfully.'

IN the ſaid ſermon, he further ſaith,

'I SHOULD have told you here of a 'certain *ſect* of *Hereticks* that ſpeak againſt 'this order and doctrine; they will have no 'magiſtrates, no judges on earth; here I 'have

[e] Pag. 56.

'have to tell you, what I have heard of late, 'by the relation of a credible perſon, and 'worſhipful man, of a town of this realm 'of *England*, that hath above five [hun-'dred] hereticks of this erroneous opi-'nion in it, as he ſaid.

The marginal note in the Edit. in 1607, ſays here he meaneth Anabaptiſts, *this is one of their errors, fol.* 51.

THAT the *Baptiſts* were very numerous at this time, is without controverſy: and no doubt, many of the *Martyrs* in Queen *Mary*'s days were ſuch, though hiſtorians ſeem to be ſilent with reſpect to the opinion of the *Martyrs* about baptiſm; neither can it be imagined, that the *Papiſts* would in the leaſt favour any of that *denomination* which they ſo much deteſted and abhorred: For in the examination of Mr. *Woodman*, before the biſhop of *Wincheſter*, in the church of St. *Mary Overies, Southwark*, the biſhop ſaid, '[d] Hold him a book, if he 'refuſe to ſwear, he is an *Anabaptiſt*, and 'ſhall be excommunicated.'

Q. Mary An. Dom. 1553.

An. Dom. 1555.

AGAIN, in the examination of Mr. *Philpot* before the lords of Queen *Mary*'s council, *Nov.* 6, 1555. *Rich* ſaith unto him, '[e] All *Hereticks* do boaſt of the ſpirit 'of God, and every one would have a 'church by himſelf; as *Joan* of *Kent*, 'and the *Anabaptiſts*.'

ANOTHER inſtance of their hatred and cruelty towards the *Anabaptiſts*, *Spanhe-*

An. Dom. 1556.

[d] *Fox*, p. 1578. *firſt Edit.*
[e] *Ibib.* p. 1407.

mius

mius gives us an account of. *David George*, of *Delph* in *Holland*, being driven from his own country by perſecution, fled to the city of *Bazil*, where he lived for ſome time in great reputation, and by his modeſt dreſs, liberal table, honeſt attendance, and prudent converſation, gained the favour both of high and low: He died in the year 1556, and was honourably buried in St. *Laurence* church. Some time after his death, it was diſcovered, that he was an *Anabaptiſt*; upon which his houſe, and thoſe of his followers were ſearched, a certain number of *Divines* and *Lawyers* appointed to examine them, his opinions were condemned by an ordinance, his picture carried about and burnt, and his corps taken up three years after buried, and burnt, &c.

David George *burnt three years after his death.*

DURING the life of this bloody Queen, which was but ſhort, two hundred and eighty four perſons were put to moſt cruel kinds of death for religion: but he that wrote the Preface to biſhop *Ridley*'s book *de Cœna Domini*, ſays, That in the two firſt years of the Queen's perſecution, there were above eight hundred perſons put to death for religion: So that Mr. *Fox* has come very ſhort in his account, as biſhop *Burnet* obſerved.

Suppoſed to be Grindal *afterwards archbiſhop of* Canterbury.

Q. Elizabeth. An. Dom. 1558.

WE come now to the reign of Queen *Elizabeth*; who, upon her acceſſion to the crown, ordered all that were impriſoned on on the account of religion to be ſet at liberty. Upon which, ‘ [d] one, ſays biſhop ‘ *Burnet*, that uſed to talk pleaſantly, told ‘ her the four *Evangeliſts* continued ſtill ‘ priſoners, and that the people longed much ‘ to ſee them at liberty. She anſwered ſhe ‘ would talk with *themſelves*, and know ‘ their own mind.’

SIR *Francis Walſingham* wrote a long letter to a *Frenchman*, given him an account of all the ſeverities of the Queen's government, both againſt *Papiſts* and *Puritans*. The ſubſtance of which is, ſays biſhop *Burnet*, ‘ [e] That the Queen laid down two ‘ maxims of ſtate: the one was, *not to force* ‘ *conſciences*; the other was, *not to let* ‘ *factious practices go unpuniſhed*, becauſe ‘ they were covered with the pretences of ‘ conſcience. At firſt ſhe did not revive ‘ thoſe ſevere laws paſt in her father's time, ‘ by which the refuſal of the oath of *Supre-* ‘ *macy* was made *treaſon*; but left her peo- ‘ to the freedom of their thoughts, and ‘ made it only penal to extol a foreign ‘ juriſdiction. She alſo laid aſide the word ‘ *ſupreme head*; and the refuſers of the ‘ oath were only diſabled from holding ‘ benefices or charges during their refuſal. ‘ Upon *Pius* the Vth's excommunicating ‘ her, though the rebellion in the north

Sir Francis Walſingham's *letter*.

[d] *Abridgment*, lib. iv. p. 340.
[e] *Ibid*. p. 382.

'was chiefly occaſioned by that, ſhe only 'made a law againſt the bringing over, or 'publiſhing of *Bulls*, and the venting of '*Agnus Dei's*, or ſuch other love-tokens, 'which were ſent from *Rome* on deſign 'to draw the hearts of her people from 'her, which were no eſſential parts of 'that religion; ſo that this could hurt 'none of their conſciences. But after the '20th year of her reign, it appeared that 'the king of *Spain* deſigned to invade 'her dominions, and that the *Prieſts* that 'were ſent over from the *Seminaries* beyond 'ſea, were generally employed to cor-'rupt her *Subjects* in their allegiance; by 'which treaſon was carried in the clouds, 'and infuſed ſecretly in confeſſion. Then 'pecuniary puniſhments were inflicted on 'ſuch as withdrew from the church; and 'in concluſion, ſhe was forced to make 'laws of greater rigour, but did often mi-'tigate the ſeverity of them to all that 'would promiſe to adhere to her in caſe 'of a foreign invaſion. As for the *Pu-'ritans*, as long as they only inveighed 'againſt ſome abuſes, as pluralities, non-'reſidence or the like, it was not their 'zeal againſt thoſe, but their violence, that 'was condemned. When they refuſed to 'comply with ſome *ceremonies*, and queſ-'tioned the ſuperiority of the *biſhops*, and 'declared for a *democracy* in the church, 'they were connived at with great gentle-

'neſs:

'nefs: but it was obferved, that they 'affected popularity much, and the me- 'thods they took to compafs their ends 'were judged dangerous, and they made 'fuch ufe of the averfion the nation had 'to *popery*, that it was vifible they were 'in a hazard of running from one ex- 'treme to another. They fet up a new 'model of *church-difcipline*, which was 'like to prove no lefs dangerous to the 'liberties of private men, than to the fo- 'vereign power of the prince. Yet all 'this was born with, as long as they pro- 'ceeded with thofe expreffions of duty 'which became *fubjects*. But afterwards, 'when they refolved to carry on their 'defigns, without waiting for the confent 'of the *magiftrate*, and entred into com- 'binations; when they began to defame 'the government, by ridiculous *pafquils*, 'and boafted of their number and ftrength, 'and in fome places break out into tu- 'mults; then it appeared that it was *fac- 'tion*, and not *zeal*, that animated them. 'Upon that the Queen found it neceffary 'to reftrain them more than fhe had done 'formerly. Yet fhe did it with all the '*moderation* that could confift with the 'peace of the church and ftate. And thus 'from this letter, fays *Burnet*, an idea 'of this whole reign may be juftly 'formed.'

 THE

THE ſhare the *Baptiſts* had in the ſeverities of this reign, will appear by the following inſtances. Dr. *Wall* ſays, '[f] About the 16th year of Queen *Elizabeth*, 'a congregation of *Dutch Antipædobaptiſts* 'was diſcovered without *Aldgate* in *London*, whereof twenty ſeven were taken and 'impriſoned. And the next month one '*Dutchman* and ten women were condemned.' *Marius de Aſſigny* tells us,

An. Dom. 1575. [g] That it was at *Eaſter*, *An. Dom.* 1575. which muſt have been the 17th of *Elizabeth*, that four of the former recanted at St. *Paul*'s croſs, the 25th of *May*; and that the reſt were baniſhed.

Their abjuration was in theſe words:

An abjuration of ſome Anabaptiſts.

'WHEREAS, we being ſeduced by 'the devil, the ſpirit of errror, and 'by falſe teachers, have fallen into theſe 'moſt damnable and deteſtable errors, that 'Chriſt took not fleſh of the ſubſtance 'of the Virgin *Mary*; that the *infants* of 'the faithful ought not to be baptized; 'that a chriſtian man may not be a *magiſtrate*, or bear the ſword and office 'of authority; and that it is not lawful 'for a chriſtian man to take an *oath*: 'Now, by the grace of God, and by the 'aſſiſtance of good and learned *miniſters*

[f] *Hiſt. Bap.* lib. ii. p. 212.

[g] *Myſtery of Anabaptiſm*, p. 368.

'of

'of Chriſt's church, I underſtand the ſame 'to be moſt damnable and deteſtable he'reſies; and do aſk God, before his church, 'mercy for my ſaid former errors, and 'do forſake, recant, and renounce them; 'and I abjure them from the bottom of 'my heart, proteſting I certainly believe 'the contrary. And further, I confeſs, 'that the whole doctrine, eſtabliſhed and 'publiſhed in the church of *England*, 'and alſo that is received in the *Dutch* 'church in *London*, is found true and 'according to God's word: Whereunto 'in all things I ſubmit myſelf, and will 'be moſt gladly a member of the ſaid '*Dutch* church; from henceforth utterly 'abandoning and forſaking all and every '*anabaptiſtical* error.'

THIS abjuration was taken from theſe *Walloon Anabaptiſts* by Dr. *De Laune*, who was then miniſter of the *Dutch* church in *Auguſtin Friars* in *London*. In the 18th year of Queen *Elizabeth*, *An. Dom.* 1575. Mr. *Fuller* ſaith, '[h] Now began the *Anabaptiſts* wonderfully to encreaſe in the '*land*; and as we are ſorry that *any* '*countrymen* ſhould be ſeduced with that 'opinion, ſo we are glad that the *Eng*'*liſh* as yet were free from that infection. 'For on *Eaſter-Day* was diſcloſed a *con*'*gregation* of *Dutch Anabaptiſts*, without

[h] *Ch. Hiſt.* cent. xvi. p. 104.

 '*Ald-*

'*Aldgate* in *London,* whereof ſeven and 'twenty were taken and impriſoned, and 'four bearing faggots at *Paul's Croſs*, ſo-'lemnly recanted their dangerous opinions. 'Next month, one *Dutchman* and ten wo-'men were condemned; of whom one '*woman* was converted, to renounce her 'errors; eight were baniſhed the land; '*two* more ſo obſtinate, that command 'was iſſued out for their burning in *Smith-*'*field.* But to reprieve them from ſo cruel 'a death, a *grave divine* ſent the follow-'ing letter to Queen *Elizabeth.* The letter was wrote in *Latin,* I ſhall give only the *Engliſh* tranſlation thereof.

Mr. Fox's letter to Queen Elizabeth.

MOST ſerene and happy princeſs, moſt illuſtrious Queen, the honour of our country, and ornament of the age. As nothing hath been further from my thoughts and expectation, than ever to diſturb your moſt excellent majeſty by my troubleſome interruption; ſo it grieves me very much, that I muſt break that ſilence which has hitherto been the reſult of my mind. But ſo it now happens, by I know not what infelicity, that the preſent time obliges me, contrary to my hope and opinion, to that which of all things in the world I leaſt deſired, and tho' hitherto I have been troubleſome to no body, I am now contrary to my inclination, conſtrained to be importunate, even

even with my princeſs; not in any matter or cauſe of my own, but thro' the calamity brought upon others; and by how much the more ſharp and lamentable that is, by ſo much the more I am ſpurred on to deprecate it. I underſtand there are ſome here in *England*, tho' not *Engliſh*, but come hither from *Holland*, I ſuppoſe both men and women, who having been tried according to law, publickly declared their repentance, are happily reclaimed. Many others are condemned to exile; a right ſentence in my opinion. But I hear there is one or two of theſe, who are appointed to the moſt ſevere of puniſhments, *viz. burning*, except your clemency prevent. Now in this one affair I conceive there are two things to be conſidered; the one is the wickneſs of their errors, the other, the ſharpedneſs of their puniſhment. As to their errors indeed, no man of ſenſe can deny that they are moſt abſurd: And I wonder that ſuch monſtrous opinions could come into the mind of any *Chriſtian*; but ſuch is the ſtate of human weakneſs, if we are left never ſo little a while deſtitute of the divine light, whither is it we do not fall; and we have great reaſon to give God thanks on this account, that I hear not of any *Engliſhman*, that is inclined to this madneſs. As to theſe fanatical *ſects* therefore, it is certain, they are by no means to be countenanced in a commonwealth, but in my opinion ought to be ſuppreſſed by proper correction. But to *roaſt alive* the bodies of poor wretches, that offend rather through blindneſs of judgment, than perverſeneſs of will, in *fire* and *flames*, raging with *pitch* and *brimſtone*, is a hard-hearted thing, and more agreeable to the practice of the *Romaniſts*, than the cuſtom of the *Goſpellers*; yea, is evidently of the ſame kind, as if it had flowed from the *Romiſh Prieſts*, from the firſt author of ſuch cruelty, *Innocent* the third. Oh! that none had ever brought ſuch a *Phalarian Bull* into the meek church of Chriſt! I do not ſpeak theſe things, becauſe I am pleaſed with their wickedneſs, or favour the errors of any men; but ſeeing I my ſelf am a man, I muſt therefore favour the life of man; not that he ſhould err, but that he might repent. Nay my pity extends not only to the life of man, but even to the beaſts.

FOR ſo it is perhaps a folly in me; but I ſpeak the truth, that I can hardly paſs by a ſlaughter-houſe where cattle are killing, but my mind ſhrinks back, with a ſecret ſenſe of their pains. And truly, I greatly admire the clemency of God in this, who had ſuch reſpect to the mean brute creatures, formerly prepared for ſacrifices, that they muſt not be committed to the *flames*, before their blood had been poured out at the foot of the altar. Whence we may gather

gather, that in inflicting of punishments, tho' just, we must not be over rigorous, but temper the sharpness of rigour with clemency. Wherefore if I may be so bold with the majesty of so great a princess, I humbly beg of your royal highness, for the sake of Christ, who was consecrated to suffer for the lives of many, this favour at my request, which even the divine clemency would engage you to, that if it may be, and what cannot your authority do in these cases, these miserable wretches may be spared; at least that a stop may be put to the horrour, by changing their punishment into some other kind. There are excommunications, and close imprisonment; there are bonds; there is perpetual banishment, burning of the hand, and whipping, or even slavery itself. This one thing I most earnestly beg; that the piles and flames in *Smithfield*, so long ago extinguished by your happy government, may not now be again revived: That if I may not obtain this, I pray with the greatest earnestness, that out of your great pity you would grant us a month or two, in which we may try whether the Lord will give them grace to turn from their dangerous errors; lest with the destruction of their bodies, their souls be in danger of eternal ruin.

AFTER

Confirmed by Fuller. AFTER this, *Fuller* goes on and ſaith, 'This letter was written by Mr. *John Fox*, 'from whoſe own hand I tranſcribed it; 'very loth that *Smithfield*, formerly con-'ſecrated with *martyrs aſhes*, ſhould now 'be profan'd with *hereticks*; and deſirous 'that the *Papiſts* might enjoy their own '*monopoly* of cruelty, in *burning con-'demn'd Perſons*.

'BUT tho' Queen *Elizabeth* conſtantly 'called him her *Father Fox*; yet herein 'ſhe was no *dutiful daughter*, giving him 'a flat denial [k]. Indeed damnable were their 'impieties, and ſhe neceſſitated to this ſe-'verity, who having formerly puniſhed ſome '*traitors*, if now ſparing theſe *blaſphemers*, 'the world would condemn her as being 'more earneſt in aſſerting her own ſafety, 'than God's honour. Hereupon the writ '*De hæretico comburendo*, (which for ſe-'venteen years had hung only up *in ter-'rorem*) was now taken down, and put in 'execution, and the two *Anabaptiſts* burnt
July 22. 'in *Smithfield*, died in great horror, with 'crying and roaring.'

GREAT were the hardſhips and ſufferings of the *Puritans* (of whom it may be reaſonably ſuppoſed, that ſome of them were *Baptiſts*, tho' they had not as yet form'd themſelves into diſtinct ſocieties) by

[k] *As to the ſaving of their lives, if after a month's reprieve and conference with divines, they would not recant their errors*, à *Stow*, ut prius.

the

the cruelty of the *biſhops*, inſtigated by the Queen's hatred of them. 'She had high 'notions of the ſovereign power of princes, 'and of her own abſolute ſupremacy in 'church-affairs; and being of opinion that 'all methods of ſeverity were lawful to 'bring her ſubjects to an outward unifor-'mity, ſhe countenanced all the engines of 'perſecution, as *ſpiritual courts, high com-'miſſion*[1], *and ſtar-chamber*, and ſtretch'd 'her prerogative to ſupport them beyond 'the laws, and againſt the ſenſe of the na-'tion.'

Supplication of the juſtices of Norfolk.

THAT the *Baptiſts* had no ſmall ſhare in the ſufferings of theſe times, we may gather from the ſupplication of the juſtices of the peace of the county of *Norfolk*, who upon complaint made to them of the cruelty of the biſhop of *Norwich*, with reſpect to the long and illegal impriſonment of ſome of the *Browniſts*, their worſhips were pleaſed to move the biſhop in their favour; with which his lordſhip was ſo diſſatisfied, that he drew up twelve articles of impeachment againſt the *juſtices* themſelves, and cauſed them to be ſummoned before the Queen and Council to anſwer for their *miſdemeanours*. Notwithſtanding his lordſhip's citation of them before the council, they writ again to their honours, praying to interpoſe in behalf of the injuries that were offer'd to divers godly miniſters. And

[1] *Neal's Hiſt. Puritans*, p. 602. vol. I.

in

in their ſupplication they ſay, 'We ſerve
'her Majeſty and the country as *magiſtrates*
'and *juſtices* of peace, according to law;
'we reverence the law and law-maker;
'when the law ſpeaks we keep not ſilence;
'when it commandeth we obey; by law we
'proceed againſt all *offenders* [m]; we touch
'none that the law ſpareth, and ſpare none
'that the law toucheth; we allow not of
'*Papiſts*, of the *Family of Love*, of *Ana-*
'baptiſts or *Browniſts*: No, we puniſh all
'theſe; and yet we are chriſtned with the
'odious name of *Puritans*, a term com-
'pounded of the *hereſies* above-mention'd,
'which we diſclaim.'

Anno 1589. IN the year 1589, Dr. *Some*, a man of great note in thoſe times, writ a treatiſe againſt *Barrow*, *Greenwood*, *Penry*, and others of the *puritan* ſect; wherein he endeavour'd to ſhew what agreement there was between the opinions of the *English Anabaptiſts* and theſe men.

Dr. Some's *account of the* Baptiſts. HIS method is firſt to ſhew, what was the opinion of the *Anabaptiſtical Recuſants*, as he terms them; then wherein theſe men did agree with, or differ from them; and then undertakes to confute their ſuppoſed errors.

THE opinions he charges the *Anabaptiſts* with, when they are ſtripp'd of his dreſs, are only to this purpoſe:

[m] *Neal's Hiſt. Purit.* p. 388. v. I.

THAT

THAT the *miniſters* of the goſpel ought to be maintained by the voluntary contributions of the people:

THAT the civil power has no right to make and impoſe eccleſiaſtical laws:

THAT people ought to have the right of chuſing their own *miniſters:*

THAT the high-commiſſion court was an antichriſtian uſurpation:

THAT thoſe who are qualify'd to preach, ought not to be hinder'd by the civil power:

THAT tho' the Lord's-prayer be a rule and foundation of prayer, yet not to be uſed as a form; and that no forms of prayer ought to be impoſed on the church:

THAT the baptiſm adminiſtred in the church of *Rome* is invalid:

THAT a true conſtitution and diſcipline is eſſential to a true church; and that the worſhip of God in the church of *England* is in many things defective.

HE touches but briefly on their opinion of *baptizing believers* only; and brings up the rear with ſaying, they count it blaſphemy for any man to arrogate to himſelf the title of *Doctor of Divinity*; that is, as he explains it, to be called *Rabbi*, or *lord* and *maſter* of other mens faith.

HE acknowledges, that there were ſeveral *anabaptiſtical conventicles* in *London*, and other places; that ſome of this ſort, as well as the *Papiſts*, had been bred at our univerſities; and tells a ſtory of one *T. L.* who

who at a conventicle in *London*, took upon him to expound the ſcriptures, conceive long prayers on a ſudden, and to excommunicate two perſons, who were formerly of that brotherhood, but had now left them.

Remarks thereon. IF this be what their *adverſaries* had chiefly to charge them with; what account might we have expected, had they been allowed to publiſh their own *faith*, and to tranſmit their own *hiſtory* down to poſterity? And tho' this *gentleman* ſeems to deal more favourably with this *ſect* than many *others*, yet he uſes the unfair method which I ſuppoſe they thought lawful, in writing againſt *hereticks*; that is, to aſſert they hold ſuch *opinions*, without producing any proof of it, or referring to any of their *works*, left they ſhould publiſh them, and people ſhould have opportunity to enquire what they ſay for themſelves.

HE likewiſe diſcovers too much of the ſpirit of *perſecution*, that reigned in theſe times, and endeavours to excite the *civil power* to be more ſevere againſt the *ſectaries*. ‘ If, ſays he, every particular con-‘ gregation in *England* might ſet up and ‘ put down at their pleaſure, *popiſh* and ‘ *anabaptiſtical fancies* would overflow this ‘ land; the conſequence would be dan-‘ gerous, *viz.* the diſhonour of God, the ‘ contempt of her majeſty, the overthrow ‘ of 'of the church and universities, and the 'utter confusion of this noble kingdom. 'Queen *Elizabeth*, and her honourable 'Councellours do see, and will prevent 'this mischief; it is more than time to 'look unto it.'

WITH such false representations as these, the *clergy* have been used to frighten the *court* into the practice of persecution.

Q. Elizabeth banishes the Anabaptists.

BUT to close this reign, Queen *Elizabeth* having by her proclamation commanded all *Anabaptists* and other *Hereticks* to depart the *land*, whether they were *natives* or *foreigners*, under the penalties of *imprisonment* or loss of *goods*; all that were of this *opinion* were obliged either to conceal their principles, or fly into some other country, where they might enjoy the liberty of their religion.

Queen Elizabeth's character.

UPON which many of the *dissenters* went over to *Holland*: Among whom there were not a few *Baptists*, as well *English* as *Dutch*; so that there was now no great number of *Dissenters* of any denomination, that dared openly to appear. '[n] Queen '*Elizabeth* however, with all her blemishes, says Mr. *Neal*, stands upon record, 'as a wise and politick princess; for delivering the kingdom from the difficulties in which it was involved at her Accession; for preserving the protestant re-

[n] *Hist. Puritans*, p. 602. vol I.

'formation

'formation against the potent attempts of 'the *Pope*, the *Emperor*, and king of '*Spain* abroad, and the Queen of *Scots* 'and her *popish* subjects at home; and for 'advancing the renown of the *English Na*-'*tion* beyond any of her predecessors. 'Her majesty held the ballance of *Europe*; 'and was in high esteem with all foreign 'princes, the greatest part of her reign: 'And tho' her *protestant* subjects were di-'vided about church affairs, they all dis-'covered a high veneration for her royal 'person and government; on which ac-'count she was the glory of the age in 'which she lived, and will be the ad-'miration of posterity.'

CHAP. II.

From the end of the reign of Queen Elizabeth, *to the end of the reign of King* James I.

King James I. An. Dom. 1602.

KING *James* the first next ascends the throne. '[a] He was born of *Ro*-'*man Catholick* parents; but being taken 'from his mother in his infancy, had been

[a] *Rapin*, book xviii. p. 159.

'edu-

educated in the proteſtant religion, and
‘ always profeſſed it. On the other hand,
‘ the religion he had been brought up in,
‘ tho' proteſtant, differed a little from the
‘ religion eſtabliſhed in *England*, if not in
‘ doctrine, at leaſt in diſcipline, and ſome
‘ other points of external worſhip, which
‘ were conſidered by the two churches as
‘ very important. In a word, it was the
‘ *preſbyterian* or *puritanical* religion. In
‘ fine, this prince had ſhewn on num-
‘ berleſs occaſions, that he was far from
‘ being an enemy to the *Romiſh* religion.
‘ All this formed a certian contraſt, which
‘ bred an univerſal ſuſpenſe. The *Catholicks*
‘ hoped to meet under his government
‘ with gentler treatment, and more indul-
‘ gence, than under *Elizabeth*; nay, they
‘ carried their expectation much farther.
‘ The *Preſbyterians* flattered themſelves,
‘ that *James*, who had been educated in
‘ their religion, would promote the re-
‘ forming of the church of *England* upon the
‘ plan of that of *Scotland*; and hoped ſhortly
‘ to ſee the downfal of the *eccleſiaſtical hi-
‘ rarchy*. Finally, the *Church-of-England-
‘ men* thought to have reaſon to expect
‘ that the new king would conform to their
‘ religion, ſince it was eſtabliſhed by law.
‘ But after all, the hopes of the three *par-
‘ ties* could not but be mixed with fears,
‘ ſince the king had not yet declared.

'HE must, says *Rapin*, at the time 'I am now speaking of, have conceiv- 'ed a larger notion than had been hi- 'therto formed of the power of an *English* 'king; since when he came to *Newark*, 'he ordered a *cut-purse* to be hanged, by 'his sole warrant, and without trial.'

IT cannot be expected I should be very particular with respect to the sufferings of the *Baptists* during this reign and the former part of the next, because they were involved in all the persecutions that befel the *Nonconformists*, under the general name of *Puritans:* For those who refused to conform to the church of *England*, were counted among the *Puritans*. Those who have read the correspondence that passed between our *bishops* and the foreign *Protestant* divines, may observe a great deal of good temper and good judgment in their desires to have had the church reformed from all remains and footsteps of *Popery*, and satisfaction given to scrupulous and tender consciences; but the stiffness of Queen *Elizabeth*, and that fondness for pomp and magnificence in worship among the generality, hindred the reformation from going any farther.

An. Dom. 1604. CALDERWOOD tells us, that on the 12th of *Jan.* 1604. [k] The *Bishops* were called 'upon by his Majesty, and were gravely

[k] *Hist. of the Reform. Scot.* p. 474.

'de-

'desired to advise upon all corruptions in 'doctrine, ceremonies and discipline, as 'they will answer it to God in consci-'ence, or to his majesty upon their obe-'dience; that they should return the third 'day. On that day they returned, and 'answered, they found all well; and when 'his majesty with great fervency brought 'instances to the contrary, they with great 'earnestness, upon their knees, craved 'that nothing might be altered, lest *Romish* 'recusants, punished by the statutes for 'their disobedience, and *Puritans*, punish-'ed by deprivation from callings and livings 'for *Nonconformity*, should say, they had 'cause to insult them, as men who had 'travailed to bind them to that, which 'by their own mouths was now confessed 'to be erroneous. Thus, by a most dis-'honourable resolution, they prefer their 'own fame and reputation to the peace 'of the church; and because they have 'once oppressed them, will always do 'so, rather than seem to own themselves 'fallible men [c].'

The bishops against any alteration in the church.

Now what could be expected from such men, who had drawn a weak king over to their interest, and who were resolved to continue in their errors rather than confess themselves fallible? And what *Christian*, or what *Englishman*, can, with-

[c] *Hist. account of further attempts for reformation*, p. 34.

out the utmoſt concern and reſentment, read the *hiſtories* of thoſe times, and obſerve the cruel uſage, great hardſhips and ſufferings of not a few, but a great multitude; who for their firmneſs in the propagation of a rational religion, their conſtancy in piety, and all chriſtian virtue, and their averſion to all methods of cruelty and uncharitableneſs, have been branded with the names of *Puritans*, *Preſbyterians*, *Anabaptiſts*, &c. whereby the unthinking multitude have been ſpirited up to hatred againſt all perſons under thoſe denominations, and more particularly to thoſe of the laſt denomination.

WHEN king *James* firſt came into *England*, he not only went over to the church of *England*, but even laboured to force the *Puritans* to conform, to be revenged on them for what the *Preſbyterian* ſynods had made him ſuffer in *Scotland*.

The Puritans *petition for a toleration.*

THE *Puritans* preſented a petition to him, not only for a *toleration*, but alſo to pray him, that ſundry articles of the church of *England*, with which they could not comply, might be reformed.

The biſhops oppoſe it.

THE *Biſhops* ſtrenuouſly oppoſed this petition, and entreated the king to leave religion as he found it at his acceſſion to the crown, without any innovation. The king, not to appear at firſt too partial, and to make believe he would not be determined without hearing the arguments on both

both ſides, appointed a conference between the two *parties*, wherein he would be moderator himſelf; and publiſhed a proclamation, commanding both ſides to be quiet, till matters were regulated as he ſhould judge proper. This conference was held at *Hampton-Court*, in the year 1604, and laſted three days. The *Puritans* ſoon ſaw what they were to expect.

A conference held at Hampton-Court.

DR. *Wellwood* ſays [d], 'This conference 'was but a blind to introduce epiſcopacy 'in *Scotland*; all the *Scotch* noblemen then 'at court being deſign'd to be preſent, and 'others, both *noblemen* and *miniſters*, be'ing called up from *Scotland* by the king's 'letter to aſſiſt at it.'

THE King's conduct was ſo agreeable to the *biſhops* and their friends, that beſides other palpable flatteries, *Whitgift*, archbiſhop of *Canterbury*, unwilling to miſs ſo fair an opportunity to flatter him, ſaid [e], 'He verily believed the king ſpoke by the 'Spirit of God.'

Whitgift *flatters the King.*

IN concluſion, both *parties* being preſent, the king ſaid [f], 'For the *biſhops* I 'will anſwer, that it is not their purpoſe 'preſently and out of hand to enforce obe'dience, but by fatherly admonitions and 'conferences to induce ſuch as are diſaf-

The King yields to the biſhops.

[d] *Notes on* Wilſon, *p.* 665. *Comp. Hiſt. Notes on* Rapin, *p.* 162.
[e] *Rapin*, vol. II. p. 162.
[f] *Ibidem*, p. 162.

 'fected:

'fected: But if any be of an oppoſite 'and turbulent Spirit, I will have them 'enforced to a conformity ---- I will --- 'that a time be limited by the *biſhops* of 'every *dioceſe* to ſuch, and they that will 'not yield, whatſoever they are, let them 'be removed; for we muſt not prefer the 'credit of a few private men to the ge'neral peace of the church.'

Whitgift *dies, and* Bancroft *ſucceeds him, a great enemy to the* Puritans.

SOON after this, *Whitgift* died, and was ſucceeded by *Richard Bancroft*, a prelate who never ceaſed to incenſe the king againſt the *Puritans*, and do them all the miſchief he could. Herein he was but too cloſely imitated by the reſt of the *biſhops*, who found a double advantage in deſtroying the *Puritans*. In the firſt *firſt* place, they made their court to the king, who hated them mortally. 2*dly*, They preſerv'd their *hierarchy*, which the *Puritans* were deſirous to overthrow.

A proclamation baniſhing all jeſuits and prieſts, another, enjoining the Puritans *to conform.*

THE perſecution which the *Puritans* ſuffer'd whilſt *Bancroft* was at the head of the *clergy*, induced many families to withdraw from the kingdom, to enjoy elſewhere liberty of conſcience, deny'd them at home. A proclamation is now publiſhed by the king, commanding all *Jeſuits* and other *Prieſts*, having orders from any foreign power, to depart the kingdom: which was ſoon followed by another, enjoining the *Puritans* to conform to the worſhip of the eſtabliſh'd church.

'THERE

'THERE was not seen here, says *Rapin*[g], 'the same care to justify the king's con-'duct, with respect to this sort of perse-'cution. The king intimated in the first, 'that he would have regard to the tender 'consciences of such *Catholicks* as could 'not comply with the received doctrines of 'the church of *England*; but in this 'there was not the least indulgence for the 'tender consciences of the *Puritans*. These 'were all a set of obstinate people, who 'deserved to have no favour shewn them.' Rapin's *remarks thereupon.*

BISHOP *Burnet* observes[h], 'that from 'the year 1606. to his dying-day, he con-'tinued always writing and talking against 'popery, but acting for it.'

THE persecution growing still more violent against the *Puritans*, great numbers of them resolved to go and settle in *Virginia*. Accordingly some departed for that country: But *Bancroft*, seeing many more ready to take the same voyage, obtained a proclamation, enjoining them not to go without the king's express license. The court was apprehensive this *sect* would in the end become too numerous and powerful in *America*; and was not so well affected to the *Puritans*, as to the *Papists*. *The* Puritans *settle in* Virginia.

THE *Puritans* were consider'd as enemies to the king, and to monarchy; but the *Papists* as hearty wishers, that the king

g *Hist. of England,* vol. II. p. 163.
h *History of his own time,* vol. I. p. 12.

 might

might meet with no oppoſition to his will. This was ſufficient to induce the court to countenance the *latter*, and cauſe the *former* to endure continual mortifications.

An. Dom. 1608. Enoch Clapham *writes againſt the ſeveral ſects.*

IN the year 1608, one *Enoch Clapham* writ a ſmall piece * againſt the ſeveral *ſects* of the *Proteſtants* in thoſe times. In which he repreſents, by way of dialogue, the opinions that each ſect held, and ſomewhat of their ſtate and condition at that time. He takes notice of their flying out of their own nation, to plant a church among the people of another language; and that they alledged in their defence, *Elias*'s flying in time of perſecution, and our Saviour's advice to his diſciples, *if they were perſecuted in one city, to fly into another*; and complain of thoſe who remained in *England* for leaving the publick aſſemblies, and running into woods and meadows, and meeting in bye ſtables, barns, and haylofts, for ſervice.

HE diſtinguiſhes the *Anabaptiſts* from *Puritans* and *Browniſts* on the one hand, and from the *Arians* and *Socinians* on the other; and makes all theſe zealous oppoſers of each other.

He gives a particular account of the Anabaptiſts.

THE *Anabaptiſts*, according to his account, held, that repentance and faith muſt precede baptiſm; that the baptiſm both of the church of *England* and of the *Puritans* was invalid, and that the true baptiſm was amongſt them. He ſays further, that they

* *Errors on the right-hand.*

complained

complained againſt the term *Anabaptiſt*, as a name of *reproach* unjuſtly caſt upon them. He alſo takes notice, that ſome of this opinion were *Dutchmen*, who, beſides the denial of *Infant-baptiſm*, held, that it was unlawful to bear arms: That Chriſt did not receive his human nature of the virgin, but brought it down with him from heaven; and agreed with the *Roman Catholicks* in the doctrines of reprobation, free-will, and juſtification. That there were others who went under this denomination that were *Engliſhmen*, to whom he does not ſo directly charge the former opinions, only the denial of their firſt *baptiſm*, and ſeparating both from the eſtabliſh'd *church*, and other *Diſſenters*; and ſays, that they came out from the *Browniſts*, and that there was a congregation of them in *Holland*.

WHEN the *Anabaptiſt* is aſked what religion he is of, he is made to anſwer; *Of the true religion, commonly termed Anabaptiſm, from our baptizing.*

WHEN he is aſked concerning the church or congregation he was joined to in *Holland*; he anſwers, *There be certain* Engliſh *people of us that came out from the* Browniſts.

WHEN the *Arian* ſays, I am of the mind that there is no true baptiſm upon earth; the *Anabaptiſt* replies, *I pray thee, ſon, ſay not ſo; the congregation I am of can, and doth adminiſter true baptiſm.*

WHEN

WHEN an enquirer after Truth offers, upon his proving what he has ſaid, to leave his old religion; the *Anabaptiſt* anſwers; *You may ſay, if God will give thee grace to leave it; for it is a peculiar grace to leave* Sodom *and* Egypt, *ſpiritually ſo called.*

WHEN the ſame perſon offers to join with them, and firmly betake himſelf to their faith; the *Anabaptiſt* replies: *The dew of heaven come upon you; to-morrow I will bring you into our ſacred congregation, that ſo you may come to be informed in the faith, and after that to be purely baptized.*

NOW this account being given by one that writ againſt them, may be the better depended upon. And he aſſures the reader, in his preface to theſe dialogues, that the characters which he gives of each *ſect*, were not without ſundry years experience had of them all.

THE *Diſſenters* that were driven into *Holland* by the ſeverity of the perſecutions in *England*, having their liberty there, ſet up ſeveral churches, which they formed as they thought moſt agreeable to the word of God.

A church of English *Baptiſts in* Holland.

THERE was one church of *Engliſh* exiles at *Leyden*, whereof Mr. *John Robinſon* was paſtor; another at *Amſterdam*, which had Mr. *Ainſworth* for their paſtor; and ſoon after theſe were ſet up, Mr. *Johnſon*'s and Mr. *John Smith*'s churches, the latter of which went under the name of *Anabaptiſts*;

baptists: so that to do justice to the *history*, we must now follow them into those parts; but I shall confine myself to the *English* only.

Mr. John Smith, *their pastor.*

IT was in the beginning of this reign, that the aforesaid Mr. *John Smith* left *England*. He had been for some time a minister of the established church; but disliking several things both in her discipline and ceremonies, he went over into *Holland*, and joined himself to the *English* church of *Brownists* at *Amsterdam*, of which Mr. *Ainsworth* was then the minister; and so greatly was he esteemed for his piety and learning, that he was accounted *one of the grandees of the separation* [i].

Some account of him.

BUT when his search after truth, and resolution to reform religion according to the primitive constitution and practice, had led him to entertain some principles different from his brethren, particularly that of baptizing believers only, they set themselves violently to oppose him, they cast him out of the church, representing him as one that had proclaimed open war against God's everlasting covenant, and that would murder the souls of babes and sucklings, by depriving them of the visible seal of salvation; they publish'd several books, wherein they endeavoured to expose both him and his principles to the world.

The English *exiles there oppose him.*

[i] *Pagit's Heresiography*, p. 62.

MR.

MR. *Ainſworth* wrote two books; the one called *A Defence of Scripture*; the other, *A Cenſure of a Dialogue of the* Anabaptiſts.

MR. *Johnſon*, who ſtiles himſelf paſtor of the antient *Engliſh* church ſojourning at *Amſterdam*, writ a third, entitled *A Chriſtian Plea.*

MR. *Robinſon*, miniſter of the *Engliſh* congregation at *Leyden*, publiſhed a fourth. But his moſt violent *adverſaries* were Mr. *Clifton* and Mr. *Jeſſop*. The one writ an anſwer to one of his books, which was called, *The Chriſtian Plea*; the other, who acknowledges he ſometime walked with them, publiſhed a piece againſt him, entitled, *A Diſcovery of the errors of the* Engliſh *Anabaptiſts*; which he preſented to king *James*; and 'tis eaſy to gueſs with what deſign that was done. In theſe they lay ſeveral accuſations againſt him: As that he ſought to deprive the church of the uſe of the holy Scriptures; that he look'd upon no tranſlation of the Bible to be properly the word of God, the original only being ſo in his opinion; that upon renouncing his *Infant-Baptiſm*, he baptized himſelf, ſuppoſing there was no true adminiſtrator of baptiſm to be found. But they wrote againſt him with ſo much warmth, and appearance of prejudice, that it greatly diſcredits what they ſay[k]. They call him a man of a woolviſh nature, one whom God had ſtruck with blind-

and charge him with baptizing himſelf.

[k] *Wall's baptiſm anatomized*, p. 109. 111.

blindneſs, a brute beaſt, and the like. But in theſe things they expos'd *themſelves* more than Mr. *Smith*, and brought the whole body of *Diſſenters* under reproach.

I CANNOT forbear obſerving, what improvement a certain *author*, who wrote againſt the Separatiſts quickly after, made of ſuch perſecuting meaſures, tho' he was as great an adverſary to the *Anabaptiſts* as they could be. 'Let us, I beſeech you, ſays he, 'look among the ſeparated congregations, 'and conſider their manifold diviſions, both 'in *judgment* and *practice*; and there we 'cannot but ſee even a babel of confuſion, 'ſeparating each from other, even for ſome 'ſmall differences in judgment, excom-'municating holier and better men than 'themſelves, yea, even ſuch as they can-'not legally tax either with *fornication*, '*covetouſneſs*, *idolatry*, *railing*, *drunkenneſs*, '*extortion*, or the like; and that only for 'not ſubmitting in every thing to their 'judgments, contrary to the *Apoſtles* di-'rection [m].'

MR. *Smith* writ ſeveral defences of himſelf and his opinions; as his *Character of the Beaſt*, his *Reply to Mr.* Clifton, his *Dialogue of Baptiſm*, &c. none of which have I yet been able to obtain, but by the quotations that his opponents take out of them, *He defends himſelf.*

[l] *Preface, Anabaptiſts myſtery of iniquity unmasked,* 1623. By I. P.

[m] 1 Cor. v. 11.

them, which were certainly the worſt part, he does not appear to have been a man of ſuch enthuſiaſm and odd opinions, as they would repreſent him.

His adverſaries divide among themſelves.

THE *Browniſts* in thoſe parts fell into diviſions amongſt themſelves a little after; and writ with as much bitterneſs and ſharp reflections againſt one another, as they had done againſt him. And whereas they could only charge him with *miſtaken opinions*, they themſelves were charged with groſs *immoralities*; ſome of which were proved upon oath before the *magiſtrates* at *Amſterdam*: as may be ſeen in Mr. *White*'s *diſcovery of Browniſm* and *Pagit*'s *Heresiography*.

Are charged with groſs Immoralities.

Mr. Smith'*s opinions prevailed much.*

HOWEVER it was, Mr. *Smith*'s opinions prevailed greatly, eſpecially that of denying *infant-baptiſm*; and he ſoon had *proſelytes* enough to form a diſtinct church of that perſuaſion, even among the *Engliſh* exiles.

MR. *Johnſon*, the paſtor of the *Engliſh* church, at the ſame place and time, was one of the firſt that writ againſt him. His book was publiſhed in the year 1617. And he, having ſpoken largely in defence of infant-baptiſm, apologizes for his ſo doing in theſe words: 'Of which point,, and of ſundry 'objections thereabout, I have treated the 'more largely, conſidering how great the 'error is in the denial thereof, and how great- 'ly it ſpreadeth both in theſe parts, and 'of 'of late in our own country, that is 'England.'

MR. *Pagit* ſays [n], 'that Mr. *Smith* and 'his *diſciples* do at once, as it were, ſwal-'low up all the ſeparation beſides.'

A particular enquiry into the charge of baptizing himſelf.

BUT the buſineſs of his baptizing himſelf, and the reaſons of it, if he did ſo, muſt be more particularly enquired into; becauſe the *Pædobaptiſts* make great improvement of it, and would from hence render all the baptizings among the *Engliſh Baptiſts* to be invalid, ſuppoſing them to be his ſucceſſors, and that he was the firſt adminiſtrator of it among them. Upon the revival of their opinion in theſe latter times, Mr. *Thomas Wall* calls [o] him *the beginner of baptiſm by dipping*, and *the captain of this and other errors:* And ſaith [p], 'that when the *Ana-'baptiſts* had framed ſo many devices to 'deny all infants *baptiſm*, they were con-'founded in themſelves, what to do, to 'begin baptizing in their way of bap-'tizing adult perſons only----but one *John* '*Smith*----being more deſperately wicked 'than others, baptized himſelf, and then 'he baptized others, and from this man 'the *Engliſh Anabaptiſts* have ſucceſſively 'received their new adminiſtration of bap-'tiſm on men and women only.'

'

[n] *Hereſiography*, p. 64.
[o] *Plain diſcovery*, p. 44. *and* preface.
[p] *Baptiſm anatomized*, p. 107.

THE

THE ſame *author* [q] alſo aſſerts, that he heard when he lived in *London*, that one Mr. *Spilſbury* ſhould go to *Holland*, to be baptized of this *Smith*; ſo he brought it into *England*. And, ſays he, 'If you can 'find no better an adminiſtrator, your miniſ-'try will be found to come out of the bot-'tomleſs pit, as *Rome*'s miniſtry did.'

The controverſy about a proper adminiſtrator.

'TIS certain, that when ſome of the *Engliſh Proteſtants* were for reviving the antient practice of *immerſion*, they had ſeveral difficulties thrown in their way about a proper *adminiſtrator*, to begin that method of baptizing.

THOSE who rejected the *baptiſm* of *infants*, at the beginning of the reformation in *England*, had the ſame objection made againſt them; as Biſhop *Burnet* obſerves [r].

'One thing, ſays he, was obſerved, that 'the whole world in that age, having been 'baptized in their *infancy*, if that *baptiſm* 'was nothing, then there was none truly '*baptized* in being, but all were in the 'ſtate of mere nature. Now it did not 'ſeem reaſonable, that men who were not '*baptized* themſelves, ſhould go and bap-'tize others; and therefore the firſt heads 'of that *ſect*, not being rightly *baptized* 'themſelves, ſeemed not to act with any 'authority, when they went to *baptize* 'others.'

[q] *Plain diſcovery*, p. 45.
[r] *Hiſt. Ref.* vol. II, part ii. p. 113.

Im-

In the like manner did they now argue againſt the reviving of the practice of *immerſion*, which had for ſome time been diſuſed: If *immerſion* be the eſſential form of that ordinance, then there is none truly *baptized*: and can an *unbaptized* perſon be a proper *adminiſtrator*; or can a man be ſuppoſed to give that to another, which he has not firſt received himſelf?

Did not a little perplex the English *Baptiſts.*

THIS difficulty did not a little perplex them; and they were divided in their opinions how to act in this matter, ſo as not to be guilty of any diſorder or ſelf-contradiction. Some indeed were of opinion, that the firſt *adminiſtrator* ſhould baptize himſelf, and then proceed to the baptizing of others. Others were for ſending to thoſe foreign *Proteſtants* that had uſed *immerſion* for ſome time, that ſo they might receive it from them. And others again thought it neceſſary to *baptiſm*, that the *adminiſtrator* be himſelf baptized, at leaſt in an extraordinary caſe; but that whoever ſaw ſuch a reformation neceſſary, might from the authority of Scripture lawfully begin it.

I do not find any *Engliſhman* among the firſt *reſtorers* of *immerſion* in this latter age accuſed of *baptizing himſelf*, but only the ſaid *John Smith*; and there is ground to queſtion the truth of that alſo.

MR. *Ainſworth*, Mr. *Jeſſop*, and ſome others, do indeed charge him with it;

but

The charge of Mr. Smith's *baptizing himself consider'd.*

but they writ, as has been already observed, with so much passion and resentment, that it is not unlikely such men might take up a report against him upon slender evidence, and after one had published it, the others might take it from him without any enquiry into the truth of it.

THE defences which he wrote for himself are not to be met with; and in the large quotations that his *adversaries* take out of them, I do not find one passage, wherein he acknowledges himself to have done any such thing, or attempts to justify such a practice; which surely, had there been any such, would not have escaped their notice.

THERE is one passage [s] indeed which Mr. *Clifton* quotes from a treatise of Mr. *Smith*'s, which some would make a proof out of his own mouth that he baptized himself: but being examined, it rather confirms the contrary. He is justifying, to the *Brownists*, his authority to begin a new form of baptizing, from the same principles by which they justified their beginning of new churches. And his words, according to their quotations, are these: 'There is as good warrant for a man 'churching himself; for two men singly 'are no church, jointly they are a church; 'so two men may put baptism on them-

[s] Wall's *Baptism anatomised, p.* 111, 112.

'selves.

'felves. Again, faith Mr. *Smith*, a man 'cannot baptize others into a church, him-'felf being out of the church, or being 'no member.'

HERE are two *principles* laid down by Mr. *Smith*, which contradict the account they give of him: That upon the fuppofition of the true *baptifm*'s being loft for fome time, through the difufe of it, 'tis neceffary there fhould be two *perfons* who muft unite in the revival of it, in order to begin the adminiftration thereof: And that the firft *adminiftrator* be a member of fome church, who fhall call and impower him to adminifter it to the members thereof.

NOW it is reafonable to conclude, that his practice was conformable to this. And I find mention made of one Mr. *Helwiffe*, and Mr. *John Morton*, that were of Mr. *Smith*'s opinion, and joined with him in this reformation of baptifm; and according to the rules he lays down, their method muft be this: That firft they formed a church of their *opinion* in the point of *baptifm*; then the church appoints two of thefe *minifters* to begin the adminiftration of it, by baptizing each other; after this one, or both thefe, baptize the reft of the congregation.

BUT enough of this. If he were guilty of what they charge him with, 'tis no blemifh on the *Englifh Baptifts*; who neither approved of any fuch method,

 nor

nor did they receive their *baptiſm* from him.

The methods taken by the English *Baptiſts at the revival of immerſion.*

THE two other methods that I mentioned, were indeed both taken by the *Baptiſts*, at their revival of *immerſion* in *England*; as I find it acknowledged and juſtify'd in their writings.

THE former of theſe was, to ſend over to the foreign *Anabaptiſts*, who deſcended from the antient *Waldenſes* in *France* or *Germany*, that ſo one or more receiving *baptiſm* from them, might become proper *adminiſtrators* of it to others. Some thought this the beſt way; and acted accordingly; as appears from Mr. *Hutchinſon*'s account, in the epiſtle of his treatiſe of the *Covenant and Baptiſm*, where he ſays,

Mr. Hutcheſon'*s account thereof.*

'WHEN the profeſſors of theſe nations 'had been a long time wearied with the 'yoke of ſuperſtitious ceremonies, traditions of men, and corrupt mixtures in 'the worſhip and ſervice of God; it pleaſed the Lord to break theſe yokes, and 'by a very ſtrong impulſe of his Spirit 'upon the hearts of his people, to convince 'them of the neceſſity of reformation. 'Divers pious and very gracious people, 'having often ſought the Lord by faſting 'and prayer, that he would ſhew them 'the pattern of his houſe, the goings-out 'and comings-in thereof, &c. reſolved, by 'the grace of God, not to receive or practiſe any piece of poſitive worſhip, which 'had

'had not *precept* or *example* from the 'word of God. *Infant-baptiſm* coming 'of courſe under conſideration, after long 'ſearch and many debates, it was found 'to have no footing in the Scriptures, 'the only rule and ſtandard to try doc-'trines by; but on the contrary a mere 'innovation, yea, the profanation of an 'ordinance of God. And though it was 'purpoſed to be laid aſide, yet what 'fears, tremblings, and temptations did 'attend them, leſt they ſhould be miſ-'taken, conſidering how many learned and 'godly men were of an oppoſite per-'ſuaſion? How gladly would they have 'had the reſt of their brethren gone along 'with them? But when there was no 'hopes, they concluded, that a chriſtian's 'faith muſt not *ſtand in the wiſdom of 'men*; and that *every one muſt give an ac-'count of himſelf to God*; and ſo reſolved to 'practiſe according to their light. The great 'objection was, the want of an *adminiſtra-'tor*; which, as I have heard, ſays he, was 'remov'd, by ſending certain meſſengers to '*Holland*, whence they were ſupplied.'

Mr. William Kiffin's *account thereof.*

THIS agrees with an account given of the matter in an antient manuſcript, ſaid to be written by Mr. *William Kiffin*, who lived in thoſe times, and was a leader among thoſe of that perſuaſion.

THIS relates, that ſeveral ſober and pious perſons belonging to the congregations

 of

of the *diſſenters* about *London*, were convinced that *believers* were the only proper ſubjects of *baptiſm*, and that it ought to be adminiſtred by *immerſion*, or *dipping* the whole body into the water, in reſemblance of a *burial* and *reſurrection*, according to 2 *Coloſ.* ii. 12. and *Rom.* vi. 4. That they often met together to pray and confer about this matter, and conſult what methods they ſhould take to enjoy this ordinance in its primitive purity: That they could not be ſatisfyed about any *adminiſtrator* in *England* to begin this practice; becauſe tho' ſome in this nation rejected the *baptiſm* of *infants*, yet they had not, as they knew of, revived the antient cuſtom of *immerſion*: But hearing that ſome in the *Netherlands* practis'd it, they agreed to ſend over one Mr. *Richard Blount*, who underſtood the *Dutch* Language: That he went accordingly, carrying letters of recommendation with him, and was kindly received both by the church there, and Mr. *John Batte* their teacher: That upon his return, he baptized Mr. *Samuel Blacklock*, a miniſter, and theſe two baptized the reſt of their company, whoſe names are in the manuſcript, to the number of fifty three.

So that thoſe who follow'd this *ſcheme* did not derive their *baptiſm* from the aforeſaid Mr. *Smith*, or his congregation at *Amſterdam*, it being an antient congregation of foreign

foreign *Baptists* in the *Low Countries* to whom they sent.

BUT the greatest number of the *English Baptists*, and the more judicious, looked upon all this as needless trouble, and what proceeded from the old *Popish Doctrine of right to administer sacraments by an uninterrupted succession*, which neither the church of *Rome*, nor the church of *England*, much less the modern *Dissenters*, could prove to be with them. They affirmed [t] therefore, and practised accordingly, that after a general corruption of *baptism*, an unbaptized person might warrantably baptize, and so begin a reformation.

Mr. Spilsbury's *opinion about a proper administrator.*

MR. *Spilsbury*, who was falsly reported to have gone over to *Holland* to receive *baptism* from *John Smith*, declares expresly against a man's baptizing himself, and judges it to be far from any rule in the gospel so to do; but observes, that where there is a beginning, some one must be first. 'And 'because, says he [u], some make it such an 'error, and so, far from any rule or ex-'ample, for a man to baptize others, who 'is himself unbaptized, and so think there-'by to shut up the *ordinance* of God in 'such a strait, that none can come by it 'but thro' the authoity of the *Popedom of* '*Rome*; let the reader consider who baptiz'd '*John the Baptist* before he baptized others.

[t] *Persecution for rsligion judg'd and condemn'd, p.* 41.
[u] *Treatise of baptism, p.* 63, 65, 66.

 'And

'and if no man did, then whether he did 'not baptize others, he himſelf being un-'baptized. We are taught by this what to 'do upon the like occaſions.'

'FURTHER, ſays he, I fear men put 'more than is of right due to it, that ſo 'prefer it above the church, and all other '*ordinances* beſides; for they can aſſume 'and erect a church, take in and caſt out '*members*, elect and ordain *officers*, and 'adminiſter the *ſupper*, and all a-new, 'without any looking after *ſucceſſion*, any 'further than the ſcriptures: But as for '*baptiſm*, they muſt have that ſucceſſively 'from the *Apoſtles*, tho' it comes thro' the 'hands of pope *Joan*. What is the cauſe 'of this, that men can do all from the 'word but only *baptiſm*?'

NOW is it probable that this man ſhould go over ſea to find an *adminiſtrator* of *baptiſm*, or receive it from the hands of one who *baptized himſelf*?

Mr. Tombes's *defends it.*

THE learned Mr. *Tombes* does very excellently defend this laſt method of reſtoring the true *baptiſm*. 'If, ſays he [x], no con-'tinuance of adult *baptiſm* can be proved, 'and *baptiſm* by ſuch perſons is wanting, 'yet I conceive what many *proteſtant wri-'ters* do yield, when they are preſſed by the '*Papiſts* to ſhew the calling of the firſt *re-'formers*; that after an univerſal corrup-'tion, the neceſſity of the thing doth juſtify

[x] *Add. to Apo.* p. 10.

'the

'the persons that reform, tho' wanting an 'ordinary regular calling, will justify in 'such a case, both the lawfulness of the '*minister's baptizing*, that hath not been 'rightly baptized himself, and the sufficiency of that *baptism* to the person so baptized. And this very thing, says he, that 'in a case where a *baptized minister* cannot be had, it is lawful for an unbaptized 'person to baptize, and his *baptism* is valid, is both the resolution of *Aquinas*, and 'of *Zanchius*, an eminent protestant. *Quæritur an is possit baptizare eos, quos ad 'Christum convertit, ut ipse ab alio ex illis 'a se conversis baptizetur. Ratio est, quia 'minister est verbi, à Christo extraordinem 'excitatus, eoque ut talis minister potest 'cum illius ecclesiolæ consensu, symmistam 'constituere, & ab eo, ut baptizetur curare.* Whereby, says Mr. *Tombes*, you 'may perceive that this is no new truth; 'that an unbaptized person may in some 'case baptize another, and he baptize him, 'being baptized of him.'

Esq; Laurence *also defends the same.*

I WILL only add farther what is said on this head by the honourable *Henry Laurence* Esq; another learned *Baptist*, who has excellently defended the true *baptism*, and the manner of reviving it in these later times. 'It cannot reasonably be objected, says he [y], 'that he that baptizeth should necessarily 'be himself a baptized person: For tho'

[y] *Treatise of Baptism*, p. 407.

'ordi-

'ordinarily it will be ſo, yet it is not neceſ-
'ſary to the ordinance; for not the perſonal
'*baptiſm* of him that adminiſters, but the
'due commiſſion he hath for baptizing, is
'alone conſiderable to make him a true
'*miniſter* of *baptiſm*. And here that ex-
'preſſion holds not, *One cannot give what*
'*he hath not*, as a man cannot teach me,
'that wants knowledge himſelf; becauſe
'no man gives his own *baptiſm*, but con-
'veys, as a publick perſon, that which is
'given us by Chriſt. A *poor man*, that
'hath nothing of his own, may give me
'*gold*, that is, the *money* of another man,
'by virtue of being ſent for that purpoſe.
'So if a man can ſhew his *commiſſion*, the
'writing and ſeal of him that ſent it, it is
'enough here. Elſe what would become
'of the *great baptizer*, *John the Baptiſt*,
'who had a fair commiſſion to baptize, but
'was not himſelf baptized that we read of:
'Or if he ſhould be, which cannot be af-
'firmed; yet the firſt *baptizer*, whoever he
'was, muſt at the time of his firſt *admi-*
'*niſtration* of that *ordinance* be *unbaptized*.'

THO' theſe things were publiſhed at different times, I have put them together, to end this matter at once. It was a point much diſputed for ſome years. The *Bapiſts* were not a little uneaſy about it at firſt; and the *Pædobaptiſts* thought to render all the baptizings among them invalid, for want of a proper *adminiſtrator* to begin their practice: But

But by the excellent reaſonings of theſe and other learned men, we ſee their beginning was well defended, upon the ſame *principles* on which all other *proteſtants* built their *reformation*.

KING *James*, to ſhew his zeal againſt hereſy, had now an opportunity to exerciſe it upon two of his own ſubjects; who, in the year 1611, were *burnt alive* in *Smithfield* for heretical opinions.

Bartholomew Legate *burnt in* Smithfield.

ONE was *Bartholomew Legate*, of the county of *Eſſex*, of whom Mr. *Fuller* gives this character [z]. That he was a man of a bold ſpirit, and fluent tongue, excellently ſkill'd in the ſcriptures, and of an unblameable converſation: But ſhewing his diſlike of the *Nicene* and *Athanaſius*'s creeds, and denying the plurality of perſons in the Godhead, and the divinity of Chriſt, was for theſe errors frequently ſummoned before the *biſhops* in their conſiſtory, and kept priſoner ſome time in *Newgate*. He very boldly defended his opinions, and would not be brought to deſiſt from it, tho' the king himſelf had him often brought before him, and endeavoured to recover him. At length, in an aſſembly of *biſhops* he was condemn'd as a contumacious and incorrigible *heretick*. This was on the 3d of *March*, and on the 18th of the ſame month, about noon, he was brought to *Smithfield*, and there burnt to aſhes before a vaſt number of ſpectators.

[z] *Book* x. *p*. 63.

THE

Edward Wightman *burnt at* Litchfield.

[a]THE other was one *Edward Wightman*, a *Baptiſt*, of the town of *Burton* upon *Trent*; who on the 14th day of *December* was convicted of divers hereſies before the biſhop of *Coventry* and *Litchfield*; and being deliver'd up to the ſecular power, was *burnt* at *Litchfield* the 11th of *April* following.

The hereſies he is charg'd with by his perſecutors.

MANY of the hereſies they charge upon him are ſo fooliſh and inconſiſtent, that it very much diſcredits what they ſay. If he really held ſuch *opinions*, he muſt either be an *ideot* or a *madman*, and ought rather to have had their prayers and aſſiſtance, than be put to ſuch a cruel death [b].

THAT they may be ſure to accuſe him with enough, he is condemn'd for holding the wicked hereſies of the *Ebionites*, *Cerinthians*, *Valentinians*, *Arians*, *Macedonians*, of *Simon Magus*, *Manes*, *Manichæus*, *Photinus*, and of the *Anabaptiſts*: And leſt all theſe hard names ſhould not comprehend every error held by him, 'tis added, *and of other heretical, execrable, and unheard-of opinions.* From this general account of his *hereſies*, they proceed to mention fifteen *particulars.* In one they make him ſay, That Chriſt is not the true natural Son of God in reſpect of his Godhead: In another, That he is only man, and a mere

[a] Fuller, *book* x. *p.* 64.
[b] Vid. *Commiſſion and Warrant for his burning, in the Appendix*, N° I.

creature;

creature; and yet, in the next, He took not human fleſh of the ſubſtance of his mother. One while he is repreſented as making himſelf to be Chriſt; at another time ſaying, That God had ordain'd and ſent him to perform his part in the work of the ſalvation of the world, by his teaching; as Chriſt was ordained and ſent to ſave the world, and by his death to deliver it from ſin, and reconcile it to God.

THREE of the articles are ſuch, that I cannot but wonder to find them amongſt thoſe *hereſies* for which a man is *burnt alive* by *Proteſtants, viz.* That the baptizing of *infants* is an abominable cuſtom: That the *Lord's-Supper* and *Baptiſm* are not to be celebrated as they are now practiſed in the church of *England:* That *Chriſtianity* is not wholly profeſſed and preached in the church of *England*, but only in part.

THE firſt who was put to this cruel death in *England* was *William Sawtre*, ſuppoſed upon very probable grounds to have denied *infant-baptiſm*; and this man, the laſt who was honoured with this kind of martyrdom, was expreſly condemn'd for that *opinion:* ſo that this *ſect* had the honour both of leading the way, and bringing up the rear of all the *martyrs* who were *burnt alive* in *England*, as well as that a great number of thoſe who ſuffer'd this death for their religion in the two hundred years betwixt, were of this *denomination*. *Remark.*

THIS

THIS burning of *hereticks* did much ſtartle the common people. Mr. *Fox*, in his excellent *Martyrology*, had ſo expoſed the *Papiſts* for this kind of *cruelty*, that it was generally diſliked and condemn'd, and thought unaccountable that *Proteſtants* ſhould be guilty of the ſame practice. The barbarity of the puniſhment moved compaſſion towards the ſufferers; and to ſee men with ſo much firmneſs and conſtancy ſeal their opinions with their blood, rather promoted their doctrines, than put a ſtop to them.

KING *James* choſe therefore for the future only to ſeize their eſtates, and waſte away their lives privately in naſty priſons, rather than honour them with ſuch a publick *martyrdom*, which would unavoidably go under the name of perſecution.

An. Dom. 1614.

Some Diſſenters go to New-England, *and ſettle there, among them ſome* English Baptiſts.

IN the Spring, *Anno* 1614. ſome *Preſbyterian* families reſolved to go and ſettle in *New-England*, to enjoy there that peace they could not find at home. 'The author, ſays *Rapin*[c], I juſt mention'd concerning the Earl of *Northampton*, ſays, 'Theſe *people* were notorious *Schiſmaticks* 'of ſeveral *ſects*, known by the general 'name of *Puritans*. As it was not im'poſſible, by the increaſe of *Preſbyterian* 'families, the *Engliſh* plantations might be'come nurſeries for *Nonconformiſts*, the

[c] *Hiſt.* Engl. *vol.* II. *p.* 185.

'court

'court gave orders not to let them depart; 'but afterwards ſuch as deſired to remove 'beyond ſea, being examined, ſome were 'allowed to purſue their voyage, and others 'were detained as ſureties for thoſe that 'went away.'

THAT ſome of theſe were *Baptiſts*, appears from Mr. *Cotton Mather* [d], where I find the firſt ſettlement of the *Engliſh* in this part of *America* was in the year 1620. They were certain pious *Nonconformiſts*, who had left their native country to avoid perſecution, and dwelt for ſome time in *Holland*, being members of the *Engliſh* church at *Leyden*, of which Mr. *John Robinſon* was paſtor; but not liking that country, obtained leave of king *James* to enjoy the liberty of their conſciences under his gracious protection in *America*, where they would endeavour the advancement of his majeſty's dominions, and the intereſt of the goſpel. They ſet ſail from *Southampton* in *England*, *Auguſt* 5. 1620. and arrived at *Cape-Cod* about the 9th of *November* following. Among theſe ſome few were *Antipædobaptiſts*. So that *Antipædobaptiſm* is as antient in thoſe parts as *Chriſtianity* itſelf.

LEAVING then *England* at preſent, let us follow theſe *Baptiſts*, and ſee how it fared with them there.

[d] *Eccl. Hiſt.* New-Engl. *lib.* i. *c.* 2.

MR.

Cotton Mather's *account of them.*

MR. *Cotton Mather* ſays thus[e]: 'Having done with the *Quakers*, let it not be 'miſinterpreted, if into the ſame chapter 'we put the inconveniences which the 'churches of *New-England* have alſo ſuffer'd from the *Anabaptiſts*; albeit they 'have infinitely more of *Chriſtianity* among them than the *Quakers*, and have 'indeed been uſeful defenders of *Chriſtianity* againſt the aſſaults of the *Quakers*. 'Yea, we are willing to acknowledge for 'our brethren as many of them as are 'willing to be ſo acknowledged.—All the 'world knows, ſays he, that the moſt eminent *reformers*, writing againſt the *Anabaptiſts*, have not been able to forbear 'making their treatiſes like what *Jerom* 'ſays of *Tertullian*'s polemical treatiſes, '*Quot verba, tot Fulmina.* And the noble martyr *Philpot* expreſs'd the mind of 'them all, when he ſaid, 'The *Anabaptiſts* are an inordinate kind of men, ſtirred up by the devil to the deſtruction of 'the goſpel, having neither ſcripture, nor 'antiquity, nor any thing elſe for them, 'but lies and new imaginations, feigning 'the baptiſm of children to be the Pope's 'commandment. Nevertheleſs it is well 'known, that of later time there have 'been a great many *Antipædobaptiſts* who 'have never deſerved ſo hard a character

[e] *Eccl. Hiſt.* New-Engl. *lib.* vii. *p.* 26.

'among

'among the churches of God. *Infant-baptiſm* hath been ſcrupled by *multitudes* 'in our days, who have been in other 'points moſt worthy *Chriſtians*, and as 'holy, watchful, fruitful and heavenly peo-'ple as perhaps any in the world. Some 'few of theſe people have been among the '*planters* in *New-England* from the be-'ginning, and have been welcome to the 'communion of our churches, which they 'have enjoy'd, reſerving their particular 'opinion unto themſelves.

'BUT at length it came to paſs, that 'while ſome of our *churches* uſed it may 'be a little too much of *cogency* towards 'the *brethren*, which would weakly turn 'their backs when *infants* were brought 'forth to be *baptized* in the congregation, 'there were ſome of theſe *brethren* who 'in a day of temptation broke forth into 'ſchiſmatical practices, that were juſtly of-'fenſive unto all the churches in this wil-'derneſs.

'OUR *Anabaptiſts*, when ſomewhat of 'exaſperation was begun, formed a church 'at *Boſton*, on *May* 28. 1665. beſides one 'which they had before at *Swanzey*. Now 'they declared our *infant-baptiſm* to be a 'mere nullity; and they arrogate unto them-'ſelves the title of *Baptiſts*, as if none were 'baptized but themſelves.

'THE General Court, ſays Mr. *Ma-ther*, were ſo afraid leſt matters might

The English *Baptists are persecuted there.*

'at last, from small beginnings, grow into a new *Munster* tragedy, that they enacted some laws for the restraint of *Anabaptistical* exorbitances [f]: Which laws, tho' never executed unto the extremity of them, yet were soon laid by, as to any execution of them at all. There were in this unhappy *schism* several truly *godly men*, whom it was thought a very uncomfortable thing to prosecute with severe *imprisonments*, on these controversies. And there came also a letter from *London*, to the governour of the *Massachuset*'s colony, subscribed by no less persons than Dr. *Goodwin*, Dr. *Owen*, Mr. *Nye*, Mr. *Caryl*, and nine other very reverend ministers, wherein were these among other passages.

A letter from the most eminent of the London *ministers thereupon.*

'WE shall not here undertake in the least to make any apology for the persons, opinions, and practices of those who are censured amongst you.—You know our judgment and practice to be contrary unto theirs, even as your's, wherein, God assisting, we shall continue to the end: neither shall we return any answer to the reason of the Rev. Elders for the justification of your proceedings, as not being willing to engage in the management of any the least difference with persons whom we so much love and honour

[f] *Eccles. Hist.* New-Engl. *lib.* vii. *p.* 27.

'in

'in the Lord.—But the ſum of all which 'at preſent we ſhall offer to you, is, That 'tho' the *court* might apprehend that they 'had grounds in general, warranting their 'proceedure in ſuch caſes, in the way 'wherein they have proceeded; yet that 'they have any rule or command, render- 'ing their ſo proceeding indiſpenſably ne- 'ceſſary under all circumſtances of fines 'or places, we are altogether unſatisfy'd. 'And we need not repreſent unto you how 'the caſe ſtands with ourſelves, and all 'your *brethren* and *companions* in the ſer- 'vices of theſe latter days in theſe nations. 'We are ſure you would be unwilling to 'put an advantage into the hands of ſome 'who ſeek pretences and occaſions againſt 'our liberty, and to reinforce the former 'rigour. Now we cannot deny, but this 'hath already in ſome meaſure been done, 'in that it hath been * vogued, that per- 'ſons of our way, principles, and ſpirit, 'cannot bear with diſſenters from them. 'And as this greatly reflects on us, ſo ſome 'of us have obſerved how already it has 'turned unto your own diſadvantage.

'WE leave it to your wiſdom to deter- 'mine, whether under all theſe circum- 'ſtances, and ſundry others of the like 'nature that might be added, it be not 'adviſeable at preſent to put an end unto 'the ſufferings and confinements of the 'perſons cenſured, and to reſtore them to

* *Sic origine.*

'their former liberty. You have the advantage of truth and order; you have the gifts and learning of an able ministry to manage and defend them; you have the care and vigilancy of a very worthy *magiſtracy* to countenance and protect them, and to preſerve the peace; and above all, you have a bleſſed Lord and maſter, *who hath the keys of* David, *who openeth and no man ſhutteth*, living for ever, to take care of his own concernments among his ſaints: and aſſuredly you need not be diſquieted, tho' ſome few *perſons*, through their own infirmity and weakneſs, or through their ignorance, darkneſs and prejudices, ſhould to their diſadvantage turn out of the way in ſome leſſer matters, into by-paths of their own. We only make it our hearty requeſt to you, that you would truſt God with his truths and ways, ſo far as to ſuſpend all rigorous proceedings, in corporal reſtraints or puniſhments, on perſons that diſſent from you, and practiſe the principles of their diſſent without danger or diſturbance to the civil peace of the place.'

Dated March 25. 1669.

'I CANNOT ſay, ſays Mr. *Mather*, that this excellent letter had immediately all the effect which it ſhould have had; however at length it has had its effect.'

ONE

[g] ONE *Roger Williams*, a preacher, who arrived in *New-England* about the year 1630. was first an assistant in the church of *Salem*, and afterwards pastor. This man, a difference happening between the government and him, caused a great deal of trouble and vexation. At length the *magistrates* passed the sentence of *banishment* upon him; upon which he removed with a few of his own *sect*, and settled at a place called *Providence*. 'There they proceeded, says Mr. *Mather*, 'not only unto the *gathering* of a thing like a *church*, but unto the *renouncing* their *infant-baptism*.' After this, he says [h], he turned *Seeker* and *Familist*, and the church came to nothing; yet acknowledges, that after all this, 'he 'was very instrumental in obtaining a 'charter for the government of *Rhode-island*, which lay near and with his town 'of *Providence*, and was by the people 'sometimes chosen governour, and in many things acquitted himself so laudably, 'that many judicious persons judged him 'to have had the root of the matter in 'him: That he used many commendable 'endeavours to christianise the *Indians* in 'his neighbourhood, and printed a relation 'of their language, tempers, and manners: 'That he also with much vigour maintain'd the main principles of the *Pro-*

Roger Williams *banished.*

Some account of him.

[g] *Eccl. Hist.* New-Engl. *p.* 7.
[h] *Ibid. p.* 9.

'*testant Religion* against the *Quakers*, of 'which he has published a large account 'in a book entitled, *George Fox digged out 'of his burrows*. Mr. *Mather* also acknow-'ledges that there was a good correspon-'dence always held between him and ma-'ny worthy and pious people in the *colo-'ny* from whence he had been banished; 'and that some of the *English nobility* had 'writ letters in his commendation.'

MR. *Baxter* calls this man *the Father of the Seekers in* London [i].

Some Indians *converted.*

SEVERAL of the *Indians* bordering upon the *English colonies* in *New-England*, were, by the endeavours of several pious ministers, brought to receive the Christian faith, and had the bible translated into their language, and several churches gather'd among them. Mr. *John Gardiner*, in his letter, giving an account of the *Christian Indians* of *Nantucket*, says, 'There are 'three societies or churches, two *congrega-'tional*, and one of the *Baptists*; but their 'number is small.'

Manuscript penes me.

MR. *Benjamin Keach* was used frequently to say, 'That when the *Indians* had em-'braced *Christianity*, and got the New 'Testament translated into their language, 'they were surprized that they found no 'directions there to baptize children, nor 'any instance of such a practice, therefore

[i] *Plain Script.* pr 146

'en-

'enquired of the *English* the ground of that 'practice, whereupon they rejected it as 'an human invention.'

The controversy of infant-baptism revived.

An assembly of ministers called.

THE *controversy* about the *baptism* of *children*, and the care that was to be taken of them afterwards, grew to such an height[k], that an assembly of the principal and most able *ministers* of both *colonies* was called by the *magistrates* on *June* 4. 1657. to answer the questions that were in agitation about these matters; who accordingly presented their elaborate answer to twenty one questions relating to this affair, which was afterwards printed in *London*, under the title of, *A disputation concerning church-members, and their children.* But this did not put an end to the controversy; therefore a synod was convened at *Boston* in the year 1662. in which this was the first and chief question to be determined, *Who are the subjects of baptism?*

'THERE have at several times, says 'Mr. *Mather*[l], arrived in this country more 'than a score of *ministers* from other parts 'of the world, who proved either so erroneous in their principles, or so scandalous in their practices, or so disagreeable 'to the church-order, for which the country was planted, that I cannot well croud 'them into the company of our *worthies.* 'I confess there were some of those per-

[k] Mather's *Eccl. Hist.* New-Engl. *lib.* v. *p.* 63.
[l] *Ibid. lib.* iii. *p.* 7.

'sons whose names deserve to live in our 'book for their piety, altho' their parti-'cular opinions were such, as to be disser-'viceable unto the declared and supposed 'interests of our churches. Of these there 'were some godly *Anabaptists*; as namely, 'Mr. *Hanserd Knollys*, of *Dover*, who af-'terwards removing back to *London*, late-'ly died there, a good man in a good old 'age; and Mr. *Miles* of *Swanzey*, who 'afterwards came to *Boston*, and is now 'gone to his rest. Both of these have a 'respectful character in the churches of this 'wilderness.'

Cotton Mather's *character of* Hanserd Knollys *and Mr.* Miles.

HAVING mentioned the several congregational churches at *Boston*, he adds[m]: 'And 'besides these, there is another small congre-'gation of *Antipædobaptists*, wherein Mr. '*Emlin* is the settled minister.'

And of a Baptist church in New-Plymouth *colony.*

IN his account of *New-Plymouth Colony*, he says[n]: 'Moreover there has been among 'them one church that have question'd 'and omitted the use of infant-baptism; 'nevertheless, there being many good men 'among those, that have been of this per-'suasion, I do not know that they have 'been *persecuted* with any harder means, 'than those of kind conferences to reclaim 'them.'

THE learned Mr. *John Tombes*, being acquainted with a law made in *New-Eng-*

m *Lib.* i. *p.* 27.
n *Ib. p.* 14.

land,

Mr. Tombes's *epistle, with his examen sent to* New-England.

land, and the proceedings against those that deny'd the *baptism* of *infants*, was prevailed upon to send a copy of his *examen* before it was printed, thither, designing thereby to put them upon the study of this matter more exactly, and to allay the vehemency of their spirits and proceedings against those that dissented from them; and therewith he sent this short epistle [o].

To all the elders of the churches of Christ in New-England, *and to each in particular by name: To the pastor and teacher of the church of God at* Boston, *there, these present.*

Reverend Brethren,

'UNderstanding that there is some disquiet in your churches about *pædo-baptism*, and being moved by some that honour you much in the Lord, and desire your comfortable account at the day of Christ, that I would yield that a copy of my *examen* of master *Marshall* his sermon of *infant-baptism* might be transcribed, to be sent to you; I have consented thereto, and do commend it to your examination, in like manner, as you may perceive by the reading of it, I did to master *Marshall*. Not doubting but that you will,

[o] *Apology*, p. 13.

'will, as in God's presence, and accountable to Christ Jesus, weigh the thing; 'remembering that of our Lord Christ, 'John vii. 24. *Judge not according to the 'appearance, but judge righteous judgment.* 'To the blessing of him who is your God 'and our God, your judge and our judge, 'I leave you, and the flock of God over 'which the Holy Ghost hath made you 'overseers, and rest,

Your brother and fellow-servant in the work of Christ,

From my study at the *Temple* in *London*, *May* 25th, 1645.

JOHN TOMBES.

An account of the Baptist *churches in* Pensilvania.

THAT the *Baptists* have very much increased in those parts since they have enjoyed tranquillity, I find by a letter from *Philadelphia* in the province of *Pensilvania*, wrote by Mr. *Abel Morgan*, pastor of a *Baptist church* there, giving an account of the state and number of the *Baptized churches* in that *province*, *Aug.* 12, 1714. wherein he says, 'We are now *nine* churches, having 'for the better assisting one the other, *four* 'general meetings. *1st* At *Welsh Tract*, 'where all the *Pensilvania* churches resort 'to in *May*. The *2d* is at *Cohansy*, for conveniency of those parts, where *Philadel-*

'*phia*

'*phia* aſſiſts. The 3*d* is at *Middleton*, where 'alſo *Philadelphia* aſſiſts. The 4*th* is at '*Philadelphia*, in the month of *September*, 'where all do reſort, and where moſt of 'the publick matters are ſettled to be deci-'ded by meſſengers from every *particular* 'church.

'IN theſe churches, ſays he, there are 'above five hundred members, but greatly 'ſcattered on this main land; our mini-'ſters are neceſſitated to labour with both 'hands. We hope, if it pleaſe God to ſup-'ply us with more help, we ſhall be more 'churches in a little time. Moſt churches 'adminiſter the ſacrament once a month; 'the miniſters are all ſound in the faith, and 'we practiſe moſt things like the *Britiſh* '*churches*.'

Dr. Geo. Abbot, *ſome account of him.*

To return to *England*: *Bancroft* was ſucceeded by Dr. *George Abbot*, biſhop of *London*; 'a divine, ſays Mr. *Neale* [c], of 'a quite different ſpirit from his *predeceſſor*: 'He was a ſound *Proteſtant*, a thorough '*Calviniſt*, an avowed enemy to *Popery*, 'and even ſuſpected of *Puritaniſm*, be-'cauſe he relaxed the penal laws; where-'by, ſays lord *Clarendon*, he unravelled all 'that his *predeceſſor* had been doing for 'many years.

'IF *Abbot*'s moderate meaſures, ſays Mr. '*Neal*, had been purſued, the liberties of '*England* had been ſecured, *Popery* diſ-

[c] *Hiſt. Purit.* vol. II p. 93.

'coun-

'countenanced, and the church prevented 'from running into thoſe exceſſes which 'afterwards proved its ruin.'

An. Dom. 1615. * *Perſecution judged, and condemned.*

Anno 1615. The more moderate or orthodox *Baptiſts* publiſhed a ſmall treatiſe *, wherein they endeavour'd to juſtify their ſeparation from the church of *England*, and to prove, that every man has a right to judge for himſelf in matters of religion; and that to perſecute any on that account, is illegal and antichriſtian, contrary to the laws of God, as well as to ſeveral declarations of the king's majeſty. They alſo aſſert their opinion concerning *Baptiſm*, and ſhew the invalidity of that *Baptiſm* which was adminiſtred either in the eſtabliſh'd *church*, or among the other *Diſſenters*, and clear themſelves of ſeveral *errors* unjuſtly caſt upon them. It appears to be written, or at leaſt approved of, by the whole body of *Baptiſts* who then remain'd in *England*; becauſe at the end of the preface they ſubſcribe themſelves Chriſt's unworthy *miniſters*, and his majeſty's faithful ſubjects, commonly, but moſt falſly called *Anabaptiſts*.

The Baptiſts *account of themſelves.*

FROM hence therefore we may know what was in general the *opinions* of that *denomination*, from themſelves; which is certainly the faireſt way of judging.

THEY acknowledge *magiſtracy* to be God's ordinance; and that kings, and ſuch

P *Hiſt. Purit.* vol. II. p. 49.

as

as are in authority, ought to be obeyed in all civil matters, *not only for fear*, *but alſo for conſcience-ſake* [q].

THEY allow the taking of an *oath* to be lawful; and declare, that all of their profeſſion were willing, in faithfulneſs and truth, to ſubſcribe the *oath* of *allegiance* [r].

THEY proteſt againſt the doctrine of the *Papiſts*, that princes excommunicated by the *pope* may be depoſed or murdered by their *ſubjects*; calling it a damnable and accurſed *doctrine*, which their *ſouls* abhor; and alſo againſt the error of the *Familiſts*, who to avoid perſecution, can comply with any external form of religion.

THEY confeſs, that Chriſt took his fleſh of the virgin *Mary*; and for their orthodoxy in theſe and other points, refer the reader to their *confeſſion of faith*, publiſh'd four years before this, which muſt be in the year 1611.

THEY acknowledged, that many call'd *Anabaptiſts*, held ſeveral ſtrange opinions contrary to them; but lament it, and clear themſelves from deſerving any cenſure upon that account, by ſhewing that it was ſo in the primitive church, and yet Chriſt did not condemn all for the errors of ſome.

BUT that which they chiefly inveigh againſt, is the pride, luxury, and oppreſſion of the lord *biſhops*, or pretended ſpi-

[q] *Perſecut. judg'd and condemn'd*, p. 5. [r] Ibid. p. 23.

ritual

ritual power, whereby they were exposed to great hardships and cruel persecutions [s].

IN their preface, having mentioned that text, *The kings of the earth shall give their power unto the beast*; 'If it be granted, say 'they, that the kings of this nation formerly have given their power to the *Romish beast*, it shall evidently appear, that 'our lord the king, and all magistrates 'under him, do give their power unto the 'same beast, tho' the beast be in another 'shape.'—And presently after; 'Our most 'humble desire of our lord the king is, 'that he would not give his power to 'force his faithful *subjects* to dissemble, to 'believe as he believes, in the least mea-'sure of persecution; tho' it is no small 'persecution to lie many years in filthy pri-'sons, in hunger, cold, idleness, divided 'from wife, family, calling, left in con-'tinual miseries and temptations, so as 'death would be to many less persecu-'tion.'

AGAIN, shewing how near the prelatical power and usurpation came to the bloody spiritual power of the *Roman Catholicks*, they say: 'How many, only for 'seeking reformation in religion, have been 'put to death by your power in the days 'of Q. *Elizabeth*? and how many, both 'then and since, have been consumed to

[s] *Persecution judged*, &c. p. 27.

'death

'death in prisons? Yea, since that spiritual power hath been set up, hath not hanging, burning, exile, imprisonments, and all manner of contempt been used, and all for religion, altho' some for grievous errors, and yet you see not this to be a bloody religion!'

'LET, say they in another place, Mr. *Fox*, or any others who have described the spiritual power of *Rome*, let but their description thereof be compared with the spiritual power, in all their laws, courts, titles, pomp, pride, and cruelty, and you shall see them very little differ, except in their *cruelties*, which, glory be to God, the King's Majesty, who thirsteth not after blood, hath somewhat restrained. Altho' it is most grievous cruelty to lie divers years in most noisome and filthy prisons, and continual temptations of want, their estates overthrown, and never coming out, many of them till death; let it be well-weighed, and it is little inferior to the cruel sudden death in times of the *Romish power* in this nation.'

BUT after all this, they conclude with an hearty prayer for their enemies, 'That the Lord would give them repentance, that their sins may not be laid to their charge, even for Christ's sake.'

NOTWITHSTANDING this, their sufferings were rather encreased than lessen'd: They

They were not only railed againſt in the pulpits under the names of *Hereticks*, *Schiſmaticks*, and *Anabaptiſts*, and harraſſed in the ſpiritual courts; but the temporal ſword was uſed againſt them; their goods ſeized, their perſons confined for many years in ſtinking goals, where they were depriv'd of their wives, children, and friends, till the Divine Majeſty was pleaſed to releaſe ſeveral of them by death.

An. Dom. 1618.

The firſt book in English *publiſhed againſt infant-baptiſm.*

IN the year 1618. there came forth a book, vindicating the principles of the *Baptiſts**. This was tranſlated from the *Dutch*, and is thought to be the firſt that was publiſhed in *Engliſh* againſt the baptizing of infants. The argument of this book is laid down in the following eight propoſitions:

'1. THAT Chriſt commanded his *apo-* '*ſtles*, and ſervants of the Holy Ghoſt, 'firſt of all to preach the *goſpel*, and make '*diſciples*, and afterwards to *baptize* thoſe 'that were inſtructed in the faith, in call- 'ing upon and confeſſing the name of 'God.

'2. THAT the *apoſtles* and *ſervants* of 'the Holy Ghoſt have, according to the 'commandment of the Lord Jeſus Chriſt, 'firſt of all *taught*, and then afterwards 'thoſe that were inſtructed in the myſte- 'ries of the kingdom of God were *bap-* '*tized*; upon the confeſſing of their faith.

* *A plain and well-grounded treatiſe concerning baptiſm.*

'3. THAT

'3. THAT after the *apoſtle*'s time, by 'the antient *fathers* in the primitive church, 'who obſerved and followed the *ordinance* 'of Chriſt, and the example of the *apo-* '*ſtles*, the people were commonly inſtruc- 'ted in the myſteries of faith; and after 'that they were *taught*, they were *bap-* '*tized* upon confeſſion of the ſame.

'4. THAT by the antient *fathers* in the 'primitive church, the children both of 'the faithful and others, were commonly '*firſt inſtructed* in the faith, and afterwards, 'upon acknowledging and confeſſing of 'the ſame, they were *baptized*.

'5. THAT according to the inſtitution 'of the Lord Chriſt, and the *apoſtles* and 'antient *fathers* right uſe, the teachers re- 'quired *faith* with *baptiſm*, and that he that 'was *baptized* muſt himſelf acknowledge 'and confeſs the ſame, and call upon the 'name of the Lord.

'6. THAT Chriſt neither gave com- 'mandment for *baptizing* of *children*, nor 'inſtituted the ſame; and that the *apoſtles* 'never *baptized* any *infants*.

'7. THAT the *baptiſm* of *infants* and '*ſucklings* is a *ceremony* and *ordinance* of 'man, brought into the church by teachers 'after the *apoſtle*'s time, and inſtituted and 'commanded by *councils*, *popes*, and *em-* '*perors*.

'8. THAT young *children* or *infants* 'ought not to be *baptized*; and that none 'ought to be brought, driven, or compell'd 'thereunto.'

ALL which the *author* endeavours to prove, either from ſeveral paſſages of *Scripture*, or large quotations out of the fathers.

I DO not find that this book receiv'd any anſwer till about thirty years after. Then Mr. *Thomas Cobbet*, of *New-England*, publiſhed *A vindication of childrens church-memberſhip, and right to baptiſm.*

I DO ſuppoſe the book was concealed as much as poſſible, till the civil wars produced liberty of conſcience; which occaſioned it to go ſo long unanſwered.

THOSE who diſſented from the eſtabliſh'd church at this time, were proſecuted by the laws made in this and the former reign againſt them; and thoſe deemed *Anabaptiſts* had of all others the leaſt favour ſhewn them, *fines* and *impriſonments* being uſually their lot.

An. Dom. 1620. *The Baptiſts preſent their humble ſupplication to K.* James.

IN the year 1620. they preſented an humble ſupplication to K. *James*, the parliament then ſitting; wherein they firſt acknowledge their obligation, by virtue of a divine command, *to pray for kings, and all that are in authority*; and appeal to God that it was their conſtant practice ſo to do. They ſet forth, that their miſeries were not only the taking away of their *goods*, but alſo long and lingering *impriſonments* for many years, in divers *counties* in *England*, in which many have died, leaving their *widows* and

and ſeveral ſmall children behind them, and all becauſe they dared not join in ſuch worſhip as they did not believe to be according to the will of God.

THEY challenge their *enemies* to accuſe them of any diſloyalty to his Majeſty, or of doing any injury to their neighbours; and declare their readineſs to be obedient to all the *laws* that were or ſhould be made for the preſervation of his Majeſty's perſon, and ſecurity of his government in all civil or temporal things: but that further than this they could not go, becauſe God was the Lord of mens conſciences, and only lawgiver in matters of religion.

THAT if they were in *error*, theſe cruel proceedings did no ways become the charity and goodneſs of the Chriſtian religion; but were the marks of *Antichriſt*, for what they themſelves condemned in the *Papiſts*.

THAT ſuch methods might indeed tempt men to become *hypocrites*; but that it was not in their power to command belief, or compel the heart.

AND therefore they humbly beſeech his Majeſty, his nobles and parliament, to conſider their caſe, and that according to the direction of God's word, they would *let the wheat and tares grow together in the world, until the harveſt.*

To this they ſubjoin ten ſhort chapters; wherein they endeavour to prove, that the ſacred ſcriptures are the rule of our faith,

 and

and not any *church*, *council*, or *potentate* whatſoever:

THAT the moſt neceſſary doctrines therein contained are ſufficiently plain, ſo that every one that ſearches with a ſincere and obedient mind may underſtand them:

THAT the knowledge of God's will, and practiſe of true religion, has commonly been found among thoſe that have been poor and deſpiſed in this world, while the great and learned have been in *error*, and the chief *perſecutors* both of the truth and its profeſſors:

THAT to perſecute men for their conſcience-ſake, is contrary to the law of Chriſt, as well as to ſeveral declarations that had been made by the king's majeſty, and other famous princes:

THAT both antient and modern writers, both *Proteſtants* and *Papiſts*, do condemn it as a great iniquity; and that to grant men liberty in matters of religion, can be no prejudice to any *commonwealth*, neither does it deprive *princes* of any power given them of God.

AND then they conclude the whole with prayer for the king's majeſty, for his royal highneſs the prince, and the honourable aſſembly of *parliament*; calling God, the ſearcher of all hearts to witneſs, that they were loyal *ſubjects* to his majeſty, *not for fear only*, *but for conſcience-ſake*; ſubſcribing themſelves, thoſe who are *unjuſtly called Anabaptiſts.*

BUT

BUT notwithſtanding the odium caſt upon them, and the ſeverities uſed againſt them, they kept up their ſeparate meetings, and had many *diſciples* who embraced their opinion, as is declared by thoſe who writ againſt them.

AMONG the many *proſelytes* which they had at this time, there was one at *London*, who being ſeverely reflected upon for his ſeparating from the church, and divers falſe reaſons for his ſo doing being reported, thought fit to write a letter to his *friends*, to acquaint them with the real occaſion of it; and that he might recommend his preſent *principle* and *practice* to them with the more advantage, he got one of the elders of the *Baptiſts* to draw it up for him. But before this letter came to the perſons deſigned, it fell into the hands of *one* in the communion of the church of *England*, who immediately publiſhed it, together with an anſwer thereto.

THIS letter, diſcovering ſomething of the principles and ſpirit of the *Baptiſts* of thoſe times, and the arguments by which they did then maintain their opinions; I ſhall here inſert the copy thereof [t].

Beloved Friends,

'THE antient love that I have had
' towards you, provoketh me to

[t] *Anabap. Myſtery of Iniquity unmasked, by* J. P. An. 1623.

 ' teſtify

‘ teſtify that I have not forgotten you,
‘ but am deſirous ſtill to ſhew my unfeign-
‘ ed love to you in any thing I may. I
‘ make no queſtion but you have heard
‘ divers falſe reports of me, altho’ among
‘ the ſame ſome truths; and that you may
‘ be truly informed of my ſtate, I thought
‘ good to write a few words unto you,
‘ hoping you will not ſpeak evil of that
‘ you know not, nor condemn a man un-
‘ heard. The thing wherein I differ from
‘ the church of *England*, is, they ſay at
‘ their *waſhing* or *baptizing* their *infants*,
‘ they are members, children of God, and
‘ inheritors of the kingdom of heaven.
‘ This I dare not believe, for the Scriptures
1 Cor. ‘ of God declare, that neither fleſh, nor
xv. ‘ waſhing the fleſh, can ſave. *Fleſh and*
John iii.5. ‘ *blood cannot enter into the kingdom of God*;
John i.12. ‘ for *that which is fleſh is fleſh*; and *we*
‘ *cannot enter into the kingdom of God, ex-*
‘ *cept we be born again*. They that have
1 Pet. iii. ‘ prerogative to be the ſons of God, muſt
21. ‘ be *born of God*, even believe in his name;
Gal.vi.15. Matt. ‘ and *the waſhing off the filth of the fleſh* is
xxviii.19. ‘ not *the baptiſm that ſaveth*; but a *good*
‘ *conſcience* maketh requeſts to God. *If*
Mar. xvi. ‘ *any man be in Chriſt, he is a new creature*.
15, 16. ‘ The conſequence of this is, that *infants*
‘ are not to be baptized, nor can be *Chri-*
‘ *ſtians*; but ſuch only as confeſs their faith,
‘ as theſe Scriptures teach. There is nei-
‘ ther command, example, or juſt conſe-
‘ quence

'quence for *infants baptiſm*, but for the Acts ii.
'baptizing of *believers*. There is beſides, 38, 41.
'of the church of God, to be conſider'd — viii. 12, 37.
'what it is; it will plainly appear, that *in-* — ix. 18.
'*fants* cannot be of it; they that know — x. 47.
'the language from whence the word *church* — xvi. 31.
'is taken, can witneſs that it ſignifieth *a* — xviii. 8.
'*people called out*, and ſo the church of Chriſt — xix. 3.
'is a company called out of their former eſ- Rev. xviii.
'ſtate, wherein they were by nature; out of 4.
'*Babylon*, wherein they have been in ſpiritual 2 Cor. vi.
'bondage to the power of Antichriſt, and 14.
'from having fellowſhip in ſpiritual wor-
'ſhip with unbelievers and ungodly men: 1 Pet. i. 5.
'From all, whoſoever cometh out, they Eph. ii. 22.
'are fit timber for his ſpiritual building, Gal. ii. 10.
'which is *a habitation of God by the Spirit*,
'and *the houſhold of faith*. Thoſe thus come Heb. iii. 6.
'out of nature, *Egyptian* bondage, and 1 Cor. xii.
'the fellowſhip of the children of *Belial*, 13.
'being *new creatures*, and ſo *holy brethren*, Eph. i.
'are made *God's houſe*, or *church*, through 22, 23.
'being knit together by the Spirit of God,
'and baptized into *his body, which is the*
'*church*. This being undeniable the church
'of Chriſt, *infants* cannot be of it, for
'they cannot be called out, as aforeſaid.
'Known wicked men cannot be of it, be- Rev. xviii.
'cauſe they are not called out, nor anti- 2. 4.
'chriſts ſpiritual bondage cannot be of it,
'becauſe that is *a habitation of devils*, and
'all God's people muſt go out of that.

Gal. iii. ‘ WHAT can be objected againſt this?
26. ‘ Are not all *the ſons of God by faith?* If
2 Cor. v. ‘ any be in Chriſt, or a Chriſtian, muſt he
17. Gal. vi. ‘ not be a *new creature?* I pray you, do
15. ‘ not take up that uſual objection which
‘ the *Antichriſtians* have learned of the
‘ *Jews*, “ What telleſt thou us of being
“ made *Chriſtians* only by faith in the Son,
John viii. “ and ſo being made free? we are the
3. “ children of *Abraham*, and of believers;
Gen. xvii. “ we are under the promiſe, I will be the
“ God of thee and thy ſeed: Thus are we
“ and our children made free, whenas
“ they neither do nor can believe in the
“ Son.” This is a *Jewiſh* antichriſtian fa-
Read Gal. ‘ ble. For *Abraham* had two ſons, which
iv. 22. *and* ‘ were types of the two ſeeds, to the which
conſider it in the fear ‘ two covenants are made: The one *born*
of God. ‘ *after the fleſh*, typing out the fleſhly *Iſ-*
‘ *raelites,* which were the inhabitants of
‘ material *Jeruſalem,* where was the ma-
Heb. ix. ‘ terial temple, and the performance of
9, 10. ‘ thoſe carnal rites which endured unto the
Rom. iv. ‘ time of reformation: The other *by faith*,
3, 19. ‘ typing out the children of the faith of
‘ *Abraham*, which are the inhabitants of
‘ the ſpiritual *Jeruſalem*, the New Teſta-
‘ ment, in which is the ſpiritual temple,
‘ the church of the living God, and the
‘ performance of all thoſe ſpiritual ordi-
‘ nances which Chriſt Jeſus, as prophet and
Heb. xii. ‘ king thereof, hath appointed, which re-
28. ‘ mains, and cannot be ſhaken or alter’d.

‘ Now

‘ Now if the old covenant be aboliſhed, Heb. viii.
‘ and all the appertainings thereof, as it is, 13. —ix. 19,
‘ as being ſimilitudes of heavenly things ; 24.
‘ even the covenant written in the book,
‘ the people, the tabernacle or temple, and
‘ all the miniſtring veſſels ; and a better
‘ covenant, eſtabliſh’d upon better promiſes,
‘ and better temple and miniſtring veſſels —viii. 6.
‘ came inſtead thereof, procured and pur-
‘ chaſed by the blood of Jeſus Chriſt, who
‘ is the new and living way : *let us draw* —x. 19,
‘ *near with a true heart, in aſſurance of* 24.
‘ *faith, ſprinkled in our hearts from an evil*
‘ *conſcience, and baptized in our bodies with*
‘ *pure water : let us keep this profeſſion of*
‘ *hope without wavering, and have no con-*
‘ *fidence in the fleſh*, to reap juſtification or
‘ chriſtianity thereby ; but let us caſt it a-
‘ way as dung and droſs : for if ever any
‘ might plead privilege of being the child
‘ of the faithful, the Apoſtle *Paul* might, as Phil. iii. 3.
‘ he ſaith ; —*read the place*—but it was no-
‘ thing till he had the righteouſneſs of God Acts ix.
‘ through faith, then was he *baptized* into 18.
‘ Chriſt Jeſus for the remiſſion of his ſins.

‘ THIS covenant, that we as children of
‘ *Abraham* challenge, is the covenant of
‘ life and ſalvation by Jeſus Chriſt, made
‘ to all the children of *Abraham*, as it Rom. iv.
‘ is made to *Abraham* himſelf ; *to them* 24.
‘ *that believe in him that raiſed up Je-*
‘ *ſus our Lord from the dead.* As alſo,
‘ the children of the fleſh are not they ;
‘ they

Acts xiii. 26,32,39. Rom.ix.8. ' they muſt be put out, and muſt not be
' heirs with the faithful: *If they that are*
Gal. iv. 30. ' *of the law be heirs, faith is made void,*
Rom. iv. 14,16. ' *and the promiſe is made of none effect.*
' *Therefore it is by faith, that it might*
' *come by grace, and the promiſe might be*
' *ſure to all the ſeed that are of the faith*
' *of* Abraham, *who is the father of all the*
Gal. iii. 7, 9, 29. —iii. 16, 29. ' *faithful.* They are his children; the pro-
' miſe of ſalvation is not made with both
' *Abraham*'s ſeeds, but with *his own ſeed,*
' *they that are of the faith of* Abraham.'

' THESE things may be ſtrange to thoſe
Eph. iv. 28. ' that are *ſtrangers from the life of God,*
' *thro' the ignorance that is in them, becauſe*
' *of the hardneſs of their hearts.* God hath
' written them as the great things of his
' law; but they are counted of many as a
Hoſ. viii. 18. ' ſtrange thing: *but wiſdom is juſtified of all*
' *her children,* and they that ſet their hearts
' to ſeek wiſdom as ſilver, and ſearch for
' her as for treaſure, they ſhall ſee the righ-
' teouſneſs of thoſe things as the light, and
' the evidence of them as the noon-day.
' They that be wiſe will try theſe things
' by the true touchſtone of the holy ſcrip-
1 Cor. iii. 21. ' tures, and leave off rejoicing in men, to
' hang their faith and profeſſion on them;
' the which I fear not to ſupplicate God
' day and night on the behalf of you all.
' To whoſe gracious direction I commit
' you, with a remembrance of my hearty
' love to every one; deſiring but this fa-
' vour,

'vour, that for requital I may receive your 'loving anſwer.

Lond. 10 May, 1622.

'*Your's to be commanded al-* '*ways in any Chriſtian* '*ſervice,*

H. H.

'*P. S.* I have ſent to my friends a te- 'ſtimony of my love; one book to Ma- 'ſter *Stroud*, one to Goodman *Ball*, one 'to Mrs. *Fountaine*, one to *Roger Seely*, 'one to *Samuel Quaſh*, and one to your 'ſelf. I beſeech you read, conſider, and '*the Lord give you underſtanding in all* '*things.*'

THE perſon who publiſhed this letter, with an anſwer thereto, obſerves, That they ſeparated from the church, and writ many books in defence of their principles, and had multitudes of diſciples [u]: That it was their cuſtom to produce a great number of ſcriptures to prove their doctrines [x]: That they were in appearance more holy than thoſe of the eſtabliſhed church [y]: That they diſſuaded their *diſciples* from reading the churchmens books, hearing in their aſſemblies, or conferring with their learned

[u] *Anabapt. Myſtery of iniquity unveil'd, p.* 61.

[x] *Advertiſement to the reader.*

[y] *Unmaſking the man of ſin,* p. 113.

men:

men[z]: That besides the denyal of *infant-baptism*, they denied also the doctrine of predestination, reprobation, final perseverance, and other truths; but of their opposing these he gives no express proof, but says[a], 'Tho' their letter question them not, 'yet I suppose their seeds are sown among 'you, so well by their *apostles* as books.'

THIS indeed has ordinarily been their treatment, to be accused only upon supposition, and have their whole *party* branded with the errors or miscarriages of a few.

THE said author further observes from this letter[b], that the *Baptists* do allow of just consequences from scripture as a sound way of arguing: And as for express command or example for *baptizing* of *infants*, he does not pretend to bring any; but rather attempts to justify that practice from *human* authority.

HE reckons that the age in which a person is to be baptized, the place of washing, whether in a river or an artificial font; the manner of washing, whether the whole body, or but a part; whether by sprinkling, or rubbing with the hand; and whether after washing, to wipe the body with a cloth, &c. are things which Christ hath left to the disposing of the church[c].

[z] *Advert. to the reader.*

[a] *Anabapt. Myst. p.* 42, 65.

[b] *Ibid. p.* 38.

[c] *Ibid. p.* 136.

HE ſays, moreover, in his *advertiſement to the reader*, ‘ if there were not a warrant in holy ſcripture, in direct words, ‘ or plain conſequence, for baptizing *infants*; yet inſomuch, as it is an *ordinance* ‘ *of man*, which croſſeth not any command ‘ of God, it is to be obeyed by Chriſtians, ‘ and that by command of God: for he ‘ that is not againſt Chriſt, is for Chriſt.’ It muſt however be granted, that this *controverſy* is ſet in a much clearer light, and managed after a more accurate manner on both ſides, in the preſent age, than it was in thoſe times.

IN the year 1624. there came forth much greater *champions* in defence of *infant-baptiſm*. An. Dom. 1624.

THE famous *Dod* and *Cleaver* [d] united their ſtrength, and joined together in publiſhing a ſmall treatiſe againſt the erroneous poſitions of the *Anabaptiſts*, as they term'd them.

IN the *preface* they apologize for their ingaging in this *controverſy*, by alledging, that thoſe of the contrary opinion were very induſtrious, and took great pains to propagate their doctrine: That divers perſons of good note for piety had been prevailed upon by them: That ſeveral had entreated their help and aſſiſtance, and that they had been engaged already in private debates about this matter.

[d] *The patrimony of Chriſtian children.*

THIS

THIS *pamphlet* being ſcarce, very few have or can now obtain a ſight of it; I ſhall therefore obſerve two or three things in it that are uncommon.

IN the *preface* they repreſent the *Baptiſts* of thoſe times as agreeing with the *Arminians* only in ſome opinions.

WHEN they anſwer the objections of the *Baptiſts*, which they ſay [e] are recited out of their own books *verbatim*, they politickly conceal both the names of the *authors*, and the *titles* of the books, except one; which if it was done to prevent examining the truth of their quotations, keep the knowlege of ſuch writings from the world, hinder perſons from reading their arguments at length, and with their connection, or that they might the better charge the whole party with the opinion of ſome particular perſons; all theſe muſt be owned very unfair in diſputants.

THEY charge it upon the *Baptiſts* as a great error held by them, that no *infants* dying in infancy are damned with the wicked in hell, which ſalvation they have by the merits of Chriſt [f].

WHEN they alſo charge upon them, the denial of *original ſin*, as the occaſion of their error in *baptiſm*, they themſelves run into as great an error, to avoid the force of the others arguments, *viz.* that the ſoul of

[e] Page 22.
[f] Page 49.

man

man is by propagation; affirming, that *Adam* was the father of men, in respect of their souls as well as their bodies; that as other creatures beget the whole of their offspring, so do men; and that when God is called *the father of spirits*, and men *the fathers of our flesh*, it does not denote any different original of soul and body[g]. Besides these, I do not find any thing but what is common upon the controversy.

BUT to close this reign, Mr. *Neal* says[h], 'That it is hard to make any judgment of 'King *James*'s religion: For one while he 'was a *Puritan*, and then a zealous *Church-*'*man*; at first a *Calvinist* and *Presbyterian*, 'afterwards a *Remonstrant* or *Arminian*; 'and at last a half, if not an entire doc-'trinal *Papist*.'

Rapin says[i], 'he was neither a sound '*Protestant*, nor a good *Catholick*; but 'had form'd a plan of uniting both 'churches, which must effectually have 'ruin'd the *protestant* interest; for which 'indeed he never expressed any real con-'cern.'

[g] Page 73, 74.
[h] *Hist. Purit.* vol. II. p. 151.
[i] *Hist. Eng.* vol. II. p. 236.

CHAP.

CHAP. III.

From the end of the reign of King James I. *to the reſtoration of King* Charles II.

Charles I. An. Dom. 1625.

KING *Charles* I. ſucceeded his father, and being tinctur'd from his infancy with the principles concerning the regal authority and prerogative royal, ſo much improved by the deceaſed king during his life [a], kept the ſame *favourite*, the ſame *council*, the ſame *miniſters*, and all the places at court, and in the kingdom, ſtill continued in the hands of the duke of *Buckingham*'s creatures; ſo that the ſufferings and hardſhips of the *Puritans* were ſtill continued: For, like the king his father, he was very fond of *arbitrary power* and had no *favourites* or *miniſters* but what were of the ſame principles.

The privy-council.

HIS *privy-council* became by degrees an abſolute court, which thought itſelf above the laws. The *ſtar-chamber* was another court, the moſt rigorous that ever was; the

Star-chamber.

[a] *Rapin*, vol. II. p. 237.

ſeve-

ſeverity whereof fell chiefly upon thoſe who pretended to diſpute the prerogative royal. The *high-commiſſion-court* perfectly ſeconded the *council* and *ſtar-chamber*; and under a colour of putting a ſtop to *ſchiſm*, oppreſſed as *Puritans* thoſe that refuſed to ſubmit to a deſpotick power. *Laud* had almoſt the ſole direction of this *high-commiſſion-court*, after the archbiſhop of *Canterbury* was excluded on account of *Sibthorp*'s ſermon. He ſo managed therefore, to prevent the growth of *Preſbyterianiſm*, that the king ſent certain *inſtructions* to the archbiſhops, with a command to impart them to the *biſhops* of their *provinces*, in order to their being obſerved. The chief ends of theſe *inſtructions* were, to hinder any *Preſbyterian* from creeping into the church of *England*, and to diſcover the careleſs obſervers of the rites preſcribed by the canons.

High-commiſſion court.

Oppreſs the Puritans.

WE do not find in the principles and doctrines of the church of *England*, any thing repugnant to charity, or tending to violence; but it was wholly owing to the character and deſigns of the *court-prelates*, of the king's *miniſters* and *counſellors*, who meant to carry the royal authority to the higheſt degree [c]. They thought nothing could more conduce to that end, than the humbling, or rather the utter ruin of the

[b] *Rapin*, vol. II. p. 285.
[c] *Ibid*, p. 287.

Puritans, and unfortunately considered as such, all that opposed their design.

THE *Presbyterian* party, tho' very numerous, as plainly appeared afterwards, laboured then under great oppressions. They had against them the *king*, the *ministers*, the *council*, the *star-chamber*, the *high-commission*, the principal heads of the church of *England*, the *Arminians*, the *Papists*, the *lord-lieutenants* of the *counties*, the *judges* of the realm, and all the *magistrates* in general; notwithstanding all which, they daily gained ground.

Yet they gain ground.

'THIS would seem, says *Rapin* [d], incre-
'dible, if it was not considered, that the
'court themselves were the chief cause of
'their increase. The court looked upon
'as *Puritans* all who did not shew sub-
'mission enough to the king, or would not
'allow sufficient extent to the prerogative-
'royal; and by oppressing them as such,
'or by refusing them all kinds of employ-
'ments, engaged them unavoidably to turn
'to the *Presbyterians*. As the king's pre-
'tensions, with regard to government, were
'not approved by the majority of the na-
'tion; it happen'd by degrees, that almost
'all *England* became *Presbyterian*, accord-
'ing to the sense given by the court to that
'term.'

[d] *Hist.* England, vol. II. p. 292.

Sir

SIR *Benjamin Rudyard*, a member of the houſe of *commons*, to intimate that there was a ſettled deſign to bring in *popery* and arbitrary power in *England*, expreſſed himſelf in the *houſe* after this manner [e]. 'They 'have ſo brought it to paſs, that under the 'name of *Puritans* all our religion is bran-'ded: ---- whoſoever ſquares his actions by 'any rule, either divine or human, he is 'a *Puritan*; --- he that will not do what-'ſoever other men would have him do, he 'is a *Puritan*, *&c.*"

Sir Benj. Rudyard's *ſpeech.*

IN ſhort, the reign of K. *Charles* I. was more violent in perſecuting the *Puritans*, than that of his father *James*: *Laud* being made biſhop of *London*, and afterwards archbiſhop of *Canterbury*, and one of the prime miniſters, uſed all his induſtry and credit to humble the *Puritan party*; that is, not only the *Preſbyterian*, but alſo the *Calviniſts*, and ſuch as would not patiently bear the yoke of ſervitude.

Matthew Wren, biſhop of *Norwich*, the biſhop of *Bath* and *Wells*, and *Coſins*, prebendary of *Durham*, being all of the ſame principles, ſeconded him in his deſign.

IN the year 1633, the *Baptiſts*, who had hitherto been intermixed among other *Proteſtant Diſſenters*, without diſtinction, and ſo conſequently ſhared with the *Puritans* in all the *perſecutions* of thoſe times, began now to ſeparate themſelves, and form diſtinct *ſo-*

An. Dom. 1633. *The* Baptiſts *begin to form diſtinct ſocieties.*

[e] *Rapin Hiſt.* England, vol. II. p. 353.

cieties of thoſe of their own perſuaſion. Concerning the firſt of which I find the following account collected from a manuſcript of Mr. *William Kiffin.*

'THERE was a congregation of Proteſtant *Diſſenters* of the *independant* Perſuaſion in *London*, gather'd in the year 1616, whereof Mr. *Henry Jacob* was the firſt paſtor; and after him ſucceeded Mr. *John Lathorp*, who was their miniſter at this time. In this ſociety ſeveral perſons, finding that the congregation kept not to their firſt principles of ſeparation, and being alſo convinced that *baptiſm* was not to be adminiſtred to *infants*, but ſuch only as profeſſed faith in Chriſt, deſired that they might be diſmiſſed from that communion, and allowed to form a diſtinct congregation, in ſuch order as was moſt agreeable to their own ſentiments.

'THE church, conſidering that they were now grown very numerous, and ſo more than could in theſe times of perſecution conveniently meet together, and believing alſo that thoſe perſons acted from a principle of conſcience, and not obſtinacy, agreed to allow them the liberty they deſired, and that they ſhould be conſtituted a diſtinct church; which was perform'd the 12th of *Sept.* 1633. And as they believed that *baptiſm* was not rightly adminiſtred to *infants*, ſo they look'd 'look'd upon the *baptiſm* they had receiv'd 'in that age as invalid: whereupon moſt 'or all of them received a new *baptiſm*. 'Their miniſter was Mr. *John Spilſbury*. 'What number they were is uncertain, because in the mentioning of the names of 'about twenty men and women, it is added, *with divers others*. *Records of that church.*

'IN the year 1638, Mr. *William Kiffin*, 'Mr. *Thomas Wilſon*, and others, being of 'the ſame judgment, were upon their re-'queſt, diſmiſſed to the ſaid Mr. *Spilſbury*'s 'congregation. An. Dom. 1638.

'IN the year 1639, another congrega-'tion of *Bapiſts* was formed, whoſe place 'of meeting was in *Crutched-Fryars*; the 'chief promoters of which were Mr. *Green*, 'Mr. *Paul Hobſon*, and Captain *Spencer*.'

IN the beginning of the year 1640, a war againſt the *Scots* was reſolved on, and thought ſo reaſonable and neceſſary to the King's honour, that it might be ventured with an *Engliſh* Parliament. Which being laid before the council, was chearfully agreed to, and after twelve years interval, a parliament was ſummoned to meet *April* 13. and being met, inſtead of beginning with the ſupply, appointed *committees* for *religion* and *grievances*; which diſobliged the King ſo much, that after ſeveral fruitleſs attempts to perſuade them to begin with the ſubſidy bill, he diſſolved them An. Dom. 1640. *A parliament ſummoned, and diſſolved.*

in anger, without paſſing a ſingle act, after they had ſat about three weeks.

The convocation continues ſitting,

'THE convocation that ſat with this 'parliament, was opened *April* 14. with 'more ſplendor and magnificence[f], ſays 'Mr. *Neal*, than the ſituation of affairs 'required.'

THO' the convocation, according to antient cuſtom, ſhould have broke up at the ſame time with the parliament, yet they continued ſitting, and paſſed ſeventeen canons, approved by the privy council, and ſubſcribed by as many of both houſes of convocation as were preſent. That the canon againſt *ſectaries*, may be better underſtood, it will be neceſſary to tranſcribe an abſtract of that againſt *Popery*, *viz.* 'All eccleſiaſtical perſons, within their ſeveral pariſhes or juriſdictions, 'ſhall confer privately with *popiſh recuſants*; [g] but if private conference prevail 'not, the church muſt and ſhall come 'to her cenſures; and to make way for 'them, ſuch perſons ſhall be preſented at 'the next viſitation, who come not to 'church, and refuſe to receive the holy 'euchariſt, or who either ſay or hear 'maſs, and if they remain obſtinate after 'citation, they ſhall be excommunicated. 'But if neither conference nor cenſures 'prevail, the church ſhall then complain of

and paſs ſeventeen canons.

Canon 3.

[f] *Hiſt. Purit.* vol. II. p. 342.
[g] *Ibid.* p. 347.

'them

'them to the civil power, and this ſacred 'ſynod does earneſtly entreat the reverend '*juſtices* of aſſize to be careful in exe- 'cuting the laws as they will anſwer it to 'God.

'THE ſynod decrees, that the canon 'above mentioned againſt *Papiſts*, ſhall be in 'full force againſt all *Anabaptiſts*, *Brown- 'iſts Separatiſts*, and other *Sectaries*, as 'far they are applicable.' Canon 5.

WHEN the canons of this arbitrary (who call themſelves ſacred) ſynod were made publick, they were generally diſliked; and had not the execution of them been ſuſpended by the prevailing of the *Nobility* and *Gentry* with the king at *York*, *Laud* might have been more famous (or rather infamous) than even *Bonner* himſelf in the *Marian* days.

IN the year 1641. one Mr. *Edward Barber* put forth a ſmall piece in defence of immerſion; intituled, *A treatiſe of baptiſm or dipping; wherein is clearly ſhewed, that our Lord Chriſt ordained dipping; and that ſprinkling of children is not according to Chriſt's inſtitution; and alſo the invalidity of thoſe arguments that are commonly brought to juſtify that practice.* Anno Dom. 1641. Edward Barber.

IN the year following another treatiſe came forth, written by *A. R.* intituled, *the vanity of childrens baptiſm.* This *author* attempts to prove theſe two points againſt the eſtabliſhed church, *viz.* that *dipping* is neceſſary to the right adminiſtration of *baptiſm*, and that this ſacrament is not to be given to *infants*.

Mr. Francis Cornwell *proſelyted to the* Baptiſts.

ABOUT this time there was a conſiderable proſelyte made to the opinion of the *Baptiſts*; namely, Mr. *Francis Cornwell*, *M. A.* and ſometime ſtudent of *Emanuel College* in *Cambridge*. Whether he received his conviction from the treatiſes abovenamed, or whether he was only by them put upon examination of the *controverſy*, and upon ſearch of the *ſcripture*, and firſt *fathers* of the church, found the truth to be on their ſide, I cannot ſay; but this is evident, when he had found out the truth himſelf, he was willing to help others to do ſo likewiſe; and therefore publiſhed a ſmall treatiſe, dedicated to the houſe of commons, intituled *the vindication of the royal commiſſion of king Jeſus*. Wherein he lays down ſeveral arguments to prove, that the practice of *chriſtening children* oppoſes the commiſſion granted by our Lord and Saviour; that it is a *Romiſh* or *Antichriſtian* cuſtom, and was eſtabliſhed by pope *Innocent* III. who made a decree, that the *baptiſm* of *infants* of believers ſhould ſucceed *circumciſion*.

A diſpute between Dr. Featly *and four* Anabaptiſts *in* Southwark.

THIS year alſo, in the month of *October*, was that diſpute between Dr. *Featly* (the favourite *author* of the reverend Mr. *Neal*) and four *Anabaptiſts* in *Southwark*; of which ſome have made ſo great a noiſe ſince,

ſince, and Mr. *Neal* ſeems willing ſhould not be buried in oblivion.

I DO not find that any have publiſhed an account of this *diſputation* but the Doctor himſelf, or that there was any *amanuenſis* to take down perfectly what was ſpoken at that time; but only ſhort notes taken by himſelf, or one of his friends, which the Doctor filled up according to his own memory. And he did not publiſh it neither, till about two years after, when beſides his fixed prejudice againſt the *Diſſenters*, he was put out of humour, by being deprived of two livings, which he enjoyed before the unhappy difference between the King and parliament. And he tells the *Reader* in his *dedication*, that he could hardly dip his pen in any thing but gall. How fair and impartial an account ſuch a man was like to give, and what credit Mr. *Neal* has got to himſelf by becoming his *diſciple*, let the reader judge. For after all, by the Doctor's own account of this *diſputation*, his antagoniſts do not appear ſo very deſpicable; nor did he gain any great advantage of them. An indifferent reader will clearly ſee the force and ſimplicity of the argument on the one hand, and the art and ſhuffling that was uſed on the other.

ONE of the *Anabaptiſts*, whom he calls a *Scotchman*, began the diſcourſe after this humble and modeſt manner.

'MASTER

'MASTER doctor, we come to dispute 'with you at this time, not for contention 'sake, but to receive satisfaction: 'We hold that the *baptism* of *infants* cannot be proved lawful by the testimony of '*scripture*, or by *apostolical* tradition. If 'you therefore can prove the same either 'way, we shall willingly submit unto 'you.'

THE doctor presently breaks forth into *exclamations*: Are you then *Anabaptists?* and insults over them as *Hereticks*, who were *mechanic* and *illiterate* men, by whose habit he could judge they were not fit to dispute; that they could not dispute on *authority*, because they understood not the *original*; nor by *reason*, because such must understand how to conclude *syllogistically* in mood and figure; with abundance of such *pedantick* stuff, that savoured of nothing but pride and a bad cause.

HE that will take the pains to read his own account of this *disputation*, will easily perceive how the *Doctor* endeavours through the whole to fly from the argument proposed, thereby to entangle the innocent men, and escape giving good proof for the points. One while he proposes difficulties to them about the *doctrine* of the *Trinity*; then again about the form of a true church: presently, he goes about to prove, that *magistrates* have power to impose religion; afterwards, that we ought to use forms of

prayer;

prayer; anon, that none ought to preach without epiſcopal ordination; with a many other impertinent digreſſions.

HE that would have an account of his *fooliſh pictures*, may ſee a book which came out preſently after the Doctor's, intitled, *Brief conſiderations on Dr.* Featly's *book*, by *Samuel Richardſon.*

ABOUT this time it was, that the pious Mr. *Hanſerd Knollys*, who had been forced to fly to *New-England* to eſcape the perſecution of the high-commiſſion-court, returned back again to *London*; where by his plain and faithful way of preaching, there was ſoon gathered a congregation of chriſtians *baptized* upon the profeſſion of their faith, over whom he was alſo ordained paſtor, and of whom we ſhall have occaſion to ſay more as we go on.

THE King's affairs being now brought to the utmoſt extremity, and he finding it impoſſible to carry on the war againſt the *Scots*, appointed commiſſioners to treat with them at *Rippon*; who agreed for a ceſſation of *arms* for two months, and the treaty to be adjourned to *London*, where a free parliament was immediately to be called.

The long parliament.

'SAD and melancholly, ſays Mr. *Neal* [h], 'was the condition of the *prime miniſters*, 'when they ſaw themſelves reduced to 'the neceſſity of ſubmitting their conduct

[h] *Hiſt. Purit.* vol. II. p. 357.

to

'to the examination of an *Engliſh parliament*, ſupported by an army from *Scotland*, and the general diſcontents of the 'people. Several of the *courtiers* began to 'ſhift for themſelves; ſome withdrew 'from the ſtorm, and others having been 'concerned in one illegal project or other, 'deſerted their maſters, and made their 'peace, by diſcovering the King's counſels 'to the leading members of *parliament*; 'which diſabled the junto from making 'any conſiderable efforts for their ſafety. 'All men had a veneration for the perſon 'of the King, tho' his majeſty had loſt 'ground in their affections by his ill uſage 'of his *parliaments*, and by taking the 'faults of his *miniſters* upon himſelf.

'BUT the queen was in no manner of 'eſteem with them, who had the *Proteſtant religion* and the liberties of their coun-'try at heart.

'THE *biſhops* had ſunk their character 'by their high behaviour in the ſpiritual 'courts; ſo that they had nothing to expect 'but that their wings ſhould be clipp'd. And 'the *judges* were deſpiſed and hated for 'abandoning the laws of their country, 'and giving a ſanction to the illegal pro-'ceedings of the *council* and *ſtar-chamber*. 'As his Majeſty had but few friends of cre-'dit or intereſt among the people at home, 'ſo he had nothing to expect from abroad. '*France* and *Spain* were pleaſed with his

'diſtreſs,

'distress. The foreign *Protestants* wished 'well to the oppressed people of *England*. 'They published their resentments against 'the *bishops* for their hard usage of the *Dutch* 'and *French* congregations; and gave it as 'their opinion, that a *Protestant* king that 'countenanc'd *Papists*, and at the same 'time drove his *Protestant* subjects out of 'the kingdom, was not worthy the assist-'ance of the reformed churches, especially 'after he had renounced communion with 'them, and declared openly that the reli-'gion of the church of *England* was not 'the same with that of the foreign *Pro-'testants*.'

MR. *Whitelock* observes [i], that tho' the court labour'd to bring in their friends, yet those who had most favour with them, had least in the country: And it was not a little strange to see what a spirit of opposition to the court-proceedings was in the hearts and actions of most of the people; so that very few of that *party* had the favour of being chosen *members* of this *parliament*.

Claren-don's *account of them.*

The earl of *Clarendon*, speaking of this *parliament*, admits that there were many great and worthy patriots in the house, and as eminent as any age had ever produced, men of gravity, of wisdom, of great and plentiful fortunes, who would have been satisfy'd with some few amend-

[i] *Pag.* 37.

ments

ments in church and ſtate. As to their religion, ſays this noble *hiſtorian*[k], 'They 'were all members of the eſtabliſh'd *church*, 'and almoſt to a man for epiſcopal govern-'ment; tho' they were undevoted enough 'to the *court*, they had all imaginable du-'ty for the king, and affection for the go-'vernment eſtabliſh'd by law or antient 'cuſtom; and without doubt the majority 'of that body were perſons of gravity and 'wiſdom, who being poſſeſſed of great and 'plentiful fortunes, had no mind to break 'the peace of the kingdom, or to make 'any conſiderable alterations in the govern-'ment of the church or ſtate.'

DR. *Welwood* affirms[l], that no age produced greater men than thoſe that ſat in this parliament.

And Lewis Du Moulin.

DR. *Lewis du Moulin*, who lived thro' theſe times ſays: 'That both lords and com-'mons were moſt, if not all, peaceable, 'orthodox church of *England* men; all con-'forming to the rites and ceremonies of '*epiſcopacy*, but greatly averſe to *Popery* 'and *Tyranny*, and to the corrupt part of 'the church, that inclined towards *Rome*.'

'THIS is further evident, ſays Mr. *Neal*[m], 'from their own order of *Nov.* 20, 1640. 'that none ſhould ſit in their houſe but 'ſuch as would receive the communion ac-

k *Vol.* I. p. 184.
l *Welwood's Memoirs*, p. 42.

'cording

'cording to the usage of the church of 'England.'

Persecution abated.

THE difference between the king and this parliament put a stop to the hot persecution which had hitherto been carry'd on against the *Dissenters*; so that men might now judge freely in matters of religion, and every one pursued the sentiments of his own mind without danger.

Antipædobaptism had not been without its *proselytes* in the worst of times, but now it began very much to prevail; and those of that *persuasion* having separated themselves, and formed distinct societies, were become several churches of this opinion in *London*, besides those that continued in communion with *Pædobaptists*.

Baxter's *first acquaintance with the* Baptists.

IT seems to have been about this time, that Mr. *Baxter* became first acquainted with any of this opinion; of whom he gives an account in these words [n], *viz.*

'WHILST I was at *Gloucester*, I saw 'the first contentions between the *Mini*-'*sters* and *Anabaptists*, that ever I was ac-'quainted with; for these were the first '*Anabaptists* that ever I had seen in any 'country, and I heard but of few more in 'those parts of *England*. About a dozen 'young men, or more, of considerable 'parts, had received the opinion against '*infant-baptism*, and were re-baptized, and

[m] *Hist. Purit.* vol. II. p. 362.
[n] *Life and Time*, p. 41. Part I.

'laboured

'laboured to draw others after them, not 'far from *Gloucester*, and the minister of 'the place, Mr. *Winnel*, being hot and 'impatient with them, harden'd them the 'more: He wrote a considerable book a-'gainst them at that time; but *England* 'having then no great experience of the 'tendency and consequence of *Anabap-'tistry*, the people that were not of their 'opinion did but pity them, and think it 'was a conceit that had no great harm in 'it, and blamed Mr. *Winnel* for his vio-'lence and asperity towards them.'

Dr. Featley's *account of them.*

THE great increase of the *Baptists* about this time, is acknowledged and bewailed by their adversaries. Dr. *Featly* says [o], 'This 'fire in the reigns of Queen *Elizabeth* and 'King *James*, and our gracious sovereign, 'till now was cover'd in *England* under the 'ashes; or if it brake out at any time, by 'the care of the ecclesiastical and civil *ma-'gistrates* it was soon put out. But of 'late, since the unhappy distractions which 'our sins have brought upon us, the tem-'poral sword being other ways employed, 'and the spiritual lock'd up fast in the 'scabbard, this *sect*, among others, hath 'so far presumed upon the patience of the 'state, that it hath held weekly conven-'ticles, re-baptized hundreds of men and 'women together in the twilight, in *ri-*

[o] *Dippers dipp'd, pr face.*

vulets

'*vulets* and ſome arms of the *Thames*, and 'elſewhere, dipping them over head and 'ears. It hath printed divers pamphlets in 'defence of their hereſy; yea, and chal-'lenged ſome of our *preachers* to diſpu-'tation.'

Dr. Wall's account of them.

IT was, ſays Dr. *Wall*[p], 'During the 'rebellion againſt King *Charles* I. and the 'uſurpation of *Oliver Cromwel*, that this 'opinion began to have any great number 'of converts to it. In thoſe times of ſtirs 'they boaſted in their books, that that pro-'phecy was fulfilled, *Many ſhall run to and* '*fro, and knowledge ſhall be increaſed.*' Dan. xiii. 4.

Fuller's account of them.

Jan. 18. 1640-1, ſays Mr. *Fuller*[q], 'This 'day happen'd the firſt fruits of *Anabap-*'*tiſtical* inſolence; when eighty of that '*ſect* meeting at a houſe in St. *Saviours* in '*Southwark*, preached, that the ſtatute in 'the 35th of *Elizabeth*, for the admini-'ſtration of the *Common-prayer*, was no 'good law, becauſe made by *biſhops*; that 'the king cannot make a good law, be-'cauſe not perfectly *regenerate*; that he 'was only to be obeyed in civil matters. 'Being brought before the *lords*, they con-'feſſed the articles, but no penalty was in-'flicted upon them.' But this is a very imperfect and partial account of this mat-

p *Hiſt. Bap.* vol. II. p. 214.

q *Church Hiſt. Book* XI. p. 172

ter, as appears by the church-book, or journal kept by this people.

IT was not an *Anabaptiſt* but an *Independent* congregation, tho' there might be ſome few among them holding that opinion. They met in *Deadman's-place*, having at that time one Mr. *Stephen More* for their paſtor; and being aſſembled on the Lord's-day, for religious worſhip as uſual, tho' not with their former ſecrecy, they were diſcovered and taken, and by Sir *John Lenthal*, the marſhal of the *King's-bench*, committed to the *Clink* priſon.

THE next morning ſix or ſeven of the men were by an order from above, carried up to the houſe of Lords. It was alledged againſt them, as *Fuller* ſays, that they had preached againſt the King's ſupremacy in eccleſiaſtical matters, and againſt the Statute of the 35th of *Elizabeth*, that eſtabliſhes the Common-prayer, and forbids all aſſembling for religious worſhip, where it is not uſed.

THE lords examined them ſtrictly concerning their principles; and they as freely acknowledged, that they owned no other head of the church but Jeſus Chriſt; that no prince had power to make laws to bind the conſciences of men; and that laws made contrary to the law of God were of no force.

As things now ſtood, the lords could by no means diſcountenance theſe principles; and therefore, inſtead of inflicting any penalty, they treated them with a great deal of reſpect and civility: and ſome of the houſe enquired, where the place of their meeting was, and intimated, that they would come and hear them. And accordingly three or four of the *Peers* did go to their meeting on the Lord's-day following, to the great ſurprize and wonder of many. The people went on in their uſual method, having two ſermons; in both which they treated of thoſe principles for which they had been accuſed, grounding their diſcourſes on the words of our Saviour, *All power is given unto me, in heaven and in earth.* After this they received the Lord's-ſupper, and then made a collection for the *poor*; to which the lords contributed liberally with them; and at their departure ſignify'd their ſatiſfaction in what they had heard and ſeen, and their inclination to come again. But this made too much noiſe, and gave too great an alarm to the mob, for them to venture a ſecond time. And perhaps this was the firſt diſſenting meeting, that ever had ſo great an honour done it.

Matth. xxviii. 18.

THIS church, as appears by their records, was conſtituted about the year 1621. The firſt paſtor thereof was one Mr. *Hubbard*, or *Herbert*, a learned man, of epiſcopal or-

 dination;

dination; who having left the church of *England*, took upon him the paſtoral care of this church, and with them went into *Ireland*, and there died. They returned again into *England*, and ſettled about *London*; and choſe Mr. *John Cann* (famous for filling up a bible with marginal notes, much valued to this day) to be their paſtor; who attended that ſervice for ſome time, and at length, with ſome of the members, left the church, and went to *Amſterdam*, and there continued with the *Engliſh* church many years: and tho' he came into *England* afterwards, yet he returned to *Amſterdam*, and there died. After his deceaſe, the church here choſe Mr. *Samuel How*, who was a *Baptiſt*, tho' his predeceſſors were not; for this church ſeems from the beginning, or at leaſt very early, to have kept mix'd communion.

HE ſerved in this miniſtration about ſeven years, and died very much lamented. In his time they were perſecuted beyond meaſure by the clergy and biſhops courts; and he dying under the ſentence of excommunication, chriſtian burial, as it was termed, was denied him; and a conſtable's guard ſecured the pariſh ground at *Shoreditch*, to prevent his being buried there. At length he was buried at *Agnes-la-cleer*; and ſeveral of his members, according to their deſire, were afterwards interred there alſo. He wrote that little book ſo often printed, called

called *How's Sufficiency of the Spirit's teaching*, &c. and was very famous for his vindication of the doctrines of ſeparation; and both he and his people were much haraſſed for it by their enemies, and were forc'd to meet together in fields and woods to avoid them. It was ſome conſiderable time after his deceaſe, that the church choſe Mr. *Stephen Moore*; who was their paſtor when the diſturbance happened which is mentioned by *Fuller*. He ſeems to have been a *Pædobaptiſt*; had been a deacon of their church, as appears by their records; was well gifted for the work of the miniſtry, and a man of good reputation, and poſſeſſed of an eſtate.

Some famous writers ſpeak favourably of the English Baptiſts.

IT contributed not a little to the increaſe of *Antipædobaptiſm* in theſe times, that ſome of the greateſt writers for reformation ſpoke favourably of that opinion, and the reaſonableneſs of granting liberty to thoſe that held it.

The right honourable Robert *lord* Brook

THE right honourable *Robert* lord *Brook*, wrote a treatiſe [r] about this time, wherein he gives this favourable account of the *Anabaptiſts* and their opinion.

I MUST confeſs, ſays he, I begin to ' think, there may be perhaps ſomewhat ' more of God in theſe which they call ' *new ſchiſms*, than appears at firſt glimpſe.

[r] *Epiſcopacy*, p. 96.

'I will not, I cannot, take on me to de-
'fend that which men uſually call *Ana-
'baptiſm*; yet I conceive, that *ſect* is two-
'fold: ſome of them hold free-will, com-
'munity of all things, deny magiſtracy,
'and refuſe to baptize their children; theſe
'truly are ſuch *hereticks* or *atheiſts*, that
'I queſtion whether any divine ſhould
'honour them ſo much as to diſpute with
'them: Much rather ſure ſhould *Alexan-
'der*'s ſword determine here, as of old at
'the gordian knot, where it required this
'motto, *Quæ ſolvere non poſſum, diſſe-
'cabo*; what I cannot untie, I will cut
'aſunder.

'THERE is another ſort of them who
'only deny baptiſm to their children till they
'come to the years of diſcretion, and then
'they baptize them; but in other things
'they agree with the church of *England*.
'Truly theſe men are much to be pitied,
'and I could heartily wiſh, that before they
'are ſtigmatized with the opprobrious brand
'of *ſchiſmaticks*, the truth might be clear'd
'to them; for I conceive, to thoſe that
'hold we may go no further than Scrip-
'ture, for doctrine or diſcipline, it may
'be very eaſy to err in this point now in
'hand, ſince the Scripture ſeems not to
'have clearly determined in this matter.

'THE analogy which baptiſm now hath
'with circumciſion in the old law, ſays
'this

'this *noble lord*[s], is a fine rational argument 'to illustrate a point well proved before; 'but I somewhat doubt whether it be 'proof enough for that which some 'would prove by it, since besides the vast 'difference in the ordinance, the persons 'to be circumcised, are stated by a positive 'law, so express, that it leaves no place for 'scruple; but it is far otherwise in bap-'tism, where all the designation of per-'sons fit to be partakers, for ought I 'know, is only such as believe, for this is 'the qualification which with exactest 'search I find the Scripture requires in per-'sons to be baptized; and this it seems to 'require in all such persons. Now how 'infants can properly be said to believe, 'I am not yet fully resolved.'

Mr. Daniel Rogers.

MR. *Daniel Rogers*, a divine of very great fame in these times, made a publick confession to the world, in his book of the *Sacrament*[t], that he was yet unconvinced by any demonstration of Scripture, for *infant baptism*.

Bishop Taylor.

DR. *Jeremy Taylor*, Bishop of *Down* and *Connor*, was another who very much promoted the opinion of *Antipædobaptism*, by this method. He wrote a treatise, when religion was in this unsettled state, called the *Liberty of prophesying*; wherein he shews

[s] *Danvers*, p. 176.

[t] Part I. p. 79.

 the

the unreaſonableneſs of preſcribing to other mens faith, and the iniquity of perſecuting differing opinions. For the church clergy were againſt *perſecution*, when it came to be their turn to bear it.

AMONG many other excellent arguments to this purpoſe, he makes uſe of this, *viz.*

THAT many opinions, condemned as erroneous, had a great probability of truth on their ſide; at leaſt ſo much might be ſaid for them, as to ſway the conſcience of many honeſt enquirers after truth, and abate the edge of their fury, who ſuppoſe they are deceived.

The Pædobaptiſts *diſpleaſed therewith.*

FOR this purpoſe, he particularly conſiders the opinion of *Antipædobaptiſm*; and under a pretence of reciting what may be ſaid for that error, as he calls it, draws up a very elaborate ſyſtem of arguments againſt *infant-baptiſm*, and ſets it forth with ſuch advantage of ſtyle, that he was thought to have ſaid more for the *Baptiſts* than they were able to ſay for themſelves.

DR. *Hammond* declared to the world '[u] That it is the moſt diligent collection ' and the moſt exact ſcheme of the argu- ' ments againſt *infant-baptiſm*, that he ' had ever met with; and that he has therein ' in ſuch manner repreſented the arguments

[u] *Six caſes Infant-baptiſm, ſect.* 49. 139.
[w] *Wall's Inf. Bap.* vol. II. p. 16.

' for

'for and againſt, that the latter have 'ſeemed to many to be ſucceſsful and 'victorious.'

x OTHERS ſuſpect him of being a real favourer of that opinion, and deſigning to promote it, and therefore call upon him, in the words of *Joſhua* to the man with his drawn ſword: *Art thou for us, or for our adverſaries?* Joſhua v. 13.

SO much were the advocates of *Infant-Baptiſm* alarmed and enraged at this performance, that they compared him to an unfaithful ſubject, who for private ends and intereſt carries arms and ammunition to known and profeſſed enemies; and they complained of it in the words of the prophet, *Thus was I wounded in the houſe of my friends.* Nay, a batchelor in divinity has the aſſurance to call ſo great and learned a man to repentance and recantation.

'y WHAT this *author*'s counſel was, 'thus to write, that which himſelf condemns, ——I know not; but do heartily 'wiſh, that if he have not yet *repented* 'of digging this pit, whereinto divers have 'fallen, not without great and apparent 'hazard to their ſouls, he timely may. If 'he have come to ſome ſecond better 'thoughts, he may do commendably to 'cover it with ſome ſeaſonable endeavour

x *Readings antidotes pref.*
y *Ibid. id.*

'that

'that no more may fall by the ſtumbling-
'block which he hath laid before them.'

SOME of the greateſt divines of thoſe times ſet themſelves to anſwer him; but ſuſpecting the inſufficiency of all other anſwers, would not let the learned biſhop reſt, till he had anſwered himſelf alſo. Yet it is the opinion of ſome, he could never remove the difficulties which he had advanced.

An. Dom. 1643. *The* Baptiſts *publiſh a Confeſſion of faith.*

THERE were ſeveral books wrote about this time by the *Baptiſts* themſelves, in defence of their principles; and in the year 1643. they publiſhed a *confeſſion of their faith*, becauſe it was the conſtant practice of their oppoſers to repreſent them as a people that held moſt dangerous errors, beſides their denial of *infant-baptiſm*; and they were frequently termed both from the pulpit and preſs, *Pelagians*, *Socinians*, *Arminians*, *Soul-ſleepers*, and the like.

BUT in this they clear themſelves fully of all theſe erroneous *tenets*, and ſhew their near agreement with all other chriſtians and proteſtants, in the fundamental points of religion. It is the firſt that was ever publiſhed by the *Engliſh Baptiſts*, and contains fifty two articles; the which you may find in the *appendix* N° 2. The *Baptiſts* never did any thing that more effectually cleared them from the charge of being dangerous *hereticks*, than this did. There were ſeveral *editions* publiſhed in

1644.

1644. and 1646. one of which was licensed by authority, dedicated to the high court of parliament, and put into the hands of several members[z].

Is acknowledged to be orthodox

THEIR greatest *adversaries* were forc'd to acknowledge it was in general an *orthodox confession*, and could object little against it, except the denial of *infant-baptism*, and making *immersion* necessary to the right administration of that ordinance.

By Dr. Featly,

DR. *Featly*, who writ with no small prejudice against the *Anabaptists*, says[a], 'If we 'give credit to this *confession*, and the *pre-'face* thereof, those who among us are 'branded with that title, are neither *Here-'ticks* nor *Schismaticks*, but tender-hearted '*Christians*, upon whom, thro' false sug-'gestions, the hand of authority fell heavy 'whilst the *hierarchy* stood; for they nei-'ther teach free-will, nor falling-away 'from grace, with the *Arminians*; nor 'deny original sin, with the *Pelagians*; nor 'disclaim magistracy, with the *Jesuits*; 'nor maintain plurality of wives, with the '*Polygamists*; nor community of goods, with 'the *Apostolici*; nor going naked, with the '*Adamites*; much less aver the mortality 'of the soul, with *Epicures* and *Psychopan-'nychists*.'

Mr. Marshal.

MR. *John Marshall*, one of the assembly of divines, and a great opposer of the *Bap-*

[z] *Edwards's Gangræna*, part I. p. 184.
[a] *Dippers dipp'd*, p. 177.

tists in those times, says of this confession[b], 'I acknowledge it the most orthodox of any '*Anabaptist* confession I ever read.' And we may very well believe him; for the *English Baptists* never had the liberty of publishing their faith before; and those in foreign parts are indeed represented as very *heterodox* by their enemies. He tells a story, in order to dissuade his *readers* from believing the *Baptists* in this confession of their faith, which I have not met with in any other *author*, and deserves our notice. The story is as follows:

[c]'THAT the *Anabaptists* of *Munster*, 'in the beginning of their schism, set 'forth a confession of faith every way as '*orthodox* as that which you * mention of 'the seven churches of the *Anabaptists* 'of *London*, as I am credibly inform'd by a 'reverend and learned divine, who hath 'many years ago both seen and read it 'in *Germany*;' and in the margin puts the name of Mr. *Dury*.

* *Mr.* Tombes.

Remarks. WELL then, when the *Anabaptists* in *Germany* had the liberty to publish their own faith, they appear'd a very *orthodox* people; but after they had been driven to great hardships, and at length conquer'd in war, their triumphant enemies describe them to be a wicked and erroneous sect.

[b] *Defence infant-baptism*, p. 76.
[c] *Ibid.* p. 74.

BUT

BUT ſuppoſe they were guilty of all thoſe errors or mad pranks that were charg'd upon them after this *orthodox confeſſion*; muſt no others then be believed, when they make a ſolemn confeſſion of their faith. The *Engliſh Baptiſts* have not only kept to this firſt confeſſion of their faith, but have rather improved both in their faith and piety; ſo that now theſe inſinuations are confuted by fact.

IT may be proper to obſerve here, that there have been two *parties* of the *Engliſh Baptiſts* in *England* ever ſince the beginning of the reformation; thoſe that have followed the *Calviniſtical* ſcheme of doctrines, and from the principal point therein, *perſonal election*, have been termed *Particular Baptiſts*: And thoſe that have profeſſed the *Arminian* or remonſtrant tenets; and have alſo from the chief of thoſe doctrines, *univerſal redemption*, been called *General Baptiſts*.

I SHALL not trouble myſelf to enquire into the reaſons for their thus diſtinguiſhing themſelves, ſo as to hold diſtinct communities thereupon; the ſame differing principiples being common to all the denominations of Chriſtians as well as them. But thus much I think fit to declare, that I am fully perſuaded, and clearly of opinion, that this difference in opinion is not a ſufficient or reaſonable ground of renouncing chri-

christian communion with one another, and therefore have not in the course of this history, lean'd either to one side or the other, but have taken facts as they came to my hands, without regarding to which of the parties they were peculiar. And I know that there are several churches, ministers, and many particular persons, among the *English Baptists*, who desire not to go under the name either of *Generals* or *Particulars*, nor indeed can justly *be ranked under either of these heads*; *because they* receive what they think to be truth, without regarding with what human schemes it agrees or disagrees.

THAT worthy judge and excellent divine Sir *Matthew Hale*, Knt. lord chief justice of the *King's-bench*, treating of the great work of our redemption, what it is, how effected, and for whom; concludes thus: 'Now, says he[d], concerning those 'several places in holy scripture, that seem 'to infer the universality of an intended 'redemption, *John* iii. 17. *John* xii. 47. '1 *John* ii. 2. 1 *Tim.* ii. 6. 1 *Tim.* ii. 4. '1 *Cor.* xv. 21. it may be considerable 'whether the intention of those places be, 'that the price was sufficient for all the 'world; so that whosoever shall reject the 'offered mercy, shall never have this ex'cuse, that there was not a sufficiency left 'for him: Or whether it be meant, that 'Christ by his death did fully expiate for all

[d] *Knowledge of God*, &c. p. 230.

'all that original guilt, which was contracted by the fall of *Adam* upon all mankind, but for the actual offences only of such as believed; that so, as the voluntary sin of *Adam* had, without the actual consent of his posterity, made them liable to guilt, so the satisfaction of Christ, without any application of him, should discharge all mankind from that originally contracted guilt. These disquisitions, says he, tho' fit, yet are not necessary to be known; it is enough for me to know, that if *I believe on him, I shall not perish, but have everlasting life*, John iii. 16. and that all are invited, and none excluded, but such as first exclude themselves.'

An. Dom. 1644. *Persecution of the Baptists.*

BUT to come to the persecution that was practised in these times upon those who were termed *Anabaptists*. It is a subject, I am sensible, will be ungrateful to the ears of many, and perhaps very ill improved by others. I could willingly have ended here, but, however, it is the duty of an *historian* to give a true account of things, and let the blame of them fall on whom it will; and this work would be very defective, if I should not take notice of the hardships and sufferings that the *Baptists* underwent in those times, even under those who both before and since have been their *brethren* in dissenting from the establish'd church, and suffering for it also. Nor can this be any just Reflection on the present

Pres-

Presbyterians, who do as much dislike, and detest such principles and practices as we can ourselves.

Presbyterians against liberty of conscience, and a toleration.

NOTHING is more evident than this, that the most noted divines of the *Presbyterian* persuasion, when they had the ascendant, did both preach and write zealously against *liberty* of *conscience*, or a *toleration* of different opinions in matters of religion; and that at the same time that they endeavoured to establish *Presbytery*, they were for using the *civil power* to suppress all who dissented from them.

SEVERAL passages to this purpose are collected by Sir *Roger L'Estrange*, in his treatise entitled, *The Dissenters Sayings*, and by a late pamphlet entitled, *Schism tried and condemn'd by the sentiments of the most eminent writers among the Dissenters.*

Mr. Calamy *declares against it.*

THERE was hardly a divine of greater fame in those days, than Mr. *Calamy* of *Aldermanbury*: And he in a sermon before the house of commons, *Oct.* 22. 1644. says to them thus [e], 'If you do not labour 'according to your duty and power to suppress the *errors* and *heresies* that are spread 'in the kingdom, all these *errors* are your '*errors*, and these *heresies* are your *heresies*; 'they are your sins, and God calls for a parliamentary repentance from you for them 'this day. You are the *Anabaptists*, you 'are the *Antinomians*, and 'tis you that

[e] *Schism try'd and condemn'd*, p. 9.

'hold

'hold that all religions are to be tolerated, *&c.*'

DR. *Burgess* to the commons, *Apr.* 30. 1645. after he had admonished them to beware of compliances with, and indulgences to all sorts of *sects* and *schisms* then pleaded for, says [f]: *Also Dr.* Burgess. An. Dom. 1645.

'AND is it persecution and antichristia-
'nism to engage all to *unity* and *unifor-*
'*mity?* Doth *Paul* bid the *Philippians* to Phil. iii. 2.
'*beware of the concision?* doth he beseech
'the *Romans to mark those which cause di-*
'*vision and offences, contrary to the doctrine*
'*which they had received, and avoid them,*
'&c. doth he, writing to the *Galatians,*
'wish, *I would they were cut off that trou-* Gal. v.
'*ble you*; and is it such an heinous offence 12.
'now, for the faithful servants of Christ to
'advise you to the same course? *Oh hea-*
'*vens!*'

THE famous Mr. *Baxter,* tho' more moderate than many, yet was not wholly free in this point. *And Mr.* Baxter.

IN his first book against the *Anabaptists,* he says [g]: 'The divisions and havock of the 'church is our calamity; we intended not 'to dig down the banks, or to pull up the 'hedge, and lay all waste and common, 'when we desired the *prelates tyranny* 'might cease.

[f] *Ibidem,* p. 12, 13.
[g] *Plain Scrip. Proof,* p. 151.

'[h] AGAIN, my judgment in that much 'debated point of *liberty* of religion, I have 'always freely made known, *I abhor unlimited liberty*, or *toleration of all.*

AND in his cure of church-divisions, he says; 'We must either tolerate all men 'to do what they will, which they will 'make a matter of conscience or religion; 'and then some may offer their *children* in 'sacrifice to the *devil*, and some may think 'they do God service in killing his servants, '*&c.* or else you must tolerate no *error* or '*fault* in religion; and then you must ad'vise what measure of *penalty* you will in'flict.'

Mr. Prynn. MORE plain still was Mr. *Prynn*, who in his answer to *John Goodwin* says:

'IF the parliament and synod shall by 'publick consent establish a *Presbyterial* 'church-government, as most consonant to 'God's word; *Independents* and all others 'are bound in *conscience* to submit unto it, 'under the pain of obstinacy, singularity, '*&c.*'

Mr. *Edwards.* MR. *Edwards*, lecturer at *Christ-Church*, a most inveterate enemy to the *sectarians*, as he terms them, directs both *ministers* and *magistrates* how they should act to establish *Presbytery* without liberty of conscience to others: and as if he had the pen

[h] *Page* 246.
[i] *Dissenters Sayings*, Part II. p. 2.
[k] *Ibidem*, p. 5.

of

of an inſpired writer, predicts the conſequences of granting a *toleration.* All which is now confuted by fact, and he appears to have been a lying prophet; for the experience which theſe nations have had is argument ſufficient, that *toleration* of different opinions is ſo far from diſturbing the publick peace, or deſtroying the intereſts of princes and commonwealths, that it does advantage to the publick, and ſecures peace. This author in the epiſtle dedicatory to his book, entitled *Gangrena*, calls upon the higher powers to rain down all their vengeance on the *ſectaries:* And to ſhew his malice againſt them, he ſays[1]; 'That *mi-*'*niſters* in our times may be a means to 'prevent and ſuppreſs *errors*, *hereſies*, and '*ſchiſms*, they muſt not only often preach 'againſt them, but they ſhould ſet them-'ſelves againſt all the ways by which *er-*'*rors* are come in, and are further coming 'in upon us, and oppoſe them by preach-'ing and writing; as laymens preaching, 'the gathering of churches, and above all 'a *toleration*; for that would be an open 'door at which all kinds of *hereſies* would 'come in, and no man could keep them 'out: And therefore if *miniſters* will wit-'neſs for truth, and againſt errors, they 'muſt ſet themſelves in a ſpecial manner 'againſt a *toleration*, as the principal inlet to

[1] *Gangræna*, Part I. p. 85.

'all *heresy* and *error*: And if a *toleration* 'be granted, all preaching will not keep 'them out. If a *toleration* be granted, the 'devil will be too hard for us, though we 'preach never so much against them. A '*toleration* will undo all; first bring in 'scepticism in doctrine and looseness of life, 'and afterwards all atheism. The patrons 'of *error*, because they cannot at first plead 'for such and such doctrines, *in terminis*, 'and yet hold them, and would have them 'propagated, therefore they plead for a '*toleration*; which once being granted, 'they will come in then of course: O let 'the *ministers* therefore oppose *toleration*, 'as being that by which the devil would 'at once lay a foundation for his kingdom 'to all generations! witness against it in 'all places; possess the *magistrates* of the 'evil of it; yea, and the people too; shew-'ing them, how if a *toleration* were grant-'ed, they should never have peace in their 'families more, or ever after have com-'mand of wives, children, servants, but 'they and their posterities after them, are 'like to live in discontent and unquiet-'ness of mind all their days. 'Tis the 'saying of *Luther*, says he, that *ministers* '*first care ought to be the name of God*, '*and the next, of the salvation of others.* '*When any thing is done, by which of neces-*'*sity either of these must suffer, and fall to* '*the ground; let the Pope perish, let wicked* *magi-*

' *magistrates perish, let the patrons of wick-* ' *ed opinions perish, let the whole world pe-* ' *rish,* ' *and let God's glory, his word, his* ' *church, his worship be saved,* Amen. Now ' neither of these can be safe, says Mr. *Ed-* ' *wards,* if there should be a *toleration*; for ' a *toleration* is very destructive to the glory ' of God, and the salvation of souls; and ' therefore whosoever should be for a *tole-* ' *ration, ministers* ought to be against it: ' if the parliament, city, yea, all the peo- ' ple were for a *toleration* of all the *sects,* ' *Anabaptists, Antinomians, Seekers, Brown-* ' *ists, Independents* (which I speak, not to ' cast the least aspersion upon them, as if ' they would be, for I believe the contrary) ' but supposing it; yet *ministers* ought to ' present their reasons against it, preach ' and cry out of the evil of it, never consent ' to it, but protest against and withstand it, ' by all lawful ways and means, within our ' callings and places, venturing the loss of ' liberties, estates, lives, and all, in that ' cause, and to inflame us with zeal against ' a TOLERATION, the great *Diana* of the ' *sectaries.*

' Now, says he [m], the opposing the *sects* of ' these times, and that great desire of a *tole-* ' *ration* of all religions, pleaded for so much ' by many, are points will bear us out be- ' fore God; and all who come after us (if

[m] *Ibid.* p. 92.

'ever a *toleration* ſhould be granted) will ſay, 'when they ſee and feel the miſchiefs of a '*toleration*, theſe were good and wiſe men, 'that had their eyes in their heads, and 'look'd afar off. As often as new evils 'ariſe in the kingdom upon a *toleration*, 'this which they have done againſt a *tole-*'*ration* will be ſpoken with honour of 'them throughout all generations, and in 'other chriſtian kingdoms.

'[n] *Miniſters* muſt pray much to God, 'and call upon him night and day, that he 'would prevent and caſt out of his church 'all the *errors*, *hereſies*, *roots of bitterneſs*, '*poiſonous principles* got in among us, and 'to give a miſcarrying womb to the *ſecta-*'*ries*, that they may never bring forth that 'miſhappen baſtard-monſter of a TOLE-'RATION.'

HE directs the *magiſtrates*, and tells them, '[o] They ſhould execute ſome exemplary pu-'niſhment upon ſome of the moſt notorious '*ſectaries* and ſeducers, and upon the wil-'ful abettors of theſe abominable errors; 'namely, the printers, diſperſers, and licen-'ſers, and ſet themſelves with all their 'hearts to find out ways to take ſome 'courſe to ſuppreſs, hinder, and no longer 'ſuffer theſe things; to put out ſome decla-'ration againſt the errors and ways of the '*ſectaries*; as their ſending emiſſaries in-

[n] *Page* 93.
[o] *Page* 98.

'to all parts of the kingdom, to poiſon 'the countries; as their *dipping* of perſons 'in the cold water in winter, whereby 'perſons fall ſick, die, *&c.* declaring, that 'they ſhall be proceeded againſt as *vagrants* 'and *rogues*, that go from country to country; and if any fall ſick upon their *dipping* and die, they ſhall be indicted upon 'the ſtatute of killing the king's ſubjects, 'and proceeded againſt accordingly.

More particularly againſt the Baptiſts.

THUS he particularly inveighs againſt the *Baptiſts*, and in another place carries his reſentment againſt them much higher. For ſays he [p], 'I could wiſh with all my heart, 'there were a publick diſputation, even in 'the point of *pædobaptiſm* and of *dipping*, 'between ſome of the *Anabaptiſts*, and 'ſome of our *miniſters*. But if upon diſputation and debate, the *Anabaptiſts* ſhould 'be found in an *error*, as I am confident 'they would, that then the parliament 'ſhould forbid all *dipping*, and take ſome 'ſevere courſe with all *Dippers*, as the ſenate of *Zurick* did.'

Remark.

THE precedent he refers to plainly diſcovers the ſpirit of the man. And he might well call it ſome *ſevere courſe*. For an *edict* was publiſhed at *Zurick* in the year 1530. making it *death* for any to baptize by *immerſion*; upon which law, ſome call'd *Anabaptiſts* were ty'd back to back, and thrown

[p] *Gangræna*, Part III. p. 177.

into the ſea, others were *burnt alive*, and many ſtarved to *death* in priſon.

BUT enough of the ſpirit and principles of perſecution as it then appeared in particular perſons. We find that whole communities of men, both *layety* and *clergy*, declared againſt *liberty of conſcience*, and petitioned for *perſecution*.

The city of London *petition againſt it.*

ON the 26th of *May*, 1646. the lord mayor, court of aldermen, and common-council, preſented a petition to the parliament, uſually called *the city remonſtrance*; in which they deſired, 'That ſome ſtrict 'and ſpeedy courſe might be taken for the 'ſuppreſſing all private and ſeparate con-'gregations; that all *Anabaptiſts*, *Browniſts*, *Hereticks*, *Schiſmaticks*, *Blaſphemers*, and all other *Sectaries*, who con-'form not to the publick diſcipline eſta-'bliſhed, or to be eſtabliſhed by parlia-'ment, may be fully declared againſt, 'and ſome effectual courſe ſettled for pro-'ceeding againſt ſuch perſons; and that 'no perſon diſaffected to *Preſbyterial* go-'vernment, ſet forth or to be ſet forth by 'parliament, may be employed in any place 'of publick truſt.'

The aſſembly of divines againſt it, and appoint a committee of accommodation.

HOWEVER, the *clergy* went before the *layety* in theſe *rigid* methods, and ſo led them the way. For when *preſbytery* was about to be eſtabliſhed, the aſſembly of divines at *Weſtminſter* appointed a committee to hear and anſwer the petitions of thoſe

thoſe who could not conform to the government. This was called *the committee for accommodation.*

The Independents requeſt to the committee, An. Dom. 1645.

To theſe the *Independants* preſented their requeſt, *Dec.* 4. 1645. which was only this:

'[q] THAT they may not be forced to communicate as members in thoſe pariſhes 'where they dwell; but may have liberty 'to have congregations of ſuch perſons 'who give good teſtimonies of their godlineſs, and yet out of a tenderneſs of 'conſcience cannot communicate in their '*pariſhes*, but do voluntarily offer themſelves to join in ſuch congregations.'

denied.

To this the aſſembly gave a flat denial, *Dec.* 15. and annexed their reaſons why ſuch a deſire was not to be granted. The *Independents* willing to be taken into the *eſtabliſhment*, made a very ſtrange *conceſſion* to them, *viz.* '[r] That they would maintain 'occaſional communion with their churches, 'not only in hearing and preaching, 'but occaſionally in baptizing their children, in their churches, and receiving the 'Lord's-ſupper there.' But all this would not prevail upon their *brethren* of the *Preſbyterian* perſuaſion to allow them ſeparate congregations. They rather improved this

Their conceſſion.

[q] *Schiſm tried and condemned,* 25.

[r] *Ibidem,* p. 27.

com-

compliance, to strengthen their arguments against granting such a liberty.

Argued against. '[s] IF, say they, they may occasionally 'exercise these acts of communion with us 'once, a second, or a third time, with-'out sin; we know no reason why it may 'not be ordinary without sin, and then 'separation and church-gathering, would 'have been needless. To separate from 'those churches ordinarily and visibly, with 'whom occasionally you may join with-'out sin, seemeth to be a most unjust se-'paration.'

Remark. THIS return upon their compliance seems to be very just. But that an assembly of such pious and grave divines, many of whom had also suffered for conscience sake themselves, should deny this liberty to their differing brethren, was very strange. And it is yet more surprizing to find them use such arguments as these for it: '[t] That 'this opened a gap for all *sects* to challenge 'such a liberty as their due: That this 'liberty was denied by the churches 'of *New-England*, and that they have 'as just ground to deny it as they: [u] That 'this desired forbearance is a perpetual 'division in the church, and a perpetual 'drawing away from the churches under 'the rule; for upon the same pretence,

More against them

[s] *Ibidem*, p. 28.
[t] *Ibidem*, 29.
[u] Page 31.

'those

'those who scruple *infant-baptism* may 'withdraw from their churches, and 'so separate into another congregation; 'and so in that, some practice may be 'scrupled, and they separate again. Are 'these *divisions* and *subdivisions*, say they, 'as lawful as they may be infinite? or 'must we give that respect to the errors 'of mens consciences, as to satisfy their 'scruples by allowance of this liberty to 'them? x That scruple of conscience is no 'cause of separation; nor doth it take off 'causeless separation from being schism, 'which may arise from errors of con-'science, as well as carnal and corrupt 'reason; therefore we conceive the causes 'of separation must be shewn to be such '*ex natura rei*, as will bear it out; and 'therefore we say, that the granting the 'liberty desired will give countenance to 'schism.'

The whole body of London *ministers against a toleration.*

ANOTHER instance of the spirit of *persecution* that prevailed in these times, appeared in the whole body of the *London* ministers; for they met together, *Dec.* 18. 1645. at *Sion-College*, to draw up a letter to the assembly of divines at *Westminster*, which was also presented *Jan.* 1. following.

IN this they pretend to shew the unreasonableness, the sin, and the mischievous conse-

x *Ibidem*, p. 32.

quences

quences of granting *toleration*, or liberty of conſcience; and caſt ſeveral bitter reflections on the *Independents*, and others for deſiring it; but their principles and ſpirit will be ſufficiently diſcovered, by citing a paſſage or two in the concluſion.

'[y] THESE, ſay they, are ſome of the 'many conſiderations which make a deep 'impreſſion on our ſpirits againſt that great '*Diana* of *Independents*, and all the *ſectaries*, ſo much cried up by them, in theſe 'diſtracted times, *viz.* a *toleration*, a *toleration*. We cannot diſſemble, how upon 'the forementioned grounds, we deteſt and 'abhor the much endeavoured *toleration*. 'Our bowels, our bowels are ſtirred within us, and we could even drown ourſelves in 'tears, when we call to mind how long 'and ſharp a travail this kingdom hath 'been in for many years together, to bring 'forth that bleſſed fruit of a pure and 'perfect *reformation*; and now at laſt, after 'all our pangs, and dolours, and expectations, this real and thorough *reformation* 'is in danger of being ſtrangled in the 'birth by a lawleſs *toleration*, that ſtrives 'to be brought forth before it.'

AFTER this they pretend to pay the *aſſembly* a very great complement, which, if true, was a ſhame to them, rather than an encomium.

[y] *Ibidem*, p. 44.

'[z] NOT

'[z] NOT, ſay they, that we can harbour 'the leaſt jealouſy of your zeal, fidelity, 'or induſtry, in the oppoſing and extir'pating of ſuch a root of gall and bitter'neſs as *toleration* is, and will be, both in 'preſent and future ages.'

ANOTHER inſtance of the ſame bitter ſpirit appears in a book entitled, *A vindication of the Preſbyterial government and miniſtry; with an exhortation to all miniſters, elders and people, within the bounds of the province of* London, *&c. Publiſhed by the miniſters and elders, met together in a provincial aſſembly*, Nov. 2. 1649. *and printed at* London, *according to order*, 1650. The words are theſe; '[a] Whatſoever doctrine is *contrary 'to godlineſs*, and opens a door to liber'tiniſm and prophaneneſs, you muſt reject 'it as *ſoul poiſon*.——Such is the doctrine 'of an *univerſal toleration of all religion*.' This book in page 175, concludes thus; *Subſcribed in the name and by the appointment of the aſſembly*;

George Walker, *Moderator*.

Arthur Jackſon,
Edmund Calamy, } *Aſſeſſors*.

Roger Drake,
Eliad Blackwell, } *Scrib.*

[z] *Ibidem*, p. 45.
[a] Page 121.

AND

AND as face anſwers to face in a glaſs, ſo did the ſpirit of *perſecution* in the country miniſters anſwer to that which appeared in thoſe at *London.*

The Lancaſhire *miniſters alſo againſt it.*

THOSE in *Lancaſhire* publiſhed a paper in 1648. ſubſcribed by eighty four of them, entitled, *The harmonious conſent of the* Lancaſhire miniſters *with their brethren at London*; in which are theſe expreſſions:

'[b] A *toleration* would be the putting a 'ſword in a madman's hand; a *cup of* '*poiſon* into the hand of a child; a letting 'looſe of *madmen* with *firebrands* in their 'hands; and appointing a city of refuge in 'mens conſciences, for the *Devil* to fly 'to; a laying of a ſtumbling-block before 'the blind; a proclaiming liberty to the 'wolves to come into Chriſt's fold, to 'prey upon the lambs: Neither would 'it be to provide for tender conſciences, 'but to take away all conſcience.'

And alſo the Warwickſhire *miniſters.*

IN the ſame year another paper was publiſhed, ſubſcribed by forty three miniſters, entituled, *The* Warwickſhire *miniſters teſtimony to the truth of Jeſus Chriſt, and to the ſolemn league and covenant; as alſo againſt the errors, hereſies and blaſphemies of theſe times, and the toleration of them; ſent in a letter to the miniſters within the province of* London, *ſubſcribers of the former*

[b] *L'ſtrange Diſſ. Sayings*, part II. p. 1.

teſti-

teſtimony. In which they expreſs themſelves thus:

Reverend and beloved brethren,

'WE, your fellow-labourers in the 'goſpel of Jeſus Chriſt, within 'the city of *Coventry* and county of *Warwick*, have peruſed your late publick '*Teſtimony to the truth of Jeſus Chriſt, 'and to our ſolemn league and covenant, 'as alſo againſt the errors, hereſies, and 'blaſphemies of theſe times, and the toleration of them*; and ſo greatly are we 'affected therewith, that with our ſouls 'we bleſs the Lord God of our fathers, 'and the father of our Lord Jeſus Chriſt, 'who hath put ſuch a thing as this into 'your hearts —— and further, to this 'your good confeſſion we hereby ſet our 'ſeals; withal heartily profeſſing all readineſs and reſolution to ſtick to this teſtimony with you, even unto death. Moreover, we do you to wit, that we look upon 'this your *teſtimony* as the voice of God, 'ſo to awaken all the Lord's watchmen thorough the land, that they ſhall not quietly ſuffer the enemy to ſow his tares 'among the wheat; remembring what the 'great reformer *Luther* ſaid, *It is almoſt 'a ſin againſt the Holy Ghoſt, to be mealmouthed, when ſuch pernicious libertines 'poiſon the bread of the houſhold of faith.*

'And

'And for the people, we find them so 'heart-taken with this your seasonable zeal, 'that they long for a way to give their 'publick *amen* to the same. Yea, we do 'for your encouragement assure you, that 'although the door of *liberty* stands in a 'manner open for every man to do what 'he will with the things of *Christ*, yet 'through his grace (and to his glory we 'speak it) errors and schisms are not very 'catching among our flocks, but they 'rather take faster root in the faith by these 'religion-winds that shake some.'

THE teaching of these rigid principles, and presenting such zealous petitions against liberty of conscience, prevailed so far as to procure several laws to be made for suppressing and persecuting the *sectaries*, that is, such as would not come into the *Presbyrian* establishment.

An ordinance of parliament

THE first attempt of this nature was an *Ordinance* of *Parliament* for the silencing all such preachers as were not *ordained ministers*, either in the *English*, or in some of the foreign *Protestant* churches. It bore date the 26th of *April*, 1645; and run in this form.

'[c] IT is this Day ordained and declared 'by the Lords and Commons assembled in 'parliament, that no person be admitted 'to preach, who is not ordained a mi-

[c] Hall's *pulpit guarded*, p. 31.

'nister

'nister, either in this or some other re-'formed church, except such, as intend-'ing the ministry, shall be allowed for the 'trial of their gifts, by those who shall 'be appointed thereunto by both houses of parliament.

'IT is this day ordered by the Lords 'and Commons assembled in parliament, 'that this *ordinance* be forthwith printed, 'and published, and sent to Sir *Thomas* '*Fairfax*, with an earnest desire and re-'commendation from both houses, that 'he take care that this *ordinance* may 'be duly observed in the *army*; and that if 'any shall transgress this *ordinance*, that he 'make speedy representation thereof to both 'houses, that the offenders may receive con-'dign *punishment* for their contempt, &c.'

The Baptists prosecuted thereupon.

UPON the coming forth of this *ordinance*, several *mayors*, *justices* and other *officers*, who longed to be at *persecution*, apprehended several *ministers*, who were called *Separatists* and *Lay-preachers*, and returned their names to the parliament, to answer for their contempt, among whom were several *Baptists*; and the parliament appointed a committee to hear and determine such cases. But they could make little of it by this law; for many of the *preachers* in separate congregations had been ordained in the church of *England*, either in times of *Episcopacy*, or since *Presbytery* had obtained the ascendant; and those

O that

that had not, alledged, that the congregations, who had called and appointed them to preach, were true churches, and as much reformed as any in the world: nor did this *ordinance* affix the crime upon those that took upon them to preach without ordination, but such as should admit them so to do; neither did it impower *magistrates* to take the *offenders* into custody.

Another ordinance to explain the former. An. Dom. 1646.

THIS *ordinance* therefore falling short of their purpose, another was made *Dec.* 26. 1646. which explained the former, and provided for those things wherein that was defective. For in this it was expresly said: The commons assembled in 'parliament do declare, that they do dislike 'and will proceed against all such persons 'as shall take upon them to preach, or expound the scriptures in any *church*, or '*chapel*, or any other publick *place*, except 'they be ordained, either here or in some 'other reformed church, as it is already 'prohibited in an order of both houses of the '26th of *April*, 1645. and likewise against all such *ministers*, or others, as 'shall publish or maintain, by preaching, 'writing, printing, or any other way, 'any thing against, or in derogation of 'church government which is now established by authority of both houses of 'parliament: and all justices of peace, sheriffs, mayors, bayliffs, and other head 'officers of corporations, and all officers 'of 'of the *army*, are to take notice of this 'declaration, and by all lawful ways and 'means, to prevent offences of this kind, 'and to apprehend the *offenders*, and give 'notice thereof to this houſe, that there-'upon courſe may be ſpeedily taken, for 'a due puniſhment to be inflicted on 'them'

THIS was a more ſevere law againſt the *Diſſenters* than the former, and would have expoſed them to very great hardſhips, had the times permitted a ſtrict execution of it.

IT was not enough, that ſuch *miniſters* as had not been ordained in the national church, ſhould be kept out of the *church* and *chapels*; but they muſt not be allowed to preach or expound the Scriptures in any publick *place*, nor would ordination itſelf be ſufficient, but they muſt be tied from ſpeaking or writing any thing againſt or contrary to the *directory* and diſcipline eſtabliſhed; and this reſtraint to extend, not only to *miniſters*, but all other *perſons*; and 'tis put into the power of the officers of the *army*, as well as the civil *magiſtrate*, to apprehend thoſe that ſhould tranſgreſs againſt this *ordinance*.

THE *Baptiſts* were as much aimed at, and as many of them proſecuted, by theſe laws, as any others who were called *ſectaries*; yet by ſome means or other they obtained a very great *indulgence* from the paliament about a year after.

An. Dom. 1647.

WHETHER it was the great number of this opinion, that were at this time, both in the *army*, and in moſt corporations in *England*; or that ſome of thoſe great men who about this time entertained the opinion againſt *infant-baptiſm*, did intercede in their behalf, I cannot ſay. But on *Mar.* 4. 1647. a declaration of the lords and commons was publiſhed, in which were theſe words:

A declaration of the lords and commons in favour of the Baptiſts.

'THE name of *Anabaptiſm* hath indeed contracted much *odium*, by reaſon of the extravagant opinions and practices of ſome of that name in *Germany*, tending to the diſturbance of the government and peace of all ſtates, which opinions and practices we abhor and deteſt: But for their opinion againſt the baptiſm of *infants*, it is only a difference about a circumſtance of time in the adminiſtration of an *ordinance*, wherein in former ages, as well as this, learned men have differed both in opinion and practice. And though we could wiſh that all men would ſatisfy themſelves, and join with us in our judgment and practice in this point; yet herein we held it fit that men ſhould be convinced by the word of God, with great gentleneſs and reaſon, and not beaten out of it with force and violence.' This indeed diſcovered a true chriſtian ſpirit,

rit, and is the method which the goſpel directs to take with thoſe who err. And had they kept to this, it would have been to their immortal honour.

BUT it muſt be recorded, to the ſhame of this very parliament, or rather of thoſe who had the chief influence in publick affairs, that about a year after this, a more ſevere law paſſed againſt *hereſy* and *error*, than any that has been made in *England* ſince the *Reformation*. Nay, I may challenge any one to produce a more cruel and bloody law in the times of *popery*, except the act *de heretico comburendo*. It bore date *May* the 2d, 1648. and was entituled, *An ordinance of the lords and commons aſſembled in parliament, for the puniſhing of blaſphemies and hereſies.* An. Dom. 1648.

IN this there is firſt a catalogue of *hereſies*, any of which whoſoever did maintain and publiſh, with obſtinacy therein, he was to ſuffer the pains of death, as in caſe of *felony*, without benefit of the *clergy*. Then an enumeration of certain *errors*, any of which whoſoever ſhould publiſh or maintain, and be thereof convicted before two juſtices of the peace, without the privilege of a jury, or liberty of an appeal, he ſhould be obliged to renounce his ſaid errors in the publick congregation; and in caſe he refuſed, or neglected this, at the time and place appointed, the ſaid *juſtices* are to commit him to *priſon*, until he ſhall find two ſufficient ſureties, that he ſhall not publiſh or maintain the ſaid error or errors any more.

AMONG the errors ſpecified are theſe, *viz.* 'That the baptizing of infants is un-'lawful, or that ſuch baptiſm is void, and 'that ſuch perſons ought to be baptized 'again, and in purſuance thereof ſhall 'baptize any perſon formerly baptized: 'That the church government by presby-'tery is antichriſtian or unlawful.'

THIS being the moſt ſhocking law I have met with, and plainly proving that the governing *Preſbyterians* in thoſe times would have made a terrible uſe of their power, if it had been ſupported by the ſword of the civil *magiſtrate*; I ſhall therefore oblige the reader with a tranſcript of the whole. The words of the ordinance are as followeth:

AN

Die Martis, 2. Maii, 1648.

AN

ORDINANCE

OF THE

LORDS and COMMONS

Assembled in

PARLIAMENT,

For punishing Blasphemies and Heresies.

'FOR the preventing of the growth and spreading of heresy and blasphemy, be it ordained by the lords and commons in this present parliament assembled: That all such persons as shall from and after the date of this present ordinance, willingly, by preaching, teaching, printing, or writing, maintain and publish that there is no God, or that God is not present in all places, doth not know and foreknow all things, or that he is not almighty, that he is not perfectly holy, or that he is not eternal; or that the father is not God, the son is not God, or that the Holy Ghost is not God; or that they three are not one eternal God; or that

London, *printed for* Edw. Husband, *printer to the honourable House of Commons.* 1648.

'ſhall in like manner maintain and pub-
'liſh that Chriſt is not God equal with the
'Father; or ſhall deny the manhood of
'Chriſt, or that the Godhead and man-
'hood of Chriſt are ſeveral natures; or
'that the humanity of Chriſt is pure and
'unſpotted of all ſin; or that ſhall main-
'tain and publiſh as aforeſaid, that Chriſt
'did not die, nor riſe from the dead, nor
'is aſcended into heaven bodily; or that
'ſhall deny his death is meritorious in the
'behalf of believers; or that ſhall main-
'tain and publiſh as aforeſaid, that Jeſus
'Chriſt is not the ſon of God, or that
'the holy Scripture, *viz.* of the old teſta-
'ment, *Geneſis, Exodus, Leviticus, Num-*
'*bers, Deuteronomy, Joſhua, Judges,*
'*Ruth,* 1 *Samuel,* 2 *Samuel,* 1 *Kings,*
'2 *Kings,* 1 *Chronicles,* 2 *Chronicles, Ezra,*
'*Nehemiah, Eſther, Job, Pſalms, Pro-*
'*verbs, Eccleſiaſtes, The Song of Songs, I-*
'*ſaiah, Jeremiah, Lamentations, Ezekiel,*
'*Daniel, Hoſea, Joel, Amos, Obadiah,*
'*Jonah, Micah, Nahum, Habbakuk, Ze-*
'*phaniah, Haggai, Zechariah, Malachi;*
'of the new teſtament, the goſpels ac-
'cording to *Matthew, Mark, Luke, John,*
'the *Acts of the apoſtles, Paul's epiſtles to*
'*the Romans, Corinthians the firſt, Co-*
'*rinthians the ſecond, to Timothy the firſt,*
'*to Timothy the ſecond, to Titus, to Phi-*
'*lemon, the epiſtle to the Hebrews, the e-*
'*piſtle of James, the firſt and ſecond epiſtles*
'*of*

' *of Peter, the first, second and third epistles* ' *of John, the epistle of Jude, the Revelation of John*, is not the word of God; ' or that the bodies of men shall not rise ' again after they are dead; or that there ' is no day of judgment after death; all ' such maintaining and publishing of such ' error or errors, with obstinacy therein, ' shall by virtue hereof be adjudged felony; and all such persons, upon complaint and proof made of the same, in ' any of the cases aforesaid, before any ' two of the next justices of the peace for ' that place or county, by the oaths of ' two witnesses, (which said justices of ' peace in such cases shall hereby have ' power to administer) or confession of ' the party; the said party so accused shall ' be by the said justices of the peace committed to prison, without bail or mainprize, until the next goal-delivery, to ' be holden for that place or county; ' and the witnesses likewise shall be bound ' over by the said justices unto the said ' goal-delivery, to give in their evidence; ' and at the said goal-delivery the party ' shall be indicted for felonious publishing and maintaining such error: And ' in case the indictment be found, and ' the party upon his trial shall not abjure ' his said error, and defence and maintenance of the same, he shall suffer the ' pains of death, as in case of felony,

' with-

'without benefit of clergy. But in caſe 'he ſhall recant, or renounce and abjure his ſaid error or errors, and the maintainance or publiſhing of the ſame; he 'ſhall nevertheleſs remain in priſon until 'he ſhall find two ſureties, being ſubſidy 'men, that ſhall be bound with him 'before two or more juſtices of the 'peace or goal-delivery, that he ſhall not 'thenceforth publiſh or maintain, as aforeſaid, the ſaid error or errors any more; 'and the ſaid juſtices ſhall have power 'hereby to take bail in ſuch caſes.

'AND be it further ordained, that in 'caſe any perſon formerly indicted for 'publiſhing and maintaining of ſuch erroneous opinion or opinions, as aforeſaid, 'and renouncing and abjuring the ſame, 'ſhall nevertheleſs again publiſh and maintain his ſaid former error or errors, as 'aforeſaid and the ſame proved as aforeſaid; the ſaid party ſo offending ſhall be 'committed to priſon as formerly, and at 'the next goal-delivery ſhall be indicted, 'as aforeſaid. And in caſe the indictment 'be then found upon the trial, and it ſhall 'appear that formerly the party was convicted of the ſame error, and publiſhing 'and maintaining thereof, and renounced 'and abjured the ſame, the offender ſhall 'ſuffer death, as in caſe of felony, without benefit of clergy. Be it further ordained by the authority aforeſaid, that

'all

'all and every perſon or perſons, that ſhall 'publiſh or maintain as aforeſaid, any of 'the ſeveral errors hereafter enſuing, *viz.* 'that all men ſhall be ſaved; or that man 'by nature hath free-will to turn to God; 'or that God may be worſhipped in or by 'pictures or images; or that the ſoul of 'any man after death goeth neither to 'heaven or hell, but to purgatory; or that 'the ſoul of man dieth or ſleepeth when 'the body is dead; or that revelations or 'the workings of the Spirit are a rule of 'faith or chriſtian life, though diverſe 'from, or contrary to the written word of 'God; or that man is bound to believe 'no more than by his reaſon he can com-'prehend; or that the moral law of God 'contained in the ten commandments, is 'no rule of chriſtian life; or that a believer 'need not repent or pray for pardon of 'ſins; or that the two ſacraments of bap-'tiſm and the Lord's-ſupper, are not or-'dinances commanded by the word of 'God; *or that the baptizing of infants is* '*unlawful, or ſuch baptiſm is void, and* '*that ſuch perſons ought to be baptized* '*again, and in purſuance thereof, ſhall* '*baptize any perſon formerly baptized*; or 'that the obſervation of the Lord's-day, as 'it is enjoined by the ordinances and laws 'of this realm, is not according, or is con-'trary to the word of God; or that it is 'not lawful to join in publick prayer or

'family

'family prayer, or to teach children to 'pray; or that the churches of *England* 'are no true churches, nor their miniſters 'and ordinances true miniſters and ordi-'nances; or that the church government 'by presbytery is antichriſtian or unlaw-'ful; or that magiſtracy, or the power of the 'civil magiſtrate by law eſtabliſhed in *Eng-*'*land*, is unlawful; or that all uſe of arms 'though for the publick defence (and be 'the cauſe never ſo juſt) is unlawful: And 'in caſe the party accuſed of ſuch publiſh-'ing and maintaining of any of the ſaid 'errors, ſhall be thereof convicted to have 'publiſhed and maintained the ſame, as 'aforeſaid, by the teſtimony of two or 'more witneſſes upon oath, or confeſſion 'of the ſaid party, before two of the next 'juſtices of the peace for the ſaid place 'or county, whereof one to be of the '*quorum* (who are hereby required and 'authorized to ſend for witneſſes and ex-'amine upon oath in ſuch caſes in the 'preſence of the party, the party ſo con-'victed ſhall be ordered by the ſaid juſtices 'to renounce his ſaid errors in the publick 'congregation of the ſame pariſh from 'whence the complaint doth come, or 'where the offence was committed; and 'in caſe he refuſeth or neglecteth to per-'form the ſame, at, or upon the day, 'time and place appointed by the ſaid 'juſtices, then he ſhall be committed to

'priſon

'prison by the said justices, until he shall 'find two sufficient sureties, before two 'justices of peace for the said place or 'county (whereof one shall be of the *quo-* '*rum*) that he shall not publish or main- 'tain the said error or errors any more. 'Provided always, and be it ordained by 'the authority aforesaid, that no attainder 'by virtue hereof shall extend either to the 'forfeiture of the estate, real or personal, 'of such person attainted, or corruption 'of such person's blood.

JOHN BROWN, *Cler' Parliament.*

IT is easy to discern by this *ordinance*, that expresly all the *Anabaptists*, falsely so called, of whom there were not a few thousands in *England* at this time, all the *Independents* or *Separatists*, all *Episcoparians*, all the *Arminians*, yea, in a word, all *England*, save rigid *Presbyterians*, are expresly condemn'd. And doubtless, these rigid principles and severe laws would have been follow'd with a violent persecution, had not the confusions of the times, and the great number of the *Dissenters* prevented. And altho' the supreme power might design these *ordinances* only *in terrorem*; yet the mayors, justices, and other subordinate magistrates, were for practising these methods, as far as it was in their power, or whenever they had the least encouragement for so doing,

doing, as appears plainly enough by the following proſecutions.

[d] BY this act *John Bidle* the *Socinian* was indicted and try'd in *Weſtminſter-hall.* He was firſt ſent to the *Compter*, and from thence to *Newgate*, *July* 3. 1655. and try'd for his life the next ſeſſions. To the indictment he pray'd counſel might be allowed him to plead the illegality of it; which being deny'd him by the judges, and the ſentence of a mute threatned, he at length gave into court his exceptions, engroſs'd in parchment; and with much ſtruggling, had counſel allow'd him; but the trial was deferred to the next day.

THE *protector*, well knowing it was not for the intereſt of his government, either to have him condemn'd or abſolv'd, takes him out of the hands of the law, and ſends him away to the iſle of *Scilly*, Oct. 5. 1655.

FOR, on the one hand, the *Preſbyterians*, and all enemies to liberty of religion (of which there appear'd a great number at his trial) would be offended at his releaſe; and all that were for liberty (among whom many congregations of *Anabaptiſts* eſpecially) had petition'd the *protector* for his diſcharge from proſecution upon that *ordinance*, by which all their liberties were threatned and condemn'd,

[d] Vide *his Life.*

and

and the capital articles of the protector's government infringed; which run thus: *That such as profess faith in God by Jesus Christ (tho' differing in judgment from the doctrine, worship or discipline publickly held forth) shall not be restrained from, but shall be protected in the profession of the faith and exercise of their religion*, &c. Art. 37. *That all laws, statutes, ordinances*, &c. *to the contrary of the aforesaid liberty, shall be esteemed as null and void*; Art. 38. In this exile he continued about three years, notwithstanding all the endeavours of his friends for his liberty, and his own letters, both to the *protector* and to Mr. *Calamy*, an eminent *Presbyterian* minister, to reason them into compassion. At length, through the importunity of friends, and other occurrences, the *protector* suffered a writ of *habeas corpus* to be granted out of the *Upper-bench-court*, as it was then called, and to be obey'd by the governour of *Scilly*, whereby the prisoner was brought thence, and by that court set at liberty, as finding no legal cause of detaining him.

He did not long enjoy this liberty, for about five months after *Oliver* died, and his son *Richard* succeeding, call'd a parliament, dangerous to *John Bidle*; which being foreseen, he was forced by the importunity of a noble friend, to retire into the country during their session. But that parliament being dissolv'd, he return'd to his wonted station,

ſtation, and continued undiſturb'd till the firſt of *June*, 1662. When he was haled out of his lodgings, where he was convened with ſome few of his friends for divine worſhip, and carried before Sir *Richard Brown*, who forthwith committed them all to the publick priſon; *John Bidle* to the *dungeon*, where he lay for five hours, and was denied the benefit of the law, which admitted offenders of that ſort to bail for their appearance; there they lay till the *recorder*, mov'd with more reverence of the laws, took ſecurity for their anſwering to their charge next ſeſſions; which they performed accordingly. But when the court could not find any ſtatute whereon to form any criminal indictment againſt them, they were referred to the ſeſſions following, and then were proceeded againſt, by pretext of an offence againſt common law (the rules of which lie moſtly in the judges breaſts) and thereupon fined, every one of the *hearers* in the penalty of twenty pounds, and *John Bidle* in one hundred, to lie in priſon till paid. Now, though the ſheriff would generouſly have been ſatisfied with ten pounds for him, and he would have paid it; yet the enmity of Sir *Richard Brown* was ſuch, as he could not be induced to conſent thereto upon any terms, but threatned him with a ſeven years impriſonment, tho' he ſhould pay the whole hundred pounds. This was the cauſe of his con-

continuing in priſon. But he had not been there full five Weeks, till by reaſon of the noiſomneſs of the place, and pent air, he contracted a diſeaſe, which in a few days put a period to his life.

THE chief proſecutors [e] of this man, I find, were certain *bookſellers* of St. *Paul's church-yard*, notoriouſly known for their prepoſterous zeal, and former oppoſition unto chriſtian liberty, under the name of *Beaeon-firers*. The *author* of the narrative of the proceedings againſt *John Bidle*, ſays [f]: 'If we enquire further into the 'converſation of theſe men, we ſhall find 'them to have been chief *city remonſtrants*, 'that thereby ſet the nation into an actual 'flame, made diviſion between the *parliament* and *army*, and were the occaſion of 'the war between them; it was the *Preſbyterian* intereſt which theſe men eſpouſed, 'that occaſioned the uproar that *Maſſey*, and '*Pointze*, and the *apprentices* made, whereof they are never to be forgotten, and ever 'to be thankfully acknowledged: If the 'providence of Almighty [God] had not interpoſed, this nation might by this time 'have become a deſolate wilderneſs. Theſe 'actings were ſo highly diſpleaſing to the 'parliament, that they voted that no perſon that had a hand therein, ſhould be capable of any place or office within the 'commonwealth.'

[e] Tho. Underhill, Luke Fawn, Nath. Webb. [f] *Page* 7.

THE author of *the humble advice to the right honourable the lord-mayor, the recorder, and the reſt of the juſtices of the honourable bench*, ſpeaking of Mr. *Bidle*, ſays g: 'If 'you ſhall ſeriouſly and deliberately weigh 'all circumſtances touching the man and 'his opinions, he is ſo free from being 'queſtioned for any the leaſt blemiſh 'in his life and converſation, that the *in-'formers* themſelves have been heard to 'admire his ſtrict exemplary life, full of 'modeſty, ſobriety, and forbearance, no 'ways contentious, touching the great 'things of the world, but altogether taken 'up with the things of God revealed in 'the holy ſcriptures; wherein his ſtudy, 'diligence and attainments have been ſo 'great, that his knowledge therein is of as 'ready uſe as a concordance, no part 'thereof being named, but he preſently 'cites the book, chapter, and verſe, 'eſpecially throughout the books of the 'New Teſtament, where all the epiſtles he 'can ſay by heart out of the *Greek tongue*, 'and withal can read the *Greek* in *Engliſh*, 'and the *Engliſh* in *Greek* ſo readily as a 'man can do the mere *Engliſh*; ſo carefully 'hath he been rightly to underſtand them. 'As to the juſtice and integrity of his heart, 'his ways have manifeſted that he would 'not diſſemble, play the hypocrite, or

g *Page* 7.

'deal

'deal fraudulently with any man to ſave 'his life; ſuch is he certainly, as is known 'to very many perſons of worth and cre-'dit in *London*. So as he is far from be-'ing ſuch a monſter as many have believed 'him to be, through the uncomely and 'unchriſtian-like clamours of his ac-'cuſers.'

THE author of *the true ſtate of the caſe of liberty of conſcience in England*, gives this teſtimony of Mr. *Bidle*'s converſation [h], 'We 'have, ſays he, had intimate knowledge 'thereof for ſome years; but we think he 'needs not us, but may appeal even to his ene-'mies, for his vindication therein. Let thoſe 'that knew him at *Oxford* for the ſpace 'of ſeven or eight years, thoſe that knew him 'at *Glouceſter* about three years, thoſe that 'knew him at *London* theſe eight or nine 'years, (moſt of which time he hath been a 'priſoner) ſpeak what they know, of un-'righteouſneſs, uncleanneſs, unpeaceableneſs, 'malice, pride, profaneneſs, drunkenneſs, 'or any the like iniquity, which they can 'accuſe him of; or hath he, (as the man-'ner of hereticks is,) 2 *Pet*. ii. 3. *Through* '*covetouſneſs, with feigned words made* '*merchandiſe of any*? Hath he not herein 'walked upon ſuch true grounds of chriſ-'tian ſelf-denial, that none in the world 'can ſtand more clear and blameleſs here-

[h] *Page* 5.

 in

'in alſo? He having ſhunned to make any 'of thoſe advantages which are eaſily made 'in the world, by men of his parts and 'breeding, languages and learning, that (if 'any known to us) he may truly ſay as the 'apoſtle, *I have coveted no man's ſilver, or* '*gold, or apparel; yea, ye yourſelves know,* '*that theſe hands have miniſtred to my ne-* '*ceſſities*; he ever accounting it *a more* '*bleſſed thing to give than receive.*

'AND that he ſhould, in holding or 'republiſhing any opinions in religion, 'wilfully ſin, doing the ſame againſt his 'own conſcience and judgment, and ſo 'ſhould fall under that character of an '*Heretick*, to be condemned of himſelf, '*Tit.* iii. 10, 11. we cannot imagine 'that his moſt zealous enemies do ſuppoſe, 'much leſs charge him with ſuch groſs 'wickedneſs; however for ourſelves that 'know him, we crave leave upon know-'ledge to affirm, that he lives conſtantly 'in ſuch a filial fear of God, with ſo much 'watchfulneſs over his ways, and lays ſo 'great a weight upon wilful ſin, that it is 'impoſſible he can be guilty of ſo abhorred 'an evil; being ſo far from *ſelf-condemn-*'*ing*, that we are perſuaded, he would 'not hold, or publiſh any opinion or 'doctrine which to his underſtanding he 'did not judge to have clear grounds in 'holy Scripture, though thereby he might 'gain the whole world: Such confidence

'have

'have those that know him, of his clear-
'ness in those particulars, of *wilful-sinning*,
'or *self-condemning*.

'AND indeed, since he hath found 'cause to differ in his judgment from the 'multitude, he hath not only diligently 'examined the Scriptures himself, but also 'hath desired and sought the knowledge 'and discourse of any learned and good 'man he could hear of, for his further 'information. But though he hath dis-'coursed with many, yet never received 'he an admonition from any, to change 'his judgment or opinion.

'SO that these things well-weighed in 'the true ballance of Scripture-truth, and 'true christian charity, we hope it will 'appear, though he may err in some part 'of his judgment, yet can he not by any 'means, be esteemed less than a believer 'in God through Jesus Christ, and one that '*exerciseth himself to have always a good* '*conscience, void of offence toward God and* '*men*; having hope of the resurrection 'both of the just and unjust; and so not 'an *Heretick*, the characters of such an 'one not all appearing in him; and much 'less a *blasphemer*, having never been 'known to be either a curser, or swearer, 'or railer against acknowledged truths. 'Insomuch that were he in a true uner-'ring church of Christ, they could not so 'much as excommunicate him out of their

'fellowſhip as an *Heretick*, much leſs per-
'ſecute him to impriſonment, or other
'puniſhment; it clearly appearing that if he
'be miſtaken in any thing (as who in ſome
'meaſure is not?) it is neceſſarily from the
'entanglement of his underſtanding, and
'not in the leaſt of wilfulneſs. Nor could
'we ever perceive, but that even in thoſe
'things wherein he moſt differed from
'the ſtream of interpreters, in thoſe high
'points of *Trinity in Unity, and Unity in
'Trinity*, that he contended therein out
'of curioſity, or vain glory, but con-
'ſcientiouſly, and to the clearing of the
'truth to him ſo appearing, and vindica-
'tion of the honour of God therein, which
'we believe to be the ſupreme end of
'all his endeavours. And though he ſhould
'ſomewhat miſtake the way, yet doubtleſs,
'God, who often accepteth the will for
'the deed, will look upon it as an error
'of his zeal and love, and receive him to
'his mercy.

'AND as we have undertaken (as be-
'ing moved in conſcience thereto) to vin-
'dicate Mr. *Bidle* from any *hereſy* in faith,
'or licentiouſneſs in practice, that might ren-
'der him juſtly uncapable of liberty of con-
'ſcience promiſed in the government; ſo
'in particular we can boldly defend him a-
'gainſt the charge of abuſing his liberty to
'the civil injury of others, or any manner
'of way endeavouring the diſturbance of
'the

'the publick peace or civil government upon any pretence. Doth he not in the 17th chapter of his *Catechism* deliver his judgment for subjection to government, and *paying tribute even for conscience-sake?* What needs more, seeing all that know him, know his practice to be conformable thereunto?'

Mr. William Kiffin *prosecuted by the same ordinance.*

ANOTHER, who was prosecuted by the force of this *ordinance*, was the Rev. Mr. *William Kiffin*, pastor of a *Baptized congregation* in the city of *London*. He was convened before the Lord-mayor at *Guildhall*, on *Thursday* the 12th of *July* 1655. and there charged with the breach of this *ordinance*, for preaching, *That the baptism of infants is unlawful:* But the Lord-mayor being busy, the execution of the penalty in the act upon him was referr'd till the *Monday* following.

THE author of *The Spirit of Persecution again broke loose*, makes the following observations on the justices partiality with respect to their management of the prosecutions against Mr. *Bidle* and Mr. *Kiffin*.

'MR. *Bidle*, says he, must be sent for by a warrant, Mr. *Kiffin* by summons of a messenger; Mr. *Bidle* must be committed by one justice without a *mittimus*, and by one justice with a *mittimus*, but Mr. *Kiffin* must not be proceeded against upon the same ordinance without two justices; he must have three or four days space 'given him; the other muſt be ſent to priſon in ſuch haſte, that a *mittimus* could not be writ to be ſent with him, but it muſt be ſent after him. And in the paſſages, ſays he, at Mr. *Kiffin*'s proſecution, you may note further, that my Lord-mayor aſked the proſecutors why they did not proſecute Mr. *Kiffin* ſooner, ſeeing they knew of this ordinance, and Mr. *Kiffin*'s practice long ago. To which they made anſwer, that they thought the ordinance had been made null and void, till the other day they perceived one was committed to priſon upon it. What made you think, ſaid my Lord, that it was void? there is no time ſet when it ſhould expire. True, ſaid the proſecutors, but there is the inſtrument of government that ſaith, *That whoſoever profeſſeth faith in God by Jeſus Chriſt, though differing in judgment from the doctrine, worſhip, and diſcipline publickly held forth, ſhall not be reſtrained from, but protected in the profeſſion of the faith and exerciſe of the religion,* &c. *and all acts and ordinances to the contrary are to be eſteemed null and void.* Would any man think that the Lord-mayor of *London* ſhould be ignorant of the fundamentals in the government? Surely thoſe that ſlight one part of the governmen, then chiefeſt, would make void all, if they could or durſt.'

THE

THE fury of theſe times ſeemed to be more eſpecially turn'd againſt the oppoſers of *infant-baptiſm*, as will appear by the following account of their ſufferings, both before and after the making of theſe laws.

Sufferings of the English Baptiſts.

I SHALL mention, in the firſt place, Mr. *Vavaſor Powell*, that faithful miniſter and confeſſor of *Jeſus Chriſt*. Hard was the meaſure he met with from wicked and debauched perſons, by often lying in wait for his life, and by many buffetings and ſtripes which he received from them, whilſt attending and pleading Chriſt's cauſe and goſpel; inſomuch that it may be truly ſaid of him,
as the *apoſtle* ſpake of himſelf; *That in all* 2 Cor. vi.
things he approved himſelf a miniſter of God, 4, &c.
in much patience, in afflictions, in neceſſities, in diſtreſſes, in ſtripes, in impriſonments, in tumults, in labours, in watchings, in faſtings; by honour and diſhonour, by evil report and good report, as a deceiver yet
true. He was in journeyings often, in perils 2 Cor. xi.
of waters, in perils of robbers, in perils by 26.
his own countrymen, in perils in the city, in perils among falſe brethren, in wearineſs and painfulneſs, in watchings often, in hunger, and thirſt, &c.

HE was taken about the year 1640. when preaching in a houſe in *Brecknockſhire*, about ten o-clock at night, and ſeized with fifty or ſixty of his hearers, by many

[i] *Page* 86.

lewd

lewd fellows, under pretence of a warrant they had from juſtice *Williams*, and ſecured in a church, where at midnight he performed divine ſervice, and preached from

Matt. x. 28. thoſe words, *Fear not them which kill the body.* And it was obſerved, that one of the chiefeſt and vileſt of his troublers did weep ſorely.

THE next morning he was brought to the juſtice's houſe; who being not at home, whilſt waiting, he preached there, at which the juſtice, when he came in, was much enraged, to find him at ſuch work in his houſe; but two of the juſtice's daughters, who ſeemed to reliſh the word, begged him not to do any thing againſt him and his companions, but he preſently committed them to the conſtable's hands; and the next day, having with him two or three more juſtices, and ſix or ſeven *prieſts*, ſent for them again to examine them further; where, after much conference, and many threatnings, he diſcharged them all at that time.

AFTER this, preaching at *Launger* in *Radnorſhire*, in the field, becauſe the publick place was not big enough to contain his auditory, Mr. *Hugh Lloyd* the high ſheriff with a band of men, ſeized him, and after examination committed him, and charged ſixteen or ſeventeen conſtables preſent, to execute his *mittimus*. They all but one refuſed it; who taking him into his cuſtody, the

priſon

prifon being at a great diftance, and Mr. *Powell's* houfe being in the way, he permitted him to lodge there that night, and was fo affected with his family duty, that he would proceed no farther, and left Mr. *Powell* at home, but for fear of the cruelty of the juftice, abfconded.

MR. *Powell*, to prevent damage to the man, bound himfelf with two fufficient fureties to appear at the next affizes at *Radnorfhire*; and accordingly appeared there, and three bills of indictment were preferred againft him, from which, upon the traverfe, he was acquitted, and the judges invited him to dinner with them, defiring him to give thanks, one of them faid, *it was the beft grace he ever heard in his life.*

THIS proved much to the furtherance of the gofpel in thofe parts, to the great offence of the high fheriff, who afterwards upon the coming on of the war, perfecuted him out of the country.

Mr. Edward Barber *impri-fon'd.*

MR. *Edward Barber*, minifter to a fmall congregation of *Baptifts* at *London*, was in the year 1641. kept eleven months in prifon, for *denying* the *baptifm* of *infants*, and that to pay *tithes* to the clergy is God's ordinance under the gofpel; but thefe feem to have been before the *epifcopal* power was laid afide[k].

[k] *Preface to his treatife of Baptifm.*

MR.

Mr. Benj. Cox *imprisoned.*

MR. *Benj. Cox*, a biſhop's ſon, and ſome time miniſter of *Bedford*, was committed to *Coventry* goal, for preaching and diſputing againſt *infant-baptiſm* in the year 1643.

The occaſion of it.

THE occaſion of it was this. Several pious and godly people at *Coventry*, having embraced the opinion of *Antipædobaptiſm*, reſolved to form themſelves into a diſtinct ſociety or church, and for their direction and aſſiſtance in this ſettlement, they ſent for this Mr. *Cox*, being an antient *miniſter*, and of good reputation both for piety and learning, as his adverſaries acknowledge.

THERE were alſo at the ſame time in this city, ſeveral *Preſbyterian* miniſters, who had fled thither for *refuge*; among whom the Rev. Mr. *Baxter* was one. Theſe were not a little alarmed and diſpleaſed at this increaſe of the *Baptiſts*, and eſpecially at ſo great a man's coming to encourage and vindicate them.

BESIDES the pulpits ringing againſt the error of *Anabaptiſm*, Mr. *Baxter* ſends a challenge to Mr. *Cox*, to diſpute with him about the points in difference; which was accepted, and carried on *viva voce*, and then by writing. Tho' no account of this is preſerv'd, but by Mr. *Baxter* himſelf, yet it is eaſy to judge which ſide gained the advantage. For there comes out an order from the *committee*, requiring Mr. *Cox* to depart

depart the *city*, and promiſe to come there no more; and upon his refuſing to do this, he is immediately committed to *priſon*.

THIS was complain'd of as very hard and illegal uſage; and Mr. *Baxter* was reflected upon as having procur'd his impriſonment; for he had a great intereſt in the *committee*, dwelt at the *governour*'s houſe, and was his intimate *friend*.

MR. *Baxter* indeed denies [l], that he ever ſpoke a word for the putting him into priſon. But if he had diſlik'd ſuch proceedings, 'tis plain he might have prevented it; for when he had been ſome time in *priſon*, upon Mr. *Pinſon*'s applying himſelf to Mr. *Baxter* for his releaſe, it was ſoon procured.

Mr. Henry Denne *ſent to priſon.*

MR. *Henry Denne*, who had been educated at *Cambridge*, ordain'd a *miniſter* by the biſhop of St. *David*'s, and enjoyed the living of *Pyrton* in *Hertfordſhire* about ten years, upon changing his opinion about *baptiſm*, was in the year 1644. apprehended in *Cambridgeſhire*, by the committee of that county, and ſent to *goal*, for preaching againſt *infant-baptiſm*, and preſuming to baptize thoſe again who had received no other.

AFTER he had been confined ſome time, through the interceſſion of his friends, his caſe was referred to a committee of parliament; and he was ſent up to *London*, and kept a *priſoner* in the lord *Peter's*

[l] *Introduct. plain proofs.*

houſe

houſe in *Aderſgate-ſtreet*, till the committee had heard his caſe, and releaſed him.

HE was a ſecond time taken up, and committed at *Spalding* in *Lincolnſhire*, in *June* 1646. for preaching and baptizing by *immerſion*. His chief proſecutors here were two juſtices of peace. They ſent the conſtable to apprehend him on the Lord's-day morning, and keep him in cuſtody, that ſo he might not preach; for the people reſorted to him very much, which was no ſmall occaſion of their taking offence. Upon the hearing his caſe, there was but one *witneſs* of his pretended crime, *viz. dipping*; for he himſelf refuſed to be his own accuſer.

IT will give the *reader* a better view of the proceedings in thoſe times, to ſee the two examinations that were taken on this occaſion.

The examination of Anne Jarrat, *of* Spalding, *ſpinſter*, June 22. 1646. *before maſter* Thomas Irbie, *and maſter* John Harrington, *commiſſioners of the peace.*

'THIS examinate ſaith, on *Wedneſday* laſt in the night about eleven or 'twelve of the clock, *Anne Stennet* and '*Anne Smith*, the ſervants of *John Mackerneſſe*, did call out this examinate to go

[a] Edward's *Gangræna, p.* 3. *p.* 86.

' with

'with them to the little croft, with whom 'this examinate did go; and coming thi-'ther, master *Denne*, and *John Macker-'nesse*, and a *stranger* or *two* followed after: 'And being come to the *river* side, mas-'ter *Denne* went into the water, and there 'did baptize *Anne Stennet*, *Anne Smith*, '*Godfrey Roote*, and *John Sowter* in this 'examinate's presence.'

ANNE JARRAT (W) *her mark.*

June 21. 1646. Lincolne Holland, Henry Denne *of* Caxton *in the county of* Cambridge, *examined before* John Harrington *and* Thomas Irby, *Esqrs*; *two of his Majesty's justices of the peace.*

'THIS examinate saith, that he liveth 'at *Caxton* aforesaid, but doth ex-'ercise at *Elsly* within a mile of his own 'house; and saith that he took orders a-'bout sixteen years since from the bishop of '*St. Davids*, and that on *Monday* last he 'came to *Spalding*, being invited thither 'by *John Mackernesse* to come to his house. 'And that he hath exercised his gifts about 'four times in several places in *Spalding*, '*viz.* at the house of *John Mackernesse* 'and Mr. *Enston*'s. As for baptizing of 'any, he doth not confess.

JOHN HARRINGTON.

IF

IF it be thought a crime to perform ſuch a ceremony in the *night*, the ſeverity of the times muſt bear the blame of it, which obliged him to take ſuch a ſeaſon. The Primitive Chriſtians held their aſſemblies and perform'd moſt of their ſocial worſhip in the *night*, when under perſecution; and for his not confeſſing the baptizing of any, the rule of common law will excuſe him, *Nemo tenetur ſeipſum accuſare.*

Mr. Coppe *impriſoned.*

ABOUT this time alſo Mr. *Coppe*, a miniſter in *Warwickſhire*, and ſome time preacher to the gariſon of *Compton-houſe* in the ſaid county, was committed to *Coventry* goal for rebaptizing.

Mr. Baxter's *account of him.*

MR. *Baxter* ſays of this man [n], 'That he 'was a zealous *Anabaptiſt*, and continued 'ſo for many years, and rebaptized more 'than any one man he ever heard of in the 'country. Witneſs, ſays he, *Warwickſhire*, *Oxfordſhire*, part of *Worceſterſhire*, '&c. That when himſelf was preacher to 'the gariſon at *Coventry*, which was near 'him, he heard of no opinions that he 'vented or held, but the neceſſity of rebaptizing, and independency: But afterwards he fell into the errors and vile practices of the *Ranters*, for which he was 'put again into *Coventry* goal.'

BUT Mr. *Baxter* acknowledges, that his former impriſonment was for his rebap-

[n] *Scrip. Proofs*, p. 148.

tizing;

tizing; and that thoſe who committed him were repreſented as *perſecutors* for ſo doing.

UPON the publiſhing of the *ordinance of parliament* in 1645. againſt unordained preachers, before recited, the Lord-mayor of *London* ſent his officers to the *Baptiſt-meeting* in *Coleman-ſtreet*, being inform'd that certain *laymen* preach'd there. When they came, they found two miniſters there, Mr. *Lamb*, the elder of the church; and a young man, who was a *teacher* among them.

Mr. Lamb *and another taken into cuſtody.*

THE congregation were greatly provoked that they ſhould be thus diſturbed in their worſhip, for it was on the Lord's-day, and ſome uſed very rough language to the officers; but Mr. *Lamb* treated them very civilly, and deſired they would permit them to finiſh their exerciſe, and gave his word that they would both appear before the Lord-mayor at ſix o-clock, to anſwer for what they did.

THE officers accepted this, and went their way; and Mr. *Lamb* with his aſſiſtant met them at his lordſhip's houſe, at the time appointed.

WHEN they were brought before the mayor, he demanded by what authority they took upon them to preach; and told them, they had tranſgreſſed an *ordinance* of *parliament*. Mr. *Lamb* replied, No, for they were called and appointed to that office by as reformed a church as any in the world, alluding to the words of the *ordinance*; and they acknowledg'd to him, that they were ſuch as rejected the *baptiſm* of *infants* as invalid.

Bound over by the Lord-mayor, and committed to priſon.

AFTER examination, his lordſhip bound them over to anſwer it before a committee of parliament; who, after hearing of them, committed them both to *goal*, where they lay for ſome time. At length, by the interceſſion of their friends, they were ſet at liberty.

Mr. Hobſon *taken into cuſtody.*

THE ſame year, and by virtue of the ſame *ordinance*, Mr. *Paul Hobſon*, a *Baptiſt miniſter*, was taken into cuſtody by the governour of *Newport-Pagnel*, for preaching againſt *infant-baptiſm*, and reflecting upon the order againſt *lay-mens* preaching.

Sent a priſoner to London.

AFTER ſome ſhort time of confinement there, the governour, Sir *Samuel Luke*, ſent him priſoner to *London*. His caſe was ſoon brought before the committee of examination; and having ſeveral great friends, he was immediately, after his being heard, diſcharged; and preached publickly at a meeting-houſe in *More fields*, to the great mortification of his perſecutors.

Mr. Hanſerd Knollys *taken into cuſtody.*

AMONG the ſufferers for *Antipædobaptiſm* in theſe times, the pious and learned Mr. *Hanſerd Knollys* muſt be number'd, tho' he had been ordained a miniſter by the biſhop of *Peterborough*, and now was a zealous

zealous oppoſer both of epiſcopacy and common prayer, yet all this could not exempt him from the rage of the *Preſbyters*; [nor will Mr. *Neal*'s invidious repreſentation do any harm to his character] becauſe he was a *Sectary* and an *Anabaptiſt*. Once he was taken up for preaching againſt *infant-baptiſm* at *Bow* church in *Cheapſide*. The occaſion was this: The churchwardens of that pariſh wanting a miniſter to preach on the Lord's-day enſuing, apply'd themſelves to Mr. *Knollys*. They renewed their requeſt three days, one after another, and were denied. At length, their earneſtneſs and great want of a ſupply prevailed with him. When he was preaching, his ſubject led him to ſay ſomething againſt the practice of baptizing *infants*. This gave ſo great an offence to ſome of his *auditory*, that they complained of him to the parliament, and a warrant from the committee for plunder'd miniſters, was ſent to the keeper of *Ely-houſe*, to apprehend him, and bring him in ſafe cuſtody before them. Hereupon he was preſently ſeized, and kept ſeveral days in *priſon*, his crime being too great to admit of bail when it was offered. At length his caſe was brought to a hearing before the committee: There were about thirty of the aſſembly of divines preſent; and Mr. *White* the chairman of the committee examined him about his authority to

The occaſion of it.

Was impriſoned.

preach, the occaſion of his preaching in *Bow* church, and the doctrine he had there delivered.

Anſwers for himſelf before the committee, and is acquitted.

TO all theſe he gave ſuch full anſwers, that they ſeemed *aſhamed* of what they had done; and ordering him to withdraw, called in the *goaler*, reproved him ſharply for refuſing bail, and threatned to turn him out of his place: ſo he was diſmiſs'd without any blame, or paying of fees, which was a ſmall reward for falſe impriſonment. Not long after this, he went into *Suffolk*, where he preached in ſeveral places, as he had opportunity and was deſired by his friends; but he being counted an *Antinomian*, and an *Anabaptiſt*, this was looked upon to be *ſedition* and *faction*, and the rabble being encouraged by the high-conſtable, ſet themſelves zealouſly to oppoſe him. At one time when he was preaching, they ſtoned him out of the pulpit. At another time, when he was to have preached, they got into the church firſt, and ſhut the doors, both againſt him and the people, upon which he preach'd in the church-yard; but this was deemed a very great and an unſufferable crime.

Is taken into cuſtody again, and ſent priſoner to London.

At length he was taken into cuſtody; and firſt he was proſecuted at a petty *ſeſſions* in the country, then ſent up a *priſoner* to *London*, with articles of complaint againſt him to the parliament. But when his caſe came to be heard before the committee of examination,

mination, he made it appear by witnesses of good reputation, that he had neither sowed *sedition*, nor raised *tumults*, and that all the disorders which had happen'd, were owing to the rage and malignity of his opposers, who had acted contrary both to law and common civility: He produc'd the copies of his sermons which he had preach'd in those parts, and afterwards printed them.

Answers for himself before the committee of examination.

Christ alone exalted, &c.

HIS answers were so full and satisfactory, that when the committee made their report to the house, he was not only discharged, but a vote passed, that he might have liberty to preach in any part of *Suffolk*, when the minister of the place did not preach there himself. But this business put him to a great deal of trouble and expence. He has left it under his own hand, that it cost him threescore pounds.

Is discharged, and a vote of the house passed in his favour.

WHEN Mr. *Knollys* found that his preaching in the churches, tho' but occasionally, gave so much offence, and brought so much trouble on himself, he set up a separate meeting in *Great St. Helens, London*, where the people flock'd to hear him, and he had commonly a *thousand* auditors. But this was rather a greater offence to his *Presbyterian* brethren, than his former method. Now they complain'd that he was too near the church, and that he kept his meetings at the same times

He sets up a meeting in Great St. Helens.

that they had their publick worſhip. And firſt they prevail'd upon his landlord, to warn him out of that place; next he was ſummon'd to appear before a committee of divines, which uſed to ſit at *Weſtminſter*, in the room called the *Queen's court*, to anſwer for his conduct in this matter. Upon his examination, Mr. *Leigh* being chairman, he aſked him why he preſumed to preach without holy orders. To which he replied, that he was in holy orders. Hereupon one of the committee ſaid to the chairman, that he had renounc'd his *ordination* by the biſhop before the committee for plunder'd miniſters. Mr. *Knollys* confeſſed that he did ſo; but ſaid, he was now ordain'd, in a church of God, according to the order of the goſpel, and then declar'd to them the manner of *ordination* uſed among the *Baptiſts*. At laſt, the chairman in the name of the committee, commanded him to preach no more; but he told them he would preach the Goſpel, both publickly and from houſe to houſe; ſaying it was more equal to obey Chriſt who commanded him, than thoſe who forbad him, and ſo went his way.

Is ſummoned before a committee of divines.

Is forbid to preach.

ONE thing that made the *Preſbyterians* more violent againſt this good man, ſeems to have been a letter that he writ from *London*, to one Mr. *John Dutton* in *Norwich*, in which there were ſome ſharp reflections upon their attempts to ſuppreſs all religion

A reaſon of the Preſbyterians *hatred.*

ligions but their own. This coming into the hands of ſome of the committee of *Suffolk*, was ſeized, ſent up to *London*, and preſently after publiſh'd by one of the chief promoters of perſecution in thoſe times. It being but ſhort, I ſhall here inſert it for the *reader*'s ſatisfaction.

Beloved brother,

'I Salute you in the Lord. Your letter I
'received the laſt day of the week;
'and upon the firſt day I did ſalute the
'brethren in your name, who re-ſalute you
'and pray for you. [a]The city *Preſbyterians*
'have ſent a letter to the ſynod, dated
'from *Sion-College*, againſt any *toleration*;
'and they are faſting and praying at *Sion-*
'*College* this day, about further contrivings
'againſt God's poor innocent ones; but
'God will doubtleſs anſwer them accord-
'ing to the *idol* of their own hearts. To-
'morrow there is a faſt kept by both hou-
'ſes, and the ſynod at *Weſtminſter*. They
'ſay it is to ſeek God about the eſtabliſhing
'of worſhip according to their covenant:
'They have *firſt vowed, now they make en-*
'*quiry*. God will certainly *take the crafty*
'*in their own ſnare*, and *make the wiſdom*
'*of the wiſe, fooliſhneſs*; for *he chooſeth the*
'*fooliſh things of this world to confound the*
'*wiſe, and weak things to confound the*

[a] Edwards's *Gangræna*, Part III. p. 48.

'*mighty*. My wife and family remember
'their love to you. Salute the brethren
'that are with you. Farewel.

London, the 13th day of the 11th Month, called January, 1645.

Your brother in the faith and fellowship of the gospel,

HANSERD KNOLLYS.

I FIND it was a common practice in those times, for such as were in *authority*, to seize the letters which the *Sectaries*, as they term them, sent one to another, and divulge them, either to expose their weakness, or to take advantage of any thing in them relating to publick affairs, in order to turn the government against them.

John Sims *seized.*

WE have a notable instance of this in the case of *John Sims*, a *Baptist minister* at *Hampton*. This man, in a journey to *Taunton* in *Somersetshire*, was prevailed upon to preach in the parish-church of *Middlesey*; which gave such offence to the *Presbyterians*, that he was presently seized by virtue of the act against unordain'd ministers; and five letters, which he was carrying from some of his religious acquaintance to others, were taken from him. These, with his examination, were sent up to London, by way of complaint against him; and the government

His letters taken from him, and pubished.

ment not taking that notice which was expected of them, the next thing was to publish them, in a book written by a *Presbyterian* minister against the sectaries.

HIS crimes are specify'd in the examination, which were these great ones; *viz. preaching* and denying *infant-baptism.* And to aggravate these, they added, That he took a text, and preach'd before two *Presbyterian ministers:* For this is the form of it.

'[b] SONDAY, the last of *May*, he preach-'ed in the parish-church of *Middlesey*, took 'his text out of the iii. *Col.* 1. one master '*Mercer*, and master *Esquier*, ministers, 'with a hundred more persons; and being 'desired to know how he durst presume 'to teach so publickly, being not called, 'and an *ordinance* of parliament to the 'contrary, answered, *If* Peter *was called,* '*so was he.*

2. 'BEING desired to know, why he 'teached contrary to the law of God, and 'the laws of the land, answered, Why 'are they suffered to teach in *London*, so 'near the parliament-house? and that he 'would allow of the parliament, as far 'forth as they go with his doctrine.

3. 'BEING desired to know whether 'he allowed of our *baptism*, answered, No: 'that for his part he was baptized a year 'since, by one master *Sickmoore*; and his

[b] Edwards's *Gangræna*, Part III. p. 50.

'manner

'manner of baptizing was, that the afore-
'said *Sickmoore* went firſt into the water,
'and he after him, ſo that he for his part
'would not allow of our *baptiſm*.'

As to the letters, there appears neither *hereſy* nor *rebellion* in them, unleſs baptizing by *immerſion*, and rejoicing that the *Preſbyterians* did not obtain that unlimited power they petition'd for, might be deemed ſuch.

IN one of theſe letters, written by *William Hayward*, are theſe words[c]:

'I NEED not tell you of the oppo-
'ſitions here in *Taunton*. Our brother will
'tell you the particular paſſages; our go-
'vernour does labour to beat us down,
'and doth ſay, that any meeting in pri-
'vate, is merely to croſs the publick meet-
'ings, and that it is not out of tenderneſs
'of conſcience, but *damnable pride* that
'we do; but this doth not any way cauſe
'us to draw back, or ſadden our ſpirits,
'for our ſpirits are carried above the fear
'of men.'

IN another Mr. *Collier* ſays[d],

'THE unlimited power of the *Preſby-*
'*terians* is denied them, of which you
'ſhall hear more ſhortly.'

AND the chief deſign of the laſt, is to comfort and ſtrengthen the ſaints againſt perſecution, and to aſſure them, that by

c *Ibid*. p. 53.
d *Ibid*. p. 51.

the

the ſame power by which they were brought into the way of holineſs, they ſhould be aſſiſted, and carried on to the end.

THIS year alſo, *Andrew Wyke* was taken up in the county of *Suffolk*, for preaching and *dipping*. When he was brought before the committee of the county, to be examined about his authority to preach, and the doctrines that he held, he refuſed to give them any account of either; alledging, that a freeman of *England* was not bound to anſwer any *interrogatories*, either to accuſe himſelf or others; but if they had ought againſt him, they ſhould lay their charge, and produce their proofs. This was look'd upon as great obſtinacy, and an high contempt of authority; and therefore he was preſently ſent to *goal*.

Andrew Wyke *taken into cuſtody.*

Is ſent to priſon.

How long he continued there I cannot find; but during his impriſonment, a pamphlet was written, either by himſelf, or ſome of his friends, giving a particular account of the proceedings againſt him, and exclaiming againſt the committee for their perſecuting principles and illegal practices. [e] It was entitled, '*The innocent in priſon* '*complaining*; *or*, *a true relation of the pro*-'*ceedings of the committee of* Ipſwich, *the* '*committee at* Bury St. Edmonds *in the* '*county of* Suffolk, *againſt one* Andrew

[e] Edwards's *Gangræna*, Part III. p. 170.

Wyke,

'Wyke, *a witneſs of* Jeſus *in the ſame* 'county, *who was committed to priſon* June 3. '1646.'

I SUPPOSE the reader's patience almoſt tired with accounts of this nature. I will only add one more; and I take it to be one of the chief and baſeſt attempts againſt the practice of *immerſion* in *baptiſm*, of any in thoſe times.

Mr. Sam. Oaes.

MR. *Sam. Oates*, a very popular preacher, and great diſputant, taking a journey into *Eſſex* in the year 1646. preach'd in ſeveral parts of that county, and baptized by *immerſion* great numbers of people, eſpecially about *Bockin*, *Braintree*, and *Tarling*. This made the *Preſbyterians* in thoſe parts very uneaſy; eſpecially the *miniſters*, who complained bitterly that ſuch things ſhould be permitted; and endeavouring to ſpur on the *magiſtrates* all they could to ſuppreſs him, one writes after this manner [f]:

'No magiſtrate in the country dare med-'dle with him; for they ſay they have 'hunted theſe out of the country into their 'dens in *London*, and impriſon'd ſome, and 'they are releaſed and ſent like *decoy-ducks* 'into the country to fetch in more; ſo that 'they go on in divers parts of *Eſſex* with 'the greateſt confidence and inſolency that 'can be imagined.'

[f] *Ibidem*, Part II. p. 3

How-

HOWEVER, at length they got ſomething againſt him, which they thought would effectually anſwer their end, and therefore endeavoured to purſue it to the uttermoſt.

IT happen'd that among the hundreds which he had baptized in this county, one died within a few weeks after; and this they would have to be occaſioned by her being dipp'd in cold water.

ACCORDINGLY they prevailed upon the *magiſtrates* to ſend him to *priſon*, and put him in *irons* as a *murderer*, in order to his *trial* at the next *aſſizes*. *Is ſent to priſon, and put in irons.*

THE books written againſt the *Baptiſts* frequently repreſented the practice of *immerſion* to be extremely dangerous; and ſome termed them a cruel and murdering *ſect* for uſing it. Now if they could but have carry'd this point, it would have confirm'd their cenſures, fix'd an eternal *odium* on the practice, and frightened many timorous perſons from complying with their duty.

GREAT endeavours were therefore uſed that he might be brought in *guilty*: Nay, ſo fond were ſome of this ſtory, that they publiſhed it for a truth before it had been legally examined, and added theſe circumſtances to it, *viz.* '[g] That he held her ſo 'long in the water, that ſhe fell preſently 'ſick: That her belly ſwell'd with the

[g] Edwards's *Gangræna*, Part II. p. 121.

'abun-

'abundance of water ſhe took in, and with-'in a fortnight or three weeks died; and up-'on her death-bed expreſſed her *dipping* 'to be the cauſe of her death.' All which was afterwards made appear to be notorious lies.

Tried for his life.

THEY did indeed carry it ſo far, as to have him arraigned for his *life* at *Chelmsford* aſſizes. But upon his trial ſeveral credible witneſſes were produced, among which the *mother* of the maid was one; who all teſtified upon *oath*, that the ſaid *Anne Martin* (that being her name) was in better health for ſeveral days after her *baptiſm* than ſhe had been for ſome years before; and that ſhe was ſeen to walk abroad afterwards very comfortably. So that notwithſtanding all the deſign and malignity that appear'd in this trial, he was in the end, brought in *not guilty*, to the great mortification of his enemies.

And honourably acquitted.

Remark.

HOW many children have died, either at their *baptiſm*, or immediately after it? And yet none ever aſcrib'd it to their fright at the time, or the coldneſs of the water thrown upon them; and it muſt, of the two, be more dangerous, to dip tender and new-born infants, than thoſe who are grown to maturity. And yet that was the practice of the church of *England* for ſeveral hundred years, even till the reign of King *James* I. when the faſhion altered; and of the thouſands of weakly perſons, who

who have been baptized by *immersion* since the revival of that practice in *England*, among the *Baptists*, it does not appear that any one received any prejudice by it. Could but one instance of that nature have been produced, you may very easily judge by this story, how much it would have been published and improved against them by their enemies.

Sir John Floyer *proves* dipping *both safe and useful.*

SIR *John Floyer*, an eminent physician, publish'd an essay to prove cold bathing both safe and useful; wherein he gives an account of many great cures done by it, and presents the world with an alphabetical catalogue of diseases against which it has been successful: And on this account, in the *epistle dedicatory*, and in his second letter, he laments the disuse of the *baptismal immersion* in *England*, which he says, continued till the year 1600. Indeed, he says, he will not concern himself in any theological disputes, whither *immersion* be essential to baptism, *&c.*

'[h] FOR all that I shall aim at, says he, is 'to shew, that *immersion* was generally 'practised by the *antients*; and that in this 'church it continued in use till the beginning of the last age; and that there is 'not that danger in it, as parents apprehend; but instead of prejudicing the health 'of their children, *immersion* would prevent

[h] Stennet *against* Russen, *p.* 134.

'many

'many hereditary diseases, if it were still 'practised.'

[i] HE closes his letter with observing, 'that 'the church of *England* continued the 'use of *immersion* longer than any other 'christian church in the *western* parts of 'the world. For the *eastern* church, saith 'he, yet use it; and our church still re-'commends the *dipping* of *infants* in her '*rubrick*, to which, I believe, the *English* 'will at last return, when physick has 'given them a clear proof by divers ex-'periments, that cold baths are both safe 'and useful. And, he says, they did great 'injury to their own children, and all poste-'rity, who first introduc'd the alteration of 'this truly antient ceremony of *immersion*, 'and were the occasion of a degenerate, 'sickly, tender race ever since.'

Some Baptists *abused by the rabble.*

BUT to return. When the *Presbyterians* found they could do nothing to Mr. *Oates* by due course of law, they endeavoured to raise the *mob* against him; and in this they were more successful. For a little after, some who were known to be *Baptists*, going occasionally to *Wethersfield* in that county, there was presently an alarm given, that *Oates* and his companions were come to that town; upon which the *rabble* were raised, and seized those innocent people. And for no other crime, but because they were

[i] *Ibid.* p. 134.

Anabap-

Anabaptiſts, they were dragged to a *pump*, and treated like the worſt of *villains*; neither was *Oates*, the perſon againſt whom they were chiefly enraged, amongſt them.

NOT long after this, *Oates* himſelf went to *Dunmow* in *Eſſex*. When ſome of the zealots for *infant-baptiſm* in that town heard where he was, without any other provocation but that of his daring to come there, they dragged him out of the houſe, and threw him into a *river*, boaſting they had thoroughly *dipt* him.

Mr. Oates *thrown into a river.*

ABOUT this time Mr. *Edward Hutchinſon*, a learned and ingenious defender of the practice of baptizing *believers* only, in his *epiſtle dedicatory* to thoſe of the *baptized congregations*, put at the beginning of his treatiſe, *concerning the covenant and baptiſm*, gives the following account of the beginning and increaſe of that people in theſe latter times.

Mr. Hutchinſon's *account of the* Engliſh Baptiſts.

'YOUR *beginning*, ſays he, in theſe nations of late years was but ſmall; yet, when it pleaſed the Lord to diſpel thoſe clouds that over-ſhadowed us, and ſcatter ſome beams of the *goſpel* amongſt us, he gave you ſo great an increaſe, that *Sion* may ſay with admiration, *Who hath begotten me theſe*, &c.

'NOR is it leſs obſervable, that whereas other *reformations* have been carried on by the *ſecular arm*, and the countenance and allowance of the *magiſtrate*; as in *Luther's* 'time, by ſeveral *German* princes; the pro- 'teſtant reformation in *England*, by King '*Edward*, Queen *Elizabeth*, &c. the *Preſ-* '*byterian* reformation, by a parliament, 'committee of eſtates, aſſembly of divines, 'beſides the favour and aſſiſtance of great 'perſonages; you have had none of theſe 'to take you by the hand; but your pro- 'greſs was againſt the impetuous current of 'human oppoſition, attended with ſuch ex- 'ternal diſcouragements, as beſpeak your 'embracing this deſpiſed truth an effect of 'heart ſincerity, void of all mercenary 'conſiderations. Yea, how active has the '*accuſer of the brethren* been, to repreſent 'you in ſuch frightful figures, expoſing 'you by that miſchievous artifice to popu- 'lar *odium*, and the laſh of *magiſtracy*, in- 'ſomuch that the name of an *Anabaptiſt* 'was crime enough, which doubtleſs was a 'heavy obſtacle in the way of many pious 'ſouls? And what our diſſenting brethren 'have to anſwer upon that account, who, 'inſtead of taking up, have laid ſtumbling 'blocks in the way of *Reformation*, will 'appear another day. Yet, notwithſtand- 'ing the ſtrenuous oppoſitions of thoſe 'great and learned ones, the mighty God of '*Jacob* hath taken you by the hand, and 'ſaid, *Be ſtrong*.'

BUT to return, whilſt the *Preſbyterians* had the aſcendant, the *perſecution* againſt the *ſectaries* continued; the members of the houſe

house of Commons, which now compos'd the parliament, had possess'd themselves of the supreme authority; the violence they had used to their colleagues, the king's tragical death, the change of the monarchy into a commonwealth, and the taxes impos'd on the people for an unnecessary war, had render'd them *odious* to the whole kingdom.

PETITIONS are made to them, in which their dissolution is demanded: They vote against a dissolution, and prepare a bill, by which all persons are forbid to present such petitions, under pain of being declared guilty of *high treason*.

IT could not be doubted, that the members who had set more than twelve years, and had but too much abused their power, would always retain the *supreme authority* in their hands, under colour of being the representatives of a republick, which properly consisted only of themselves. An. Dom. 1653.

Cromwel being therefore very certain this parliament was odious to the people, went to the house, *April* 20. 1653. attended with some *officers* and *soldiers*; and without any ceremony told them, he was come to put an end to their power, of which they had made an ill use, and therefore they were to be immediately dissolved. A little after, he publishes a *declaration*, to justify the dissolution of the parliament; makes choice of an hundred and forty four Cromwel *dissolves the long parliament.*

 persons

persons, to take care of the government; and requires them to assemble at *Whitehall*, *July* 4. ensuing. These persons, when assembled, made no scruple to call themselves *a parliament*, and chose one *Rouse* for their speaker. They did nothing considerable in a session of more than five months. At last, on the 12*th* of *December*, the speaker, with a good number of the members, dissolv'd themselves, and return'd the *sovereign power* into the hands of *Cromwel* and the council of officers, beseeching them to take care of the government.

Is made protector. TWO days after, the council of *officers*, by virtue of the *authority* lately given them by the parliament, declared that for the future the government of the republick should reside in a single person, *viz. Oliver Cromwel*, captain-general of the forces of *England*, *Scotland* and *Ireland*, who should have the title of protector of the three kingdoms, and be assisted by a council of twenty one persons.

An. Dom. 1657. THUS an end was put to the *Presbyterian* establishment, and *Cromwel* was confirmed in his *protectorship*, by a parliament, in the year 1657. with more power than was annexed to it by the council of *officers*. This was done by a solemn *instrument*, called *the humble petition and advice*; the parliament thereby shewing, it was not a law to be imposed on him, but an advice, which was submitted to his judgment and discretion, with

with freedom to accept or refuſe it, as he ſhould think proper. I ſhall only tranſcribe from thence what concerned religion. 'That his *highneſs* would encourage a 'godly *miniſtry* in theſe nations; and that 'ſuch as do revile, and diſturb them in 'the worſhip of God, may be puniſh'd ac-'cording to law, and where laws are de-'fective, new ones to be made [i]: 'That 'the proteſtant chriſtian religion, as it is 'contain'd in the old and new teſtament, 'be aſſerted and held forth for the publick 'profeſſion of theſe nations, and no other: 'And that a confeſſion of faith be agreed 'upon, and recommended to the people of 'theſe nations; and none to be permitted 'by words or writing, to revile or reproach 'the ſaid confeſſion of faith.'

Welwood, as quoted by *Rapin* [k], tells us, 'That as to the morals and conduct of the '*protector*, as a private perſon, they may 'be ſaid to have been very regular. He 'was guilty of none of the vices, to which 'men are commonly addicted; *gluttony*, '*drunkenneſs*, *gaming*, *luxury*, *avarice*, 'were vices with which he was never re-'proached; on the contrary, it is certain, 'he promoted virtuous men; as on the 'other hand, he was inflexible in his pu-'niſhments of vice and ill actions. It is 'true, his own preſervation oblig'd him

Welwood's *character of him.*

[i] *Rapin*, vol. II. p. 597.
[k] *Ibid*. p. 600.

'sometimes to employ men of ill prin-
'ciples; but this is not uncommon to those
'who are at the head of a government.

'THO' as to his religion he was an *Independent*, his principle was to leave every man at liberty in the religion he had chosen, and never persecuted any person on that account. He even connived at the private meetings of those who remained attached to the church of *England*, tho' he was well informed of them. If they were not favour'd with the free and publick exercise of their religion, it was because they were consider'd by him as *Royalists*, always ready to form plots in the king's favour, and from whom consequently he had great reason to secure himself. Tho' he was in the sentiments of the *Independents*, and therefore averse to all union with the national church, he however consider'd all protestant churches as part of the protestant church in general; and without aiming to establish *Independency* by force and violence, he expressed on all occasions an extreme zeal for the protestant religion.'

BISHOP *Burnet* says[1]: 'A great design *Cromwel* had intended to begin his *kingship* with, if he had assumed it; he resolv'd to set up a council in opposition to the congregation *de propaganda fide* at *Rome*.

[1] *Hist. of his own time*, p. 77.

'He

'He intended it ſhould conſiſt of ſeven 'counſellors, and four ſecretaries for different provinces. The ſecretaries were to 'have 500 l. ſalary a piece, and to keep 'a correſpondence every where, to know 'the ſtate of religion all over the world; 'that ſo all good deſigns might be by 'their means protected and aſſiſted. Stoupe 'was to have the firſt province. They 'were to have a fund of 10,000 l. a 'year at their diſpoſal for ordinary emergencies; but to be farther ſupplied, as 'occaſions ſhould require it.'

AND he further adds, that *Cromwel* ſaid once in council[m], 'That he hoped he 'ſhould make the name of an *Engliſhman* 'as great as ever that of a *Roman* had 'been.'

WELL might the biſhop then ſay, with reſpect to his government, as he does[n], 'If 'it be compar'd with thoſe of the two laſt 'kings, there will appear a very great diſparity with regard to the glory and reputation of the *Engliſh nation*. *James* I. and '*Charles* I. ſeemed to have ſtudied to diſgrace the *Engliſh* name; whereas *Cromwel* in the ſpace of four or five years 'carried the glory of his nation as far as 'poſſible, and in that reſpect was not 'inferiour to *Elizabeth*.'

[m] *Page* 81.
[n] *Vid.* Rapin, vol. II. p. 600.

HE is by his enemies charg'd with cruelty, for having, whilſt *protector*, put ſome men to death, for conſpiring againſt his perſon and government: 'That is, according to this reproach, ſays *Rapin* [o], he 'ſhould have patiently ſuffered the plots 'againſt him, and when one failed, liberty ſhould have been given for a ſecond 'and a third, till ſome one had ſucceeded. 'This deſerves no confutation. But to ſhew 'that *Cromwel* was not for an unneceſſary 'effuſion of blood, we need only recite 'what is owned by the earl of *Clarendon*, 'who aſſures us [p],

'THAT when it was propoſed in a 'council of *officers*, that there might be a 'general *maſſacre* of the *Royaliſts*, *Cromwel* would never conſent to it.

'To form a juſt and rational idea of *Cromwel*'s character, ſays *Rapin* [q], his conduct and 'actions in themſelves muſt be examined, 'and joined to the juncture of the time, independently of the opinions of his enemies. I ſhall only obſerve, ſays he, that 'the confuſion which prevail'd in *England*, 'ſoon after the death of *Cromwel*, clearly 'ſhews the neceſſity of this uſurpation. In 'general it can't be denied, that *Cromwel* 'was one of the greateſt men in his age, if 'it is conſider'd, that without the advantages

[o] *Vol.* II. *p.* 602.
[p] *Hiſt. Rebel.* vol. III. p. 509.
[q] *Rapin*, vol. II. *p.* 602.

'of *birth* or *fortune*, he rose so near a 'throne, that it was in his power to mount 'it. *History* furnishes very few instances 'of this kind. *Cromwel's* death was fol-'lowed with so much alterations in the 'government, that the interval between 'that and the restauration may be justly 'called a time of true *anarchy*. *Cromwel* 'should have had a successor like himself, 'to finish what he had so ably begun. But 'two so great men are not commonly 'found so near one another, nor often in 'the same age.'

A LITTLE before his death, a discovery was made of a conspiracy of the *Royalists*, forming in *England*, in favour of the king; upon which *Cromwel* erected a high court of *justice*, for trial of the criminals, and especially of the three principal ones, *viz. John Mordaunt*, brother of the earl of *Peterborough*; Sir *Henry Slingsby*, a rich and popular man in the county of *York*; and Dr. *Hewit*, a minister of the church of *England*[r].

An. Dom. 1658. *A conspiracy against him.*

MR. *Mordaunt* escaped death by the means of his wife, who bribed some of the judges, and prevailed with colonel *Mallory*, one of the two witnesses against her husband, to make his escape. Sir *Henry Slingsby* and Dr. *Hewit* were condemned and executed, *June* 8. 1658. Before the same court were

Some executed for it.

[r] *Ibid.* p. 599.

tried,

tried, condemned, hanged, and quartered for the ſame crime, *Aſhton*, *Stacey*, and *Battely*. Some others were condemned and pardon'd by *Cromwel*. Not to multiply any more the number of his enemies, it is certain he had a great many, and that thoſe who had been moſt attached to him while he was believ'd to be in their view, hated him mortally when they found themſelves deceived. The earl of *Clarendon* relates [s] on this occaſion a long addreſs to the king, from ſeveral *Independents*, *Quakers*, and *Anabaptiſts*, brought him by a young gentleman, of an honourable extraction and great parts; by whom they made many extravagant propoſitions, and ſeemed to depend very much upon the death of *Cromwel*, and thereupon to compute their own power to ſerve the king; who gave ſuch an anſwer only to them, as might diſpoſe them to hope for his favour, if he received ſervice from them, and ſo believe, that he did not intend to perſecute or trouble any men for their opinions, if their actions were peaceable; which they pretended to effect.

'SINCE the ſpirit, humour, and language, ſays the noble hiſtorian, of that 'people, and in truth of that time, cannot 'be better deſcribed and repreſented by that 'petition and addreſs which was never pub- 'liſhed, and of which there remains no

[s] *Hiſt. Rebel.* vol. III. p. 489.

'copy

'copy in any hand that I know of, but 'only the original which was presented to 'the king (it being so dangerous a thing 'for any man who remained in *England* 'to have any such transcript in his custody) 'it will not be amiss, says he, in this place 'to insert the petition and the address in the 'very words in which it was presented to 'his majesty, with the letter that accompanied it, from the gentleman mentioned 'before, who was an *Anabaptist* of special 'trust among them, and who came not 'with the petition, but expected the king's 'pleasure upon the receipt of it; it being 'sent by an officer who had served the 'king in an eminent command, and was 'now gracious among those sectaries, without swerving in the least degree from his 'former principles and integrity; for that 'people always pretended a just esteem and 'value of all men, who had faithfully adhered to the king, and lived soberly and 'virtuously.'

THE noble historian further says, 'That the gentleman who brought this address, &c. brought likewise with him a 'particular letter to the king, from the 'gentleman that is before described, upon 'whose temper, ingenuity, and interest, 'the messenger principally depended, having had much acquaintance and conversation with him; who tho' he was an '*Anabaptist*, made himself merry with 'the

'the extravagancy and madneſs of his 'companions; and told this gentleman that 'though the firſt addreſs could not be 'prepared but with thoſe demands, which 'might ſatisfy the whole party, and 'comprehend all that was deſired by any 'of them, yet if the king gave them ſuch 'an encouragement as might diſpoſe them 'to ſend ſome of the wiſeſt of them to 'attend his majeſty, he would be able, 'upon conference with them, to make 'them his inſtruments to reduce the reſt 'to more moderate deſires, when they 'ſhould diſcern that they might have 'more protection and ſecurity from the 'king, than from any other power that 'would aſſume the government.

'THE king, adds he, believed that 'theſe diſtempers might in ſome con-'juncture be of uſe to him; and there-'fore returned the general anſwer that is 'mentioned before; and that he would be 'willing to confer with ſome perſons of 'that party, truſted by the reſt, if they 'would come over to him; his majeſty 'being then at *Bruges*. Upon which that 'young gentleman came over thither to 'him, and remained ſome days there con-'cealed. He was a perſon of very extra-'ordinary parts, ſharpneſs of wit, readineſs 'and volubility of tongue, but an *Anabap-'tiſt*. He had been bred in the univer-'ſity of *Cambridge*, and afterwards in the

'inns

'inns of court, but being too young to 'have known the religion, or the government of the precedent time, and his father having been engaged from the beginning against the king, he had sucked 'in the opinions that were most prevalent, 'and had been a soldier in *Cromwel's* life-guard of horse, when he was thought to 'be most resolved to establish a republick; 'but when that mask was pulled off, he 'detested him with that rage, that he was 'of the combination with those who resolved to destroy him by what way soever, and was very intimate with *Syndercome*. He had a great confidence of the 'strength and power of that party, and 'confessed that their demands were extravagant, and such as the king could not 'grant; which, after they were once engaged 'in blood, he doubted not they would 'recede from, by the credit the wiser men 'had amongst them. He returned into '*England* very well satisfy'd with the 'king, and did afterwards correspond very 'faithfully with his professions, but left 'the king without any hope of other benefit from that party, than by their increasing the faction and animosity against '*Cromwel*; for it was manifest, they expected a good sum of present money from 'the king, which could not be in his 'power to supply.'

THE

THE *addreſs*, *propoſitions*, and *letter* I have put into the *appendix*, Nº V.

I MUST now return a little back, being unwilling for the ſake of the exact order of time, to break in upon ſo remarkable a part of our civil *hiſtory*, with matters of ſo different a kind, which could have no connection therewith; and obſerve, that in the year 1654. the Rev. Mr. *William Britten*, who had embraced the principles of the *Baptiſts*, publiſhed a treatiſe, intituled, *The Moderate Baptiſt*; *briefly ſhewing ſcripture-way for that initiatory ſacrament of baptiſm*; *together with divers queries*, *conſiderations*, *errors and miſtakes*, *in and about the work of religion: Wherein may appear*, *that the* Baptiſts *of our times hold not thoſe ſtrange opinions as many heretofore have done*; *but as the ſcriptures are now more clearly underſtood*, *ſo they deſire to come nearer to walk by the ſame light.* He in the *Epiſtle Dedicatory* apologizes for its publication, and aſſigns the cauſes which chiefly induced him thereto; and then gives a ſhort account of *himſelf* to his countrymen, the well-affected people of *Northamptonſhire*; the which you will find annexed to the *Epiſtle Dedicatory* of the ſaid book; to which I refer you.

IN the year 1656. the *Baptiſt* churches in the county of *Somerſet* publiſhed a confeſſion of their faith, the which I have put in the *appendix*, Nº III.

IN

In the *Epiſtle Dedicatory* they apologize for their ſo doing; by ſaying, ‘ It may ‘ with ſome ſeem altogether needleſs and ‘ uſeleſs to bring to publick view a nar‑ ‘ rative of faith in ſuch a day as this is; eſ‑ ‘ pecially their having been the like brought ‘ forth by ſeveral *baptized* congregations ‘ formerly. Unto which we reply, that ‘ our publiſhing this *narrative* of our faith ‘ and practice, is not from any diſlike we ‘ found with the former confeſſion of our ‘ beloved brethren, whom we own, and ‘ with whom we are one both in faith and ‘ practice; neither is there any thing in ours ‘ contradictory to our brethren, that we ‘ know of, that have gone before us.

We mean the narrative publiſhed by the ſeven churches in London.

‘ We can ſay, when the Lord ſet us firſt ‘ upon this work, we did not think of ‘ bringing it to publick view; but did it ‘ rather for a trial of our unity in the faith, ‘ for our more clear fellowſhip one with ‘ another, from our harmony in faith and ‘ practice.

‘ Yet having finiſhed it according to ‘ our apprehenſions (and we believe a mea‑ ‘ ſure of the teachings of the Lord) now ‘ judge there is a more than ordinary ne‑ ‘ ceſſity for us thus to publiſh our faith.

‘ 1. In regard of the general charge ‘ laid upon our profeſſion, as if none in ‘ the *countries*, that profeſſed *baptiſm*, were ‘ of our brethrens judgment that publiſhed ‘ that confeſſion of faith in *London*, but ‘ hold

‘ hold free-will, falling away from grace, ‘ *&c.* all which, through the grace of ‘ God we diſclaim; and not only we, but ‘ to our knowledge, many other churches ‘ in the adjacent counties, who ſtand faſt ‘ in the profeſſion of the unchangeable ‘ love of God in Jeſus Chriſt to his people.

‘ 2. BEING very ſenſible of the great ‘ diſtractions and diviſions that are amongſt ‘ profeſſing people in this nation, the many ‘ ways and wiles of *Satan* to ſeduce and ‘ deceive ſouls, the great departing from the ‘ faith, and that under glorious notions of ‘ ſpiritualneſs and holineſs, *Satan* trans- ‘ forming himſelf into an angel of light, ‘ and his miniſters into miniſters of righte- ‘ ouſneſs; we could not but judge it our ‘ bounden duty, in this our day, to come ‘ forth in a renewed *declaration* of our ‘ faith, as a publick teſtimony before all ‘ men, that through grace we do with ‘ one ſoul deſire to cleave to the Lord, ‘ contending earneſtly for the faith that ‘ was once given to the ſaints: for this ‘ being the great deſign of *Satan*, to de- ‘ ſtroy the faith and practice of the goſpel- ‘ churches, we judge nothing more ſuit- ‘ able and proper to us as churches of our ‘ Lord, wherein we might bear our wit- ‘ neſs for him (in this day of temptation) ‘ in print as well as in practice, than this ‘ our teſtimony to the faith and truth as it ‘ is in Jeſus.’

Richard

Richard Cromwel was in the year 1658. without any opposition, proclaimed *protector* of the commonwealth of *England*, *Scotland*, and *Ireland*; and addresses were presented to him from all parts, signed by many thousands, to congratulate him upon his accession to this dignity, and to assure him they would willingly hazard their lives and fortunes to support him. But such *addresses* are not always to be depended upon; experience having often shewn, they are far from being sincere, tho' carefully express'd in the strongest terms.

Richard Cromwel *proclaimed protector.*

THUS *Richard* was install'd *successor* to his father *Oliver*, and took the same oath; but his *protectorship*, which was but short, was one entire series of anarchy and confusion, and pav'd the way for the restoration of King *Charles* II.

BISHOP *Burnet* observes [g] upon the new parliament (or convention as it was afterwards called) 'That such unanimity appeared in their proceedings, that there 'was not the least dispute among them, but 'upon one single point. Yet that was a very 'important one. *Hale*, afterwards the famous chief-justice, moved, that a committee might be appointed to look into 'the propositions that had been made, and 'the concessions that had been offered by 'the late king during the war, particu-

The convention parliament. Bishop Burnet's *observation thereon.*

[g] *Hist. of his own time*, p. 88, 89.

'larly at the treaty of *Newport*, that from 'thence they might digeſt ſuch propoſitions 'as they ſhould think fit to be ſent over to 'the king. This was ſeconded, but, ſays 'the biſhop, I do not remember by whom. 'It was foreſeen that ſuch a motion might 'be ſet on foot; ſo *Monk* was inſtructed 'how to anſwer it, whenſoever it ſhould be 'propoſed. He told the houſe, that there 'was yet, beyond all mens hope, an uni-'verſal quiet all over the nation; but there 'were many incendiaries ſtill on the watch, 'trying where they could firſt raiſe the 'flame. He ſaid, he had ſuch copious in-'formations ſent him of theſe things, that 'it was not fit they ſhould be generally 'known. He could not anſwer for the 'peace, either of the nation or of the ar-'my, if any delay was put to the ſending 'for the king. What need was their of 'ſending propoſitions to him? might they 'not as well prepare them, and offer them 'to him when he ſhould come over? He 'was to bring neither *army* nor *treaſure* 'with him, either to fright them or to 'corrupt them. So he moved, that they 'would immediately ſend commiſſioners to 'bring over the king, and ſaid, that he muſt 'lay the blame of all the blood or miſ-'chief that might follow, on the heads of 'thoſe who ſhould ſtill inſiſt on any mo-'tion that might delay the preſent ſettle-'ment of the nation. This was eccho'd

'with

'with ſuch a ſhout over the houſe, that 'the motion was no more inſiſted on. 'This, ſays the biſhop, was indeed the 'great ſervice that *Monk* did-----To the 'king's coming in without conditions may 'be well imputed all the errors of his reign.' And it may be added, many miſchiefs that followed afterwards.

CHAP. IV.

Containing an account of ſome of the moſt eminent and leading men among the ENGLISH BAPTISTS.

IT is well known, that nothing has been more common than for the *writers* in in general againſt the *Baptiſts*, to repreſent them to the world as *ignorant* and *illiterate* men. Thus Mr. *Ruſſen* triumphs over them, at the cloſe of his firſt argument, in the fifth chapter of his treatiſe, entitled, *Fundamentals without a Foundation.*

'IF any of their leading teachers, ſays 'he [a], cannot read this laſt paragraph with'out an interpreter, I do not think them 'fit men to diſpute about ſuch principles:

[a] Stennet *againſt* Ruſſen, p. 121.

'let them lay aside learning, which their 'ignorance betrays, and follow their trades, 'wherein they are better skilled.'

AND towards the close of his *preface*, he insults them for their supposed ignorance of *grammar*. 'If here, says he[b], 'they cavil at my *moods*, *participles*, *tenses*, 'and *distinctions*; if they carp at some 'sentences of *Latin* scattered here and 'there, let them blame their own *igno-*'*rance!* 'Tis for want of such *human ad-*'*vantages*, that they so strangely wrest 'the Scriptures, and know not rightly to 'divide the word of truth.'

THE vanity of this *author* is sufficiently exposed by his *answerer*, the reverend and learned Mr. *Stennet*; and I may venture to say, that the opinion of the *Baptists* in general in this affair is well expressed by the reverend Mr. *Keach* and Mr. *Delaune*, who say[c], ''Tis certain, that no sort of men 'have more need of *learning*, than the '*ministers* of the gospel, because their em-'ployment is of the highest concern, *viz.* '*rightly to divide the word of truth*; and 'therefore that sacred office is not to be 'intruded into, but by persons duly qua-'lified and called. And most certain it is, 'that human literature, without grace, is 'a dangerous enemy to the true christian

[b] Stennet *against* Russen, p. 18.

[c] Keach *and* Delaune *to the reader*, Sacred Philology, Book II.

'religion;

'religion; and barely considered in itself, 'gives no right to the exercise of that sacred function, any more than the meanest 'of mechanick arts. For, as Dr. *Carlton*, 'formerly bishop of *Chichester*, well says, 'a *layman*, that hath the Spirit of God, is 'better able to judge of the church and its 'members, than a man in *ecclesiastical* 'function, that hath not the Spirit of God. 'And *Justin Martyr* excellently, *Infelix* '*est sapientia extra verbum Dei sapere:* so 'that it is not the formality of *academical* degrees, nor any *philosophical* dexterity, 'which is to be exercised in the things that 'may be known by the light of natural 'reason, nor variety of *languages*, that 'qualifies a *preacher:* for if things will 'travel beyond their road, and must needs 'be defining things beyond their sphere or 'reach, they become extravagant and saucy.'

CONCERNING *unlearned* mens *wresting the holy Scriptures*, it may be proper to consider in what sense they are *unlearned*; for men may be learned or unlearned in divers respects. A man may be learned in *arithmetic*, that is unlearned in *logic*; or he may be learned in *grammar*, and unlearned in *geometry*; and learned in *philosophy*, though unlearned in *divinity*. For if a man should attain to some perfection in the seven liberal arts and sciences[d],

[d] *Grammar, Logic, Rhetoric, Music, Arithmetic, Geometry, Astronomy.*

and besides these should gain the knowledge of several languages, and be a proficient in moral and natural philosophy, these would be rare accomplishments, make him a lovely man, useful, and set him in a station above his fellows; but yet he might be ignorant in the things of God, and consequently an *unlearned* man in the account of St. *Peter*. For all that wisdom is no more than St. *Paul* speaks of, even *the wisdom of this world*. Therefore a great *scholar* in secular or human *learning* may possibly be *unlearned* in *divinity*, yea, tho' he can read *Greek* and *Hebrew*.

THE reverend bishop *Taylor* observed, that *Hebrew* and *Greek* scholars are not blessed with an assured knowledge of divine truth, above such as can only read the Scriptures in *Latin* and *English*. 'For 'says he [e], I know no man that says, that 'the *Scriptures* in *Hebrew* and *Greek* are 'easy and certain to be understood, and 'that they are hard in *Latin* and *English*. 'The difficulty is in the thing, however it 'be expressed; the least is in the *language*. 'If the *original* languages were our mother-tongue, *Scripture* is not much the 'easier to us; and a natural *Greek* or a '*Jew*, can with no more reason or authority obtrude his interpretations upon other 'mens *consciences*, than a man of another 'nation.'

[e] *Polemic. Disc.* p. 974. Hook's *Apol.* p. 59.

IT

It is to be feared, too many, by their plausible deportments, and the favour of their friends, get into *orders*, and profess to be *ministers* of Christ, before they believe in him, or love him, or have any good-will to his interest; who must be acknowledged *scholars*, but yet *unlearned*, that is, better acquainted with the writings of *Aristotle* than the epistles of St. *Paul*; learned in *philosophy*, but unlearned in *divinity*; learned in *languages*, *arts* and *sciences*, but unlearned in the *Scriptures* of truth. And such as these are like enough to *wrest the Holy Scriptures, to their* own and other mens *hurt*. *Tertullian* observed long ago, that *philosophers* have been the chief fathers of *hereticks*. And a learned bishop of the church of *England* [f], who wrote upon the knowledge of the tongues, says, 'There 'hath not been a greater *plague* to the 'christian religion, than *school* divinity; 'where men take upon them the liberty 'to propose new questions, make nice di-'stinctions, and rash conclusions of divine 'matters, tossing them up and down with 'their tongues like *tennis* balls. And from 'hence proceeded all the dangerous *here-'sies*, and cruel bickerings about them, 'falling from words to blows. The first '*divinity* school we read of, was set up 'at *Alexandria*, by *Pantænus*, and from

[f] *Naked truth*, p. 5, 6. Keach's *Parables*, *Preface*.

'thence ſoon after ſprang up that damnable *hereſy* of the *Arians*, which overrun all chriſtendom, and was the cauſe of the deſtruction of ſo many millions of chriſtians, both of body and ſoul, which before this were ſo groſs and ſenſual, that none took them up but diſſolute or frantick people, and ſoon vaniſhed. But after this ſchool, ſubtle way of arguing was brought into chriſtianity, *hereſy* grew more refined, and ſo ſubtle, that the plain and pious *fathers* of the church knew not how to lay hold of it, the ſchool diſtinctions and evaſions baffled them, and ſo thoſe *ſophiſters*, proud of their conqueſt, triumphed, and carried away a ſpecious appearance of truth as well as *learning*, or rather *cunning*, inſomuch, that many godly perſons were deluded, and fell into them; and many of their *hereſies* continue unto this day.'

LET men therefore take heed how they cry up man's wiſdom. The knowledge of the tongues none will or can deny to be uſeful; but it is that ſtreſs which is by ſome laid upon it, rendring it eſſential to a *miniſter*, that gives the offence. So then, we acknowledge this kind of *literature* is good, as a hand-maid, *Hagar* like; but if it muſt needs be *miſtreſs*, and uſurp *authority* in the family, if, like ſcoffing *Iſhmael*, it will mock at the ſpirit and the ſimplicity of the goſpel, let it be caſt out.

I SHALL

I SHALL now give a brief account of ſome of the *Baptiſt* miniſters who lived in the times to which the preceding hiſtory refers, whereby it will appear, that men of the greateſt *learning* and *piety*, have neither been aſhamed nor afraid in the worſt of times to ſtand up in vindication of a principle truly *apoſtolical*, though ever ſo much deſpiſed and hated. Mr. *John Smith*, of whom mention is made in the foregoing hiſtory, was a divine of the church of *England*, and did in the former part of the reign of King *James* I. embrace the opinion of the *Baptiſts*. I can find no account of him but from his enemies [g]; and yet they acknowledge he was a man of right eminent parts. He began firſt with a diſlike of the ceremonies of the church, and the uſe of preſcribed forms of prayer; and on this occaſion had a diſpute with Mr. *Hilderſham* and others; but his diſſatisfaction ſtill remaining, and having publiſhed ſomething againſt theſe things, he was forced to fly out of the land, to eſcape the ſeverity of the *perſecution* then in *England*. And ſo well was he beloved and reſpected by thoſe that were inclined to nonconformity, that a great company followed him out of their native country to *Leyden* in *Holland*.

John Smith.

HERE he at firſt joined himſelf with the *Engliſh* congregation, who were called

[g] Baylie's *Diſſuaſive*, p. 15.

Browniſts;

Brownists, and his *piety* and *learning* ſoon procured him the reputation of being one of the *grandees* of the ſeparation [h].

BUT being now more zealouſly ſet to ſearch out the truth, and in a country where he might ſafely divulge his *opinions*, he quickly after declared againſt ſeveral of the *principles* and *practices* of the *Browniſts*, and among the reſt that of their *baptizing infants*. This expoſed him to the hatred and cenſures of his brethren of the ſeparation. And though they were in exile themſelves, for the liberty of their conſciences, yet they could not, with that charity and moderation as they ought, bear that others ſhould differ from them: they caſt him out of the church for his errors, with all that adhered to him. They repreſented him to be one that had proclaimed war againſt God's everlaſting covenant, and a murderer of the ſouls of babes and ſucklings, by depriving them of the viſible ſeal of ſalvation. They publiſhed ſeveral books againſt him; wherein they endeavoured to expoſe both him and his opinions to the world. Two were written againſt him by Mr. *Ainſworth*, elder of the church which caſt him out; one was publiſhed againſt him by Mr. *Johnſon*, paſtor of the antient *Engliſh* church at *Amſterdam*; and another by Mr. *Robinſon*, mi-

[h] Pagit's *Hereſiography*, p. 62.

nifter of the *Engliſh* congregation at *Leyden*; with ſome others.

IN theſe they lay ſeveral groſs things to his charge. As that he was againſt reading the Scriptures in publick worſhip; that he would not allow any tranſlation to be the word of God, but the original only; that he *baptized himſelf*, ſuppoſing there was then no right *adminiſtrator* in being. They call him a man of a wolfiſh nature; one whom God had ſtruck with blindneſs; a brute beaſt, and the like, as hath been before obſerved.

BUT it is to be obſerved, that at the ſame time that they accuſe him after this manner, they are forced to acknowledge that he was more refined than the common ſorts of the *Anabaptiſts*, and that he did not go with that heretical ſect. Nay more, that he had ſuch a diſlike and averſion to their groſs errors, that his conſcience would not permit him to be re-baptized by any of them. And if, according to their accuſation, which, as I have ſhewn, is very unlikely, he *baptized himſelf*, it was this that led him to it. The *Engliſh* refugees were ſuch, as in his opinion had no true *baptiſm* themſelves, having only been ſprinkled in their *infancy*; and the foreign *Anabaptiſts* were ſuch as denied Chriſt's having taken fleſh of the virgin *Mary*, the lawfulneſs of *magiſtracy*, and the like, which he and his followers looked upon as very great

great *errors*. So that neither the *one* nor the *other* could be thought by him to be proper *adminiſtrators* of *baptiſm*.

HOWEVER it was, Mr. *Smith*'s opinions prevailed much, eſpecially, that of baptizing *believers* only; and he ſoon had *proſelytes* enough to form a diſtinct *church* of that *perſuaſion*, even among the *Engliſh* exiles.

Mr. Tho. Helwiſſe, *Mr.* John Moreton.

He baptized two *miniſters*, who after his deceaſe came into *England*, brought ſeveral of his congregation with them, and very much promoted this opinion at *London* both by their preaching and writings.

HE writ ſeveral treatiſes, which are not now to be met with; as *The Character of the Beaſt*; *A Dialogue of Baptiſm*; his *Differences with the Brethren of the Antient Separation*; and his *Reply to Mr.* Clifford'*s Chriſtian Plea*.

THE time of his death does not appear: but by a book written by Mr. *Robinſon* in the year 1614. it appears he was then dead, and that a great part of his congregation were returned into *England*, with the aforeſaid perſons.

IN which book mention is made of a a *confeſſion* of *faith*, which I have put in the *appendix*, No IV. publiſhed by the remainder of Mr. *Smith*'s church after his death. This was publiſhed in the year 1611. ſo that its probable he died in *exile* about the year 1610.

THE

THE order of time leads me to give some account of Mr. *Tho. Helwisse*. He had not, as the former, the advantage of a learned education, but appears by his writings to have been a man of good natural parts, and not without some acquired. *Mr.* Tho. Helwisse.

THE first thing we meet with concerning him is, that he was a member of the antient church of *Separatists*, which had been founded at the establishment of the Reformation in the beginning of Queen *Elizabeth*'s reign; and was very serviceable to that people when they transported themselves out of *England* into *Holland*, to escape *persecution* [i].

WHILE he continued among them, which was some time, he was esteemed a man of eminent faith, charity and spiritual gifts. But when Mr. *Smith* had occasioned the controversy about *infants baptism* to be revived among them, he was one of those who was convinced of the invalidity and unlawfulness of such *baptisms*, and was accordingly excommunicated with the rest of that persuasion [k].

HE received his baptism from Mr. *Smith*, and was one of the first in the constitution of his church, and after his death had the care of that people committed to him. He did not go on with the same comfort and *Baptized by Mr.* Smith.

[i] Robinson *of Com.* p. 41.
[k] Johnson's *Enquiry*, p. 63.

success

ſucceſs as Mr. *Smith* had done; yet they who upbraided him on this account, did at the ſame time acknowledge [l], that his preaching and writings had made ſome *proſelytes* to his opinions, and occaſioned them to reject their *infant* baptiſm.

Is oppoſed by the Browniſts.

THE chief oppoſers of Mr. *Helwiſſe* and his church were the *Browniſts*; from whom they had ſeparated. Theſe people writ againſt them with great warmth, and called them *Hereticks*, *Anabaptiſts*, *Freewillers*, &c. and yet, in the ſame writings, they made ſeveral conceſſions in their favour, which cleared them from thoſe extravagant opinions which ſome held who went under thoſe names.

FOR they acknowledge, that Mr. *Helwiſſe* and his people diſclaimed free-will, or power in a man's ſelf to work out his own ſalvation: That though they excluded *infants* from *baptiſm*, and from being members of the viſible church, yet they were ſo charitable, as to believe that all *infants*, dying before they had committed actual ſin, were ſaved: That they held an election of certain perſons to eternal life, upon the foreſight of faith and holineſs; and agreed with the *Browniſts* in the main truths of the goſpel. And as to their furniture and morals, they ſay, they were ſuch as had come to ſome degree of knowledge and godlineſs: that they had a *zeal for God*, tho' in their

l Robinſon *of Com.* p.48.

opinion

opinion, *not according to knowledge*; and that when they found a perſon in their communion guilty of ſin, they proceeded to cenſure him for it [m].

ONE would think that a *people* of whom all this could be ſaid, ſhould have met with better treatment and more kind uſage than they did, tho' they might differ from their *brethren* in ſome leſſer points of religion.

A LITTLE after Mr. *Smith*'s death, Mr. *Helwiſſe* and his people publiſhed a confeſſion of their faith. This, if it could be met with, would give us a true account of their opinions. It was ſuppoſed to have been chiefly drawn up by Mr. *Smith* himſelf, before his deceaſe; but it was called, *The Confeſſion of Faith, publiſhed in certain concluſions, by the remainder of Mr.* Smith'*s company*, and came out in the year 1611. At the end of it there was an *appendix*, giving ſome account of Mr. *Smith*'s laſt ſickneſs and death. *Publiſhes a confeſſion of faith.*

MR. *Robinſon*, the paſtor of an *Engliſh* congregation of *Browniſts* at *Leyden*, publiſhed three years after, his *Remarks* upon it; and has therein collected thoſe paſſages which were thought the moſt obſcure or erronious in it.

ABOUT the ſame time alſo Mr. *Helwiſſe* began to reflect upon his own conduct, and that of the other *Engliſh* diſſenters, in leaving their own country and

[m] Robinſon *of communion*, p. 73, &c.

friends,

friends, and flying into a ſtrange land to eſcape perſecution: whether this did not proceed from fear and cowardice; and whether they ought not rather to return, that they might bear a teſtimony for the truth, in their own land, where it was in danger of being wholly extinguiſhed; and that they might alſo encourage and comfort their brethren who were there ſuffering *perſecution* for Chriſt's ſake. The concluſion of this was, that he and his church quickly left *Amſterdam*, and removed to *London*; where they continued their church ſtate, and aſſemblies for worſhip, as publickly as the evil of the times would permit. And to juſtify this conduct, he wrote a treatiſe, entitled, *A Short Declaration*, &c. wherein he endeavours to ſhew in what caſes it was unlawful to fly in times of *perſecution.*

Leaves Holland, *and with ſome others comes to* London.

BUT this greatly provok'd his *brethren* the *Nonconformiſts* in exile. They aſcribed it to his natural confidence under the appearance of ſpiritual courage. They cenſured it as vain glory, ſo to challenge the king and ſtate to their faces, and call it avowing wilful perſecution; and Mr. *Robinſon* writ an anſwer to him, from whence this account is collected.

Publiſhes a treatiſe, entitled, Perſecution judged and condemned.

IN the year 1615. Mr. *Helwiſſe* and his church at *London*, publiſhed a treatiſe, entitled, *Perſecution for Religion judged and condemned.* 'Tis true, there is no author's name

name to it. But at the end of the *Epiſtle Dedicatory* inſtead of names, it is ſubſcribed thus, *By Chriſt's unworthy witneſſes, his Majeſty's faithful ſubjects, commonly, but moſt falſly, called Anabaptiſts.* But it appears to be theirs, becauſe towards the end of the book, to clear themſelves from thoſe groſs errors held by ſome *Anabaptiſts*, and to prove their *orthodoxy* in the point of Chriſt's incarnation, the lawfulneſs of magiſtracy, *&c.* they refer the reader to the *confeſſion of faith* beforementioned, printed four years before this, and call it *their confeſſion.*

IN this, beſides their expoſing, by ſeveral excellent arguments, the great ſin of *perſecution*, they take the opportunity of clearing themſelves of ſeveral falſe charges caſt upon them, and of making known ſome of their chief opinions. They reject the *baptiſm* of *infants*, as being a practice that has no foundation in Scripture; and all *baptiſm* received either in the church of *Rome* or *England*, they looked upon to be invalid, becauſe received in a falſe church, and from *antichriſtian miniſters.*

THEY aſſert, that every man has a right to judge for himſelf in matters of religion; and that to perſecute any on that account, is illegal and antichriſtian.

THEY acknowledge *magiſtracy* to be God's *ordinance*, and that kings, and ſuch as are in authority, ought to be obeyed in

T all

all civil matters, not only for fear, but alſo for conſcience ſake.

THEY allow the taking of an *oath* to be lawful: and declare, that all of their profeſſion were willing in faithfulneſs and truth to ſubſcribe the oath of allegiance.

THEY proteſt againſt that doctrine of the *Papiſts*, that princes excommunicated by the *pope* may be depoſed or murdered by their ſubjects; calling it a *damnable* and *curſed* doctrine, which their ſouls abhor; and alſo againſt the error of the *Familiſts*, who, to avoid *perſecution*, can comply with any external form of religion.

THEY own, that ſome called *Anabaptiſts* held ſeveral ſtrange opinions contrary to them; and endeavour to clear themſelves from deſerving any cenſure on that account, by ſhewing, that it was ſo in ſome of the primitive churches: as ſome in the church of *Corinth* denied the reſurrection of the dead; ſome in the church at *Pergamos* held the doctrine of the *Nicolaitans*; and yet Chriſt and his apoſtles did not condemn all for the errors of ſome. But that which they chiefly inveigh againſt, is the pride, luxury, and oppreſſion of the *lordly* biſhops, and the pretended ſpiritual power, by which, they ſay, many were expoſed to confiſcation of goods, long and lingering impriſonments, hanging, burning, and baniſhment.

How

HOW long Mr. *Helwiſſe* lived, and continued the elder of this church of *Baptiſts* at *London*, I cannot find. The books wrote againſt them about this time ſhew, that they went on with great courage and reſolution; and notwithſtanding the ſeverities uſed againſt them by the civil power, increaſed very much in their numbers.

ONE *author*, to prove their doctrines plain and eaſy to be underſtood, particularly that of *Baptiſm*, ſays, [n] 'witneſs the 'multitude of their diſciples.' And when the famous *Dod* and *Cleaver* united their forces, to confute their ſuppoſed *error*, they apologized for their attempt, alledging, that the people of this perſuaſion took great pains to propagate their doctrine; and that divers perſons of good note for piety had been prevailed upon by them, as has been before obſerved.

AMONG their other *proſelytes* about this time, there was one at *London*, who being ſeverely reflected upon for his leaving the church of *England*, and joining with ſuch an heretical people, as they were then eſteemed, wrote a letter to inform his relations of his real opinion, and what he had to offer in defence of it. This letter falling into the hands of a zealous ſon of the church, before it came to the perſons intended, he immediately publiſhed it, with an anſwer to it. He ſays it was in-

[n] *Anabaptiſm unmaſked, by* J. P. p. 61.

dited by a principal elder of that ſeparation; and if ſo, in all probability Mr. *Helwiſſe* was the *author* of it. It bears date at *London* the 10th of *May* 1622. and contains in a little compaſs, the ſtate of this controverſy. The ſpirit and management of the *Baptiſts* in thoſe times, is very well repreſented by it, as you may ſee by turn-back to *page* 133. of this *hiſtory*, where the ſame is recited.

Mr. John Morton.

Mr. *John Morton* was another of Mr. *Smith*'s diſciples, and contemporary with Mr. *Helwiſſe*. I can find but very little concerning him.

IN the *preface* to the two publick diſputations, about *infant-baptiſm*, between Dr. *Gunning* and Mr. *Denn*, I find, after Mr. *Denn* had mentioned ſeveral *authors* who had written in defence of *infant-baptiſm*, he adds 'Have we not had alſo 'many who have laboured not a little on 'the oppoſite party, and both by their 'pens and ſufferings teſtified againſt the '*baptiſm* of *infants*? As *Morton*, with ſome 'others contemporary, the miniſters of '*Tranſilvania*, and ſince of later years '*Blackwell*, *Tombes*, *Cornwall*, *Fiſher*, *Lamb* 'ſenior, *Lamb* junior, *Writer*, *Haggar*, 'with many others.' So that this *Morton*, who lived before the civil wars, did both write and ſuffer for the cauſe of the *Baptiſts*; though a particular account of theſe things cannot now be obtained.

ALTHOUGH

ALTHOUGH this man might after his return from *Holland*, ſtay ſome time at *London* with Mr. *Helwiſſe* and his church; yet there appears a probability of his ſetling afterwards in the country, and preaching to ſome people there: for at the beginning of the civil wars, when they were demoliſhing an old *wall* near *Colcheſter*, there was found hid in it the copy of a book, written by *J. Morton*, ſuppoſed to be the ſame perſon.

THE *General Baptiſts* were very fond of it, ſoon got it printed, and it has ſince received ſeveral impreſſions.

THE *author* of this book appears to have been a man of conſiderable learning and parts, one that underſtood the *oriental* languages, and was acquainted with the writings of the *fathers*, but a very zealous *Remonſtrant* or *Arminian*. It is entitled, *Truth's Champion*; and contains thirteen chapters on the following heads:

1. THAT Chriſt died for all men.
2. OF his dying for all, to ſave all.
3. OF his power given out to all.
4. OF predeſtination.
5. OF election.
6. OF free-will.
7. OF falling away.
8. OF original ſin.
9. OF baptizing, or baptiſm.
10. OF the miniſtry.
11. OF love.

12. OF thoſe that hold that God hath appointed or deſtinated unavoidably all the actions of men, and the ſad effects that follow.

13. OF the man *Adam*, and of the man Chriſt; with anſwer to divers objections on the ſame.

IT is written in a very good ſtile, and the arguments are managed with a great deal of art and ſkill; ſo that thoſe who follow the *Remonſtrants* ſcheme of doctrines, do not value it without a cauſe.

BUT leaving this *Gentleman*, let us come to thoſe times that are nearer us, in which we may have a more particular account of the chief perſons of this perſuaſion; and we ſhall find, that as *knowledge* and *liberty* has increaſed, ſo there have been ſtill men of greater learning and reputation, who have embraced the *opinion* of the *Baptiſts*.

Mr. John Tombes.

MR. *John Tombes*, B. D. did about the beginning of the civil wars embrace this *opinion*; and by his learned writings promoted it more than any one man of thoſe times.

HE was born at *Bewdly* in *Worceſterſhire*, in the year of our Lord 1603, and his parents deſigning him for the ſacred function of the miniſtry, took care to have him timely inſtructed at the grammar-ſchool; where he proved ſo good a proficient, that at fifteen years of agė he was found

found fit for the *University*, and accordingly was then sent to *Oxford*, and educated in *Magdalen-hall*, under the famous Mr. *William Pemble*, author of *Vindiciæ Gratiæ*, and several other learned treatises.

HERE, by his good genius, his diligent studies, and the advantage of such an accomplished tutor, his improvements were uncommon, and he quickly gained the reputation of a person of incomparable parts and learning; and therefore, upon the decease of his tutor, which happened in 1624. he was chosen to succeed him in the catechetical lecture in this hall, when he was yet but twenty one years of age, and of six years standing in the university. But notwithstanding this, he approved himself an excellent disputant, and good divine, upon the principles of the Anti-remonstrants.

Is chosen catechetical lecturer at Magdalen-hall, Oxford.

HE held this lecture about seven years, and then left *Oxford*, and went to *Worcester*, and after that to *Lemster* in *Herefordshire*; at both which places he made himself very popular by his preaching. I do not find that he had any settlement in the former of these places; only was very famous in that city, about the year 1630. for his having a more powerful way of preaching than ordinary. But he was possessed of the living at *Lemster*, and enjoyed it several years. This, though a large parish, yet was but a poor cure, such as would hardly afford him a maintenance, and what some

Leaves Oxford.

Obtains the living at Lemster.

thought much below his merit. But the Lord Viscount *Scudamore*, who had a great respect for him, was pleased to make some addition to it, of which Mr. *Tombes* made a thankful acknowledgment in the first book that he published [o]. He was among the first of the clergy of those times, who endeavoured a reformation in the church, and the purging out of all human inventions in the worship of God; and while he continued in this parish, preached an excellent sermon on that subject, which was afterward printed by an order of the House of Commons. But this exposed him to the rage of the church party; and therefore at the very beginning of the civil wars, some of the king's forces coming into that country, he was in 1641. drove from his habitation, and plundered of almost all he had in the world [p].

Is plundered there.

Goes to Bristol.

UPON this he fled to *Bristol*, which was in the parliament's possession; and general *Fiennes*, who then had the command of that city, gave him the living of *All-Saints* there, in consideration of his great losses.

HE had not been there above a year, before the city was besieg'd by prince *Rupert* and his army, and a plot formed by their friends within, to deliver up the city, to burn the houses, and *massacre* the inhabitants.

[o] *Christ. Com. against scandalizers*, 1641

[p] *Præcursor*, p. 25.

bitants. But this was very ſeaſonably diſcovered and prevented. Mr. *Tombes* on the day of publick thankſgiving obſerved by the city on this occaſion, preached two very ſuitable ſermons, and drew a ſhort account of this bloody plot, and the happy means of its being prevented; which with the ſermons was ſent up to *London*, and printed by an order of parliament.

BUT this had like to have coſt him dear. For the next year following, the city was taken by the king's party, his wife and children again plundered, and a ſpecial warrant out for the apprehending of him; ſo that it was with great difficulty, and by a ſpecial providence of God, that he eſcaped, and got ſafe to *London* with his wife and children, on *Sept*. 22. 1643 [q].

Is plundered again, eſcapes to London.

WHEN he had been a little time at *London*, and acquainted himſelf with ſeveral miniſters, who were now come from all parts, to form the aſſembly of divines at *Weſtminſter*, he took opportunity to divulge to them his ſcruples concerning *infant-baptiſm*. It appears, he had entertained ſome doubts about this practice very early; for in the year 1627. when he was lecturer at *Magdalen-hall* in *Oxford*, being led by the courſe of theſe lectures to examine this point, he then diſcovered the inſufficiency of all the common arguments uſually brought

Divulges his ſcruples about infant-baptiſm.

[q] *Apology*, p. 7

to

to juſtify that practice; and reſted wholly
1 Cor. vii. 14. upon thoſe words of the *apoſtle*, *Elſe were your children unclean, but now are they holy.* And when he held the living at *Lemſter*, which obliged him to practiſe the *baptizing* of *infants*, he declares this was the only ſcripture that he built upon; and frequently told his *auditors*, that that text was the only warrant for it.

[r] BUT when he was at *Briſtol*, he met with an ingenious *Baptiſt*, who, in a diſpute with him, did ſo fully anſwer his argument from that only *text*, as put him to a ſtand. He would not raſhly and all at once, caſt off an opinion and practice ſo univerſally received; and yet, as a man that durſt not oppoſe the truth, whoever brought it, he reſolved to conſider the matter more fully, and that if ever he came to *London*, where he ſhould have a greater advantage both of men and books, he would more ſtrictly examine the hiſtory of *Pædobaptiſm*, and conſult his brethren of the aſſembly about this matter.

BEING therefore now come to *London*, he put his reſolution into practice, by reading *Voſſius*'s *Theſes de Pædobaptiſmo*; and examining the antient teſtimonies therein, he found, that in point of *antiquity*, the matter was not ſo clear as he had taken it to be; that *infant-baptiſm* began firſt to be

[r] *Apology*, p. 6.

practiſed

practised in cases of *supposed necessity* only, conceiving that it conferred grace, and saved all that received it, and that afterwards it grew to be the ordinary practice. And as to the holiness of *believers* children, that only *text* he had so long hung upon, he thought that no *protestants* of learning had expounded it of *legitimation*; but meeting with *Camerarius*'s notes, then newly printed at *Cambridge*, and afterwards with *Musculus*, *Melancthon*, and *Beza*, who were all of that *opinion*, and prove by good arguments, that this must be the *apostle*'s meaning, and that no other sense is suitable to the case he was there resolving; he thereupon became fully satisfied, that *infant-baptism* was without any real foundation, either from *scripture* or *antiquity*.

Consults some divines thereupon.

[s] HOWEVER, he still resolved to consult the most learned of his *brethren*, and hear the utmost that could be said on the other side; and accordingly there was a meeting of the *London* ministers in *January* 1643. The great Dr. *Holmes*, Mr. *Marshal*, Mr. *Blake*, and Mr. *Hen. Scudder*, are particularly mentioned as present at it.

THE question proposed was, what *scripture* there was for *infant-baptism*? Mr. *Tombes* told them plainly, he doubted there was none. The place they chiefly insisted

[s] *Apology*, p. 8.

upon

upon was *Mat.* xix. 14. *For of ſuch is the kingdom of heaven.* But this he ſhewed them was on many accounts inſufficient for that purpoſe.

Is miſrepreſented by them.

THE whole iſſued without any ſatisfaction to Mr. *Tombes:* and he complained that ſeveral of them did afterwards miſrepreſent him, as to what then paſſed.

THE *aſſembly* of divines were now ſitting at *Weſtminſter*, and had declared, that their deſign was to reform religion, in *England* and *Scotland*, according to the word of God, and the example of the beſt reformed churches. And Mr. *Tombes* was alſo informed, by one of that *aſſembly*, that they had appointed a *committee* to conſider the point of *infant-baptiſm.*

Delivers his reaſons to the committee.

WHEREUPON he drew up in *Latin*, the chief reaſons of his doubting the lawfulneſs of that practice, and ſent them to Mr. *Whittaker* the chairman of that *committee*; hoping that an *aſſembly* of ſuch grave and learned *divines* would either anſwer the ſcruples of a *brother* in the miniſtry; or, if they appeared to be juſtly founded, that they would according to their profeſſions and covenant, endeavour to reform this abuſe of the *ordinance* of *baptiſm.*

But receives no anſwer.

HE waited many months, but could get no anſwer, or hear that the *point* was ſo much as admitted to a debate in the *aſſembly*. Inſtead of that, he found that ſome of the *aſſembly*, both by *ſermons* and *pamphlets*

phlets, endeavoured to render odious to the people those that should deny *baptism* to *infants*; that they passed a vote, tending to explode, if not censure, any that should but dispute against it; and that instead of considering his arguments impartially, his papers were tossed up and down from one to another, in order to expose him [t].

BUT that which was still worse, being now *minister* of *Fenchurch* in *London*, care was taken to prejudice his parishioners against him, under the notion of his being an *Anabaptist*. Though he medled not with any thing of this matter in the *pulpit*, they refused to come and hear him, and resolved at the expiration of the year, to withold his maintenance from him. It happened, just after his *stipend* was taken away at *Fenchurch*, for not practising the *baptism* of *infants*, that the honourable societies of the *Temple* wanted a preacher; whereupon some who knew Mr. *Tombes* to be a man of great learning, and an excellent preacher, sollicited for the bringing of him thither. This was at length obtained for him; but not without great difficulty, and a promise that he would not meddle with the controversy about *infant-baptism* in the pulpit. Which promise he made; but upon these two conditions: That no one did preach for the *bap-*

His maintenance witheld from him.

He is chosen by the templers.

[t] *Apology*, p. 9, 10.

tizing

tizing of infants in his pulpit; and that no laws were likely to be enacted, to make the denial of *infant-baptiſm* penal.

And diſmiſſed from them.

[u] HE continued in this place about four years; and then was diſmiſſed, for publiſhing his firſt *Treatiſe* againſt *infant-baptiſm*; which contained his objections againſt that practice, before ſent to the *aſſembly* of divines, and his *examen* of Mr. *Marſhal's* ſermon on *infant-baptiſm*.

FOR this he was cenſured as a man of a reſtleſs ſpirit, and one that had a mind to encreaſe the diviſions and confuſions of the times; and others repreſented it as a breach of his promiſe of ſilence in this matter. But in his *apology* he clears himſelf very handſomely from all theſe charges; and ſhews, that he had ſuch provocations, as made his publiſhing of this both *juſt* and *neceſſary*. He had waited nine months for the *aſſembly's* anſwer to his doubts; but inſtead of receiving any, his papers were handed about, and by ſome publickly expoſed in their pulpits.

WHEN he had long ſollicited Mr. *Marſhal's* anſwer to the remarks he had made upon his ſermon, the beſt return he could get was, that ſince he had a *place* for his miniſtry, without *baptizing* of *infants*, he expected him to be quiet.

[u] *Præcurſor*, p. 25.

WHEN

WHEN he wanted the *aſſembly*'s approbation of him as a *miniſter*, he was told by the *examiner*, that there were many of the *aſſembly* that did ſcruple in conſcience the giving approbation to him, becauſe of his *opinion*. He was alſo informed, that in *New England* there was a law made, and ſome proceedings thereupon, againſt thoſe that denied the *baptiſm* of *infants*: That here in *England*, the *directory*, which enjoins the *baptizing* of *infants*, was publiſhed with an *ordinance* of parliament, to make the not uſing of it *penal*; and that many godly, learned, and prudent perſons, both of thoſe that differed from him, as well as of thoſe that agreed with him in this *point*, earneſtly requeſted the publiſhing of his papers. And from theſe conſiderations he ſays, [k] he thought himſelf obliged to it, both in *faithfulneſs* to God, and in *charity* to men.

BUT all this could not ſave him from being turned out of the *Temple*. See his *apology*, printed in the year 1646. of which Mr. *John Bachiler* ſays: 'Having peruſed this mild *apology*, I conceive that the ingenuity, learning, and piety, therein contained, deſerve the preſs.'

AFTER this, the people of *Bewdly* in *Worceſterſhire*, the town of his nativity, choſe him for their miniſter. And now he be- *He is choſen miniſter of* Bewdly.

[k] *Apology*, p. 15.

gan

gan to preach and diſpute publickly againſt *infant-baptiſm*, and to put his opinion into practice, being baptized by *immerſion*, on a perſonal profeſſion of faith. And ſeeing no proſpect of any reformation in the eſtabliſhed church in this *point*, he there gathered a *ſeparate* church of thoſe of his own *perſuaſion*, continuing at the ſame time miniſter of the pariſh[y].

And gathers a church of Baptiſts there.

HIS ſociety of *Baptiſts* was not very large, but conſiſted of ſuch who were of good eſteem for their piety and ſolid judgment; and three eminent miniſters of that perſuaſion were trained up in it, *viz.* Mr. *Richard Adams*, Mr. *John Eccles*, and one Capt. *Boylſton*; and it continued till about the time of the king's reſtoration.

BESIDES his living at *Bewdly*, which was made ſmall by the ſtate's ſelling the lands belonging to the dean and chapter of *Worceſter*, from whence great part of his income aroſe, he had the parſonage of *Roſſe* given him. There was a vicar endowed there; but the rectory and parſonage-houſe being leaſed out, they beſtowed the rent upon him, expecting him only to preach there now and then as he could.

The maſterſhip of the hoſpital at Ledbury *given to him.*

SOMETIME after, the maſterſhip of the hoſpital in *Ledbury* was beſtowed upon him, upon which he gave up his intereſt at *Roſſe*; and when the affections of the

[y] Fiſher. Baby. *Bap.* p. 417.

people

people at *Bewdley* were alienated from him, becaufe of his different opinion concerning *baptifm*, he was reftored to his firft living at *Lemfter*. This variety of places occafioned fome of his opponents, through miftake, to accufe him of holding *pluralities*; a thing that he abhorred, and from which he publickly cleared himfelf [z]. The two latter, which are both in *Herefordfhire*, he held indeed till the reftoration; but then the mafterfhip of the hofpital did not oblige him to the cure of fouls.

Is reftored to his living at Lemfter.

IN the year 1653. as there was fome alteration made in the form of the *civil* government, fo there was likewife in the *ecclefiaftical*. A certain number of men were authorized to examine and approve all fuch as fhould be allowed the publick exercife of the miniftry, and were therefore called *Tryers*. Mr. *Tombes* being known to be a perfon as well qualified for fuch a poft, as moft men then in *England*, was, notwithftanding his different opinion, appointed to be one of them. And among other good effects that followed hereupon, this was one, *viz.* the commiffioners agreed to own the *Baptifts* as their *brethren*, and that if any fuch applied to them for probation, and appeared in other refpects to be duly qualified, they fhould not be rejected for holding this *opinion* [a]. And hence

Is made one of the Tryers.

[z] *Præcurfor*, p. 26.

[a] Woodward's *corruption corrected*, p. 4.

it came to paſs, that at the *reſtoration* ſeveral pariſhes were found to have *Baptiſt* miniſters fixed in them.

THE reputation that Mr. *Tombes* had of being a great ſcholar, and a perfect maſter in controverſy, occaſioned his being frequently drawn into publick diſputations, and of writing upon moſt controverſies that prevailed in his time; but his chief ſubject was about *infant-baptiſm*, againſt which practice he has writ more books than any one man in *England*.

Has ſeveral publick diſputes with the Pædobaptiſts.

HE alſo held ſeveral publick diſputes againſt it: One with Mr. *Baxter* at *Bewdly*; another with Mr. *Tirer* and Mr. *Smith* at *Roſſe*; a third with Mr. *Cragg* and Mr. *Vaughn* at *Abergavenny*; and a fourth at *Hereford*. And many who were far enough from approving his opinion, acknowledged he had the advantage of his opponents, both as to learning and argument [b].

UPON the reſtoration of King *Charles* II. he readily fell in with *monarchical* government, and writ a treatiſe the ſame year to juſtify and encourage the taking the *oath* of *ſupremacy*. But a little after, when he found the ſpirit of *perſecution* again revived, and the former government and ceremonies of the church impoſed; he not only quitted his places, but laid down the *miniſtry* alſo, and having not long before married

He quits his places, and laid down his miniſtry.

[b] Nelſon's *life of biſhop* Bull, p. 251.

married a rich widow at *Salisbury*, by whom he enjoyed a good estate, he was resolved to live at rest and peace in his old age.

HE conformed to the church afterwards, its true, as a *lay communicant*, and writ a *treatise* to prove the lawfulness of so doing; nevertheless he continued in his judgment as much a *Baptist* as ever, and publickly defended that *opinion* afterward. Nor could he be prevailed upon to accept any benefice or dignity in the church, though it was offered to him, and by such as were able to have preferred him very high, for he was well beloved by several great men both in church and state.

THE earl of *Clarendon* took an opportunity soon after the restoration to speak to his majesty in his favour, and gave a great character of him from his own knowledge: by which means he was protected from having any trouble given him for any thing he had written or acted during the *rebellion*. And when he published his book of *oaths*, which was dedicated to the king, the same noble peer being then Lord Chancellor, introduced him to present it into his majesty's own hand [c]. *Was very much esteemed.*

THE learned and judicious bishop *Sanderson* had a great esteem for him; as had also one of his successors, bishop *Barlow*; and living chiefly at *Salisbury* the latter part of his life, he was observed to make

[c] *Saints no Smiters.*

frequent visits to Dr. *Ward*, bishop of that place, who respected him very much for his great learning. And at this town it was that he died, *May* 25. 1676. being seventy three years of age.

Some Pædobaptists *testimonies of his character.*

THE character that is given of this great man, by those who have zealously opposed his particular *opinion*, and so cannot be suspected of any partiality, is sufficient to convince the world that he was a person of extraordinary abilities.

MR. *Baxter*, who was personally engaged to dispute and write against him, calls him the chief of the *Anabaptists*; and says, he was the greatest and most learned writer against *infant-baptism* [c]. And though in the warmth of disputation, he published some unhandsome things against him, when he grew cooler, he professed himself heartily sorry, and publickly asked pardon both of God and Mr. *Tombes* [d].

MR. *Wood*, the *Oxford* biographer, says [e], 'That there were few better disputants in 'his age than he was.' Mr. *Nelson*, that zealous churchman, says [f], 'It cannot be 'denied, but that he was esteemed a per- 'son of incomparable parts.' And a little further: '*Tombes* was the head of the '*Anabaptists*, and *Baxter* of the *Presby-* '*terians*. The victory, as it is usual, was

[c] *Life*, *Append.* p. 72. 80.
[d] *Confirmation*, p. 256.
[e] *Life*, *Append.* p. 58. *Ath. Oxon.*
[f] *Life of bishop* Bull, p. 249, 251.

'claimed

'claimed by both ſides, but ſome of the 'learned who were affected to neither of 'them, yielded the advantage both of learning and argument to the former, while 'yet they were as far from approving his 'cauſe, as even Mr. *Baxter* himſelf could be.'

DR. *Calamy*, in the life of Mr. *Baxter*, ſpeaking of Mr. *Tombes*, ſays, 'whom all 'the world muſt own to have been a very 'conſiderable man, and an excellent ſcholar, how diſinclined ſoever they may be 'to his particular opinions [g].'

MR. *Wall*, in his elaborate *hiſtory* of *infant-baptiſm*, ſays [h], 'Of the profeſſed *Anti-'pædobaptiſts*, Mr. *Tombes* was a man of 'the beſt parts in our nation, and per-'haps in any.' But that which will perpetuate his memory yet more than all this, is, that character of him which the Houſe of Lords have been pleaſed to publiſh. For in their conference with the Commons upon the bill to prevent *occaſional conformity* in 1702. to prove that receiving the ſacrament in the church does not neceſſarily import an entire *conformity*, they fix upon him as an inſtance, and thus expreſs themſelves [i]: 'There was a very learned and famous man, 'that lived at *Saliſbury*, Mr. *Tombes*, 'who was a very zealous *conformiſt* in all 'points but in one, *infant-baptiſm*.'

g *Life of* Baxter, p. 345.
h Vol. II. c. 2. § 15. p. 29.
i *Account of the proceedings*, p. 21.

AND now, to finiſh our account of him; That he juſtly deſerved all theſe great encomiums, will appear to any unprejudiced perſon, that ſhall conſult the learned and ingenious books which he has written. And though they are many, and ſome of them now very difficult to be met with; yet, I think, the following is a compleat *catalogue* of them, and ſet down in the order in which they were publiſhed:

His works. 1. *Chriſt's Commination againſt ſcandalizers; a treatiſe wherein the neceſſity, nature, ſorts and evils of ſcandalizing are cleared and fully handled.* 8vo 1641

2. Fermentum Phariſæorum; *or, The Leaven of Phariſaical Will-Worſhip, declared in a ſermon on* Mat. xv. 9. publiſhed by order of parliament. 4to 1643

3. Jehovah Jireh; *or, God's Providence in delivering the godly*; in two thankſgiving ſermons publiſhed by order of parliament. 4to 1643

4. Anthropolatria; *or, The Sin of glorying in Men, eſpecially in eminent Miniſters of the Goſpel.* 4to 1645

5. *An Exercitation about Infant-Baptiſm; preſented to a chairman of a committee of the aſſembly of divines.* 4to 1646

6. *An Examen of the ſermon of Mr.* Stephen Marſhal *about infant-baptiſm.* 4to 1646

7. *An Apology or Plea for the aforegoing treatiſes concerning Infant-Baptiſm.* 4to 1646

8. *An*

8. *An Antidote againſt the Venom of a Paſſage in the Epiſtle Dedicatory of Mr.* Baxter's *book*, entitled, *The Saints Everlaſting Reſt*; which contains a ſatyrical invective againſt *Anabaptiſts.* 4to 1650

9. *An Addition to the Apology, for the two treatiſes concerning Infant-Baptiſm*; in anſwer to Mr. *Robert Bailie.* 4to 1652

10. *Præcurſor*; *or*, *A Forerunner to a large Review of the Diſpute concerning Infant-Baptiſm.* 4to 1652

11. *Antipædobaptiſm*; *or*, *No plain nor obſcure Scripture-Proof of Infant-Baptiſm*; being the firſt part of the full Review. 4to 1652

12. *Refutatio Poſitionis, ejuſque Confirmationis, Pædobaptiſmum eſſe licitum, affirmantis, ab Henrico Savage, SS. T. D.* 4to 1653

13. *A Plea for Antipædobaptiſts*; in anſwer to a book, entitled, *The Anabaptiſts anatomiſed and ſilenced, in a publick diſpute at Abergavenny.* 4to 1654

14. *Antipædobaptiſm*; or, the ſecond part of the full Review of the diſpute concerning infant-baptiſm.

15. *Antipædobaptiſm*; or, the third part of the full Review. 4to 1657

16. *Animadverſiones quædam in Aphoriſmos* Richardi Baxter, *de Juſtificatione.* 1658

17. *A ſhort Catechiſm about Baptiſm.* 4to 1658

18. *Felo de ſe*; *or, Mr.* Baxter's *Self-Deſtroying*, manifeſted in twenty arguments againſt infant-baptiſm out of his own writings. 4to 1659

19. *True Old-Light exalted above pretended New-Light*; a treatiſe of Jeſus Chriſt, as he is *the Light that enlightens every one that comes into the World*, againſt the *Quakers* and *Arminians*; and recommended by Mr. *Baxter.* 4to 1660

20. *Romaniſm diſcuſſed*; an anſwer to the nine firſt articles of *H. T.*'s Manual of Controverſies, recommended by *R. Baxter.* 4to 1660

21. *A ſerious Conſideration of the oath of the King's Supremacy.* 4to. 1660

22. *A Supplement to the ſerious Conſideration*, &c. 4to 1660

23. *Sepherſheba, or, The Oath-Book*; a treatiſe concerning ſwearing, containing twenty catechetical lectures on the third commandment. 4to 1662

24. *Saints no Smiters*; a treatiſe againſt the fifth monarchy men. 4to 1664

25. *Theodulia*; or, A Juſt Defence of hearing the Sermons, and other Teachings of the preſent Miniſters of *England.* 8vo 1667

26. *Emanuel, or God-man*; wherein the doctrine of the firſt *Nicene* and *Chalcedon* councils is aſſerted againſt the *Socinians.* 8vo 1669

27. A

27. *A Just Reply to the books of Mr.* Wills, *and Mr.* Blinman, *for Infant-Baptism*; in a Letter to *Henry Danvers*, Esq; 8vo 1675

28. *Animadversiones in Librum Georgii Bulli, cui titulum fecit, Harmonia Apostolica.* 8vo 1676

ANOTHER *champion* in the cause of the *Baptists*, contemporary with the former, was Mr. *Henry Denne*, who signalized himself by his preaching and writing, disputing and suffering for this opinion. *Mr.* Henry Denne.

HE was from his childhood designed for the ministry; and to qualify him the better for that great employment, was educated at the university of *Cambridge*, and when he came from thence, received orders from the bishop of St. *David's*, about the year of our Lord 1630.

THE first living he obtained was that of *Pyrton* in *Hertfordshire*, which cure he held for about ten years; and being a more frequent and lively preacher than the generality of the *clergy* of those times, was greatly beloved and respected by his parishioners.

IN 1641. there was a visitation held at *Baldock* in this county; and Mr. *Denne* was the person fixed upon to preach the sermon to the *clergy* and *gentry* that assembled on this occasion. This proved a great means of making him so publick and *Preaches the visitation sermon at* Baldock.

and famous as he became afterwards. For he entertained them with an uncommon difcourfe, and fuch a one, as procured him both a great many *friends* and *enemies*.

HE had always been fufpected as a perfon puritanically inclined; and the difference that was now between the king and parliament gave fuch perfons an opportunity of declaring their minds more freely, and puihing on for fuch a reformation of religion as before they defired and wifhed for. Mr. *Denne* took this to be fuch an opportunity for him, and refolved now to expofe the fin of *perfecution*, the vices of the clergy, and the corruptions in doctrine and worfhip, which he apprehended to be in the eftablifhed church.

HIS introduction to his text on this occafion was fo fingular in its kind, and will give the reader fuch a tafte of the ingenuity and fpirit of the man, that I conclude it will not be an offenfive digreffion, to give the whole of it in his own words.

The introduction to it.

AFTER he had concluded his prayer, he thus addreffed himfelf to his learned and numerous *auditory*. '*Holy brethren* and '*fathers*, I am at this prefent time fur'prized with three paffions; with joy, 'with fear, and with grief. My forrow 'fympathizeth with yours. I am forry, 'in the firft place, that you have not a 'wifer man to fpeak unto you this day, 'efpecially fo many fitting by; and for 'this

'this I preſume you are as ſorrowful as I. 'I am right ſorry, in the ſecond place, 'that I ſhall this day trouble you with ſo 'large a diſcourſe, as neither the quantity 'nor quality of the day will well permit. 'As a remedy for this, let me intreat your 'chriſtian patience to tire me. This is 'my grief. My fear is, beſides that ordi-'nary fear which doth uſually follow me 'at ſuch exerciſes, eſpecially at extraordi-'nary times, and in unaccuſtomed places, 'I have yet another fear, that I ſhall this 'day be miſtaken; not that I fear the mi-'ſtaking of my words, for that were to 'call your judgments into queſtion; but I 'fear leſt you ſhould miſtake the inten-'tions of my heart, and that I ſhall be 'thought to aim at ſome particular per-'ſons. To clear this, I call the Searcher 'of all hearts to record, before whom I 'proteſt this day, that I aim not at any 'man's perſon; but I deſire to be free 'from envy and malice, and to be in per-'fect charity with all men. And I do 'here again proteſt, that what I ſhall ſpeak 'this day, is againſt the errors and vices, 'not againſt the perſons of men. This 'is my fear. My joy is founded upon your 'fervent charity, joined with your ſound 'judgment. In reſpect of your charity, I 'count it a part of my happineſs, ſeeing 'it is as it is, to ſpeak before you, who 'will be ready to cover my infirmities,

'and

'and to pardon my failings, and gently to 'admoniſh me, if any thing be amiſs. In 'reſpect of your judgment, I do count it 'a further happineſs, that I have this 'day an opportunity to make confeſſion 'of my faith, and to communicate my 'doctrine unto ſo learned, judicious, and 'indifferent *auditors*, which that I may 'do, I betake myſelf with ſpeed to a por-'tion of ſcripture, ſelected for this pre-'ſent occaſion, written *John* v. 35. *He 'was a burning and a ſhining light, and 'ye were willing for a ſeaſon to rejoice in 'his light.*'

WHOEVER will be at the pains to read the ſermon itſelf, will find the ſame briſkneſs of ſtile, and chain of thought, running through the whole; and that there was great occaſion for ſome ſuch apology as this, to a diſcourſe, wherein the chief evils of the time are ſo freely cenſured, and the vices of the *clergy* ſo plainly laid open; particularly, their *pride*, their *covetuouſneſs*, their *pluralities*, and *non-reſidence*, which about this time were riſen to a great height. And his applications are ſometimes very particular and biting. Of which let me give this one inſtance. The court for receiving preſentments againſt ſuch as break the *eccleſiaſtical laws*, being held at theſe viſitations, after he had enumerated ſome of the moſt flagrant crimes of the clergy, he takes the freedom to ſay, 'I muſt

'I muſt call upon thoſe in *authority*, that 'they would make diligent ſearch after 'theſe *foxes*. If the courts had been ſo 'vigilant to find out *theſe*, as *nonconformable miniſters*, ſurely by this time 'the church would have been as free 'from *them*, as the land from *wolves*. 'But they have preferred the traditions of 'men before the commandments of Almighty God. I tell you, that *conformity* hath ever ſped the worſe for their 'ſakes, who breaking the commandments 'of God, think to make amends with '*conformity* to the traditions of men.'

THE clergy had much ado to ſit the hearing of theſe things; and a great noiſe was afterwards made about it, and many falſe *reports* given out both againſt him and his ſermon; ſo that he was obliged to print it in his own defence. And from this time he began to be taken notice of, not only as a man of extraordinary parts, but alſo a proper perſon to help forward the deſigned *reformation*. Mr. *Diſborough*, a man that had a great hand at that time in publick affairs, ſaith of him; 'He is 'the ableſt man in the kingdom, for 'prayer, expounding, and preaching.'

MR. *Edwards*, who is never to be ſuſpected of partiality to any that were called *Sectarians*, acknowledges [k], That he had

[k] Gangræna, *part* 1. *page* 23.

a very

a very affectionate way of preaching, and took much with the people.

THE revolutions which happened about this time in the ſtate, neceſſarily brought on ſome alterations in religion; and the government having declared their deſign to reform religion in theſe kingdoms according to the word of God, and the example of the beſt reformed churches; this put Mr. *Denne*, as well as many other learned men, upon making a diligent and impartial ſearch after truth, and bringing ſome points of religion into ſtrict examination, which before they had only taken for granted, and received from the influence of cuſtom. Among the reſt, he found that the practice of *baptizing children* was without any foundation from *ſcripture*, or the writings of the chriſtians for the two firſt *ages* after Chriſt. And accordingly, about the year 1643. he publickly profeſs'd himſelf to be a *Baptiſt*, and was baptized by *immerſion* at *London*, and joined himſelf to the congregation of that perſuaſion there, of which Mr. *Lamb* was the paſtor. This of courſe expoſed him to the reſentment of thoſe who now ſat at the *helm* of *eccleſiaſtical affairs*. And the next news we hear of him is, that he was taken up in *Cambridgeſhire*, and committed to *priſon* by the *committee* of that county, for preaching againſt *infant-baptiſm*, and preſuming to *rebaptize* ſome in thoſe

He profeſſes himſelf to be a Baptiſt.

Is thereupon impriſoned.

thoſe parts. Mr. *Denne* appealed to the parliament; upon which he was, by an order from the houſe, brought up to *London*, and, till his caſe could be heard, was kept *priſoner* in the lord *Peter*'s houſe in *Biſhopſgate-ſtreet*.

IT happened, that there was in this *priſon*, at the ſame time, the great Dr. *Featly*, famous for his oppoſing the *Anabaptiſts*, and who had but juſt before publiſhed his book, called *the Dippers Dipt; or, the Anabaptiſts duck'd, and plunged over head and ears*, at a *diſputation* in *Southwark*.

THIS book, aſſoon as Mr. *Denne* came into the *priſon*, was laid before him in his apartment.

Challenges Dr. Featly *to diſpute.*

HAVING read it, he looked upon himſelf obliged to defend the principle and practice for which he now ſuffered; and therefore ſent to the *doctor*, offering to diſpute with him upon the arguments he had laid down in his book. The doctor at firſt accepts the *challenge*; but when they had only diſcourſed on the firſt of his ten *arguments*, he found he had now another kind of *opponent* to deal with, than thoſe he triumph'd over at *Southwark*[1]; and therefore declined going any further, on pretence it was not ſafe ſo to do without *licence* from the *government*;

[1] Denn's *Antichriſt unmask'd, pref.*

but

but however, bid him write, and ſaid he would defend his own *arguments.*

UPON this Mr. *Denne* ſet himſelf to writing, and drew up a very learned and ingenious anſwer, dating his book from this priſon, as the doctor had done his, and tho' the doctor's was publiſhed before he
Jan. 10. 1644. came thither, ſo quick was he with his
Feb. 22. 1644. anſwer, that there is but a little above a month's difference in the date of them. But I do not find that ever the doctor, according to his promiſe, made any reply to it.

He obtains the pariſh of Elſly. AFTER Mr. *Denne* was ſet at liberty, notwithſtanding his oppoſing the common opinion in this particular, he obtained by ſome means or other the pariſh of *Elſly* in *Cambridgeſhire*[m], where he preached publickly in the church, and enjoyed the means belonging to it for ſome time, and was very much followed for his popular preaching.

BUT this gave great offence to ſome of the *Preſbyterian* party, who now began to think none ought to be admitted into publick *livings* but *themſelves.* And more eſpecially the neighbouring *miniſters* were greatly prejudiced againſt him. Being once to preach on a lecture day at *St. Ives,* an order was obtained from the committee of the county againſt it; whereupon he went

[m] Gangræna, *part* 1. *page* 23.

into

into a churchyard a little diſtance, and preached under a tree, and to the mortification of his oppoſers, a great number of the people followed him thither. He was alſo in the year 1646. taken up by two juſtices of the peace at *Spalding* in *Lincolnſhire*, and committed to priſon, for having *baptized* ſome perſons in a river there, as has been before obſerved. By ſuch proceedings as theſe, Mr. *Denne* was obliged to quit his living; and finding ſuch laws enacted, as would hinder his being uſeful, or enjoying any benefice in the church, he went into the *army*; and being a man of great courage and zeal for the liberties of his country, took upon him the profeſſion of the *ſoldier* as well as the *divine*, and behaved himſelf ſo well, as to gain a reputation, not inferior to many, in both theſe characters.

Quits his living, and went into the army.

As to his opinion in other points, he ſeems to have taken that which is called the middle way; being properly neither *Calviniſt* nor *Arminian*. For tho' he held the doctrine of *perſonal election*, and the ſpecial efficacy of grace to ſome, yet he as zealouſly oppoſed the doctrine of *abſolute reprobation*; aſſerting, that by the death of Chriſt, all men were put into the poſſibility of ſalvation, and were to have the offers of it: ſo that the deſtruction [n] and ruin

[n] *Drag-net*, p. 106.

of thoſe that periſh, is only of *themſelves.*

THE ſame ſcheme was vindicated by biſhop *Uſher*, Dr. *Davenant*, and of late by the famous Dr. *Tillotſon.* But for this Mr. *Denne* was accuſed by ſome who wrote againſt him, of being a great *Antinomian*, and a *deſperate Arminian* [*].

ONE of the moſt remarkable paſſages of this man's life, that wherein he moſt ſerved the *Baptiſts*, and gave the greateſt proofs of his being a good *ſcholar*, and a compleat *diſputant*, was that publick diſpute which he held for two days with Dr. *Gunning* in St. *Clement*'s church, without *Temple-Bar*, concerning *infant-baptiſm*, in the year 1658. which was afterwards printed. He died a little after the reſtoration, and upon his grave was put, by a *clergyman* of his acquaintance, this epitaph.

To tell his wiſdom, learning, goodneſs unto men,
I need to ſay no more, but here lies Henry Denne.

THOSE that deſire to ſee a confirmation of this character, will find it by reading his works: which are,

[*] Gangræna, *part* 1. *p.* 22.

1. *The*

1. *The doctrine and conversation of* John *the* Baptist; a visitation sermon. 8vo 1642 *His works.*

2. *The foundation of childrens baptism discovered and rased*; an answer to Dr. *Featley* and Mr. *Marshal.* 4to 1645

3. *The man of sin discovered, whom the Lord will destroy with the brightness of his coming.* 4to 1645

4. *The drag-net of the kingdom of heaven*; or, Christ's drawing all men. 8vo 1646

5. *The levellers design discovered*, a sheet, 1649.

6. *A contention for truth*, in two publick disputations at St. *Clement*'s church, between Dr. *Gunning* and *Henry Denne*, concerning infant-baptism. 4to 1658

ANOTHER famous man of this denomination, was the learned, humble, and very pious Mr. *Henry Jessey*, M. A. *Mr. Henry Jessey.*

HE was born on the 3d of *September*, 1601. at *West-Routon* in the North Riding of *Yorkshire*, his father being minister of that place. When he was seventeen years of age, he was sent to the university, and educated in St. *John*'s college at *Cambridge*, where he continued about six years, and commenced, first batchelor, and then master of arts. But that which is most remarkable, is, that while he was under the teachings of men, and eagerly pursuing after human learning in this place, God himself was pleased to teach him, and enrich his

his ſoul with divine learning, working effectually in him, by his Holy Spirit, the knowledge of ſin, and faith in Chriſt; ſo that he dates his converſion to God, while he was yet at the *univerſity*, and but of twenty one years of age; a very rare and uncommon inſtance! However, this put no ſtop to the progreſs of his education; for he followed his ſtudies as cloſely as ever, only he now ſteered the courſe of them more directly to qualify him for the *miniſtry* of the goſpel; having determined from this time to devote himſelf to that ſacred employment. When he removed from the univerſity, old Mr. *Bramton Gurdon*, of *Aſſington* in *Suffolk*, famous for his having three ſons parliament-men, took him to be chaplain in his family. And in this worthy family he continued nine years, where he had the opportunity of perfecting his ſtudies, and qualifying himſelf yet better for more publick ſervice.

Is firſt a chaplain to a private family.

IT was in the year 1627. that he received *epiſcopal ordination.* And tho' after this he was frequently ſolicited to accept of ſome promotion in the church, yet could not be prevail'd upon until the year 1633. and then the living of *Aughton* in *Yorkſhire* was given to him. Here he found that his predeceſſor Mr. *Alder*, had been remov'd for *nonconformity*, and he knew that his principles would not permit him to conform ſo far as the other had done, and therefore

Obtains the living of Aughton.

fore expected no long continuance in this place. And it proved according to his expectation: for the very next year he himself was remov'd for not using all those *ceremonies* enjoin'd by the *rubrick* and *canons*, and for presuming to remove a *crucifix* set up there. *Is removed from thence.*

AFTER this, Sir *Matthew Bointon*, in the same county, took him into his family; by whom he also was introduc'd to preach frequently both at *Barneston* and *Rowsby*, two parishes near adjoining in *Yorkshire*; and began every day to be more and more taken notice of for his piety, humility, and excellent preaching.

IN the year 1635. he came up to *London* with his patron; and he had not been long here, before he was earnestly solicited to take the pastoral care of a congregation of *protestant dissenters* in this city, which had been form'd ever since the year 1616. by one Mr. *Henry Jacob*. They had often heard him preach to their great satisfaction; and it was now well known, that he would accept no preferment in the establish'd church, but look'd upon the imposition of *ceremonies*, and *oaths* of *episcopal* and *canonical* obedience to be unwarrantable and sinful. His great modesty caus'd him to decline it for some time; but at length, after many prayers to God, and consultations with his brethren, he accepted of this charge in the year 1637. and in this vineyard did he continue a faithful and la- *He comes to* London. *Accepts of an* Independent *congregation.*

borious ſervant of Jeſus Chriſt, unto the day of his death.

Several of his congregation embrace the opinion of the Baptiſts.

IT happen'd that every now and then ſeveral of this congregation were embracing the opinion of the *Baptiſts*, and going off from them on that occaſion. In 1638. the year after his coming among them, ſix perſons of note eſpous'd it; in 1641. a much greater number; and in 1643. it was reviv'd again, and prevail'd more than ever.

MANY of theſe were ſuch as Mr. *Jeſſey* very much reſpected for their piety and ſolid judgment, and the alteration of their opinions occaſion'd frequent debates in the congregation about it; ſo that he was by theſe things neceſſarily put upon the ſtudy of this *controverſy*: and when, upon a diligent and impartial examination of the *holy ſcriptures* and *antiquity*, he found occaſion to alter his *opinion*; yet he did not do it without great deliberation, many prayers, and divers conferences with pious and learned men of a different perſuaſion.

HIS firſt *conviction* was about the *mode of baptizing*: for he quickly diſcern'd that *ſprinkling* was a modern corruption, brought in without any juſt ground either from *ſcripture* or *antiquity*; and therefore in the year 1642. the church being aſſembled, he freely declared to them, that *immerſion*, or *dipping* the whole body into the water, appeared to him to be the right manner of adminiſtring *baptiſm*, this being the import

He himſelf declares for immerſion in baptiſm, and practiſes it.

mport of the original word Βαπτίζω, this agreeing with thoſe examples of *baptiſm* recorded in the holy ſcriptures, and this beſt repreſenting thoſe *ſpiritual myſteries* ſignified by it, *viz.* the *death* and *reſurrection* of Chriſt, and our *dying* to ſin, and *riſing* again to newneſs of life. And therefore he propoſed, that thoſe who were *baptized* for the future, ſhould receive it after this manner. And tho' he continued for two or three years after this, to *baptize children*, his manner was to *dip* them into the water.

BUT about the year 1644. the *controverſy* about the *ſubjects* of *baptiſm* was again reviv'd, and ſeveral debates held in the *congregation* about it; by which not only ſeveral private chriſtians were convinced that *infant-baptiſm* was an unſcriptural practice, but Mr. *Jeſſey* himſelf alſo came over to this opinion. However, before he would abſolutely determine in the point, and practiſe accordingly, he reſolved to conſult with divers learned and judicious *miniſters* of thoſe times; and therefore had a meeting with Dr. *Goodwin*, Mr. *Philip Nye*, Mr. *Jer. Burroughs*, Mr. *Walter Craddock*, and ſeveral others. But theſe giving him no ſatisfaction, he was in *June* 1645. baptized by Mr. *Hanſerd Knollys*; and it proved no ſmall honour and advantage to the *Baptiſts*, to have a man of ſuch

Is further convinced that it belongs not to infants;

And is baptized by Hanſerd Knollys.

ſuch extraordinary piety, and ſubſtantial learning among them.

Yet held mixed commu- nion.

BUT notwithſtanding his differing from his *brethren* in this, or any other point, he maintained the ſame chriſtian love and charity to all ſaints as before, not only as to a friendly converſation, but alſo in reſpect of *church-communion*. He had always ſome of the *Pædobaptiſt perſuaſion*, and blamed thoſe that made their particular opinion about *baptiſm* the boundary of church communion. He publiſhed the reaſons of his opinion in this caſe; and when he travelled thro' the *north* and *weſt* parts of *England* to viſit the churches, he made it his principal buſineſs to excite them to love and union among themſelves, notwithſtanding their differing from one another in ſome opinions; and was alſo the principal perſon that ſet up, and preſerved for ſome time, a meeting at *London* of ſome eminent men of each denomination, in order to maintain peace and union among thoſe chriſtians that differed not fundamentally; and this catholick ſpirit procured him the love and eſteem of the good men of all *parties*.

His ſtated labours.

HE divided his labours in the *miniſtry*, according to the extenſiveneſs of his principles. Every lord's-day in the afternoon he was among his own people; in the morning he uſually preach'd at St. *George*'s church

church in *Southwark*, being one of the fixed *miniſters* in that pariſh; and once in the week days he preached at *Ely-Houſe*, and in the *Savoy* to the maimed ſoldiers.

BESIDES his conſtant labours, thus, in the work of the miniſtry, there was another profitable work, wherein his ſoul was engaged, and in which he took great pains for divers years; and this was no leſs than the making a new and more correct tranſlation of the Holy Bible.

He attempts a more correct tranſlation of the Bible.

HE was very induſtrious, in the firſt place, to underſtand fully thoſe languages in which it was written: the *Hebrew* and *Greek* teſtaments he conſtantly carried about him, frequently calling one *his ſword and dagger*, and the other his *ſhield and buckler*. And beſides the *Hebrew* and *Greek*, he ſtudied the *Syriack* and *Chaldee* dialects, which the unlearned *Jews* ſpoke in their captivity. But notwithſtanding his qualifications in this, and many other reſpects, he had not the vanity to think this a work fit for any ſingle man to encounter with; and therefore ſent letters to many learned men of this and other nations, deſiring their aſſiſtance and joint labours with him in this great deſign. And by his perſuaſions many perſons of great note for their learning, faithfulneſs, and piety, did engage in it; particularly Mr. *John Row*, the *Hebrew* profeſſor at *Aberdeen*, took great pains with him herein. The writer of Mr. *Jeſſey*'s life ſays,

ſays, that he made it the maſter ſtudy of his life, and would often cry out, ' Oh, ' that I might ſee this done before I die!'

IN that book there is a ſpecimen given of the *errors* he took notice of in the preſent *tranſlation*, the rules he obſerved in correcting them, and the progreſs that was made in this work.

IT appears, that it was almoſt compleated, and wanted little more than the appointing commiſſioners to examine it, and authorize its publication, which was what he always attended, and of which he had from the firſt ſome aſſurances given him. But the great turn that was given to publick affairs both in church and ſtate, by the *reſtoration*, cauſed this great and noble deſign to prove *abortive*.

IT was not however loſt labour to himſelf, if the world ſhould never be favoured with it; for by this thorough ſtudy of the *Scriptures*, he was made an excellent *textuary*, was well ſkilled in the *hiſtory* and *chronology* thereof, and became ſo familiar with its *language* and *phraſeology*, that it was to him like his *mother-tongue*, both in preaching and converſation. This way of ſpeaking he thought moſt ſavoury, and beſt becoming thoſe that profeſs'd chriſtianity; therefore, as he uſed it to great advantage himſelf, ſo he exhorted all chriſtians to uſe themſelves to the like practice. And for their aſſiſtance herein, he began

began in the year 1645. to ſet forth *a ſcripture-calendar*, as a guide to ſpeak and write in ſcripture-ſtile; and continued it yearly to 1664.

IN this, beſides the day of the month, age of the moon, progreſs of the ſun, quarter-days, and the like, common to vulgar almanacks; there was, peculiar to his deſign, the ſcripture-account of hours, days, night-watches, months and quarters; alſo the weights and meaſures therein mentioned; with a brief chronology and church hiſtory; and ſtill every year entertained the publick with ſomething new on theſe ſubjects, compriſing the whole in two ſheets. Theſe are ſome of thoſe methods by which this great and good man endeavoured, according to the nature of his office, to ſerve the ſouls of men, and improve their minds in knowledge and holineſs. Something alſo in juſtice ought to be ſaid of his labours of love towards their bodies, and care to promote their temporal intereſts. *His work,*

HE choſe a *ſingle life*, that ſo not being incumbered with *wife* or *family*, he might be the more entirely devoted to his ſacred work, and the better enabled to do good, and communicate to the relief of others. And beſides his own *alms*, he was a conſtant ſolicitor and agent for the poor, with others whom he knew able to ſupply their wants; for this purpoſe he carried about him *And labour of love* him a liſt of the names of the moſt eminent objects of charity known to him, adding to each name their ages, infirmities, afflictions, charges and graces; and by this method he raiſed conſiderable ſums for their relief. There were above *thirty families*, who had all their ſubſiſtance from him, and were after his death expoſed to great difficulties.

NOR did he limit his charity within the narrow compaſs of his own congregation or opinion; but, according to the rule, *did good to all*, as well as *more eſpecially to the houſhold of faith*, ſo that many hundreds of poor, beſides his own people, were refreſhed by him. And where it was not charity *to give*, but might be ſo on ſome ſpecial occaſions *to lend*, he would do it freely, without taking *intereſt* or *ſecurity* from the party.

His charity to the diſtreſſed Jews *at* Jeruſalem.

ONE of the moſt famous inſtances of his charity, and what is perhaps without precedent, was that which he ſhewed to the poor and diſtreſſed *Jews* at *Jeruſalem*. The love that the *Jews* had for the *holy land*, and particularly the place where the famous city of *Jeruſalem* had ſtood, drew a great number of that religion to inhabit in thoſe parts, though they were obliged to pay conſiderable ſums to the *Turks* for liberty ſo to do. Theſe being generally poor, and dwelling in a place where there was now no trade or merchandize, they were chiefly

chiefly ſupported by their rich and trading brethren in other countries. The *Jews* in *Hungary*, *Poland*, *Lithuania* and *Pruſſia*, were wont to ſend them fifteen millions of rixdollars yearly, for the maintenance and training up of *learned rabbi's*, and for the relief of decriped men and antient widows: but a war which happened between the *Swedes* and *Poles*, cut off this means of their ſubſiſtance; ſo that about the year 1657. they were reduced to great extremity, four hundred of their poor widows were *ſtarved to death*, others ſuffered much by hunger and nakedneſs; and their *elders* and *rabbi's* were committed to *priſon*, and uſed very cruelly by ſcourging and otherwiſe, becauſe they owed between four and five thouſand pounds for their liberty of dwelling there, and other occaſions. And they were aſſured by the *rulers* in thoſe parts, that they ſhould all be ſold for *ſlaves*, if payment was not ſpeedily made.

IN this deplorable caſe, all the proſpect of relief they had left, was to ſend to ſome of their brethren at *Venice* and *Amſterdam*; but theſe could help them to little more than what would pay the intereſt of their debts. However, the *chriſtians* in *Holland* hearing their caſe, had compaſſion on them, and ſent them five hundred rixdollars; and ſome there knowing Mr. *Jeſſey* to be a man of a publick ſpirit, and one that delighted in charitable actions,

tions, and alſo that he had formerly been very helpful in procuring liberty for the *Jews* to trade and inhabit in *England*, on ſuch limitations as might render it ſafe both for the government and merchants, they therefore ſend a repreſentation of this caſe to him, earneſtly deſiring him to ſet forward a collection for them in *England.*

WHEN Mr. *Jeſſey* had received full ſatisfaction concerning the truth of this relation, and that there was a ſafe way of conveying what might be collected to them, he immediately communicated the matter to his brethren the *London-miniſters*, and in a ſhort time three hundred pound was gathered and ſent to them, and a bill of receipt with thanks returned.

TO this act of hoſpitality he was influenced not only by that common compaſſion which we ought to ſhew to all human nature, but from the conſideration of their having antiently been God's *peculiar* and *beloved people*, and that there are ſeveral *predictions* of their being called in the latter days, and bringing great glory to the goſpel-church.

IN the year 1650. when the *Jews* were permitted to return and trade in *England* as formerly, Mr. *Jeſſey* wrote an excellent *treatiſe* on purpoſe to remove their prejudices, and convince them that Jeſus was the true Meſſiah, which was recommended very highly by the hands of ſeveral of the

aſſembly

assembly of *divines*, and afterwards turned into *Hebrew*, to be dispersed among the *Jews* of all nations.

AND to promote the same good design of their conversion to christianity, there were letters sent with this charity; *one* signed by all the *ministers* that had been concerned in raising this money for them, *others* written particularly by Mr. *Jessey*; the copies of both which may be seen in his life.

IT is easy to suppose, that a man of such great piety, learning, and extensive charity, must be very much crouded with visitors; and tho' Mr. *Jessey* was no courtier, yet, according to the modern phrase, he had a very great *levee*; some to converse with him as a *friend*, some to consult him as a *casuist*, and others to get relief from him as a common *benefactor* to the distressed.

HE was however resolved to have to himself sufficient time for his private devotions and necessary studies. And as he hated idle talk and fruitless visits, so he took all possible methods to avoid them. Among the rest, that his friends might know his desire and resolution in this case, he put over his study door, the place where he usually received his visitors, this writing [p].

[p] Jessey's *life*, p. 103.

Amice,

Amice, quisquis huc ades;
Aut agito paucis; aut abi;
Aut me laborantem adjuva.

Whatever friend comes hither,
Dispatch in brief, or go,
Or help me busied too.
By HENRY JESSEY.

DURING the time that *episcopacy* was laid aside in *England*, Mr. *Jessey* was a man always had in esteem, and free from all degrees of *persecution*; a favour that very few *Baptists* enjoyed besides himself. But in the little time he lived both before and after this, he had his share of those *persecutions*, which fell upon the *Nonconformists*.

He was ejected from his living, and died in prison.

UPON the *restoration* he was ejected from his living at St. *George's*, *Southwark*, silenced from his *ministry*, and being committed to *prison* for his religion, he died there, full of peace and joy, on the 4th of *Sept.* 1663. having that day compleated the sixty third year of his age. He was buried three days afterwards from *Woodmongers* hall; and there appeared an uncommon number of mourners at his funeral, several thousands of pious persons of all denominations attending his obsequies, each bewailing their loss in that particular wherein he had been useful to them, and one of his learned acquaintance writ this epitaph on his death.

'In

In mortem domini HENRICI JESSEY.

Post varios casus, & per dispendia vitæ
Plurima, devictis hostibus, ille jacet.
Sub tumulo, invictus victor, sub pace triumphans,
Præmia virtutis possidet ille suæ.
Cymba fides, remique preces, suspiria venti
Cum quibus Elysiis per Styga fertur agris.

THOSE that desire to know more of this great and good man, may read his life, published in 1671. But perhaps one testimony of his great learning and piety from a *Pædobaptist*, may go further with some men, than all that can be said by those of his own persuasion.

I WILL therefore add the *character* that is given of him by *Obediah Wills*, M. A. who has writ with as much zeal and warmth against Mr. *Jessey*'s particular opinion, as any man; yet when he is commending love and union among Christians of different sentiments, he says [r], Mr. Wills' *character of him.*

'AND such a frame of spirit was there
'in that man of God, Mr. *Jessey*,— He, to
'my knowledge, was an *Anti-pædobaptist*
'of long standing, as holy I conceive, as
'any of that judgment; of good learning

[q] Jessey's *life*, p. 97. [r] *Inf. Bapt. preface.*

'and of a very tender conſcience; and of 'ſo healing and uniting a ſpirit, that 'he eſteemed it his duty, and preſſed o-'thers to it, to keep up chriſtian com-'munion with thoſe that feared God, tho' 'they differ'd about *baptiſm*. We have 'his arguments for the ſame publiſhed in 'print, and grounded on *Romans* xiv. 1. 'which are ſo clear, and have in them 'ſuch ſtrength of evidence, that I never 'yet could hear them anſwered, nor do 'ever expect it. I wiſh there were more 'ſuch *Anti-pædobaptiſts* as he.

THE books written by him are as follows.

His works. 1. *A ſtore-houſe of proviſion to further reſolution in ſeveral caſes of conſcience, and queſtions now in diſpute.* 8vo 1650

2. *A ſcripture calendar*, publiſhed yearly, from 1645, to 1660.

3. *The glory and ſalvation of Jehudah and Iſrael*; a treatiſe to reconcile Jews and Chriſtians in the faith of the Meſſiah. 1650

4. *An eaſy catechiſm for children*; in which the anſwers are wholly in the words of ſcripture.

5. *The exceeding riches of grace, advanced by the Spirit of grace, in Mrs.* Sarah Wright. 8vo 1658

6. *The Lord's loud call to* England; being an account of ſome late various and wonderful judgments. 4to 1660

7. *Miſ-*

7. *Miſcellania Sacra*, or divers neceſſary truths. 8vo 1665

A looking-glaſs for children; being a narrative of God's gracious dealings with ſome little children. 8vo 1672

Mr. Wil. Dell.

William Dell, M. A. was another profeſſed *Baptiſt*, famous in the time of the late civil wars. [f] He was trained up at the univerſity of *Cambridge*, accepted a living in the eſtabliſhed church, and before the civil wars, ſeemed well enough pleaſed with epiſcopacy and the ceremonies: But when the change in the ſtate brought on a reformation in religion, he appeared among the forwardeſt for the promoting of it, and would have had it carried on much farther than many others deſigned, or would allow of. Tho' this created him many enemies, and expoſed him to the cenſure of the prevailing party, yet he exclaimed againſt making a whole kingdom a church, and called it *the myſtery of iniquity*. He thought, that no power belonged to the church and clergy, but what is ſpiritual; and took pains to ſhew [t], that the blending the civil and eccleſiaſtical powers together has conſtantly been the method of ſetting up a *ſpiritual tyranny*, and of ſupporting the anti-chriſtian church and prelacy. He zealouſly oppoſed all

[f] Love's *animad.* p. 49. [t] *Right reform. preface.*

all compulsion in matters of religion; and held, that every particular person, and societies of christians, ought to have the liberty of worshipping God according to the best of their knowledge, and in that manner which they thought most agreeable to his word.

Opposes the Presbyterians.

THESE principles led him necessarily to oppose the *Presbyterians* in their attempts to get the civil power over entirely to themselves, and to establish their articles of faith, and directory for worship and discipline, suppressing all others. And there was no man stood more in their way than he did, so that he obtained the name of *a rigid Anti-presbyterian*, and a *famous sectary* [u].

HE writ a book against *uniformity*, wherein he calls the imposing of it antichristian, about the same time as they were getting their directory confirmed by parliament, which greatly enraged them; but he was protected against their resentment, by the favour of some great men.

HE had the living at *Yeldon*, in the county of *Bedford*, a place worth about two hundred pound a year. But some other officiated for him; for about the year 1645. he became *chaplain* to the *army*, constantly attending on Sir *Thomas Fairfax*, and preaching at the head quarters.

Goes into the army.

[u] Love's *animad.* p. 4. Gangræna *part* 3. *p.* 213.

THIS

THIS poſt they envied him more than the other; not for the profit of it, but becauſe it gave him an opportunity of ſpreading his *principles* among ſome of the leading men in the ſtate, and enabled him to make the greater ſtand againſt their deſired eſtabliſhment of *Presbytery*. Mr. *Baxter* himſelf went into the *army* for ſome time, to counterwork Mr. *Dell* and others, whom he eſteemed as *ſectarians*; and endeavoured to perſuade other miniſters to follow his example, but met with little ſucceſs, as he himſelf acknowledges [y].

WHEN his method failed [z], they endeavoured to blacken his *character*, by repreſenting him to be an [a] *Antinomian*, a *Socinian*, a *Sectarian*, and one that oppoſed reaſon [b], ſound doctrine, order and concord [c]; but chiefly ſought occaſion to catch ſomething from his diſcourſes, that might expoſe him to the government, and render him odious to the common people. Several inſtances of this might be collected out of the *hiſtories* of thoſe times. I will only take notice of the two moſt remarkable.

His enemies endeavour to expoſe him.

ONE was, from a diſcourſe which he preach'd at *Marſton*, then the head quarters of the *army* before *Oxford*.

[y] *Life*, p. 53, 56.
[z] Love's *animad.* p. 18.
[a] Ibid. p. 6.
[b] Gangræna, *part* 3. p. 213.
[c] Baxter's *life*, p. 64.

SOME who were ſuppoſed to come from *London* to be ſpies upon the army to expoſe them, being preſent, were greatly provoked; and inraged by what he delivered: whereupon they drew up their charge againſt him, and in ſeveral heads, ſigned it with their names, and returning to *London*, copies of it were put into the hands of ſeveral members of both houſes of parliament, and divers eminent citizens of *London*, in order to carry on their deſign againſt him.

IT ſhews the ſpirit of thoſe times, and the unhappy ſtruggles that were among the contending parties; and being ſhort, I ſhall here inſert it.

MR. *Dell* expounding the ſeven laſt verſes of the 54th of *Iſaiah*, in *Marſton* church near *Oxford*, before the general and other commanders and ſoldiers, *June* the 7th 1646. being ſabbath day in the forenoon, uſed theſe or the like words, in effect.

Their charge againſt him.

'1. [d] THERE are no more of the church 'of God in a kingdom than there be of 'ſuch as have the Spirit of God in that 'kingdom.

'2. NEITHER Old nor New Teſtament 'do hold a whole nation to be a church.

[d] Edwards's Gangræna, *part* 3. *p.* 63

3. WHAT-

'3. WHATSOEVER a ſtate, an aſſem-'bly, or council ſhall ſay, ought not to 'bind the ſaints, further than the judg-'ments of thoſe ſaints ſhall lead them.

'4. THE ſaints are thoſe that are now 'ſtiled *Anabaptiſts*, *Familiſts*, *Antinomi-'ans*, *Independants*, *Sectaries*, &c.

'5. The power is in you the people; 'keep it, part not with it.

'6. THE firſt party that roſe againſt you, 'namely, the profane ones of the land, 'are already fallen under you, and now 'there is another party, *Formaliſts* and '*Carnal-Goſpellers* riſing up againſt you; 'and I am confident they ſhall fall under 'you.

'7. THEY are willing to become ſub-'jects to make the ſaints ſlaves; nay, they 'are willing to become ſlaves themſelves, 'that they may tread upon the necks of 'the ſaints.

'8. HIS ſermon, or expoſition, for the 'greateſt part of it, tended meerly to di-'viſion and ſedition.

'9. BEING ſpoken with after his ſer-'mon, by ſome of his hearers, touching 'theſe things, and ſuch like paſſages, he 'ſaid to this effect; his intentions were 'not according to his expreſſions, and he 'thought he had preached only to ſoldiers.

Peter Mills, *Nicholas Widmergole*,
Henry Potter, *Theophilus Smith*.
John Haine,

4 THIS

THIS proceeding obliged Mr. *Dell* to print his ſermon in his own vindication. He declares in the prèface, that it contained the whole of what was then delivered, exactly ſet down, and nothing abated; and appeals to ſeveral hundreds of perſons, ſome of which were of great worth and piety, who were ready to confute the falſhood and untruths of their charge.

HE does indeed therein ſhew his diſlike of making every man in a kingdom a member of the church, and taking thoſe into Chriſt's flock that are none of his ſheep; and endeavours to expoſe the evil of *perſecution*, and the folly of building our faith on the opinions of any learned man, or an whole *aſſembly of divines*; and exclaims againſt the practice of abuſing good men with the odious names of *Sectaries*, *Schiſmaticks*, *Hereticks*, &c. but ſays nothing that will bear ſo ill a ſenſe as thoſe words they accuſe him with. And as to the two laſt articles of their charge, which contains their opinion of his diſcourſe, and what paſſed afterwards, he ſo fully confuted both, that in their rejoinder they dropt them.

THERE was another inſtance of this nature, which expoſed Mr. *Dell* very much to the envy of thoſe who were for eſtabliſhing an *uniformity*, and again *toleration*.

Nov.

Nov. 25. 1646. being appointed for a publick faſt, Mr. *Dell* and Mr. *Love* were choſen to preach before the houſe of commons.

Preaches before the houſe of Commons.

IT was a very critical juncture with reſpect to the ſtate of religion. The miniſters of *London*, and after their example, thoſe of other parts, had petitioned againſt *toleration*, deſiring that all *ſectaries* and *lay preachers* might be ſuppreſs'd, and *presbytery* only eſtabliſhed and allowed of; and the city of *London* had but juſt before preſented their *remonſtrance* to the ſame effect: ſo that this great affair lay now before the parliament, and was the chief ſubject of debate throughout the kingdom.

MR. *Dell* was known to be one of the heads of the oppoſite party; and having this opportunity, he thought himſelf obliged to vindicate his opinion, and defend the rights and liberties of his brethren. Accordingly preaching in the morning, from *Heb.* ix. 10. *Until the time of reformation*, he took the liberty of handling this point very freely before the parliament; ſhewing, what true goſpel reformation is, into whoſe hand the work is committed, and by what means it is to be brought about: and under this laſt head does, by ſeveral excellent arguments, expoſe the unreaſonableneſs and evil of *perſecution*,

secution, or using external force and compulsion in matters purely religious.

WHEN Mr. *Love* came to preach in the afternoon, instead of delivering the sermon he had prepared, he set himself with great warmth, and many unhandsome reflections, to confute what had been delivered in the morning; endeavouring to justify the punishing of *Hereticks* and *Schismaticks*, and to vindicate the authority of the civil *magistrate*, in imposing articles of faith, and a form of worship. The fame of this contest quickly spread itself thro' the nation, and warmed the spirit of both the parties. The *parliament* thought it most prudent for them not to give their publick approbation to either discourse, and it would have been ridiculous to have done it to both; therefore they dropt the usual ceremony in that case.

MR. *Dell* printed his sermon, and having a copy of Mr. *Love*'s, put at the end of his own a reply to Mr. *Love*'s contradictions; upon both which, Mr. *Love* quickly after wrote some *animadversions*. And thus they were made the *heads* and *champions* of the two contending parties of the nation; the *one for liberty*, the *other for persecution*.

MR. *Dell*'s discourse met with great approbation from the publick, and caused his doctrine very much to obtain. And

tho

tho' the *rigid Presbyterians* were very much [e] provok'd and offended with him, the government shew'd no resentment, nor did he lose any present or following preferment by what he had done.

[f] In the year 1649. when several were turned out of the universities for refusing to take the oaths to the government, he was made master of *Caius* college at *Cambridge*; and this, with his living at *Yeldon*, he held, till he was ejected by the act of *uniformity*, made quickly after the restoration.

Dr. Calamy's charge against him.

Dr. *Calamy*, in his account of the ejected ministers, calls him *a very unsettled man*; and says, he was challenged with three contradictions in his life. 1. For being professedly against *Pædobaptism*, and yet he had his own *children* baptized: 2. For preaching against *universities*, when yet he held the *headship* of a college: 3. For being against *tithes*, and yet taking 200 *l. per annum* at his living at *Yeldon*.

Confuted.

Dr. *Calamy* takes no notice of this in his first edition: but however it is now fixed upon as a brand of infamy on the character of this learned defender of the peoples religious liberties. And as these things are laid down, they do indeed shew a *contradiction* between *principles* and *practice*; and the doctor's *impartiality* and *in-*

[e] *I use the term* rigid *to distinguish them from the other* Presbyterians *who dislike such proceedings.*

[f] Baxter's *life*, p. 64.

genuity

genuity towards the *Baptiſts* may be eaſily ſeen, where he is neceſſitated to mention them. But if ſome circumſtances are conſidered, the *contradictions* will in a great meaſure diſappear, and the crime of them be wholly taken away.

HE that believes *infant-baptiſm* to be no inſtitution of Chriſt, yet for the ſatiſfaction of a *pious wife*, or ſome other near relations who eſteem it ſo, may permit them to get his *children* baptized; or if he don't eſteem it a religious rite, may admit it as a title to ſome *civil privilege*; as *Paul* circumciſed *Timothy*.

As to the ſecond, I do not find that he was againſt *univerſities* as *ſeminaries* of *learning*, and proper places for the education of youth; but making ſuch an education *eſſential* to a goſpel miniſter, and preferable to the gifts of the Spirit.

Nor, 3dly, can I ſee any evil or *contradiction* in it, for a perſon who aſſerts that there is no divine right for *tithes* under the goſpel, but that miniſters ſhould be maintained by the voluntary contributions of the people, to accept of a living raiſed by *tithes*, till ſuch a reformation can be obtained, and other methods fixed for their ſupport. It rather beſpeaks a man's virtue to oppoſe a practice and deſire the reformation of it, tho' it was ſo beneficial to himſelf. And had he not made conſcience of practiſing nothing in religion but what was conſiſtent with

the

the ſentiments of his own mind, he would never have loſt two ſuch great *livings* for his *nonconformity* as he did; and yet the doctor himſelf aſſerts, that this was the only reaſon of his ejectment. It muſt be granted, that he was ſomewhat tinctured with the *enthuſiaſm* that prevailed in thoſe times; but was however a man of ſubſtantial learning, of real piety, and a noble defender of the rights and liberties of conſcience.

The tracts which he publiſhed, were, *His works.*

1. *Power from on high; or the power of the Holy Ghoſt diſperſed thro' the whole body of Chriſt, and communicated to each member.* Two Serm. 4to 1645

2. *Right reformation.* A ſermon before the houſe of Commons, *Nov.* 25. 4to 1646

3. *The building and glory of the truly chriſtian and ſpiritual church*; repreſented in an expoſition on *Iſaiah* 45. 4to 1647.

4. *The doctrine of baptiſm reduced from its antient and modern corruptions.* 4to 1648.

5. *A treatiſe againſt uniformity.* I am not certain but this may be the ſame with the firſt.

THE next I ſhall mention, is one whoſe memory is ſtill very precious to many godly perſons, both of this and other denominations; *viz.*

THE

Mr. Hanserd Knollys.

THE pious and learned Mr. *Hanserd Knollys*. He was born at *Chalkwell* in *Lincolnshire*, and descended from religious parents, who took care to have him trained up in good literature, and instructed betimes in the principles of religion. For this end they kept a tutor in their house for him and his brother, till he was fit for the *university*; and then he was sent to *Cambridge*, where he continued some time and became a *graduate* [f], tho' he is so modest, as to take no notice of it in the account he has left of his life under his own hand. His mind was tinctured with piety, before he came hither: but by some sermons which he heard here, he was effectually convinced of sin, and brought more to mind the salvation of his soul, than formerly.

His behaviour at the university.

THE manner of his behaviour, and the spending of his time here, is worthy of notice, as a rare instance and good example for all *academicks*. He prayed every day, and heard all the godly ministers he could. His chief study was the holy scriptures, tho' he read other useful books. He affected to get acquaintance with the most sober and gracious christians, tho' called *Puritans*. He frequently kept days of fasting and prayer alone, to humble his soul

[f] Tomb's *answ. to* Bailie *p.* 21.

for

for his ſins, and to ſeek pardon and grace of God, thro' Jeſus Chriſt; was ſtrict in performing the duties of religion, and examined himſelf every night to call to mind the ſins of the day, that he might confeſs them, mourn for them, and ſeek pardon, and maintained an indignation againſt all actual ſins, whether committed by himſelf or others. From ſuch an hopeful beginning much good might be expected; and happy would it be for this nation, if our *univerſities* and private *academies* were filled with ſuch *ſtudents*.

WHEN he came from the univerſity, he was choſe *maſter* of the free-ſchool at *Gainſborough*, which he held but a little time.

IN *June* 1629. he was ordained by the biſhop of *Peterborough*, firſt a *deacon*, than a *presbyter* of the church of *England*. Soon after which, the biſhop of *Lincoln* gave him the living at *Humberſtone*. When he had held this cure two or three years, he began to ſcruple the lawfulneſs of ſeveral *ceremonies* and *uſages* of the *national* church; as the *ſurplice*, the *croſs* in *baptiſm*, the admitting *wicked* perſons to the *Lord's-ſupper*, &c. whereupon he reſolved to reſign his living to the biſhop who had beſtowed it upon him; for he told the biſhop plainly, that he could not in *conſcience* conform any longer; however ſaid, he was willing to continue preach-

Is ordained by a biſhop, and a living given him.

Reſigns his living.

ing

ing, tho' he could not hold any *cure*, or read their *ſervice*. And accordingly after this, for two or three years, he frequently preached in divers pariſhes, and was connived at by his *dioceſan* in ſo doing. But about the year 1636. he left the church entirely, and join'd himſelf to the *Diſſenters*, and was expoſed to many difficulties and hardſhips for his *non-conformity*, both before and after the civil wars, beſides the ill treatment he met with, even during that time, for his being a *Baptiſt*; of which an account has been already given.

WHEN the epiſcopal *hierarchy* was laid aſide, and univerſal liberty granted, Mr. *Knollys* came to *London*, and for ſome time preached to the publick churches with great approbation. But when ſome other perſons got into the ſaddle, this could not be born with, becauſe he was againſt a *national church*, an *eſtabliſhed uniformity*, and *infant-baptiſm*. Whereupon he ſet up a *meeting-houſe* in great *St. Helens*, and was very much crowded after, having ſeldom leſs than a thouſand hearers.

And ſet up a meeting-houſe. Gathers a church of Baptiſts, *and was ordained their paſtor.*

HE publickly owned his *opinion*, and frequently preached and diſputed againſt *infant-baptiſm*, and many were convinced by him of the unwarrantableneſs of that practice; among whom, were ſome learned *miniſters* as well as others; particularly the learned Mr. *Jeſſey* was his diſciple in this point, and was baptized by him; and he

he ſoon gathered a ſufficient number to form a diſtinct church of this *denomination* at *London*; of which he was ordained the *paſtor* in the year 1645. And with this people he continued in the faithful diſcharge of that *office*, until the day of his death, except when he was forced from them by violent *perſecution*, or abſent upon juſt occaſions.

HE was very diligent and laborious in the work of the *miniſtry*, both before and after his ſeparation from the eſtabliſhed church. While he was a *Conformiſt*, he often preached three times and ſometimes four on the Lord's-day; at *Holton* at ſeven in the morning, at *Humberſtone* at nine, at *Scartho* at eleven, and at *Humberſtone* again at three in the afternoon; beſides his preaching every *holiday*, and at every *burial*, as well of the *poor* as of the *rich*.

NOR was he leſs diligent in his work after he became a *Nonconformiſt*. For above forty years ſucceſſively he preached three or four times every week, whilſt he had health and liberty: and when he was in *priſon*, it was his uſual practice to preach every day. One thing is very remarkable, while he continued to preach in the *eſtabliſhed church*, which was about five or ſix years, he ſays [t], he was not, as he knew of, inſtrumental to the converſion of

[t] *Life*, p. 9.

one *ſoul* to God, which occaſioned him not only to queſtion, but reject the call and commiſſion he had received to preach the goſpel. But when he ſet out upon another *foundation*, and experienced more of God's teachings and aſſiſtance in the work, he quickly found to his comfort, that many *ſinners* were converted, and many *believers* eſtabliſhed by his *labours*, and that from henceforward he continued to receive many *ſeals* of his *miniſtry*.

HE was as excellent and ſucceſsful in the gift of prayer as of preaching; for God was pleaſed to honour him with ſeveral remarkable anſwers to his prayers: eſpecially during the time of the plague at *London*, divers ſick perſons being ſuddenly reſtored, even while he was praying with them.

ONE very remarkable inſtance of this kind he thought fit to leave to poſterity, which is publiſhed in his life, to which I refer you, it being too long to be inſerted here.

He was often compelled to change his place of abode.

THE frequent revolutions that happened within the compaſs of this good man's long life, occaſioned a great variation in his circumſtances and place of abode. Sometimes he was worth ſome hundreds of pounds, at other times he had neither houſe to dwell in, food to eat, nor one peny to buy any; and frequently was he hurried about from place to place, by the *evil* of the

the *times*, and the *envy* of his *perſecutors*.

FIRST he and his family were forced from *Lincolnſhire* to *London*, then from *London* to *New-England*, and thence back again. Another time they were obliged to remove from *England* into *Wales*, and after this twice from *London* to *Lincolnſhire*. Another circuit was from *London* to *Holland*, from thence into *Germany*, and thence to *Rotterdam*, and then to *London* again. Theſe frequent *removings*, and different *circumſtances* of life, tended very much to the exerciſe of his graces, the increaſe of his experiences, both in temporal and ſpiritual things; and furniſhed him with frequent inſtances of the great love and goodneſs of God, in the courſe of his providence.

WHEN he was with his people, he always received a contribution from them according to their ability; believing it to be his *right* and their *duty*: but the chief means of his *ſubſiſtance*, was by teaching *ſchool*. He was well acquainted with the learned languages, and had an extraordinary way of inſtructing youth: ſo that when the times would permit him to follow this employment, he never wanted ſufficient encouragement; and many eminent perſons, both for piety and learning, were trained up by him.

HE lived to a good old age, and went home as a ſhock of wheat that is gathered in its ſeaſon. And though he was of ſo great an age, yet he did not lie ſick long, nor keep his bed many days. All the time of his illneſs, he behaved himſelf with extraordinary patience and reſignation to the divine will, longing to be diſſolved and to be with Chriſt, not ſo much to be freed from pain and trouble, as from all ſin: and according to his deſire, he departed this life in a great tranſport of joy, on the 19th day of *September* 1691. and *ætatis ſuæ* 93.

And died at London *in the* 93*d. year of his age.*

MR. *Keach* writ an *elegy* on his death, and beſides the funeral-ſermon that was preached for him to his own congregation, Mr. *Tho. Harriſon* preached a ſermon on this occaſion at *Pinners-hall*, where Mr. *Knollys* kept up a morning-lecture every Lord's-day. This was publiſhed, and contains an excellent character of this old diſciple and eminent miniſter of the goſpel. I ſhall give it in his own words.

Mr. Harriſon's *character of him.*

'1. *His accurate and circumſpect walking.* 'I do not ſay, that he was wholly free 'from ſin; ſinleſs perfection is unattainable 'in a mortal ſtate: but yet he was one 'who carefully endeavoured to avoid it. 'He, with the apoſtle *Paul*, did herein '*exerciſe himſelf to have always a conſcience* '*void of offence, towards God and towards* '*men.* He walked with that caution, that 'his greateſt *enemies* had nothing againſt

'him,

'him ſave only in the matters of his God. 'That holy life which he lived, did com-'mand reverence even from thoſe who 'were enemies to the holy doctrine which 'he preached. He was a preacher out of 'the pulpit as well as in it: not like thoſe 'who preſs the form of godlineſs on a 'Lord's-day, and openly deny the power 'of it the remainder of the week; who 'pluck down that in their converſations, 'which they build up in their pulpits.

"2. *His univerſal love to Chriſtians.* 'He had a great reſpect to Chriſt's new 'commandment, which he gave to his 'diſciples, *to love one another.* He loved 'the image of God whereſoever he ſaw 'it. He was not a man of a narrow and 'private, but of a large and publick ſpirit: 'the difference of his fellow-chriſtians opi-'nions from his, did not alienate his af-'fections from them. He loved all his 'fellow-travellers, though they did not 'walk in the ſame particular path with 'himſelf. He embraced thoſe in the arms 'of his love upon earth, with whom he 'thought he ſhould join in ſinging the ſong 'of the Lamb in heaven. It would be 'well, if not only private chriſtians, but 'alſo miniſters, did imitate him therein: 'there would not then be that ſourneſs of 'ſpirit, which is too often, with grief be 'it ſpoken, found among them.

' 3. '*His meekneſs and humility.* He was
' not of a proud and lofty temper, but like
' that maſter whom he profeſſed to ſerve,
' *meek and lowly.* He was willing to bear
' with, and forbear others; to ſtoop and
' condeſcend to others, and to paſs by thoſe
' injuries which he received from them.

' 4. *His labouriouſneſs in that work which
' he was engaged in.* He was not a loiterer,
' but a labourer: he was willing to *ſpend
' and to be ſpent* in the ſervice of his Lord,
' and for the good of poor ſouls. It is
' true, old age and youth did as it were
' meet in him: God had bleſſed him
' with an extraordinary meaſure of bodily
' ſtrength; and he was not an unfaithful
' ſteward of this talent wherewith God
' had entruſted him. Yea, *when his fleſh
' and his heart ſeemed to fail*; when
' his fleſh was ſo weak, that he could
' hardly bear to ſtand in a pulpit, and his
' voice ſo low, that he could ſcarcely be
' heard; his affections were ſo much en-
' gaged in his work, that he was very un-
' willing to leave it.

' 5. *His couragious and chearful ſuffering
' for his maſter's and the goſpel's ſake.* He
' chearfully went about ſuffering as well
' as preaching work. He was not unwil-
' ling *to take up his croſs, and follow* his
' Lord and Maſter in the thorny road of
' tribulation. In theſe things, let us imi-
' tate and follow the example of this holy

' man,

'man, who I question not, says Mr. *Harrison*, is gone to the assembly of the first-born, to that glorious company of prophets, who having finished their work on earth, are wearing their crowns in heaven.'

COMPARE this character, supported by the forementioned facts, with what Mr. *Neal* says of this worthy *Gentleman*, and let the world judge which has done most *justice* to his *memory*.

His works are these, *viz.*

1. *Christ exalted*; *a lost sinner sought and saved by Christ*; *God's people an holy people*; being the sum of divers sermons preached in *Suffolk*. 4to 1646 *His works.*

2. *The shining of a flaming fire in Zion*; an answer to Mr. *Saltmarsh*, his thirteen exceptions against the grounds of new baptism, in his book, entitled, *The smoke of the temple*. 4to 1646

3. *The world that now is, and that which is to come*. 8vo

4. *Grammaticæ Latinæ, Grecæ & Hebraicæ, compendium*; *rhetorica adumbratio*; *item radices Grecæ & Hebraicæ, omnes quæ in Sacra Scriptura veteris & novi Testamenti occurrunt*. 8vo 1665

5. *The parable of the kingdom of heaven expounded*, being an exposition of the first three verses of the 25th chapter of *Matthew*. 8vo 1664

6. *An essay of sacred rhetoric*, used by the Holy Spirit in scripture of truth. 8vo 1675

7. *An expoſition of the whole book of the revelations.* 4to 1668

8. *A ſmall piece in defence of ſinging the praiſes of God.* 8vo

9. A preface to Mr. *Collier*'s book, entitled, *The exaltation of Chriſt.* 8vo 1647

10. A preface to Mr. *Keach*'s *Inſtructions for children.* 12mo

11. His *laſt legacy to the church*; written a little before his death.

12. *Some account of his life*, written with his own hand, to the year 1672

THE two laſt mentioned, were publiſhed after his death.

Mr. Francis Cornwell.

THE next I ſhall mention, though ſo particular an account cannot be given of him as ſome others, is *Francis Cornwell.* M. A.

HE was trained up at *Cambridge*, and was ſome time ſtudent of *Emanuel* college, and commenced *maſter* of *arts* in that *univerſity.* When he left the *univerſity*, he was prefer'd to a living in the eſtabliſhed church, and at the beginning of the civil wars, was *miniſter* at *Orpington* in *Kent* [u].

Profeſſes himſelf a Baptiſt.

I CANNOT find the certain time or means of his embracing the opinion of the *Baptiſts.* But in the year 1643. he publickly profeſs'd that *principle*, and wrote in defence it. His book was intitled,

[u] Vide *his two queries.*

The

The vindication of the royal commiſſion of King Jeſus. In this he attempts to prove by ſeveral arguments, that the practice of *chriſtning* children was a *popiſh* tradition, and an *antichriſtian* cuſtom, contrary to the commiſſion given by our bleſſed Saviour, *&c.* It was dedicated to the parliament, and given away at the door of the houſe of Commons to divers of the members [x], which cauſed it to make a great noiſe, and be much handed about, to the great offence of thoſe of a different *opinion.*

DR. *Featley* [y] makes ſeveral remarks upon it, and pretends to anſwer the main arguments in it. There was alſo about the ſame time another piece publiſhed in anſwer to it, called a *Declaration againſt the Anabaptiſts* [z]. But neither of theſe convinced Mr. *Cornwell,* or ſtopp'd the ſpreading of his *opinion,* which prevailed much at this time among the learned, as well as the common people [a].

THE doctor calls him [b], *a new Anabaptiſtical proſelyte.* Whence it ſhould ſeem, that he had but lately entertained this *opinion.* However, having found the *truth* himſelf, he was willing to help others to do ſo

x Edward's *Gangræna,* part 3. p. 98.
y *Dipper Dipp'd.*
z *Ibid.* p. 48.
a *Ibid. Preface.*
b *Ibid.* p. 45.

likewiſe

likewiſe; at leaſt, to ſee whether his *brethren* in the *miniſtry* could anſwer his *arguments*, and reſolve the *doubts* he had concerning the lawfulneſs of that *practice*. And according to this, we find after he has examined the *ſcriptures* and *antiquity* concerning this *point*, he makes this appeal in his book: 'Oh, that the learned '*Engliſh miniſtry* would inform me, leſt 'my blood, like *Abel*'s, cry aloud from 'heaven for vengeance, for not ſatisfy'ing a troubled conſcience! How ſhall I 'admit the *infant* of a *believer* to be 'made a viſible member of a particular 'church, and be *baptized*, before it be 'able to make confeſſion of its *faith* and '*repentance*?'

Appeals to the Engliſh *miniſtry for information.*

AFTER the publiſhing of his book, and finding no ſatisfactory anſwer returned to his arguments, he went on to preach and propagate his opinion, notwithſtanding the dangerous conſequence that it might be of to himſelf.

In a ſermon before divers miniſters, he declares his ſentiments.

IN the year 1644. being to preach a ſermon at *Cranbrook* in *Kent*, before divers *miniſters* in thoſe parts, he took the liberty of declaring his ſentiments freely in this point; and told them, *pædobaptiſm* was an *antichriſtian innovation*, a human tradition, and a practice for which there was neither *precept*, *example*, or true *deduction* from the word of God. At this ſeveral of the *miniſters* were not only very much ſtartled, but

but greatly offended: and when they had debated the matter together afterwards, they agreed to re-examine this *point*, and to bring their collections together, at the next meeting, which was to be within a fortnight.

MR. *Christopher Blackwood*, who was one of them, took a great deal of pains, and studied the question closely, and began to suspect that it was indeed, as had been said, no more than an *human tradition*, and that it was attended with more evil consequences than he had ever before considered. When they met again, according to agreement, he brought in his arguments, which determined against *pædobaptism*: but there was none had brought any thing in defence thereof. One said, that they sought for truth and not victory; and therefore proposed, that they might have his papers to examine the arguments. The other approving of this motion, the papers were accordingly left with them; and after he had waited a long time, and could get no answer, he sent for them again, and after some correction and enlargement, sent them to the press [b].

Mr. Blackwood *becomes his proselyte.*

THUS, by Mr. *Cornwell*'s means, the *controversy* was revived in that county, the truth gained ground, and he had the honour of making a very ingenious and learned proselyte to his opinion.

[b] Blackwood's *storm. antich.* p. 1.

HE

HE did not continue long after this in the *national church*, though it was now much reformed to what it had been. For besides his denial of *infant-baptism*, he disliked both *national* and *parochial* churches; and taught, that the true church was to consist only of such as professed *repentance* from dead works, and *faith* in the Lord Jesus Christ, and were *baptized* according to his commands; this being after the pattern of the first churches in *Judæa* [c]. And such a church or society of christians was quickly gathered by him in *Kent*.

HE was also a very zealous opposer of *persecution*, and an imposed uniformity. And when the *ordinance of parliament* was made, to silence all *lay-preachers*, that is, as they explained it, all that had not *episcopal* or *presbyterian ordination*, or that should preach any thing contrary to the articles of *faith*, and *directory* for publick worship, published by the *assembly*, he publickly opposed it, and wrote a small *piece* to discover the evil and unchristian spirit of such proceedings, and entitled it, *Two Queries worthy of consideration*; because the whole goes upon these two questions, which he proposes therein to the ministers both of church and state.

Q. I. WHETHER that ministry that preacheth freely the gospel-faith, that the

[c] *Two queries*, p. 5.

Lord Jeſus is the Chriſt, as the apoſtle Acts ii.
Peter did, be not truly *orthodox?* 36.

Q. 2. WHETHER it be agreeable to the word of God, contained in the ſacred ſcriptures, to ſilence or inhibit any *miniſters* of Jeſus Chriſt, for preaching this goſpel-faith freely?

AS a loyal covenanter for a pure reformation in *England*, (theſe are his words) he affirms the *former*, and endeavours to maintain it by ſeveral arguments. The *latter* he denies, and intimates, that whoſoever ſhall be guilty of any ſuch practice, would act as the *Jews* of old did, who caſt the blind man out of their ſynagogue, for confeſſing that Jeſus was the Chriſt.

THERE were, if Mr. *Edwards* may be depended upon, divers pamphlets put forth by this learned man: but all I can meet with, are the two already mentioned. He continued a faithful ſhepherd of that flock, which had been gathered by his miniſtry in *Kent*, unto the day of his death; and was ſucceeded in that place and office, by a ſon who was of his own name and principles. His writings are reckoned theſe which follow:

1. *A Vindication of the Royal Commiſſion of King Jeſus.* *His works,*

2. *Two Queries worthy of conſideration,* &c.

3. *A*

3. *A Conference between Mr.* John Cotton, *and the Elders of* New-England. 8vo 1646

4. *A Deſcription of the Spiritual Temple*; or, *The Difference between the Chriſtian and Antichriſtian Church.* 8vo 1646

MORE of this gentleman's character may be ſeen in the prefaces to the two laſt mentioned books.

Mr. Chriſt. Blackwood.

IT will be very natural in the next place, to give ſome account of Mr. *Chriſtopher Blackwood*, who was the diſciple of the former in the point of baptiſm. The firſt thing that I can meet with concerning him is, that he was a *miniſter* ſomewhere in *Kent*, and was poſſeſſed of a *parochial* charge in that county at the beginning of the *civil wars.* From whence, as well as from his writings, it may be concluded, that he had a learned education, and was probably trained up at one of our *univerſities.* The time and means of his receiving this *opinion* is already related from the account which he himſelf gave of it. And he did not, after the change of his judgment, continue long in the *eſtabliſhed church*; for he was as zealous againſt *national churches*, as againſt *infant-baptiſm* [d].

CAPTAIN *Dean*, who lived in thoſe times, reckons him among thoſe of his

[d] *Letter*, p. 8, 9.

acquaintance,

acquaintance, who voluntarily left their *parochial* charges and *benefices*, as not approving the *baptizing* of *infants*, and concerning whom he further ſays, they were *worthy guides, well qualified in all reſpects for the miniſtry.*

THE *Preſbyterians* of thoſe times wrote againſt him with ſome warmth [e], becauſe he was an advocate for *liberty of conſcience*, and oppoſed their attempted *eſtabliſhment*, as well as their *infant-baptiſm* [f]. In the firſt book he writ, he joined theſe two together, *infants baptiſm* and *compulſion of conſcience*; and called them, *the two laſt and ſtrongeſt garriſons of antichriſt.*

WHEN his *principles* occaſioned him to leave the *national church*, I do not find that he collected a diſtinct congregation of ſuch as agreed with him in this doctrine of *baptiſm*, as many others did. It rather appears from the *dedications* of ſome of his *books*, that he went into the *army*, and that in the year 1653. he went into *Ireland* with the *army*, under the command of general *Fleetwood* and lieutenant *Ludlow*. He lived till after the *reſtoration*, was then at *London*, and put his hand to the apology publiſhed by the *Baptiſts* in 1660. declaring againſt *Venner*'s inſurrection.

[e] Edwards's *Gangræna*, part 3. p. 98.
[f] Blake's *Infant-Bapt.*

HE

HE has publiſhed ſeveral tracts; as,

His works. 1. *The ſtorming of Antichriſt in his two laſt and ſtrongeſt garriſons; compulſion of conſcience and infants baptiſm.* 4to 1664.

2. *Apoſtolical baptiſm; or a ſober rejoynder to a treatiſe of Mr.* Blake's, in anſwer to his former treatiſe.

3. *Four treatiſes:* The firſt ſetting forth *the excellency of Chriſt*; the ſecond, containing a *preparation for death*; the third, concerning *our love to Chriſt*; the fourth, concerning *our love to our neighbours.* 4to 1653

4. *A treatiſe concerning repentance*; wherein alſo the doctrine of *reſtitution* is largely handled: with a ſolution of many caſes of conſcience concerning it. 4to 1653

5. *A ſoul-ſearching catechiſm*; wherein is opened and explained, not only the ſix fundamental points, *Heb.* vi. 1. but alſo many other queſtions of higheſt concernment in the chriſtian religion. 2d edition. 4to 1653

6. *A brief catechiſm concerning baptiſm*; firſt publiſh'd at the end of his *Storming of Antichriſt*, afterwards reprinted for the ſatisfaction and information of the people of God in *Lancaſhire.* 1652

7. *An expoſition of the ten firſt chapters of* Matthew, delivered in ſeveral ſermons. 4to 1659

ANO-

ANOTHER who deserves to be rank'd amongst the worthies of this denomination, is Mr. *Benj. Cox*, who in his time made no mean figure amongst them. He was a bishop's son, a man of great learning, and a graduate in one of our *universities* [g]. He was for some time a *minister* in the *establish'd church*, had a parochial charge somewhere in the county of *Devon*, and was very zealous for the superstitious *ceremonies* that prevailed in bishop *Laud*'s time; of which the *Presbyterians* afterwards upbraided him when he opposed their *establishment* [h]. But notwithstanding this, when the affairs of state gave men occasion to think and speak more freely in matters of religion, Mr. *Cox* was amongst the earliest of them in promoting reformation, and was in a fair way of being a very great and famous man in this kingdom, had he not, when he came to take the model of his religion from the scriptures only, rejected the *baptism* of *infants*, as not being therein contained. For this hindred him from preferment in the established church, and prejudiced those divines against him who were at the head of *ecclesiastical* affairs [i]. However, as it was, he preserv'd even among them the character of a man of great *learning* and competent parts.

Mr. Benj. Cox.

Was first a minister in the establish'd church.

[g] Tombes's *Answ. to* Bailie, *p.* 21.
[h] Gangræna, *part* 1. *p.* 38.
[i] Baxter's *Script. Proof, Introd.*

Diſputes with Mr. Baxter,

IN 1644. he had a diſpute with Mr. *Baxter* concerning *infant-baptiſm*; firſt by word of mouth, then by writing; and was afterward *impriſoned* in the city of *Coventry* for his opinion in this point, as has been before obſerved.

and with others at Alder-manbury *church.*

THE year following he came to *London*, and was one of the principal managers, on the part of the *Baptiſts*, in the *publick diſpute* concerning *infant-baptiſm* at *Aldermanbury* church; to which a ſtop was afterwards put by the government.

HE was ſome time *miniſter* at *Bedford*, after *epiſcopacy* and the *common prayer* were laid aſide[k]. But in the year 1646. when the *ſeven churches* in *London*, called *Anabaptiſts*, publiſhed a confeſſion of their faith, and preſented it to the parliament, I find his name ſubſcribed to it in behalf of one of thoſe congregations.

I CANNOT learn certainly either his age, or the time of his death. Mr. *Baxter*, at the beginning of the civil wars, called him *an antient miniſter*[l]. He muſt therefore be very old when he died; for he lived till after the reſtoration. And tho' when the act of *uniformity* in 1662. took place, he at firſt conform'd; yet ſoon after his conſcience ſmote him for what he had done, and he threw up his *living*, and died a *Nonconformiſt* and *Baptiſt*.

k Dean's *Letter, p.* 8.
l *Script. Proofs, Introd.*

THERE

THERE were but two pieces, as I can find, publiſhed by him.

1. A DECLARATION concerning the publick diſpute which ſhould have been in the publick meeting-houſe of *Aldermanbury, Dec.* 3. 1645. concerning infant-baptiſm. *His works.*

2. GOD's ordinance the ſaints privilege, proved in two treatiſes. The firſt, *The Saints Intereſt by Chriſt in all the Privileges of Grace cleared, and the Objections againſt the ſame anſwer'd.* The ſecond, *The peculiar Intereſt of the Elect in Chriſt, and his ſaving Graces*: wherein is proved, that Chriſt hath not ſatisfy'd for the ſins of all men, but only for the ſins of thoſe that do or ſhall believe in him; and the objections againſt the ſame anſwer'd.

AMONG the worthies of this denomination, I muſt not omit the mention of that grave divine and ſolid preacher, Mr. *Daniel Dyke.* He was born at *Epping* in *Eſſex*, about the year 1617. (his father, Mr. *Jeremiah Dyke*, being miniſter of that pariſh) and had the name of *Daniel* given him in reſpect to his uncle, the famous Mr. *Daniel Dyke*, B. D. ſo well known by his excellent treatiſe, *of the deceitfulneſs of the heart*, publiſhed after his death by the father of Mr. *Dyke* who is the ſubject of this article. *Mr.* Dan. Dyke.

AFTER he had been ſufficiently inſtructed at private ſchools in the country, he was ſent to the *univerſity* at *Cambridge*, and there trained up for the *miniſtry*. And when he came to be publickly employ'd in that ſacred work, he was ſoon took notice of for his great learning and uſeful preaching, and had ſuitable preferment beſtow'd upon him.

Was made chaplain in ordinary to the protector,

HE was made one of the *chaplains* in ordinary to *Oliver Cromwel*, when he came to be lord protector of *England*. He had alſo the parochial charge of *Great Hadham* in *Hertfordſhire*, a place worth at leaſt 300 l. *per annum*. And when the government in the year 1653. appointed a certain number of men to examine and approve all ſuch as ſhould be admitted into livings in the eſtabliſhed church, Mr. *Dyke* was fix'd upon to be one of them.

and one of the Tryers.

INDEED his great learning, his ſeriouſneſs, and piety, together with his ſolid judgment, render'd him worthy, as well as fit, for ſo great a truſt; and he, with Mr. *John Tombes*, were all the *Baptiſts* that I can find to have been in this *commiſſion*.

UPON the Reſtoration, Mr. *Dyke* diſcover'd himſelf to be a man of great integrity, and faithfulneſs to his conſcience, and quitted his profitable living, rather than ſin againſt his light, by conforming to epiſcopal government, and uſing the ceremonies of the church of *England*. Nor did he he ſtay till he was forced out by the act of *Uniformity* in 1662. but voluntarily reſigned preſently after the king came in; for he foreſaw the ſtorm that was coming, and the ſnares that muſt attend a man of his principles, while he continued in ſuch a poſt. *He quits his living upon the Reſtoration.*

WHEN his intimate friend and acquaintance Mr. *Caſe*, who was one of thoſe miniſters deputed to wait on the king at the *Hague*, and one of the *commiſſioners* at the *Savoy* to treat about the ſettlement of religion, endeavoured to perſuade him to continue, and told him what a hopeful proſpect they had, from the king's behaviour, &c. Mr. *Dyke* told him plainly, 'That 'they did but deceive and flatter them-'ſelves: That if the king was ſincere in 'his ſhew of piety, and great reſpect to 'them and their religion; yet when he 'came to be ſettled, the party that had for-'merly adhered to him, and the creatures 'that would come over with him, would 'have the management of publick affairs, 'and would circumvent all their deſigns, 'and in all probability not only turn them 'out, but take away their liberty too.' And they afterwards found the truth of his words by woful experience.

DR. *Calamy* has put his name in the liſt of the *ejected* or *ſilenced miniſters*, but gives him no other *character*, than that he was an *Anabaptiſt*; which is another inſtance of the Doctor's *impartiality* and *candour* for the people of this *denomination.*

HIS resigning his living in the church, and the troubles and persecutions that followed afterwards, did not cause him to lay down the ministry of the word; but he preached afterwards as often as he had opportunity, and was generally preserved by some good providence from the rage and malice of his persecutors. And though he lived in two or three great *storms*, and had several *writs* out against him, yet was never in *prison* except one *night*.

Is ordain'd co-pastor with Mr. William Kiffin *to a* Baptist *church.*

SOMETIME after his leaving his parochial charge, he was chosen and ordain'd co-pastor with Mr. *William Kiffin* to the congregation of *Baptists* at *Devonshire-square, London*, and continued a faithful labourer in this vineyard until his death, which was in the year 1688. a little before the *happy Revolution*, when he was about seventy years of age.

HIS funeral-sermon was preached by Mr. *Waner*, at the aforesaid meeting-house, and his corps interr'd at the *Dissenters* burying-ground in *Bunhill-fields*.

HE left behind him two daughters, who may be still living; from the eldest of which this account was received in the year 1716.

HE was a man of so great modesty, and had so mean an opinion of his own abilities, that he could never be prevail'd upon

to

to publiſh any thing. Only I find his name, in company with ſome of his brethren, to two or three printed papers, in compoſing which it is ſuppoſed he had the principal ſhare. As,

1. THE *Baptiſts Anſwer to Mr.* Wills's *Appeal.* 8vo 1675 *His works.*

2. AN epiſtle recommendatory to Mr. *Cox*'s *Confutation of the errors of* Thomas Collier. 4to

3. *The Quakers Appeal anſwer'd*; or, a full relation of the occaſion, progreſs, and iſſue of a meeting at *Barbican* between the *Baptiſts* and the *Quakers.* 8vo 1674

Mr. Sam. Fiſher.

THERE was another, who though he did not perſevere in this profeſſion to the end, yet did ſo zealouſly defend it, both by diſputation and writing for ſome time, that ſhould I paſs him without notice, ſome may be ill-natured enough to ſay it was with deſign: I mean Mr. *Samuel Fiſher*, acknowledged by all parties to have been a man of eminent piety and virtue [m]. His parents deſigned him from his childhood, for a *miniſter* of the *church of England*; and in order thereunto, took care to have him, while a boy, well inſtructed at private ſchools. And when he had attained a competent meaſure of grammar-learning, he was ſent to one of our *univerſities*, where

[m] *Hiſtory of the* Quakers *by* Gerrard Croeſe.

his diligence and progreſs was ſo great, that he ſurmounted moſt of his fellows. His mind led him moſtly to the ſtudy of eloquence. Rhetoric and poetry, were the ſciences he then put the greateſt value upon. So that he became a man ſingularly learned, and wonderfully eloquent, and had an accurate knowledge of the *Greek* and *Latin* antiquities; which ſo ſtuck to him, that even after he had changed his religion, and opinion of theſe *human ornaments*, yet his writings ſavoured much of them, though contrary to his intention.

Ordained a miniſter of the church of England.

WHEN he had perfected his *academick* courſe, and taken his degrees, he was ordained, firſt a *deacon*, then a *preſbyter* of the *church of England*[n]; the former he received from a biſhop before the *civil wars*; the latter from certain *Preſbyterian* miniſters after *epiſcopacy* was laid aſide[o].

Becomes chaplain to Sir Arthur Haſelrigg.

HIS firſt preferment was to be a chaplain in the family of that noble and pious gentleman Sir *Arthur Haſelrigg*. He demeaned himſelf in this ſtation ſo well, that the report of his fame invited thoſe who knew him, to judge of his ability and ſkill for greater things, to advance him to a more high and dignified place: and accordingly he obtained a parochial living in *Kent* of 500 *l.* a year. But notwithſtanding his great learning and high preferment,

Is advanced to the living of Lidd, *in* Rumſey Marſh.

[n] *Baby Bapt.* p. 6.
[o] *Ibid.* p. 12.

he

he ſtill preſerved an humble mind, and affable carriage; and would converſe freely, not only with ſuch who were very much below himſelf, but alſo with ſerious chriſtians, who were of different, and contrary ſentiments from him.

AMONG the reſt there was a *Baptiſt* miniſter in thoſe parts, with whom he kept an intimate correſpondence. This man was frequently calling upon him to juſtify from *ſcripture* the lawfulneſs of *baptizing children*; and to ſhew by what authority they changed the antient cuſtom of *immerſion*, and uſed *ſprinkling* in that ſacrament.

THIS *perſon* was vaſtly inferior to Mr. *Fiſher* both in learning and natural parts; yet in this point he was a means of inſtructing him in the way of the Lord *more fully*; and Mr. *Fiſher* was a man of ſo much integrity and love for the truth, that he would not reject it by what hand ſoever it was brought to him. Therefore when he had diligently examined this matter, and found that the *Baptiſts* were in the right, he freely quitted his living, and returned his *diploma* back to the biſhop; was baptized according to Chriſt's inſtitution, and joined himſelf to a *baptized* congregation at *Aſhford* in *Kent*. This muſt be acknowledged, even by thoſe who reject his *opinion*, to have been an extraordinary inſtance of ſincerity and ſelf-denial.

Quits his living, and joins himſelf to a Baptiſt *congregation.*

HAVING

HAVING left so good a *living*, he now contented himself with a little he had of his own, and farmed a piece of ground in the neighbourhood, by both which he had enough to live upon. He continued however, still in the exercise of the *ministry*, and in a little time after took the pastoral charge of a congregation of *Baptists*; and the noise of so pious and learned a man turning *Baptist*, spread far and near, and contributed not a little towards the promoting of that doctrine p. Some hundreds were baptized by him; and he was frequently engaged in publick disputes with the most learned and zealous advocates for *infant-baptism*, as at *Ashford* in *Kent*, *July* 27. 1649. where he defended his principles against several noted *ministers*, in the presence of two thousand auditors.

Is frequently engaged in publick disputes.

HE had another dispute with Dr. *Channel* at *Petworth* in 1651. and at least eight other publick disputes was he drawn into within the space of three years, always coming off with good success and honour to his cause. While he continued with the *Baptists*, he was an ornament to the whole *sect*, and looked upon as one of the chief defenders of their doctrine.

ABOUT the year 1655. he was strongly attacked by two leading men of the people called *Quakers*, *Caton* and *Stubbs*; and be-

p *Baby Bapt.* p. 411.

ing

ing but an unſtable man, he was carried away with their *opinions*, and afterwards writ ſeveral books in defence of that religion, which are had in great eſteem among them.

Goes off to the Quakers.

WHILE he was among the *Baptiſts*, he wrote that elaborate treatiſe, entitled, *Baby Baptiſm mere Babiſm.* In this, he not only confutes the falſe account that had been publiſhed of his diſpute with ſeveral *miniſters* at *Aſhford*, which was the occaſion of his writing on this *controverſy*; but alſo anſwers particularly, with great learning and many witty turns, what had been written upon this ſubject, by Dr. *Featley*, Dr. *Holmes*, Mr. *Marſhal*, Mr. *Blake*, Mr. *Cotton*, Mr. *Baxter*, and others; ſo that it contains the whole of the *controverſy* as then managed, and is the only *folio* writ upon it in the *Engliſh* tongue.

THE reverend and very pious *Francis Bampfeild*, M.A. was alſo a divine of great note among this *denomination* of *Proteſtants*. He deſcended from a very antient and honourable family in *Devonſhire*, and was by his parents deſigned for the *miniſtry* from his birth, and educated accordingly. When he was but a child, he diſcovered a great delight in books and learning, and from his own inclination concurred with the deſign of his pious parents. After he had been inſtructed by ſome of the ableſt maſters in *grammar-learning*, he was

Mr. Francis Bampfeild.

Manuſcr. penes me.

was about the ſixteenth year of his age ſent to the *univerſity*, and educated at *Wadham* college in *Oxon*; where he continued between ſeven and eight years, made great improvements, and commenced *maſter* of arts. When he left the *univerſity*, he was ordained firſt a *deácon*, then a *preſbyter* of the church of *England*; the former by biſhop *Hall*, the latter by biſhop *Skinner*; and was ſoon after preferred to a living of about 100 *l.* a year in *Dorſetſhire*; where he took great pains to inſtruct the people, and promote true religion amongſt them. And having an annuity of 80 *l.* a year for life ſettled on him by his friends, he ſpent all the income of his place in acts of *charity* among his *pariſhioners*; as in giving them *bibles* and other good *books*, ſetting the *poor* to work, and relieving the *neceſſities* of thoſe that could not, and ſuffered not knowingly one *beggar* to be in his pariſh.

Is ordain'd a miniſter in the eſtabliſhed church.

Preferred to a living in Dorſetſhire.

WHILE he was here, he began to ſee, that the church of *England* needed *reformation* in many things, not only in *doctrine* and *worſhip*, but more eſpecially in *diſcipline*; and therefore, as became a ſincere chriſtian, and faithful *miniſter*, he heartily ſet about it, making the laws of Chriſt his only rule in this caſe. But he met with great *oppoſition* and trouble for ſo doing.

ABOUT the ſame time, the people at *Sherbourn*, one of the moſt populous towns in in *Dorsetshire*, wanting a *minister*, did earnestly solicit him to come thither. Here was more work and less wages; however there being a prospect of doing more good, and finding many thousands of the *people*, as well as the neighbouring *ministers*, very desirous of his removing, after about two years waiting, he accepted their call. And in this *parish* he continued, till the act of *uniformity* took place, to labour with great success, and was universally beloved by his *parishioners*.

ONE thing was very remarkable, if not singular in him; that though he joined heartily in the reformation of the church in those times, yet he was zealous against the *parliament*'s *war*, and *Oliver*'s *usurpation*; constantly asserting the *royal cause* under all those changes, and suffering for it.

Is very zealous in the royal cause:

BUT after the *Restoration*, being utterly unsatisfied in his conscience with the conditions of *conformity*, he took his leave of his sorrowful and weeping *congregation*, the Lord's-day before St. *Bartholomew* [q] in 1662. and was quickly after *imprisoned* for worshipping God in his own family.

SO soon was his unshaken loyalty to the King forgotten; nay, so far was he from having any favour shewn to him on this account, that he was more frequently *imprisoned*, and exposed to greater hardships

Yet more persecuted than other Dissenters.

[q] *Conformists 4th Plea*, p. 44.

for

for his *nonconformity*, than moſt other *Diſſenters*, as will appear in its place.

IN all the changes of the times till now, every *party* was for having a man of ſuch *piety*, ſerioufneſs and learning kept in the *miniſtry*. Beſides his being approved and ordained by the biſhops beforementioned, when that *hierarchy* was uppermoſt; he had the approbation of the aſſociated *miniſters*, both of the *preſbyterian* and *congregational* perſuaſion. When *Oliver* took the ſupreme power upon him, he voluntarily gave him licenſe and authority under his hand and ſeal. When the *Tryers* were ſet up, to examine and approve publick preachers, they without his ſeeeking for it, gave him their approbation and teſtimony alſo [r]. And beſides all this, he had an *authority* and *licence* for preaching under the hands and

Charles I. *and* II. ſeals of two Kings, not of his own ſeeking, but procured for him by his friends. But as he did not put any value upon human *authorities*, ſo now they were of no ſervice to him.

HE was reſolved however to be faithful to the commiſſion he had received from Jeſus Chriſt, and eſteemed it *more reaſonable to obey God than man*; ſo that all the oppoſition and ſufferings that he met with, neither diſcouraged him in his work, nor cauſed him in the leaſt to decline it.

[r] *Hiſtorical declaration of his life*, p. 6.

WHEN

WHEN he was in *prison*, he preached sometimes every day, and gathered a church even under his confinement. And when he was at liberty, he ceased not *to preach in the name of Jesus*. And he had the courage of being one of the first that set up separate meetings in two or three counties in *England*. In the latter part of his life he came to *London*, where he soon gathered a *congregation*, which met at *Pinner's-hall*, to whom he was *pastor*, and constantly preached, when the evil of the times would permit. But he met with the same ill-treatment here, as he had done in the countries, and was often carried from his meeting to *prison*, and at last died in *Newgate*, *Feb*. 16. 1683.

He gathers a church in prison, and died in Newgate.

ALL that knew him will acknowledge, that he was a man of great piety. And he would in all probability have preserved the same character, with respect to his learning and judgment, had it not been for his opinion in two points, *viz*. That *infants* ought not to be baptized, and that the *Jewish sabbath* ought still to be kept.

HE hath published several tracts. As,

His works.

1. *A Letter*, containing his judgment for the *observation of the Jewish*, or, *Seventh-day Sabbath*. 8vo 1672

2. *All in one:* All useful sciences and profitable arts in one book of *Jehovah*, &c. folio 1677

3. *The*

3. *The open Confessor*, and *The Free-Prisoner*; a sheet, written when he was a prisoner in *Salisbury*. 1675

4. *A Name, a new one*; or, an histo-storical declaration of his life, especially as to some eminent passages relating to his call to the ministry. 1681

5. *The House of Wisdom*, &c. for the further promoting of scripture-knowledge. 1681

6. *The Free-Prisoner*; a letter written from *Newgate*. 1683

7. *A Just Appeal from lower Courts on Earth, to the highest Court in Heaven.* 1683

8. *A Continuation* of the former *Just Appeal.* 1683

9. *A Gramatical Opening of some* Hebrew *Words and Phrases in the Beginning of the Bible.* 1684

Mr. Edward Stennett.

MR. *Edward Stennett* was another *Baptist* minister of note and learning in those times. His wife was Mrs. *Mary Quelch*, whose parents were of good repute in the city of *Oxford*. They were both very pious and worthy persons, and justly deserved the character given them in the epitaph inscribed on their tomb at *Wallingford*, which was composed by their son Mr. *Joseph Stennett* [s], and is as followeth:

[s] Stennett's *works*, vol. IV. p. 274.

Here

Here lies an holy, and an happy pair;
As once in grace, they now in glory ſhare:
They dar'd to ſuffer, but they fear'd to ſin;
And meekly bore the croſs, the crown to win:
So liv'd, as not to be afraid to die;
So dy'd, as heirs of immortality.

Reader, attend: tho' dead, they ſpeak to thee;
Tread the ſame path, the ſame thine end ſhall be.

THE part Mr. *Edward Stennett* took in the *civil wars*, being on the ſide of the *parliament*, expoſed him to the neglect of his relations, and afterwards to many difficulties. He was a faithful and laborious *miniſter*; but his diſſent from the *eſtabliſhed church*, depriving him of the means whereby to maintain his family, which was large, he applied himſelf to the ſtudy of *phyſick*; by the practice of which he was enabled to bring up his children, and to give them a liberal education, notwithſtanding he bore a conſiderable ſhare of the *perſecution* which the *diſſenters* underwent at that time. While I ſpeak of his *ſufferings*, it may not be amiſs to recite an account of one very extraordinary deliverance he met with, and which was often related by his ſon, the reverend Mr. *Joſeph Stennett*, whoſe memory is dear to many ſtill living, *viz.*

Applies himſelf to the ſtudy of phyſick.

'[t] He dwelt in the castle of *Walling-* '*ford*, a place where no warrant could 'make forcible entrance, but that of a lord 'chief justice; and the house was so situated, 'that assemblies could meet, and every 'part of religious worship be exercised in 'it, without any danger of a legal con- 'viction, unless *informers* were admitted, 'which care was taken to prevent; so that 'for a long time he kept a constant and 'undisturbed meeting in his *hall*. A *gen-* '*tleman* who was in the commission of 'the peace, and his very near neighbour, 'being highly incensed at the continuance 'of an *assembly* of this kind so near him; 'after having made several fruitless at- 'tempts to get his *emissaries* admitted into 'the house in order to a conviction, in the 'rage of a disappointment resolved, toge- 'ther with a neighbouring *clergyman*, upon 'doing it by a *subornation* of *witnesses*.

A malicious design against him.

'They accordingly hired some persons fit 'for their purpose, to swear they had 'been at those *assemblies*, and heard *prayer* 'and *preaching* there, though they had 'never been in the house on those occa- 'sions. The *clergyman*'s conduct in this 'affair was the more censured, because he 'had professed a great friendship for Mr. '*Stennett*, and was under considerable

[t] *Mr.* Joseph Stennett's *life*, p. 4, &c.

'obligations

'obligations to him; having often had his '*assistance* in the way of his *profession* as a '*physician*, for his family, without any re-'ward. Mr. *Stennett* finding an *indict-*'*ment* was laid against him on the *con-*'*venticle* act, founded upon the oaths of 'several witnesses, and being well assured 'that nothing but *perjury* could support it, 'was resolved to traverse it, and accord-'ingly did so. The *assizes* were held at '*Newbury*, and when the time drew near, 'there was great triumph in the success 'these gentlemen proposed to themselves, 'when on a sudden the scene was changed; 'news came to the justice, that his son, 'whom he had lately placed at *Oxford*, 'was gone off with a player; the con-'cern whereof, and the riding in search of 'him, prevented his attendance in the 'court. The *clergyman*, a few days be-'fore the *assizes*, boasted much of the ser-'vice which would be done to the church 'and the neighbourhood by this prosecu-'tion, and of his own determination to 'be at *Newbury* to help carry it on; but 'to the surprize of many, his design was 'frustrated by *sudden death*. One of the '*witnesses*, who lived at *Cromish*, was also 'prevented by being seized with a violent 'and sad disease, of which he died. An-'other of them fell down and broke his 'leg, and was so hindred. In short, of seven

Circumvented by providence.

'or eight persons engaged in this wicked 'design, there was but one left who was 'capable of appearing; he was a *gardiner*, 'who had been frequently employed by 'Mr. *Stennett* at day-labour, but never 'lodged in his house, nor was admitted to 'the religious assemblies held there. They 'thought to make him, as he was a ser-'vant to the family, a very material evi-'dence; and kept him in liquor for se-'veral days to that purpose. But coming 'to his reason just as the *assizes* drew on, 'he went about the town, exclaiming 'against himself for his *ingratitude* and '*perjury*, as well as against those who had 'employed him; and absolutely refused to 'go. So that when Mr. *Stennett* came to '*Newbury*, neither *prosecutor* nor *witness* 'appearing against him, he was discharged 'of course,

His family.

'MR. *Edward Stennett* had several sons, 'and one daughter, besides those who died 'young. His eldest son, *Jehudah*, after-'wards an eminent *physician* at *Henly* upon '*Thames*, wrote an *Hebrew* grammar at 'nineteen years of age; which was print-'ed, and well received by the publick. 'Another of his sons, *Benjamin*, proved a 'valuable and useful *minister*; but died 'young. His daughter, chiefly by the in-'structions of her brother *Joseph* (of whom 'I shall have occasion to treat hereafter)

'acquired

'acquired ſuch ſkill in the *Greek* and *Hebrew* languages, as to conſult the *ſcriptures* in their *originals* with eaſe and pleaſure. She was an excellent woman, and married to a worthy gentleman, Mr. *William Morton* of *Knaphill* in the county of *Bucks*.'

Mr. Vavaſor Powell.

To theſe muſt be added the famous Mr. *Vavaſor Powell*, a man of great piety and uſefulneſs, and while he lived, no ſmall honour to this *denomination* of *Proteſtants*. He was born in the year 1617. and thoſe that have men in eſteem for their pedigree, may know, that he deſcended from a very antient and honourable ſtock; his father Mr. *Richard Powell* being of a noble family, that had lived for ſome hundreds of years at *Knocklas*, in *Radnorſhire*; and his mother of the *Vavaſors*, a family of great antiquity, that came out of *Yorkſhire* into *Wales*. So that by both, he became allied to the chief and beſt families in *North-Wales*, and was ſaluted by the principal gentry in thoſe parts as their kinſman. He was trained up a ſcholar, and made a good proficiency in the learned languages; but proved a very wild and unlucky youth, and was therefore termed by his ſchool-fellows and companions *Dux omnium malorum*, which he himſelf acknowledges to have been juſt. His firſt preferment was in the *eſtabliſhed church*;

 his

Was first made curate at Clun.

his uncle Mr. *Erasmus Powell*, taking him to be curate at *Clun*, where he also kept a school to augment his income; but was still a stranger to true and unfeigned religion. And though, according to his own expression, he was *a reader of common prayers, and in the habit of a foolish shepherd*; yet was he one that slighted the *scriptures*, a stranger to secret and spiritual prayer, and a great prophaner of the *sabbath*. But by conversing with some serious and godly christians, who in contempt were called *Puritans*, and by reading their books, and hearing their sermons, God was pleased to convince him of his miserable and sinful estate, and to work a great and very remarkable conversion in him. Soon after which, he left the *episcopal church*, and joined with the *Nonconformists*; became a very lively and powerful preacher, and was the means of converting many from the error of their ways. But the more good he did, and the more popular he became, the more *enemies* he had, and with the greater rage did they persecute him. So that in the year 1642. he left his native country, and came to *London*, where there being universal liberty, he preached in several publick places with great approbation, and was some time after invited to settle at *Dartford* in *Kent*; where he went and was blessed with great success in his labours, being instrumental

He leaves the established church, and joins the Nonconformists.

inſtrumental in bringing many ſouls to Chriſt, and gathering a congregation in that town. When he had been there about two years and a half, and the nation a little better ſettled, eſpecially *Wales*, he was earneſtly ſolicited to return to his own country, there being very few able *miniſters* in thoſe parts. And beſides his having the language ſpoken there, he was in great eſteem and veneration among that people; and therefore was likely to do more good there, than where he now was.

Settles at Dartford *in* Kent.

BY theſe conſiderations he was prevailed upon to return thither. And for his further encouragement and reputation, the *ſynod* of *miniſters*, who were appointed by authority to examine and approve of all publick preachers, gave him their *certificate* and *teſtimonial.*

Returns to Wales.

THEY being, as I conceive, all *Pædobaptiſts*, whoſe *teſtimonies* in our *favour* I have a great value for; ſhall therefore inſert the copy thereof in this place [u].

'THESE are to certify thoſe whom it 'may concern, that the bearer here- 'of, Mr. *Vavaſor Powell*, is a man of a re- 'ligious and blameleſs converſation, and of 'able gifts for the work of the *miniſtry*, 'and hath approved himſelf faithful there-

[u] *The life of* Vavaſor Powell, *p.* 16.

'in; which we whose names are under written, do testify, some of our own knowledge, others from credible and sufficient information. And therefore he being now called, and desired to exercise his gifts in his own country of *Wales*, he also having the language thereof, we conceive him fit for that work, and worthy of encouragement therein. In witness whereof, we have here subscribed our names, *Sept.* 11. 1646.

Charles Herte, prolocutor.

Henry Scudder	*Stephen Marshal*
William Greenhill	*Jer. Whitaker*
Franc. Woodcock	*Arthur Salwey*
William Strong	*Peter Sterrey*
Joseph Caryl	*Henry Prince*
William Carter	*Christopher Love*
Thomas Wilson	*Tho. Froysell*
Jer. Borroughs	*Robert Bettes.*
Philip Nye	

Is very laborious in the work of the ministry.

WHEN he came down again into his native country, he applied himself to his Lord's work with great zeal and diligence; travelling from place to place, and taking all opportunities to preach the gospel, and win souls to Christ. He frequently preached in two or three places in a day, and was seldom two days in a week throughout the year, out of the pulpit, nay, he would sometimes

ſometimes ride an hundred miles in a week, and preach in every place, where he might have admittance, either night or day; ſo that there was hardly a *church*, *chapel* or *town-hall* in all *Wales*, where he had not preached; beſides his frequent preaching in *fairs* and *markets*, upon *mountains* and in ſmall *villages*. For if he paſſed at any time through any place where there was a concourſe of people, he would take the opportunity of preaching Chriſt, and recommending to them the care of their ſouls, and another world.

THE pains that he took, and the fatigues that he endured, were very great and uncommon, and ſuch as filled all that knew him with admiration. And God was pleaſed to bleſs his labours with proportionable ſucceſs. The people flocked with great zeal and deſire to attend his miniſtry, and many were by his means turned unto the Lord. And whereas, when he left *Wales* in 1642. there was not above one or two gathered churches in thoſe parts, now they began to encreaſe apace; and before the reſtoration, there was above twenty diſtinct ſocieties formed; of which ſome had two, ſome three, and ſome four or five hundred members.

Plants many churches.

THESE were chiefly gathered and planted by the care and induſtry of Mr. *Powell*, and they differed very little from one another in their faith and order. MR.

MR. *Powell* drew up a ſhort *confeſſion of faith* in thirty articles [x], which, as may be gathered from what he ſays in his *epiſtle* to the churches in *Wales*, not only contained his own opinion, but the faith and diſcipline of thoſe churches. It is publiſhed at large in the account of his life, and ſhews, that he, and thoſe churches that were planted by him, followed the *Calviniſtical* ſcheme of doctrines, in the points of *election*, *juſtification*, *effectual Calling*, *free-will and perſeverance.* And though they eſteemed none the proper *ſubjects* of *baptiſm*, but ſuch as perſonally made a profeſſion of *repentance* and *faith*, and judged that the right form of adminiſtring that *ordinace*, was by *immerſion* only, yet did not they make this a boundary of their communion; but aſſerted, that difference in perſuaſion and practice in this and many other caſes, might very well conſiſt with brotherly-love and chriſtian communion. They were alſo for ordination of elders, ſinging of pſalms and hymns in publick worſhip, laying on of hands on the newly-baptized, and anointing the ſick with oil, according to the apoſtolical direction. *James* v. 14, 15.

IN *Feb.* 1649. an act of parliament paſſed for the propagating of the goſpel in *Wales*, the deſign of which was, that the many

[x] *Treatiſe, entitled,* The Bird in the Cage.

pariſhes

pariſhes in thoſe parts that were without *miniſters* might be ſupplied, and that ſuch in livings as were *ignorant* or *ſcandalous*, might be removed, and others duly qualified put in their room.

SEVERAL gentlemen of the beſt reputation for piety and integrity in thoſe parts, as well *miniſters* as others, were appointed *commiſſioners* for the execution of this act; and among the reſt, Mr. *Vavaſor Powell* was one. By having this honour and power conferred upon him, he was put into a capacity of doing a great deal more good than otherwiſe he could have done. Yet it created him a great deal of trouble, and raiſed him up many *enemies*, who did not ſpare to load him with *reproaches*, and accuſe him with the worſt of crimes.

Is appointed one of the commiſſioners for propagating the goſpel in Wales.

THOUGH this act continued in force but for three years, yet they repreſented, that the *commiſſioners* got great eſtates by it; that the profits ariſing by *tythes*, of which by this act they were to have the diſpoſal, was put into their own pockets; that godly and learned *miniſters* were turned out, and worſe or none put in their room; inſomuch, that the generality of the people were either turned *Atheiſts* or *Papiſts*. And and all this was chiefly laid at the door of Mr. *Powell*, and not only whiſpered about privately, but publiſhed in *pamphlets*, without either author or printers name.

Is very much reproached by his enemies.

A

A VIRULENT one I have now by me, entitled, *Strena Vavasoriensis*; or, *A New-Year's-Gift for the* Welch *Itinerants*, &c. A more malicious piece could not be written, full of the most abominable *lyes* and *slanders* that malice could invent. But Mr. *Powell* was fully cleared, not only by the account which he himself gave of their whole proceedings in this affair, but also by the *testimony* of many *magistrates*, *ministers*, and other credible persons of different opinions in religion, who had the inspection of this matter, and published a vindication of him in the year 1654. entitled, *Examen & Purgamen Vavasoris*.

But honourably cleared.

HE was greatly harrassed by his *persecutors*, and kept a *prisoner* about ten years. And during the time of his last illness, though his *physician* ordered he should be kept from speaking much, yet so zealously was he affected for the glory of God, and with the love of Christ, that neither his pains, bodily weakness, or the tender advice of friends, could possibly restrain him; but he would, notwithstanding all, break forth into high and heavenly praises, sometimes by *prayer*, and sometimes by *singing*.

His last sickness and death in prison.

HIS patience under all his pains was very great. He would under the greatest pain bless God, and say, he would not entertain one bad thought of God for all the world.

world. The ſight of the pardon of ſin and reconciliation with God, was ſo clear, and without interruption, even to the laſt, that it was as a fire in his boſom till he ſpake of it; and very hardly would he be reſtrained at any time: and when he had ſpent his ſtrength in ſpeaking, then would he compoſe himſelf to get a little more ſtrength, that he might go on to ſpeak further of the grace of God towards him, and to give ſeaſonable advice to all about him; and ſo continued till God took away his ſtrength and ſpeech from him. He kept his bed about thirty days, and finiſhed his courſe, ſervice and ſufferings, on the 27th of *October* 1670. at *Karoone-houſe*, the then fleet-priſon in *Lambeth*, in the eleventh year of his impriſonment, and in the 53d of his age. Says the writer of his life,

In vain oppreſſors do themſelves perplex,
To find out acts, how they the ſaints may vex;
Death ſpoils their plots, and ſets th' oppreſſed free,
Thus Vavaſor *obtained true liberty;*
Chriſt him releas'd, and now he's join'd among
The martyr'd-ſouls, *with whom he cries,* how long?

THE ſeveral books that he publiſhed, were,

1. Chriſt

His works. 1. Chrift *and* Mofes's *excellency*; or Zion *and* Sina's *glory*. 8vo 1650

2. *A Dialogue between Chrift and a Publican; Chrift and a doubting Chriftian.*

3. *Chrift exalted by the Father; God the Father glorified; and Man's Redemption finifhed.*

4. *The Bird in the Cage, chirping.* 8vo 1661

5. *Common Prayer no Divine Service.* 4to 1660

6. *The Sufferer's Catechifm.*

7. *A Scriptural Catechifm.*

8. *Sinful and finlefs Swearing.*

9. *A Scripture Concordance.*

F I N I S.

APPENDIX.

NUMB. I.

Anno Dom. 1611. An. Reg. Jac. 9.

The commission and warrant for the condemnation and execution of Edward Wightman, *at* Litchfeild; *with an account of his heretical opinions.*

AMES, by the grace of God, King of *England*, *Scotland*, *France*, and *Ireland*, Defender of the Faith, *&c.* to our right trusty, and right well-beloved councellour, *Thomas* Lord *Ellesmere*, our chancellour of *England*, greeting. Whereas the reverend father in God, *Richard*, bishop of *Coventry* and *Litchfeild*, having judicially proceeded in the examination, hearing, and determining of a cause of heresie against *Edward Wightman*, of the parish of *Burton* upon *Trent*, in the diocese of *Coventry* and *Litchfeild*, concerning the wicked heresies of the *Ebionites*, *Cerinthians*, *Valentinians*, *Arrians*, *Macedonians*, of *Simon Magus*, of *Manes*, *Manichees*, of *Photinus*, and *Anabaptists*,

baptists, and of other heretical, execrable, and unheard of opinions, by the instinct of Satan, by him excogitated and holden, *viz.*

1. THAT there is not the Trinity of Persons, the Father, the Son, and the Holy Ghost, in the unity of the Deity. 2. That Jesus Christ is not the true natural Son of God, perfect God and of the same substance, eternity, and majesty with the Father, in respect of his Godhead. 3. That Jesus Christ is only man, and a mere creature, and not both God and man in one person. 4. That Christ our Saviour took not human flesh, of the substance of the virgin *Mary* his mother; and that that promise, *The seed of the woman shall break the serpent' head*, was not fulfilled in Christ. 5. That the person of the Holy Ghost is not God coequal, co-eternal, and co-essential with the Father and the Son. 6. That the three Creeds, *viz.* The Apostles Creed, the *Nicene* Creed, the *Athanasian* Creed, are the heresies of the *Nicolaitans.* 7. That he the said *Edward Wightman* is that prophet spoken of in the eighteenth of *Deut.* in these words, *I will raise them up a prophet*, &c. and that place of *Isaiah*, *I alone have troden the winepress*; and that that place, *Whose fan is in his hand.* are proper and personal to him the said *Edward Wightman.* 8. And that he the said *Wightman* is that person of the *Holy Ghost* spoken of in the Scriptures; and the *Comforter* spoken of in the sixteenth of St. *John*'s gospel. 9. And that those words of our Saviour Christ, *of the sin of blaspheming against the Holy Ghost*, are meant of his person. 10. And that that place, the fourth of *Mal.* of *Elias to come*, is likewise meant of his person. 11. That the soul

ſoul doth ſleep in the ſleep of the firſt death, as well as the body; and is mortal as touching the ſleep of the firſt death, as the body is: And that the ſoul of our Saviour Jeſus Chriſt did ſleep in that ſleep of death as well as his body. 12. That the ſouls of the elect ſaints departed are not members poſſeſſed of the triumphant church in heaven. 13. That the baptizing of infants is an abominable cuſtom. 14. That there ought not in the church the uſe of the Lord's Supper to be celebrated in the elements of bread and wine; and the uſe of baptiſm to be celebrated in the element of water, as they are now practiſed in the church of *England:* But that the uſe of baptiſm is to be adminiſter'd in water, only to converts of ſufficient age and underſtanding, converted from infidelity to the faith. 15. That God hath ordained and ſent him, the ſaid *Edward Wightman*, to perform his part in the work of the ſalvation of the world, to deliver it by his teaching or admonition, from the hereſie of the *Nicolaitans*, as Chriſt was ordained and ſent to ſave the world, and by his death to deliver it from ſin, and to reconcile it to God. 16. And that Chriſtianity is not wholly profeſſed and preached in the church of *England*, but only in part. Wherein he the ſaid *Edward Wightman* hath before the ſaid reverend father, as alſo before our commiſſioners, for cauſes eccleſiaſtical, within our realm of *England*, maintained his ſaid moſt perilous and dangerous opinions; as appeareth by many of his confeſſions; as alſo by a book written and ſubſcribed by him, and given to us; for the which his damnable and heretical opinions, he is by divine ſentence, declared by the ſaid reverend father, the bishop of *Coventry* and *Litchfeild*, with the advice and consent of learned divines, and others learned in the law, assisting him in judgment, justly adjudged, pronounced, and declared to be an obstinate and incorrigible heretick, and is left by them under the sentence of the great excommunication, and therefore as a corrupt member to be cut off from the rest of the flock of Christ, lest he should infect others professing the true Christian faith; and is to be by our secular power and authority, as an heretick, punished; as by the *significavit* of the said reverend father in God, the bishop of *Coventry* and *Litchfeild*, bearing date at *Litchfeild*, the fourteenth day of *Dec.* in the ninth Year of our reign, and remaining in our court of *Chancery*, more at large appeareth. And although the said *Edward Wightman* hath since the said sentence pronounced against him, been often very charitably moved and exhorted, as well by the said Bishop, as by many other godly, grave and learned divines, to dissuade, revoke and remove him from the said blasphemous, heretical, and ana-baptistical opinions; yet he arrogantly and wilfully resisteth and continueth in the same. We therefore, according to our regal function and office, minding the execution of justice in this behalf, and to give example to others, lest they should attempt the like hereafter, have determined, by the assent of our council, to will and require, and do hereby authorize and require you our said chancellour, immediately upon the receipt hereof, to award, and make out, under our great seal of *England*, our writ of execution, according to the tenour in these pre-

presents ensuing; and these presents shall be your sufficient warrant and discharge for the same.

THEN was a warrant granted by the King to the lord chancellour of *England*, to award a writ under the great seal to the sheriff of *Litchfield*, for burning of *Edward Wightman*, delivered over to the secular power by the bishop of *Coventry* and *Litchfield*.

The WARRANT.

THE King to the sheriff of our city of *Litchfeild*, greeting. Whereas the reverend father in Christ, *Richard*, by divine providence, of *Coventry* and *Litchfeild* bishop, hath signified unto us, That he judicially proceeding, according to the exigence of the ecclesiastical canons, and of the laws and customs of this our kingdom of *England*, against one *Edward Wightman*, of the parish of *Burton* upon *Trent*, in the diocese of *Coventry* and *Litchfeild*, of, and upon the wicked heresies of *Ebion*, *Cerinthus*, *Valentinian*, *Arrius*, *Macedonius*, *Simon Magus*, of *Manes*, *Manichees*, *Photinus*, and of the *Anabaptists*, and other arch-hereticks; and moreover, of other cursed opinions, belched, by the instinct of Satan excogitated, and heretofore unheard of; the aforesaid *Edward Wightman* appearing before the aforesaid reverend father, and other divines and learned in the law, assisting him in judgment, the aforesaid wicked crimes, heresies, and other detestable blasphemies and errors, stubbornly and pertinaciously, knowingly, maliciously, and with an hardened heart, published, de-

 fended

ſended and diſperſed; by definitive ſentence of the ſaid reverend father, with the conſent of divines, learned in the law aforeſaid, juſtly, lawfully, and canonically, againſt the ſaid *Edward Wightman* in that part brought, ſtands adjudged, and pronounced an heretick; and therefore, as a diſeaſed ſheep out of the flock of the Lord, leſt our ſubjects he do infect by his contagion, he hath decreed to be caſt out and cut off. Whereas therefore the holy mother church hath not further in this part what it ought more to do and proſecute, the ſame reverend father, the ſame *Edward Wightman* as a blaſphemous and condemned heretick, hath left to our ſecular power to be puniſhed with condign puniſhment; as by the letters patents of the aforeſaid reverend father the biſhop of *Coventry* and *Litchfeild* in this behalf thereupon made, is certified unto us in our *Chancery*. We therefore, as a zealot of juſtice, and a defender of the catholick faith, and willing that the holy church, and the rights and liberties of the ſame, and the catholick faith to maintain and defend, and ſuch like Hereſies and Errors every where, ſo much as in us lies, to root out and extirpate, and hereticks ſo convict to puniſh with condign puniſhment, holding that ſuch an heretick in the aforeſaid form convict and condemned, according to the laws and cuſtoms of this our kingdom of *England* in this part accuſtomed, ought to be burned with fire. We command thee, that thou cauſe the ſaid *Edward Wightman*, being in thy cuſtody, to be committed to the fire in ſome publick and open place below the city aforeſaid, for the cauſe aforeſaid, before the people; and the ſame

ſame *Edward Wightman*, in the ſame fire, cauſe really to be burned, in the deteſtation of the ſaid crime, and for manifeſt example of other Chriſtians, that they may not fall into the ſame crime. And this no ways omit, under the peril that ſhall follow thereon. Witneſs, *&c.*

NUMB. II.

A CONFESSION *of* FAITH *of ſeven congregations, or churches of Chriſt in* London, *which are commonly, but unjuſtly called* Anabaptiſts; *publiſhed for the vindication of the truth, and information of the ignorant; likewiſe for the taking off thoſe aſperſions, which are frequently, both in pulpit and print, unjuſtly caſt upon them. Printed at* London, Anno 1646.

I.

THE Lord our God is but one God, whoſe ſubſiſtence is in himſelf; whoſe eſſence cannot be comprehended by any but himſelf, who only hath immortality, dwelling in the light, which no man can approach unto; who is in himſelf moſt holy, every way infinite, in greatneſs, wiſdom, power, love; merciful and gracious, long-ſuffering, and abundant in goodneſs and truth; who giveth being, moving, and preſervation to all creatures.

1 Cor. viii. 6. Iſa. xliv. 6. —, xlvi. 9. Exod. iii. 14. 1 Tim. vi. 16. Iſa. xliii. 15. Pſal. cxlvii. 5. Deut. xxxii. 3. Job xxxvi. 5. Jer. x. 12. Exod. xxxiv. 6, 7. Acts xvii. 28. Rom. xi. 36.

II.

II.

1 Cor. i. 3. John i. 1. —— xv. 26. Exod. iii. 14. 1 Cor. viii. 6.

In this divine and infinite Being there is the Father, the Word, and the Holy Spirit; each having the whole divine Eſſence, yet the Eſſence undivided; all infinite without any beginning, therefore but one God; who is not to be divided in nature, and being, but diſtinguiſhed by ſeveral peculiar relative properties.

III.

Iſa. xlvi. 10. Eph. i. 11. Rom. xi. 33. Pſal. cxv. 3. —— cxxxv. 6. —— xxxiii. 15. 1 Sam. x. 9, 26. Prov. xxi. 6. Exod. xxi. 13. Prov. xvi. 33. Pſal. cxliv. Iſa. xlv. 7. Jer. xiv. 22. Mat. vi. 28, 30 Col. i. 16, 17. Numb. xxiii. 19, 20. Rom. iii. 4. Jer. x. 10. Eph. i. 4, 5.

God hath decreed in himſelf, before the world was, concerning all things, whether neceſſary, accidental or voluntary, with all the circumſtances of them, to work, diſpoſe, and bring about all things according to the counſel of his own will, to his glory: (Yet without being the author of ſin, or having fellowſhip with any therein) in which appears his wiſdom in diſpoſing all things, unchangeableneſs, power, and faithfulneſs in accompliſhing his decree: And God hath before the foundation of the world, fore-ordained ſome men to eternal life, through Jeſus Chriſt, to the praiſe and glory of his grace; leaving the reſt in their ſin to their juſt condemnation, to the praiſe of his juſtice.

Jude 4, 6. Prov. xvi. 4.

IV.

Gen. i. 1. Col. i. 16. Iſa. xlv. 12. 1 Cor. xv. 45, 46. Eccleſ. vii. 29. Gen. iii. 1, 4, 5. 2 Cor. xi. 3.

In the beginning God made all things very good; created man after his own Image, filled with all meet perfection of nature, and free from all ſin; but long he abode not in this honour; Satan uſing the ſubtlety of the ſerpent to ſeduce firſt *Eve*, then by her ſeducing

cing *Adam*; who without any compulsion, in eating the forbidden fruit, transgressed the command of God, and fell, whereby death came upon all his posterity; who now are conceived in sin, and by nature the children of wrath, the servants of sin, the subjects of death, and other miseries in this world, and for ever, unless the Lord Jesus Christ set them free.

1 Tim. ii. 14. Gal. iii. 22. Rom. v. 12. — xviii. 19. — vi. 22. Eph. ii. 3.

V.

God in his infinite power and wisdom, doth dispose all things to the end for which they were created; that neither good nor evil befals any by chance, or without his providence; and that whatsoever befals the elect, is by his appointment, for his glory, and their good.

Job xxxviii. 11. Isa. xlvi. 10, 11. Eccles. iii. 14. Mar. x. 29, 30. Exod. xxi. 13. Prov. xvi. 33. Rom. viii. 28.

VI.

All the elect being loved of God with an everlasting love, are redeemed, quickned, and saved, not by themselves, nor their own works, lest any man should boast, but, only and wholly by God, of his free grace and mercy, through Jesus Christ, who is made unto us by God, wisdom, righteousness, sanctification, and redemption, and all in all, that he that rejoiceth, might rejoice in the Lord.

Jer. xxxi. 3. Eph. i. 3, 7. — ii. 8, 9. 1 Thes. v. 9. Acts xiii. 38. 2 Cor. v. 21. Jer. ix. 23, 24. 1 Cor. i. 30, 31. Jer. xxiii. 6.

VII.

And this is life eternal, that we might know him the only true God, and Jesus Christ whom he hath sent. And on the contrary, the Lord will render vengeance, in flaming fire, to them that know not God,

John xvii. 3. Heb. v. 9. 1 Thes. i. 8.

John vi. 36. God, and obey not the goſpel of Jeſus Chriſt.

VIII.

THE rule of this knowledge, faith, and obedience, concerning the worſhip of God, in which is contained the whole duty of man,
Col. ii. 23. is (not mens laws, or unwritten traditions,
Mat. xv. 9, 6. but) only the word of God contained in the
John v. 39. 2 Tim. iii. 15, holy Scriptures; in which is plainly recorded
16, 17. whatſoever is needful for us to know, believe,
Iſa. viii. 20. and practiſe; which are the only rule of ho-
Gal. i. 8, 9. lineſs and obedience for all ſaints, at all times,
Acts iii. 22, 23. in all places to be obſerved.

IX.

Gen. iii. 15. THE Lord Jeſus Chriſt, of whom *Moſes*
—— xxii. 18. and the Prophets wrote, the Apoſtles preach-
—— xlix. 10. ed, he is the Son of God, the brightneſs of
Dan. vii. 13. his glory, *&c.* by whom he made the world;
—— ix. 24, *&c.* who upholdeth and governeth all things that
Prov. viii. 23. he hath made; who alſo when the fulneſs of
John i. 1, 2, 3.
Heb. i. 8. time was come, was made of a woman, of
Gal. iv. 4. the tribe of *Judah*, of the ſeed of *Abraham*
Heb. vii. 14. and *David*; to wit, of the virgin *Mary*, the
Rev. v. 5. Holy Spirit coming down upon her, the
Gen. xlix. 9, 10. power of the moſt High overſhadowing her;
Rom. i. 3. and he was alſo tempted as we are, yet with-
& ix. 10. out ſin.
Mat. i. 16.
Luke iii. 23, 26. Heb. ii. 16. Iſa. liii. 3, 4, 5. Heb. iv. 15.

X.

1 Tim. ii. 5. JESUS Chriſt is made the mediator of the
Heb. ix. 15. new and everlaſting covenant of grace be-
John xiv. 6. tween God and man, ever to be perfectly and
Iſa. ix. 6, 7. fully the prophet, prieſt, and king of the church of God for evermore.

XI.

XI.

UNTO this office he was appointed by God Prov. viii. 23.
from everlasting; and in respect of his man- Isa. xlii. 6.
hood, from the womb called, separated, and — xlix. 15.
— xi. 2, 3, 4, 5.
anointed most fully and abundantly with all — lxi. 1, 2.
gifts necessary, God having without measure Luk. iv. 17, 22.
poured out his Spirit upon him. John i. 14, 26.
—— iii. 34.

XII.

CONCERNING his mediatorship, the Scripture holds forth Christ's call to his office; for Heb. v. 4, 5, 6.
none takes this honour upon him, but he that is called of God as was *Aaron*, it being an action of God, whereby a special promise being made, he ordains his Son to this office; which promise is, that Christ should be made Isa. liii. 10, 11.
a sacrifice for sin; that he should see his seed, John iii. 16.
and prolong his days, and the pleasure of the Rom. viii. 32.
Lord shall prosper in his hand; all of meer free and absolute grace towards God's elect, and without any condition foreseen in them to procure it.

XIII.

THIS office to be mediator, that is, to be 1 Tim. ii. 5.
prophet, priest, and king of the church of Heb. vii. 24.
Dan. vii. 14.
God, is so proper to Christ, that neither in Acts iv. 12.
whole, or any part thereof, it cannot be transferred from him to any other. Luke i. 33.
John xiv. 6.

XIV.

THIS office to which Christ is called, is Deut. viii. 15.
threefold; a prophet, priest, and king: This Acts iii. 22, 23.
number and order of offices is necessary, for Heb. iii. 1.
—— iv. 14, 15.
in respect of our ignorance, we stand in need Psal. ii. 6.
of his prophetical office; and in respect of 2 Cor. v. 20.
our Acts xxvi. 18.

Col. i. 21. John xvi. 8. Psal. cx. 3. Cant. i. 3. John vi. 44. Phil. iv. 13. 2 Tim. iv. 18.

our great alienation from God, we need his priestly office to reconcile us; and in respect of our averseness and utter inability to return to God, we need his kingly office, to convince, subdue, draw, uphold and preserve us to his heavenly kingdom.

XV.

John i. 18. — xii. 49, 50. — xvii. 8. Deut. xviii. 15. Mat. xxiii. 10. Heb. iii. 1. Mal. iii. i. 1 Cor. i. 24. Col. 2. 3.

CONCERNING the prophecy of Christ, it is that whereby he hath revealed the will of God, whatsoever is needful for his servants to know and obey; and therefore he is called not only a prophet and doctor, and the apostle of our profession, and the angel of the covenant, but also the very wisdom of God, in whom are hid all the treasures of wisdom and knowledge, who for ever continueth revealing the same truth of the gospel to his people.

XVI.

John i. 18. Acts iii. 22. Deut. xviii. 15 Heb. i. 1.

THAT he might be a prophet every way compleat, it was necessary he should be God, and also that he should be man: For unless he had been God, he could never have perfectly understood the will of God; and unless he had been man, he could not suitably have unfolded it in his own person to men.

That Jesus Christ is God is wonderful clearly expressed in the Scriptures. He is called the mighty God, Isa. ix. 6. *That word was God,* John i. 1. *Christ, who is God over all,* Rom. ix. 5. *God manifested in the Flesh,* 1 Tim. iii. 16. *The same is very God,* John v. 20. *He is the first,* Rev. i. 8. *He gives being to all things, and without him was nothing made,* John i. 2. *He forgiveth sins,* Mat. ix. 6. *He is before* Abraham, John viii. 58. *He was and is, and ever will be the same,* Heb. xiii. 8. *He is always with his to the end of the world,* Mat. xxviii. 20. *Which could not be said of Jesus Christ, if he were not God. And to the Son he saith, Thy throne, O God, is for ever and ever,* Heb. i. 8. John i. 18.

Also,

Also, Christ is not only perfectly God, but perfect man, made of a woman, Gal. iv. 4. *Made of the seed of* David, Rom. i. 3. *Coming out of the loins of* David, Acts ii. 30. *Of* Jesse *and* Judah, Acts xiii. 23. *In that the children were partakers of flesh and blood he himself likewise took part with them,* Heb. ii. 14. *He took not on him the nature of angels, but the seed of* Abraham, ver. 16. *So that we are bone of his bone, and flesh of his flesh,* Eph. v. 30. *So that he that sanctifieth, and they that are sanctified are all of one,* Heb. ii. 11. *See* Acts iii. 22. Deut. xviii. 15. Heb. i. 1.

XVII.

CONCERNING his priesthood, Christ having sanctified himself, hath appeared once to put away sin by that one offering of himself a sacrifice for sin, by which he hath fully finished and suffered all things God required for the salvation of his elect, and removed all rites and shadows, &c. and is now enter'd within the vail into the holy of holies, which is the presence of God. Also, he makes his people a spiritual house, an holy priesthood, to offer up spiritual sacrifice acceptable to God through him. Neither doth the Father accept, or Christ offer to the Father, any other worship or worshippers.

John xvii. 19. Heb. v. 7, 8, 9, 10, 12. Rom. v. 19. Eph. v. 2. Col. i. 20. Eph. ii. 14 &c. Rom. viii. 34. Heb. ix. 24, —— viii. 1. 1 Pet. ii. 5. John iv. 23, 24.

XVIII.

THIS priesthood was not legal or temporary, but according to the order of *Melchisedec*, and is stable and perfect, not for a time, but for ever, which is suitable to Jesus Christ, as to him that ever liveth. Christ was the priest, sacrifice, and altar: He was a priest according to both natures; he was a sacrifice according to his human nature; whence in scripture it is attributed to his body, to his blood: Yet the effectualness of this sacrifice did depend upon his divine nature; therefore

Heb. vii. 16, &c. Heb. v. 6. —— x. 10. 1 Pet. i. 18, 19. Col. i. 20, 22. Heb. ix. 13.

it

Acts xx. 28. it is called the blood of God. He was the
Heb. ix. 14. altar according to his divine nature, it belong-
— xiii. 10, ing to the altar to ſanctify that which is offered
12, 15.
Mat. xxiii. 17. upon it, and ſo it ought to be of greater dig-
John xvii. 19. nity than the ſacrifice it ſelf.

XIX.

1 Cor. xv. 4. CONCERNING his kingly office, Chriſt
1 Pet. iii. 21, being riſen from the dead, and aſcended into
22.
Mat. xxviii. heaven, and having all power in heaven and
18, 19. earth, he doth ſpiritually govern his church,
Luke xxiv. 51. and doth exerciſe his power over all, angels
Acts i. 1. and men, good and bad, to the preſervation
— v. 30, 31. and ſalvation of the elect, and to the over-
John xix. 36.
Rom. xiv. 9. ruling and deſtruction of his enemies. By this
John v. 26, 27. kingly power he applieth the benefits, virtue,
Rom. v. 6, 7, 8. and fruits of his propheſy and prieſthood to
— xiv. 17. his elect, ſubduing their ſins, preſerving and
Gal. v. 22, 23.
Mark i. 27. ſtrengthening them in all their conflicts againſt
Heb. i. 14. Satan, the world, and the fleſh, keeping their
John xvi. 15. hearts in faith and filial fear by his ſpirit: By
Job ii. 8. this his mighty power he ruleth the veſſels
Rom. i. 21.
— xvii. 18. of wrath, uſing, limiting and reſtraining
Eph. iv. 17, them, as it ſeems good to his infinite
18. wiſdom.
2 Pet. ii.

XX.

1 Cor. xv. 24, THIS his kingly power ſhall be more fully
28. manifeſted when he ſhall come in glory to
Heb. ix. 28. reign among his ſaints, when he ſhall put
2 Theſ. i. 9, 10.
1 Theſ. iv. 15, down all rule and authority under his feet,
16, 17. that the glory of the Father may be perfectly
John xvii. 21, manifeſted in his Son, and the glory of the
26. Father and the Son in all his members.

XXI.

XXI.

JESUS Chrift by his death did purchafe falvation for the elect that God gave unto him: Thefe only have intereft in him, and fellowfhip with him, for whom he makes interceffion to his Father in their behalf, and to them alone doth God by his Spirit apply this redemption; as alfo the free gift of eternal life is given to them, and none elfe.

Eph. i. 14. Heb. v. 9. Mat. i. 21. John xvii. 6. Heb. vii. 25. 1 Cor. ii. 12. Rom. viii. 29, 30. 1 John v. 12. John xv. 13. —— iii. 16.

XXII.

FAITH is the gift of God, wrought in the hearts of the elect by the fpirit of God; by which faith they come to know and believe the truth of the fcriptures, and the excellency of them above all other writings, and all things in the world, as they hold forth the glory of God in his attributes, the excellency of Chrift in his nature and offices, and of the power and fulnefs of the Spirit in its workings and operations; and fo are enabled to caft their fouls upon this truth thus believed.

Eph. ii. 8. John vi. 29. —— iv. 10. Phil. i. 29. Gal. v. 22. John xvii. 17. Heb. iv. 11. 12. John vi. 63.

XXIII.

ALL thofe that have this precious faith wrought in them by the Spirit, can never finally nor totally fall away; feeing the gifts of God are without repentance; fo that he ftill begets and nourifheth in them faith, repentance, love, joy, hope, and all the graces of the Spirit unto immortality; and though many ftorms and floods arife, and beat againft them, yet they fhall never be able to take them off that foundation and rock, which by faith they are faften'd upon; notwithftanding, through unbelief, and the

Mat. vii. 24, 25. John xiii. 10. —— x. 28, 29. 1 Pet i. 4, 5, 6. Ifa. xlix. 13, 14, 15, 16.

temptations of Satan, the ſenſible ſight of this light and love, be clouded and overwhelmed for a time; yet God is ſtill the ſame, and they ſhall be ſure to be kept by the power of God unto ſalvation, where they ſhall enjoy their purchaſed poſſeſſion, they being engraven upon the palms of his hands, and their names having been written in the book of life from all eternity.

XXIV.

Rom. x. 17. FAITH is ordinarily begotten by the
1 Cor. i. 28. preaching of the goſpel, or word of Chriſt,
Rom. ix. 16. without reſpect to any power or agency in
Ezek. xvi. 16. the creature; but it being wholly paſſive,
Rom. iii. 12.
—— i. 16. and dead in treſpaſſes and ſins, doth believe
Eph. i. 19. and is converted by no leſs power than that
Col. ii. 12. which raiſed Chriſt from the dead.

XXV.

John 3. 14, 15. THE preaching of the goſpel to the con-
—— i. 12. verſion of ſinners, is abſolutely free; no
Iſa. lv. 1. way requiring as abſolutely neceſſary, any
John vii. 37. qualifications, preparations, or terrors of the
1 Tim. i. 15. law, or preceeding miniſtry of the law, but
Rom. iv. 5. only and alone the naked ſoul, a ſinner and
—— v. 8. ungodly, to receive Chriſt crucified, dead
Acts v. 30, 31. and buried, and riſen again; who is made a
—— ii. 36. prince and a ſaviour for ſuch ſinners as
1 Cor. i. 22, 24. through the goſpel ſhall be brought to believe on him.

XXVI.

1 Pet. i. 5. THE ſame power that converts to faith in
2 Cor. xii. 9. Chriſt, carrieth on the ſoul through all duties,
1 Cor. xv. 10. temptations, conflicts, ſufferings; and what-
Phil. ii. 12, 13. ſoever a believer is, he is by grace, and is

carri-

carried on in all obedience and temptations by the same. John xv. 5. Gal. ii. 19, 20.

XXVII.

All believers are by Christ united to God; by which union, God is one with them, and they are one with him; and that all believers are the sons of God, and joint heirs with Christ, to whom belong all the promises of this life, and that which is to come. 1 Thes. i. 1. John xvii. 21. —— xx. 17. Heb. ii. 11. 1 John iv. 16. Gal. ii. 19, 20.

XXVIII.

Those that have union with Christ, are justified from all their sins by the blood of Christ, which justification is a gracious and full acquittance of a guilty sinner from all sin, by God, through the satisfaction that Christ hath made by his death for all their sins, and this applied (in the manifestation of it) through faith. 1 John i. 7. Heb. x. 14. —— ix. 26. 2 Cor. v. 19. Rom. iii. 23. Acts xiii. 38, 39. Rom. v. 1. —— iii. 25, 30.

XXIX.

All believers are a holy and sanctified people, and that sanctification is a spiritual grace of the new covenant, and an effect of the love of God manifested in the soul, whereby the believer presseth after a heavenly and evangelical obedience to all the commands, which Christ as head and king in his new covenant hath prescribed to them. 1 Cor. xii. 1 Pet. ii. 9. Eph. i. 4. 1 John iv. 16. Mat. xxviii. 20.

XXX.

All believers through the knowledge of that justification of life given by the Father, and brought forth by the blood of Christ, have as their great privilege of that new covenant, peace with God, and reconciliation, 2 Cor. v. 19. Rom. v. 9, 10. Isa. liv. 10. —— xx.

B where-

Eph. ii. 13, 14. whereby they that were afar off are made nigh
—— iv. 7. by that blood, and have peace passing all un-
Rom. v. 10, derstanding; yea, joy in God through our
11. Lord Jesus Christ, by whom we have received the atonement.

XXXI.

Rom. vii. 23, All believers in the time of this life, are
24. in a continual warfare and combat against
Eph. vi. 10, sin, self, the world, and the devil; and are
11, &c.
Heb. ii. 9, 10. liable to all manner of afflictions, tribulations
2 Tim. iii. 12. and persecutions, being predestinated and ap-
Rom. viii. 29. pointed thereunto, and whatsoever the saints
1 Thes. iii. 3.
Gal. ii. 19, 20. possess or enjoy of God spiritually, is by faith;
2 Cor. v. 7. and outward and temporal things are lawfully
Deut. ii. 5. enjoyed by a civil right by them who have
no faith.

XXXII.

John xvi. 33. The only strength by which the saints are
—— xv. 5. enabled to encounter with all oppositions and
Phil. iv. 11. trials, is only by Jesus Christ, who is the
Heb. ii 9, 10.
2 Tim. iv. 18. captain of their salvation, being made perfect
through sufferings; who hath engaged his
faithfulness and strength to assist them in all
their afflictions, and to uphold them in all
their temptations, and to preserve them by
his power to his everlasting kingdom.

XXXIII.

Mat. xi. 11. Jesus Christ hath here on earth a spiri-
2 Thes. i. 1. tual kingdom, which is his church, whom
1 Cor. i. 2. he hath purchased and redeemed to himself
Eph. i. 1.
Rom. i. 7. as a peculiar inheritance; which church is a
Acts xix. 8, 9. company of visible saints, called and separa-
—— xxvi. 18. ted from the world by the word and spirit of
2 Cor. vi. 17. God, to the visible profession of the faith of
Rev. xviii. 4.
the

the gospel, being baptized into that faith, and joined to the Lord, and each to other, by mutual agreement in the practical enjoyment of the ordinances commanded by Christ their head and king. Acts ii. 37. —— x. 37. Rom. x. 10. Mat. xviii. 19, 20. Acts ii. 42. Acts ix. 26. 1 Pet. ii. 5.

XXXIV.

To this church he hath made his promises, and giveth the signs of his covenant, presence, acceptation, love, blessing, and protection. Here are the fountains and springs of his heavenly graces flowing forth to refresh and strengthen them. Mat. xxviii. 18, &c. 1 Cor. xi. 24. —— iii. 21. 2 Cor. vi. 18. Rom. ix. 4, 5. Psal. cxxxiii. 3. Rom. iii. 7, 10. Ezek. xlvii. 2.

XXXV.

And all his servants of all estates (are to acknowledge him to be their prophet, priest, and king;) and called thither to be enrolled among his houshold servants, to present their bodies and souls, and to bring their gifts God hath given them, to be under his heavenly conduct and government, to lead their lives in this walled sheepfold, and watered garden, to have communion here with his saints, that they may be assured that they are made meet to be partakers of their inheritance in the kingdom of God; and to supply each others wants, inward and outward; (and although each person hath a propriety in his own estate, yet they are to supply each others wants, according as their necessities shall require, that the name of Jesus Christ may not be blasphemed through the necessity of any in the church) and also being come, they are here by himself to be bestowed in their several order, due place, peculiar use, Acts ii. 41, 47. Isa. iv. 3. 1 Cor. xii. 6, 7, &c. Ezek. xx. 40, 37. Cant. iv. 12. Eph. ii. 19. Rom. xii. 4, 5, 6. Col. i. 12. — ii. 5, 6, 19. Acts xx. 32. — v. 4. — ii. 44, 45. — iv. 34, 35. Luke xiv. 26. 1 Tim. vi. 1. Eph. iv. 16.

being fitly compact and knit together according to the effectual working of every part, to the edifying of it self in love.

XXXVI.

Acts i. 23, 26.
—— vi. 3.
—— xv. 22, 25.
Rom. xii. 7, 8.
1 Tim. iii. 2, 6, 7.
1 Cor. xii. 8, 28.
Heb. xiii. 7, 17.
1 Pet. v. 1, 2, 3. iv. 15.

BEING thus joined, every church hath power given them from Christ, for their well-being, to choose among themselves meet persons for elders and deacons, being qualified according to the word, as those which Christ hath appointed in his testament, for the feeding, governing, serving, and building up of his church; and that none have any power to impose on them either these or any other.

XXXVII.

Heb. v. 4.
John x. 3, 4.
Acts xx. 28, 29.
Rom. xii. 7, 8.
Heb. xiii. 7, 17.
1 Pet. v. 1, 2, 3.

THAT the ministers lawfully called, as aforesaid, ought to continue in their calling and place, according to God's ordinance, and carefully to feed the flock of God committed to them, not for filthy lucre, but of a ready mind.

XXXVIII.

1 Cor. ix. 7, 14.
Gal. vi. 8.
Phil. iv. 15, 16.
2 Cor. x. 4.
1 Tim. i. 2.
Psal. cx. 3.

THE ministers of Christ ought to have whatsoever they shall need, supplied freely by the church, that according to Christ's ordinance they that preach the Gospel should live of the gospel by the law of Christ.

XXXIX.

Mat. xxviii. 18, 19.
John iv. 1.
Mark xvi. 15, 16.
Acts ii. 37, 38.

BAPTISM is an ordinance of the new testament, given by Christ, to be dispensed upon persons professing faith, or that are made disciples; who upon profession of faith, ought

to

to be baptized, and after to partake of the Lord's Supper. Acts viii. 36, 37, &c.

XL.

THAT the way and manner of the dispensing this ordinance, is dipping or plunging the body under water; it being a sign, must answer the things signified, which is, that interest the saints have in the death, burial, and resurrection of Christ: And that as certainly as the body is buried under water, and risen again; so certainly shall the bodies of the saints be raised by the power of Christ, in the day of the resurrection, to reign with Christ.

Mat. iii. 6, 16. Mar. xv. 9, *reads* [*into* Jordan] *in* Greek. John iii. 23. Acts viii. 38. Rev. i. 5. —— vii. 14. Heb. x. 22. Rom. vi. 3, 4, 5, 6. 1 Cor. xv. 28, 29.

The word baptizo *signifies to dip or plunge (yet so as convenient garments be both upon the administrator and subject with all modesty.)*

XLI.

THE person designed by Christ to dispense baptism, the scripture holds forth to be a disciple; it being no where tied to a particular church officer, or person extraordinarily sent, the commission injoining the administration, being given to them as considered disciples, being men able to preach the gospel.

Isa. viii. 16. Eph. ii. 7. Mat. xxviii. 19. John iv. 2. Acts xx. 7. — xi. 10. 1 Cor. xi. 2. — x. 16, 17. Rom. xvi. 2. Mat. xviii. 17.

XLII.

CHRIST hath likewise given power to his church to receive in, and cast out, any member that deserves it; and this power is given to every congregation, and not to one particular person, either member or officer, but in relation to the whole body, in reference to their faith and fellowship.

Rom. xvi. 2. Mat. xviii. 17. 1 Cor. v. 4, 11, 13. —— xii. 6. —— ii. 3. 2 Cor. ii. 6, 7.

XLIII.

Mat. xviii. 16. — xvii. 18. Acts xi. 2, 3. 1 Tim. v. 19, &c. Col. iv. 17. Acts xv. 1, 2, 3.

And every particular member of each church, how excellent, great, or learned ſo-ever, is ſubject to this cenſure and judgment; and that the church ought not without great care and tenderneſs, and due advice, but by the rule of faith, to proceed againſt her members.

XLIV.

Acts xx. 27, 28. Heb. xiii. 17, 24. Mat. xxiv. 45. 1 Theſ. v. 2, 14. Jude 3, 20. Heb. x. 34, 35. — xii. 15.

Christ for the keeping of this church in holy and orderly communion, placeth ſome ſpecial men over the church; who by their office, are to govern, overſee, viſit, watch; ſo likewiſe for the better keeping thereof, in all places by the members, he hath given authority, and laid duty upon all to watch over one another.

XLV.

1 Cor. xiv. 3, &c. Rom. xii. 6. 1 Pet. iv. 10, 11. 1 Cor. xii. 7. 1 Theſ. v. 19, &c.

Also ſuch to whom God hath given gifts in the church, may and ought to propheſy, according to the proportion of faith, and ſo to teach publickly the word of God, for the edification, exhortation, and comfort of the church.

XLVI.

Rev. ii. & iii. Chap. Acts xv. 12. 1 Cor. i. 10. Heb. x. 25. Jude 19. Rev. ii. 20, 21, 27. Acts xv. 1, 2. Rom. xiv. 1. — xv. 1, 2, 3.

Thus being rightly gathered, and conti-nuing in the obedience of the goſpel of Chriſt, none are to ſeparate for faults and corruptions (for as long as the church conſiſts of men ſub-ject to failings, there will be difference in the true conſtituted church) until they have in due order, and tenderneſs, ſought redreſs thereof.

XLVII.

XLVII.

AND although the particular congregations be diſtinct, and ſeveral bodies, every one as a compact and knit city within it ſelf; yet are they all to walk by one rule of truth; ſo alſo they (by all means convenient) are to have the counſel and help one of another, if neceſſity require it, as members of one body, in the common faith, under Chriſt their head.

1 Cor. iv. 17
—— xiv. 33, 36.
—— xvi 1.
Pſal. cxxii. 3.
Eph. ii. 12, 19.
Rev. xxi.
1 Tim. iii. 15.
—— vi. 13, 14.
1 Cor. iv. 17.
Acts xv. 2, 3.
Cant. viii. 8, 9. 2 Cor. viii. 1, 4. & xiii. 14.

XLVIII.

A CIVIL magiſtracy is an ordinance of God, ſet up by him for the puniſhment of evil-doers, and for the praiſe of them that do well; and that in all lawful things, commanded by them, ſubjection ought to be given by us in the Lord, not only for wrath, but for conſcience-ſake; and that we are to make ſupplications and prayers for kings, and all that are in authority, that under them we may live a quiet and peaceable life, in all godlineſs and honeſty.

Rom. xiii. 1, 2, &c.
1 Pet. ii. 13, 14.
1 Tim. ii. 1, 2, 3.

The ſupreme magiſtracy of this kingdom we acknowledge to be the king and parliament (now eſtabliſhed) freely choſen by the kingdom, and that we are to maintain and defend all civil laws and civil officers made by them, which are for the good of the commonwealth. And we acknowledge with thankfulneſs, that God hath made this preſent king and parliament honourable in throwing down the prelatical hierarchy, becauſe of their tyranny and oppreſſion over us, under which this kingdom long groaned, for which we are ever ingaged to bleſs God, and honour them for the ſame. And concerning the worſhip of God; there is but one lawgiver, which is able to ſave and deſtroy, Jam. iv. 12. *which is Jeſus Chriſt, who hath given laws and rules ſufficient in his word for his worſhip; and for any to make more, were to charge Chriſt with want of wiſdom, or faithfulneſs, or both, in not making laws enough, or not good enough for his houſe: Surely it is our wiſdom, duty, and privilege, to obſerve*

observe Christ's laws only, Psal. ii. 6, 9, 10, 12. *So it is the magistrates duty to tender the liberty of mens consciences*, Eccles. viii. 8, *(which is the tenderest thing unto all conscientious men, and most dear unto them, and without which all other liberties will not be worth the naming, much less injoying) and to protect all under them from all wrong, injury, oppression and molestation; so it is our duty not to be wanting in nothing which is for their honour and comfort, and whatsoever is for the well-being of the commonwealth wherein we live; it is our duty to do, and we believe it to be our express duty, especially in matters of religion, to be fully perswaded in our minds of the lawfulness of what we do, as knowing whatsoever is not of faith is sin. And as we cannot do any thing contrary to our understandings and consciences, so neither can we forbear the doing of that which our understandings and consciences bind us to do. And if the magistrate should require us to do otherwise, we are to yeild our Persons in a passive way to their power, as the saints of old have done*, Jam. v. 4. *And thrice happy shall he be, that shall lose his life for witnessing (though but for the least title) of the truth of the Lord Jesus Christ*, 1 Pet. v. Gal. v.

XLIX.

Acts ii. 40, 41. BUT in case we find not the magistrate to
—— iv. 19. favour us herein; yet we dare not suspend
—— v. 28, 29. —— xx. 23. our practice, because we believe we ought to
1 Thes. iii. 3. go in obedience to Christ, in professing the
Phil. i. 28, 29. faith which was once delivered to the saints,
Dan. iii. 16, 17. which faith is declared in the holy scriptures,
—— vi. 7, 10, and this our confession of faith a part of
22, 23. them, and that we are to witness to the truth
1 Tim. vi. 13, of the old and new testament unto the death,
14. if necessity require, in the midst of all trials
Rom. xii. 1, 8. and afflictions, as his saints of old have done;
1 Cor. xiv. 37. Rev. ii. 20. not accounting our goods, lands, wives, chil-
2 Tim. iv. 6, 7, dren, fathers, mothers, brethren, sisters;
8. yea, and our own lives dear unto us, so we
Rom. xiv. 10, 12. may finish our course with joy; remembring
2 Cor. v. 10. always, that we ought to obey God rather
Psal xlix. 7. than men, who will when we have finished
—— l. 22. our course, and kept the faith, give us the
crown of righteousness; to whom we must
give an account of all our actions, and no
man

man being able to discharge us of the same.

L.

It is lawful for a Christian to be a magistrate or civil officer; and also it is lawful to take an oath, so it be in truth, and in judgment, and in righteousness, for confirmation of truth, and ending of all strife; and that by rash and vain oaths the Lord is provoked, and this land mourns.

Acts viii. 38. — x. 1, 2, 35. Rom. xvi. 23. Deut. vi. 13. Rom. i. 9. 2 Cor. x. 11. Jer. iv. 2. Heb. vi. 16.

LI.

We are to give unto all men whatsoever is their due, as their place, age, estate, requires; and that we defraud no man of any thing, but to do unto all men, as we would they should do unto us.

1 Thes. iv. 6. Rom. xiii. 5, 6, 7. Mat. xxii. 21. Titus iii. 1 Pet. ii. 15, 17. 1 Pet. v. 5. Eph. v. 21, 23. & vi. 1, 9. Tit. iii. 1, 2, 3.

LII.

There shall be a resurrection of the dead, both of the just and unjust, and every one shall give an account of himself to God, that every one may receive the things done in his body, according to that he hath done, whether it be good or bad.

Acts xxiv. 15. 1 Cor. v. 10. Rom. xiv. 12.

The Conclusion.

THUS we desire to give unto Christ that which is his; and unto all lawful authority that which is their due; and to owe nothing to any man but love; to live quietly and peaceably, as it becometh saints, endeavouring in all things to keep a good conscience, and to do unto every man (of what

what judgment ſoever) as we would they ſhould do unto us, that as our practice is, ſo it may prove us to be a conſcionable, quiet, and harmleſs people (no ways dangerous or troubleſome to human ſociety) and to labour and work with our hands that we may not be chargeable to any, but to give to him that needeth both friends and enemies, accounting it more excellent to give than to receive. Alſo we confeſs, that we know but in part, and that we are ignorant of many things which we deſire and ſeek to know; and if any ſhall do us that friendly part to ſhew us from the word of God that we ſee not, we ſhall have cauſe to be thankful to God and them; but if any man ſhall impoſe upon us any thing that we ſee not to be commanded by our Lord Jeſus Chriſt, we ſhould in his ſtrength rather embrace all reproaches and tortures of men, to be ſtripp'd of all outward comforts, and if it were poſſible, to die a thouſand deaths, rather than to do any thing againſt the leaſt tittle of the truth of God, or againſt the light of our own conſciences. And if any ſhall call what we have ſaid hereſy, then do we with the Apoſtle acknowledge, that after the way they call hereſy, worſhip we the God of our fathers, diſclaiming all hereſies (rightly ſo called) becauſe they are againſt Chriſt, and to be ſtedfaſt and immoveable, always abounding in obedience to Chriſt, as knowing our labour ſhall not be in vain in the Lord.

Pſal. lxxiv. 21, 22.

ARISE, O God, plead thine own cauſe; remember how the fooliſh man blaſphemeth thee daily. O let not the oppreſſed return aſhamed, but let the poor and needy praiſe thy name.

Come, Lord Jeſus, come quickly.

NUMB

NUMB. III.

A CONFESSION *of the* FAITH *of ſeveral congregations of Chriſt in the county of* Somerſet, *and ſome churches in the counties near adjacent. Printed at* London, Anno 1656.

I.

WE believe that there is but one God. 1 *Cor.* viii. 6. *But to us there is but one God*, who is immortal, eternal, inviſible, only wiſe: 1 *Tim.* i. 17. *Now unto the king, eternal, immortal, inviſible, only wiſe*, &c. Holy, *Lev.* xi. 44. *And ye ſhall be holy, for I am holy.* Almighty, *Gen.* xvii. 1. *I am the almighty God.* Infinite, 1 *Kings* viii. 27. *Behold the heaven, and heaven of heavens, are not able to contain thee.* Iſa. xl. 28. *There is no ſearching of his underſtanding.* Pſalm cxlvii. 5. *Great is our Lord, and of great power, his underſtanding is infinite.* A Spirit, *John* iv. 24. *God is a ſpirit.* Glorious in holineſs, *Exod.* xv. 11. *Who is like thee glorious in holineſs.* Juſt, merciful, gracious, long-ſuffering, abundant in mercy and truth, *Exod.* xxxiv. 6, 7. *The Lord, the Lord God merciful and gracious, long-ſuffering, and abundant in goodneſs and truth.* Faithful in all things, *Deut.* vii. 9. *The Lord thy God, he is God, the faithful God.*

II.

II.

THAT this God, who is ſo in himſelf, did according to his own will in time, create all things, by, and for Jeſus Chriſt, *Heb.* i. 2. *By whom alſo he made the worlds.* Col. i. 16. *For by him were all things created that are in heaven, and that are in earth,* &c. *All things were created by him and for him,* John ii. 3. Who is the word of God, *John* i. 1. *In the beginning was the word, and the word was with God, and the word was God,* and upholds all things by the word of his power, *Heb.* i. 3.

III.

THAT God made man after his own image; *Gen.* i. 27. *So God created man in his own image, in the image of God created he him.* In an eſtate of uprightneſs and human perfection; *Eccleſ.* vii. 29. *Lo this only have I found, that God hath made man upright.*

IV.

THAT God gave *Adam* a juſt law, requiring obedience under the penalty of death; *Gen.* ii. 17. *But of the tree of the knowledge of good and evil, thou ſhalt not eat of it, for in the day that thou eateſt thereof thou ſhalt ſurely die.* Which law he brake, and brought himſelf and his poſterity under the guilt and judgment denounced, *Gen.* iii. 6. *And when the woman ſaw that the tree was good for food,* &c. *ſhe took of the fruit thereof and did eat, who gave alſo unto her husband with her, and he did eat.* Rom. v. 12. *Wherefore as by one man ſin enter'd into the world, and death by*

ſin,

sin, and so death passed upon all men, for that all have sinned. Rom. v. 17, 18, 19. *For if by one man's offence death reigned by one —— Therefore as by the offence of one judgment came upon all men to condemnation —— For as by one man's disobedience many were made sinners.*

V.

MAN being in this undone estate, God did in the riches of his mercy hold forth Christ in a promise; *Gen.* iii. 15. *And I will put enmity between thee and the woman, and between thy seed and her seed, it shall bruise thy head, and thou shalt bruise his heel.*

VI.

THAT in process of time God gave forth his laws by the hand of *Moses*, Exod. xx. John i. 17. to fallen man, *Gal.* iii. 19. *The law it was added because of transgressions,* not for justification to eternal life, *Gal.* iii. 17. *Rom.* iii. 20. *Therefore by the deeds of the law there shall no flesh be justified in his sight,* but that all might appear guilty before the Lord by it, *Rom.* iii. 19. *Now we know that what things soever the law saith, it saith to them that are under the law, that every mouth may be stopped, and all the world may become guilty before God.* Rom. v. 20. *Moreover, the law enter'd that the offence might abound.*

VII.

THAT out of this condition none of the sons of *Adam* were able to deliver themselves, *Rom.* viii. 3. *For what the law could not do, in that it was weak through the flesh.* Eph.

ii. 1, 5.

ii. 1, 5. *And you hath he quickned, who were dead in trespasses and sins, even when we were dead in sins hath quickned us together with Christ, by grace ye are saved.* Rom. v. 6. *For when we were yet without strength, Christ died for the ungodly.*

VIII.

THAT God continued and renewed the manifestation of his grace and mercy in Christ after the first promise made *Gen.* iii. in other promises, *Gen.* xxii. 18. with *Gen.* xii. 3. *Gal.* iii. 16. *And in thy seed shall all the nations of the earth be blessed.* And in types, as the passover, *Exod.* xii. 8. *And they shall eat the flesh in that night roast with fire, and unleavened bread.* And *ver.* 13. with 1 *Cor.* v. 7. *For even Christ our passover is sacrificed for us.* And the brazen serpent, *Numb.* xxi. 9. *And* Moses *made a serpent of brass, and put it upon a pole, and it came to pass that if a serpent had bitten any man, when he beheld the serpent of brass he lived.* Compared with *John* iii. 14. *And as* Moses *lifted up the serpent in the wilderness, even so must the son of man be lifted up.* With the ministry and ministration of *Moses* and *Aaron*, the sacrifices, *&c.* being all figures of Christ, *Heb.* vii. 8. and *Chapter* ix. And in prophesies, as *Isa.* ix. 6. *For unto us a child is born, unto us a son is given, and the government shall be upon his shoulder, and his name shall be called wonderful, counsellor, the mighty God, the everlasting Father, the prince of Peace.* And, *Isa.* xi. 1, 2. *And there shall come forth a rod out of the stem of* Jesse, *and a branch shall grow out of his roots, and the spirit of the Lord shall rest upon him, the spirit of wis-*

wisdom and understanding, the spirit of counsel and might, the spirit of knowledge and of the fear of the Lord. Isa. liii. 6. *All we like sheep have gone astray, we have turned every one to his own way, and the Lord hath laid on him the iniquity of us all.* Compar'd with 1 *Pet.* ii. 24. *Who his own self bare our sins in his own body on the tree.* With 1 *Cor.* xv. 3. *Christ died for our sins according to the scriptures.*

IX.

THAT God in his son did freely, without respect to any work done, or to be done by them as a moving cause, elect and choose some to himself before the foundation of the world. *Eph.* i. 3, 4. *According as he hath chosen us in him, before the foundation of the world.* 2 Tim. i. 9. *Who hath saved us, and called us with an holy calling, not according to our works, but according to his own purpose and grace which was given us in Christ Jesus before the world began.* Whom he in time hath, doth, and will call, justify, sanctify and glorify. *Rom.* viii. 29, 30. *For whom he did foreknow he also did predestinate to be conformable to the image of his son, that he might be the first born amongst many brethren. Moreover, whom he did predestinate, them he also called, and whom he called, them he also justified, and whom he justified, them he also glorified.*

X.

THAT those that were thus elected and chosen in Christ, were by nature [before conversion] children of wrath even as others. *Eph.* ii. 3. *Among whom also we all had our conversation in times past in the lusts of our flesh, fulfill-*

fulfilling the desires of the flesh and of the mind, and were by nature the children of wrath, even as others. Rom. iii. 9. *What then? Are we better than they, no, in no wise, for we have before proved both* Jews *and* Gentiles, *that they are all under sin.*

XI.

THAT those that are chosen of God, called and justified, shall never finally fall from him, but being born from above are kept by the power of God through faith unto salvation. *John* vi. 39. *And this is the Father's will which hath sent me, that of all which he hath given me I should lose nothing, but should raise it up again at the last day.* John x. 28. *And I give unto them eternal life, and they sha'l never perish, neither shall any man pluck them out of my hand.* John xi. 26. *And whosoever liveth and believeth in me shall never die.* 1 Pet. i. 5. *Who are kept by the power of God through faith unto salvation.* Psalm lxxxix. 30, 31, 32, 33, 34. *If his children forsake my laws, and walk not in my judgments. If they break my statutes, and keep not my commandments, then will I visit their transgressions with the rod, and their iniquity with stripes. Nevertheless my loving-kindness will I not utterly take from him, nor suffer my faithfulness to fail; my covenant will I not break, nor alter the thing that is gone out of my lips.* 1 John iii. 9. *Whosoever is born of God doth not commit sin, for his seed remaineth in him, and he cannot sin, because he is born of God.* John xiv. 19. *Because I live ye shall live also.* Heb. xii. 2. *Looking unto Jesus the author and finisher of our faith.* Jer. xxxi. 3. *I have loved thee with an everlasting*

lasting love, therefore with loving kindness have I drawn thee. John x. 29. *My Father which gave them me is greater than all, and no man is able to pluck them out of my Father's hand.* Psalm xxxvii. 28. *For the Lord loveth judgment, and forsaketh not his saints: They are preserved for ever.* Jer. xxxii. 40. *And I will make an everlasting covenant.* Rom. viii. 39. *Nor height, nor depth, nor any other creature, shall be able to separate us from the love of God, which is in Christ Jesus our Lord.* 1 Cor. i. 8, 9. *Who shall also confirm you unto the end— God is faithful.* Rom. viii. 30. *Whom he justified, them he also glorified. Being confident of this very thing, that he which hath begun a good work in you, will perform it until the day of Jesus Christ.* Psalm xlviii. 14. *For this God is our God for ever and ever, he will be our guide even to death.*

XII.

That when the fulness of time was come, God sent forth his Son, made of a woman, *Gal.* iv. 4, 5. according to the promises and prophesies of the scriptures; who was conceived in the womb of *Mary* the virgin by the power of the Holy Spirit of God, *Luke* i. 35. *Matt.* i. 20. And by her born in *Bethlehem*, Matt. ii. 11. Luke ii. 6, 7.

XIII.

We believe that Jesus Christ is truly God. *Isa.* ix. 6. *His name shall be called the mighty God.* Heb. i. 8. *But unto the Son he saith, thy throne, O God, is for ever and ever.* Rom. ix. 5. *Who is over all God blessed for ever.* And truly man, of the seed of *David.* 1 Tim.

ii. 5. *There is one mediator between God and man, the man Christ Jesus.* Acts xiii. 23. *Of this man's seed hath God, according to his promise, raised unto* Israel *a Saviour Jesus.* Rom. i. 3. *Made of the seed of* David *according to the flesh.*

XIV.

THAT after he came to be about thirty years of age, being baptized, he manifested himself to be the Son of God, *Luke* iii. 21, 23. with *John* ii. 7, 11. The promised Messiah, by doing such works both in his life and in his death which were proper unto, and could be done by none but the Son of God, the true Messiah. *John* i. 49. *Thou art the Son of God, thou art the king of.* Israel. *John* vi. 9, &c.

XV.

THAT this man Christ Jesus suffered death under *Pilate*, at the request of the *Jews*, Luke xxiii. 24. Bearing the sins of his people on his own body on the cross. 1 *Pet.* ii. 24. *Who his own self bare our sins on his own body on the tree*, according to the will of God. *Isa.* liii. 6. *The Lord hath laid on him the iniquity of us all.* Being made sin for us; 2 *Cor.* v. 11. *For he hath made him to be sin for us.* And so was also made a curse for us, *Gal.* iii. 13, 14. *Christ hath redeemed us from the curse of the law, being made a curse for us.* 1 Pet. iii. 18. *For Christ also hath once suffered for sin,* that we might be made the righteousness of God in him. 2 *Cor.* v. 11. And by his death upon the cross, he hath obtained eternal redemption and deliverance for his church.

Col.

Col. i. 14. *In whom we have redemption through his blood, even the forgiveneſs of ſin.* Eph. i. 7. *In whom we have redemption through his blood, the forgiveneſs of ſins, according to the riches of his grace.* Acts xx. 28. *Feed the church of God, which he hath purchaſed with his own blood.* Heb. ix. 12. *By his own blood he enter'd in once into the holy place, having obtained eternal redemption for us.* 1 Pet. i. 18, 19. *For as much as ye know ye were not redeemed with corruptible things,* &c. *but with the precious blood of Chriſt, as of a lamb without blemiſh and without ſpot.*

XVI.

THAT this ſame Jeſus having thus ſuffered death for our ſins, was buried. *Matth.* xxvii. 59, 60. *And when* Joſeph *had taken the body, he wrapped it in a clean linen cloth, and laid it in his own new tomb, which he had hewen out of the rock, and he rolled a great ſtone to the door of the ſepulchre and departed.* And was alſo raiſed by the power of God. *Eph.* i. 19. *And what is the exceeding greatneſs of his power to us-ward who believe, according to the working of his mighty power which he wrought in Chriſt when he raiſed him from the dead,* the third day according to the ſcriptures. 1 *Cor.* xv. 3, 4. *For I delivered unto you firſt of all that which I alſo received, how that Chriſt died for our ſins according to the ſcriptures, and that he was buried, and that he roſe again the third day according to the ſcriptures.* For our juſtification. *Rom.* iv. 25. *Who was delivered for our offences, and was raiſed again for our juſtification.*

XVII.

THAT after he had been ſeen forty days upon the earth, manifeſting himſelf to his diſciples. *Acts* i. 3. *To whom alſo he ſhewed himſelf alive after his paſſion by many infallible proofs, being ſeen of them forty days.* He aſcended into the heavens. *Acts* i. 9, 10, 11. *And when he had ſpoken theſe things, while they beheld, he was taken up, and a cloud received him out of their ſight: And while they looked ſtedfaſtly towards heaven, as he went up,* &c. *Heb.* iv. 14. *Seeing then that we have a great high-prieſt that is paſſed into the heavens, Jeſus the Son of God.* And is ſet on the right hand of the throne of God. *Heb.* viii. 1. *We have ſuch an high-prieſt, who is ſet on the right hand of the throne of the majeſty in the heavens.* Heb. i. 3. *When he had by himſelf purged our ſin, ſat down at the right hand of the Majeſty on high.* Whom the heavens muſt receive until the time of the Reſtitution of all things. *Acts* iii. 21. *Whom the heavens muſt receive, until the times of the reſtitution of all things, which God hath ſpoken by the mouth of all his holy prophets ſince the world began.*

XVIII.

THAT the Father having thus exalted him, and given him a name above every name. *Phil.* ii. 9. *Wherefore God alſo hath highly exalted him, and given him a name above every name.* And hath made him who is mediator, 1 *Tim.* ii. 5. Prieſt. *Heb.* x. 21. *And having an high-prieſt over the houſe of God.* Heb. viii. 1. *We have ſuch an high-prieſt.* Propher. Acts iii. 22. *A prophet ſhall the Lord*

Lord your God raise up unto you of your brethren, &c. And king to his people. Psalm ii. 6. *Yet have I set my king upon my holy hill of* Zion. *Rev.* xv. 3. *Thou king of saints.* As he is our priest, so is he our peace and reconciliation. *Eph.* ii. 14, 15. *For he is our peace,* Rom. v. 9, 10. *For if when we were enemies, we were reconciled to God, by the death of his son, much more being reconciled, we shall be saved by his life,* &c. And being enter'd into the holy place, even heaven it self, there to appear in the presence of God, *Heb.* ix. 24. Making continual intercession for us. *Heb.* vii. 24, 25. *But this man because he continueth ever, hath an unchangeable priesthood; wherefore he is able also to save them to the uttermost, that come unto God by him, seeing he ever liveth to make intercession for them.* He is become our advocate. 1 *John* ii. 1. *We have an advocate with the Father, Jesus Christ the righteous.* By whom we have boldness and access unto the throne of grace with acceptance. *Heb.* x. 19. *Having therefore, brethren, boldness to enter into the holiest by the blood of Jesus.* Eph. iii. 12. *In whom we have boldness and access with confidence, by the faith of him.* Heb. iv. 16. *Let us therefore come boldly to the throne of grace,* &c. As he is our prophet, so he hath given us the scriptures, the Old and New Testament, as a rule and direction unto us both for faith and practice. *John* v. 39. *Search the scriptures, for in them ye think ye have eternal life, and they are they which testify of me.* 1 Pet. i. 10, 11, 12. 2 *Tim.* iii. 16. *All scripture is given by inspiration of God, and is profitable for doctrine, for reproof, for correction, for instruction in righteousness,* &c. 1 *Pet.* x. 20, 21.

We have also a more sure word of prophesy, whereunto ye do well that ye take heed, as unto a light that shineth in a dark place —— Knowing this first, that no prophesy of the scriptures is of any private interpretation. For the prophesy came not in old time by the will of man, but holy men of God spake as they were moved by the Holy Spirit. Eph. ii. 20. *And are built upon the foundation of the apostles and prophets, Jesus Christ himself being the chief corner stone.* 1 Cor. xiv. 37. *If any man thinketh himself to be a prophet, or spiritual, let him acknowledge that the things that I write unto you are the commandments of the Lord.* Tit. i. 2, 3. *In hope of eternal life, which God that cannot lye promised before the world began, but hath in due time manifested his word through preaching, which is committed unto me, according to the commandment of God our Saviour.* And that he hath sent, doth and will (according to his promise) send his Holy Spirit the Comforter, by whom he leadeth us into all truth. *John* xiv. 26. *But the Comforter, which is the Holy Spirit, whom the Father will send in my name, he shall teach you all things,* &c. John xvi. 13. *Howbeit, when the Spirit of truth is come, he will guide you into all truth.* And by his continual presence with us, and in us. *John* xiv. 16, 17. *And I will pray the Father, and he shall give you another Comforter, that he may abide with you for ever, even the Spirit of truth,* &c. *He dwelleth with you and shall be in you,* teaching, opening and revealing the mysteries of the kingdom, and will of God unto us. 1 *Cor.* ii. 10, 11, 12, 13. *But God hath revealed them unto us by his Spirit, for the Spirit searcheth all things, yea the deep things of God; for*

for what man knoweth the things of a man ſave the ſpirit of man which is in him. Even ſo the things of God knoweth no man, but the Spirit of God; now we have received not the ſpirit of the world, but the Spirit which is of God, that we might know the things that are freely given us of God, which things alſo we ſpeak, not in the words which man's wiſdom teacheth, but which the Holy Spirit teacheth. Rev. ii. 29. *He that hath an ear let him hear what the Spirit ſaith to the churches.* Rev. v. 5. *And one of the elders ſaid unto me, weep not, behold the lion of the tribe of* Judah, *the root of* David, *hath prevailed, to open the book, and to looſe the ſeven ſeals thereof.* Giving gifts in his church for the work of the miniſtry, and edifying the body of Chriſt. *Eph.* iv. 8, 12. *Wherefore he ſaith, when he aſcended up on high he led captivity captive, and gave gifts unto men —— For the perfecting of the ſaints, for the work of the miniſtry, for the edifying of the body of Chriſt.* 1 Cor. xii. 4, 5, 6. *Now there are diverſities of gifts, but the ſame Spirit, and there are differences of adminiſtrations, but the ſame Lord, and there are diverſities of operations, but it is the ſame God which worketh all in all*; that through the powerful teachings of the Lord, by his Spirit in his church, they might grow up in him. *Eph.* iv. 15. be conformed to his will. *Ezek.* xxxvi. 27. *And I will put my Spirit within you, and cauſe you to walk in my ſtatutes, and ye ſhall keep my judgments and do them.* 1 Pet. i. 2. *Elect according to the foreknowledge of God the Father, through ſanctification of the Spirit unto obedience.* And ſing praiſes unto his name. *Heb.* ii. 12. *I will declare thy name unto my brethren, in the midſt of the church will*

I sing praise unto thee. 1 Cor. xiv. 15. *What is it then? I will pray with the Spirit, and I will pray with the understanding also; I will sing with the Spirit, and will sing with the understanding also.* And as he is our prophet, and king, lord, and law-giver. *Isa.* xxxiii. 22. *For the Lord is our judge, the Lord is our law-giver, the Lord is our king.* Isa. lv. 4. *Behold I have given him for a witness to the people, a leader and commander to the people.* Prince of life. *Acts* iii. 15. *And killed the prince of life, whom God hath raised from the dead.* Prince of peace, *Isa.* ix. 6. Master of his people. *Matt.* xxiii. 8. *One is your master even Christ.* Head of his church. *Col.* i. 18. *And he is the head of the body the church.* The Almighty, *Rev.* i. 8. So he hath given rules unto us, by the which he ruleth over us. *Luke* vi. 46. *And why call ye me Lord, and do not the things which I say.* John x. 16. *And other sheep I have, which are not of this fold, them also I must bring, and they shall hear my voice.* 1 John ii. 4. *He that saith I know him, and keepeth not my commandments, is a liar, and the truth is not in him.* John xiv. 15. *If ye love me keep my commandments.* Matt. 28. 20. *Teaching them to observe all things whatsoever I have commanded you.* And ruleth over all things for his church. *Eph.* i. 22. *And hath put all things under his feet, and gave him to be head over all things to the church.* Rev. xix. 16. And by the power of love ruleth by his Spirit in us. 2 *Cor.* v. 14. *For the love of Christ constraineth us.* 1 John ii. 5. *But whoso keepeth his word, in him verily is the love of God perfected.* Making us (in a measure) both able and willing to honour him. *Phil.* iv. 13. *I can*

can do all things through Christ that strengtheneth me. Heb. xiii. 21. *Make you perfect in every good work to do his will, working in you that which is well pleasing in his sight, through Jesus Christ.* Eph. vi. 10. *Finally, my brethren, be strong in the Lord, and in the power of his might.* Phil. ii. 13. *For it is God which worketh in you both to will, and to do of his good pleasure.* And bow before him, *Psal.* xcv. 6. *O come, let us worship and bow down.* Psal. cx. 3. *Thy people shall be a willing people in the day of thy power.* Rev. iv. 10, 11. *The four and twenty elders fall down before him that sat on the throne, and worship him that liveth for ever and ever, and cast their crowns before the throne, saying; thou art worthy, O Lord, to receive glory, and honour, and power.* Submitting our selves to him alone in all his commands with joy. *John* xv. 14. *Ye are my friends, if ye do whatsoever I command you.* Rev. xiv. 4. *These are they which follow the lamb whithersoever he goeth.* Rev. vii. 15. *Therefore are they before the throne of God, and serve him day and night in his temple.* Psal. cxix. 2, 47. *Blessed are they that keep his testimonies, and that seek him with the whole heart —— And I will delight my self in thy commandments which I have loved.* Rev. xv. 3, 4. *And they sung the song of* Moses *the servant of God, and the song of the lamb, who shall not fear thee, O Lord, and glorify thy name, for thou only art worthy.*

XIX.

THAT the Spirit is administred by or through the word of faith preached. *Gal.* iii. 2. *This only would I learn of you? Received ye the Spirit by the works of the law, or by the hear-*

hearing of faith. Which word was first declared by the Lord himself, and was confirm'd by them that heard him. *Heb.* ii. 3. *How shall we escape if we neglect so great salvation, which at the first began to be spoken by the Lord, and was confirmed unto us by them that heard him.* Which word is called the gospel of God's grace, *Acts* xx. 24. The word of reconciliation, 2 *Cor.* v. 19. The sword of the Spirit, *Eph.* vi. 17. The weapon of a Christian, 2 *Cor.* x. 4. A faithful, *Rev.* xxii. 6. Quick, powerful, *Heb.* iv. 12. Plain, *Prov.* viii. 9. Comfortable, *Rom.* xv. 4. Pure, *Psal.* xii. 6. Right, true, *Psal.* xxxiii. 4. Sound, *Tit.* ii. 8. And wholesome word, 1 *Tim.* vi. 3.

XX.

THAT this spirit of Christ, being administer'd by the word of faith, worketh in us faith in Christ, *John* iii. 5. 1 *Pet.* i. 22. *Seeing ye have purified your souls in obeying the truth through the Spirit.* Acts xvi. 14. Gal. v. 22. *The fruit of the Spirit is faith,* &c. *whose heart the Lord opened, that she attended unto the things which were spoken of* Paul. By virtue of which we come to receive our sonship. *John* i. 12. *But as many as received him, to them gave he power to become the sons of God, even to them that believe on his name.* Gal. iii. 26. *For ye are all the children of God by faith in Christ Jesus.* And is further administer'd unto us through faith in the promises of God. *Eph.* i. 13. *Also after that ye believed, ye were sealed with that Holy Spirit of promise.* Acts ii. 38, 39. *Then* Peter *said unto them repent, and be baptized every one of you, in the name of Jesus Christ,*

Christ, for the remission of sins, and ye shall receive the gift of the Holy Spirit. Acts i. 4. *And being assembled together with them, commanded them that they should not depart from* Jerusalem, *but wait for the promise of the Father, which, saith he, ye have heard of me.* Waiting on him in those ways and means that he hath appointed in his word. *John* xiv. 15, 16, 17. *If ye love me keep my commandments, and I will pray the Father, and he shall give you another Comforter, that he may abide with you for ever, even the Spirit of truth.* Luke xi. 9, 13. *And I say unto you ask and it shall be given unto you, seek and ye shall find, knock and it shall be opened unto you —— If ye being evil, know how to give good gifts unto your children, how much more shall your heavenly Father give the Holy Spirit to them that ask him.* This faith being the ground of things hoped for, and the evidence of things not seen, *Heb.* xi. 1.

XXI.

THAT justification is God's accounting and declaring that man justified from the guilt and condemnation of all his sin, who hath received Jesus Christ and doth believe in him (in truth and power) according to the record given of him by God in scripture. *Rom.* iv. 5. *But to him that worketh not, but believeth on him that justifieth the ungodly, his faith is counted for righteousness.* 1 John v. 10, 11. *He that believeth on the Son of God, hath the witness in himself: He that believeth not God, hath made him a liar, because he believeth not the record that God gave of his Son. But this is the record, that God hath given to us eternal life, and this life is in his Son,* Joh. iii. 36.

XXII.

XXII.

THAT justification from the guilt and condemnation of sin is only obtained through faith in that man Jesus Christ, crucified at *Jerusalem*, and by God raised from the dead. *Rom.* v. 1, 9. *Therefore being justified by faith, we have peace with God through our Lord Jesus Christ. Much more being now justified by his blood we shall be saved from wrath through him.* Acts xiii. 38, 39. Rom. iv. 25. *Who was delivered for our offences, and was raised again for our justification.* And, *Chap.* x. 9. *That if thou shalt confess with thy mouth the Lord Jesus, and shalt believe in thine heart, that God hath raised him from the dead thou shalt be saved.* And that those who bring in any other way of justification, do therein make void, and acquit themselves of having any interest in the gospel and grace of Christ. *Gal.*.ii. 21. and v. 4. *Whosoever of you is justified by the law, is fallen from grace.*

XXIII.

THAT this faith being wrought in truth and power, it doth not only interest us in our justification, sonship, and glory, but it produceth as effects and fruits, a conformity, in a measure, to the Lord Jesus, in his will, graces and virtues. *Rom.* v. 3, 4. *And not only so, but we glory in tribulations also, knowing that tribulation worketh patience, and patience experience, and experience hope.* 1 John iii. 23, 24. *And this is his commandment, that we should believe on the name of his Son Jesus Christ, and love one another, as he gave*

us

us commandment, and he that keepeth his commandments dwelleth in him, and he in him, and hereby we know that he abideth in us by the spirit which he hath given us. 2 Pet. i. 5, 6, 7. *And besides this giving all diligence, add to your faith virtue, and to virtue knowledge, and to knowledge temperance, and to temperance patience, and to patience godliness, and to godliness brotherly kindness, and to brotherly kindness charity.* Gal. v. 6. Acts xxvi. 18. 1 Thes. i. 3.

XXIV.

THAT it is the duty of every man and woman, that have repented from dead works, and have faith towards God, to be baptized. *Acts* ii. 38. *Then* Peter *said unto them, repent and be baptized every one of you, in the name of Jesus Christ, for the remission of sins.* Acts viii. 12, 37, 38. *But when they believed* Philip *preaching the things concerning the kingdom of God, and the name of Jesus Christ, they were baptized both men and women —— And* Philip *said, if thou believest with all thine heart, thou mayest, and he commanded the chariot to stand still, and they went down both into the water, both* Philip *and the Eunuch, and he baptized him:* That is, dipped or buried under the water. *Rom.* vi. 3, 4. *Know ye not, that so many of us as were baptized into Jesus Christ, were baptized into his death, therefore we are buried with him by baptism into death.* Col. ii. 12. *Buried with him in baptism.* In the name of our Lord Jesus. *Acts* viii. 16. *Only they were baptized in the name of the Lord Jesus.* Or in the name of the Father, Son, and Holy Spirit.

Spirit. *Matt.* xxviii. 19. *Go ye therefore and teach all nations, baptizing them in the name of the Father, and of the Son, and of the Holy Spirit*; therein to ſignify and repreſent a waſhing away of ſin. *Acts* xxii. 16. *Ariſe and be baptized and waſh away thy ſins.* And their death, burial, and reſurrection with Chriſt. *Rom.* vi. 5. *For if we have been planted together in the likeneſs of his death, we ſhall be alſo in the likeneſs of his reſurrection.* Col. ii. 12. *Buried with him in baptiſm, wherein alſo you are riſen with him through the faith of the operation of God, who hath raiſed him from the dead.* And being thus planted in the viſible church or body of Chriſt, 1 *Cor.* xii. 3. who are a company of men and women ſeparated out of the world by the preaching of the goſpel. *Acts* ii. 41. *Then they that gladly received his word were baptized, and the ſame day there were added unto them about three thouſand ſouls.* 2 Cor. vi. 17. *Wherefore come out from among them, and be ye ſeparate, ſaith the Lord.* Do walk together in communion in all the commandments of Jeſus. *Acts* ii. 42. *And they continued ſtedfaſtly in the apoſtles doctrine and fellowſhip, and in breaking of bread, and in prayers.* Wherein God is glorified, and their ſouls comforted. 2 *Theſ.* i. 11, 12. *Wherefore we alſo pray always for you, that our God would count you worthy of this calling, and fulfil the good pleaſure of his goodneſs, and the work of faith with power, that the name of our Lord Jeſus Chriſt may be glorified in you.* 2 Cor. i. 4. *Who comforteth us in all our tribulation, that we may be able to comfort them which are in any trouble by the comfort*

fort wherewith we our ſelves are comforted.

XXV.

THAT we believe ſome of thoſe commandments further to be as followeth.

1. CONSTANCY in prayer, *Col.* ii. 23, 24.

2. BREAKING of bread, 1 *Cor.* xi. 23, 24.

3. GIVING of thanks, *Eph.* v. 20.

4. WATCHING over one another, *Heb.* xii. 15.

5. CARING one for another, 1 *Cor.* xii. 25. by viſiting one another, eſpecially in ſickneſs and temptations, *Matt.* xxv. 36.

6. EXHORTING one another, *Heb.* iii. 13.

7. DISCOVERING to each other, and bearing one another's burdens, *Gal.* vi. 2.

8. LOVING one another, *Heb.* xiii. 1.

9. REPROVING when need is one another, *Matt.* xviii. 15.

10. SUBMITTING one to another in the Lord, 1 *Pet.* v. 5.

11. ADMINISTRING one to another according to the gift received, whether it be in ſpirituals, or temporals, 1 *Pet.* iv. 10.

12. THE offender to ſeek reconciliation, as well as the offended, *Matt.* v. 23, 24.

13. LOVE our enemies and perſecutors, and pray for them, *Matt.* v. 44.

14. EVERY one to work if he be able, and none to be idle, 2 *Theſ.* iii. 10, 11, 12.

15. THE women in the church to learn in ſilence, and in all ſubjection, 1 *Tim.* ii. 11. 1 *Cor.* xiv. 37.

16. PRIVATE admonition to a brother offending another; and if not prevailing, to take one or two more; if he hear not them,

then to tell it to the church; and if he hear not them, to be accounted as an heathen and publican, *Matt.* xviii. 15.

17. PUBLICK rebuke to publick offenders, 1 *Tim.* v. 20.

18. THE brethren in miniſtring forth their gifts, ought to do it decently and in order, one by one, that all may learn, and all may be comforted, 1 *Cor.* xiv. 31, 40.

19. A SPECIAL care to aſſemble together, that their duty to God, and the church, may not be neglected, *Heb.* x. 24, 25.

20. AND all things in the church, done in the name and power of the head, the Lord Chriſt Jeſus, *Col.* iii. 17.

21. THAT in admitting of members into the church of Chriſt, it is the duty of the church, and miniſters whom it concerns, in faithfulneſs to God, that they be careful they receive none but ſuch as do make forth evident demonſtration of the new birth, and the work of faith with power. *John* iii. 3. *Jeſus anſwered and ſaid unto him, verily, verily, I ſay unto thee, except a man be born again, he cannot ſee the kingdom of God.* Matt. iii. 8, 9. *Bring forth therefore fruits worthy amendment of life.* Acts viii. 37. *And* Philip *ſaid, if thou believeſt with all thy heart, thou mayeſt.* Ezek. xliv. 6, 7. *Let it ſuffice you of all your abominations, in that ye have brought into my ſanctuary, ſtrangers uncircumciſed in heart, and uncircumciſed in fleſh, to be in my ſanctuary to pollute it.* Acts ii. 38. *Then* Peter *ſaid unto them, repent and be baptized every one of you in the name of Jeſus Chriſt.* 2 Cor. ix. 14. *Be ye not unequally yoked together with the unbelievers, for what fellowſhip hath righteouſneſs*

teousness with unrighteousness; and what communion hath light with darkness. Psal. xxvi. 4, 5. *I have not sat with vain persons, neither will I go in with dissemblers: I have hated the congregation of evil-doers, and will not sit with the wicked.* Psalm ci. 7. *He that worketh deceit, shall not dwell within mine house.*

XXVI.

THAT those that truly repent, and believe, and are baptized in the name of the Lord Jesus, are in a fit capacity to exercise faith, in full assurance to receive a greater measure of the gifts and graces of the Holy Spirit. *Acts* ii. 38, 39. *Then* Peter *said unto them, repent and be baptized every one of you, in the name of Jesus Christ, for the remission of sins, and ye shall receive the gifts of the Holy Spirit; for the promise is unto you and to your children, and to all that are afar off, even as many as the Lord our God shall call.* Eph. i. 13. *In whom ye also trusted, after that ye heard the word of truth, the gospel of your salvation, in whom also after ye believed ye were sealed with that Holy Spirit of promise.*

XXVIII. Sic Origin.

THAT it is the duty of the members of Christ in the order of the gospel, tho' in several congregations and assemblies (being one in the head) if occasion be, to communicate each to other, in things spiritual, and things temporal. *Rom.* xv. 26. *For it hath pleased them of* Macedonia, *and* Achaia, *to make a certain contribution for the poor saints which are at* Jerusalem. *Acts* xi. 29. *Then the disciples every man according to his ability determined to send relief unto the brethren which dwelt in* Judea. *Acts* xv. 22. *Then pleased it the apostles and elders, with the whole church, to send chosen men of their own company to* Antioch, *with* Paul *and* Barnabas, *namely* Judas *sirnamed* Barsabas, *and* Silas *chief among the brethren.* Acts xi. 22. *Then tidings of these things came to the ears of the church which was in* Jerusalem, *and they sent forth* Barnabas, *that he should go as far as* Antioch.

XXIX.

THAT the Lord Christ Jesus being the foundation and corner stone of the gospel church whereon his apostles built. *Eph.* ii. 20. *And are built upon the foundation of the apostles and prophets, Jesus Christ himself being the chief corner stone.* Heb. ii. 3. He gave them power and abilities to propagate, to plant, to rule and order. *Matt.* xxviii. 19, 20. *All power is given me in heaven and in earth, go ye therefore, and teach all nations* in his name. *Luke* x. 16. *He that heareth you heareth me, and he that despiseth you despiseth me.* For the benefit of that his body, by which ministry he did shew forth the exceeding riches of his grace, by his kindness towards it in the ages to come, *Eph.* ii. 7. which is according to his promise. *Matt.* xxviii. 20. *And, lo, I am with you alway, even unto the end of the world.*

XXX.

THAT this foundation and miniftration aforefaid, is a fure guide, rule and direction, in the darkeft time of the anti-chriftian apoftacy, or fpiritual *Babylonifh* captivity, to direct, inform, and reftore us in our juft freedom and liberty, to the right worfhip and order belonging to the church of Jefus Chrift. 1 *Tim.* iii. 14, 15. *Thefe things write I unto thee, hoping to come unto thee fhortly; but if I tarry long, that thou mayeft know how thou oughteft to behave thy felf in the houfe of God.* 2 Tim. iii. 15, 16, 17. *All fcripture is given by infpiration of God, and is profitable for doctrine, for reproof, for correction, for inftruction in righteoufnefs, that the man of God may be perfect, throughly furnifhed unto all good works.* John xvii. 20. *Neither pray I for thefe alone, but for them alfo which fhall believe on me through their word.* Ifa. lix. 21. *As for me, this is my covenant with them, faith the Lord, my Spirit that is upon thee, and my words which I have put in thy mouth, fhall not depart out of thy mouth, nor out of the mouth of thy feed, nor out of the mouth of thy feeds feed, faith the Lord, from henceforth and for ever.* Rev. ii. 24. *But that which ye have already, hold faft till I come.* Ifa. xl. 21. *Have ye not known? Have ye not heard? Hath it not been told you from the beginning? Have ye not underftood?* Rev. ii. 5. *Remember therefore from whence thou art fallen, and repent, and do the firft works.* 1 Cor. xiv. 37. *If any man think himfelf to be a prophet, or fpiritual; let him acknowledge that the things that I write unto you are the command-*

ments of the Lord. Rev. i. 3. *Blessed is he that readeth, and they that hear the words of this prophesy.* 2 Thes. iii. 14. *And if any man obey not our word by this epistle, note that man, and have no company with him, that he may be ashamed.* Rev. ii. 11. *He that hath an ear let him hear what the Spirit saith to the churches.* 1 Pet. i. 25. *But the word of the Lord endureth for ever, and this is the word which by the gospel is preached unto you.* 1 John iv. 6. *We are of God, he that knoweth God heareth us: Hereby know we the spirit of truth, and the spirit of error.* 2 Pet. i. 15, 16. *Moreover I will endeavour that you may be able after my decease, to have these things always in remembrance, for we have not followed cunningly devised fables, when we made known unto you the power and coming of our Lord Jesus Christ, but were eye-witnesses of his Majesty.* Isa. lviii. 11, 12. *And they that shall be of thee, shall build the old waste places, thou shalt raise up the foundations of many generations: And thou shalt be called the repairer of the breach, the restorer of paths to dwell in.* 2 Pet. iii. 2. *That ye may be mindful of the words which were spoken by the holy prophets, and of the commandments of us, the apostles of the Lord and Saviour.* Isa. viii. 20.

XXXI.

THAT the church of Jesus Christ with its ministry may from among themselves, make choice of such members, as are fitly gifted and qualified by Christ, and approve and ordain such by fasting, prayer, and laying on of hands. *Acts* xiii. 3. *And when they had fasted and prayed, and laid their hands on them.* Acts xiv. 23. *And when they had ordained*

dained them elders in every church, and had prayed with fasting, they commended them to the Lord, on whom they believed. For the performance of the several duties, whereunto they are called, *Acts* xx. 28. *Rom.* xii. 6, 7, 8. 2 *Tim.* iv. 2. *Acts* vi. 3. *Wherefore brethren, look ye out among you seven men of honest report, full of the Holy Spirit and wisdom, whom we may appoint over this business.*

XXXII.

THAT such a ministry labouring in the word and doctrine, have a power to receive a livelihood of their brethren, whose duty it is to provide a comfortable subsistance for them, if they be able, to whom for Christ's sake they are servants. 1 *Cor.* ix. 4, 7. 1 *Tim.* v. 17, 18. *Let the elders that rule well, be counted worthy of double honour, especially they which labour in the word and doctrine; for the scripture saith, thou shalt not muzzle the mouth of the ox that treadeth out the corn: And the labourer is worthy of his hire.* Yet it is commendable in cases of necessity, for them, for example sake, and that they may be able to support the weak, to labour and work with their hands. *Acts* xx. 24, 25. *Ye your selves know that these hands have ministred unto my necessities, and to them that were with me, I have shewed you all things, how that so labouring ye ought to support the weak, and to remember the words of the Lord Jesus, how he said, it is more blessed to give than to receive.*

XXXIII.

THAT the authority of Chrift in an orderly miniftry in his church, is to be fubmitted unto. *Heb.* xiii. 17. *Obey them that have rule over you, and fubmit your felves, for they watch for your fouls.* 2 Thef. iii. 14. *And if any man obey not our word by this epiftle, note that man, and have no company with him, that he may be afhamed.*

XXXIV.

THAT as it is an ordinance of Chrift, fo it is the duty of his church in his authority, to fend forth fuch brethren as are fitly gifted and qualified through the Spirit of Chrift to preach the gofpel to the world. *Acts* xiii. 1, 2, 3. *The Holy Spirit faid, feparate me* Barnabas *and* Saul, *for the work whereunto I have called them, and when they had fafted and prayed, they fent them away.* Acts xi. 22. *and* viii. 14.

XXXV.

THAT it is the duty of us believing *Gentiles*, not to be ignorant of that blindnefs that yet lieth on *Ifrael*, that none of us may boaft. *Rom.* xi. 25. *For I would not, brethren, that you fhould be ignorant of this myftery, left you fhould be wife in your own conceit, that blindnefs in part is happened to* Ifrael, *until the fulnefs of the* Gentiles *be come in.* But to have bowels of love and compaffion to them, praying for them. *Rom.* x. 1. *Brethren, my hearts defire and prayer to God for* Ifrael *is, that they might be faved.* Expecting their calling, and fo much the rather, because caufe their converfion will be to us life from the dead. *Rom.* xi. 15. *For if the caſting away of them be the reconciling of the world, what ſhall the receiving of them be, but life from the dead.*

XXXVI.

THAT it is the will of the Lord, and it is given to the faints not only to believe in him, but to fuffer for his name. *John* xvi. 13. *In the world ye ſhall have tribulation.* Phil. i. 26. *For unto you it is given in behalf of Chriſt, not only to believe on him, but alſo to ſuffer for his ſake.* And fo to pafs through many tribulations into the kingdom of God. *Acts* xiv. 22. *Confirming the ſouls of the diſciples, and exhorting to continue in the faith, and that we muſt through much tribulation enter into the kingdom of God.* 2 Tim. iii. 12. *Yea, and all that will live godly in Chriſt Jeſus ſhall ſuffer perſecution.* 2 Tim. ii. 12. *If we ſuffer we ſhall alſo reign with him; if we deny him, he will alſo deny us.*

XXXVII.

THAT the angels of the Lord are miniftring fpirits, fent forth for the good of thofe that fhall be the heirs of falvation. *Heb.* i. 14. *Are they not all miniſtring ſpirits, ſent forth to miniſter for them who ſhall be heirs of ſalvation.* Pfal. xci. 11, 12. *For he ſhall give his angels charge over thee, to keep thee in all thy ways, they ſhall bear thee up in their hands, leſt thou daſh thy foot againſt a ſtone.* Acts xxvii. 23. *For there ſtood by me this night, the angel of God, whoſe I am, and whom I ſerve, ſaying, fear not* Paul. Luke xxii. 43. *And there appeared unto him an angel from heaven ſtrengthening him.*

XXXVIII.

THAT the wicked angels. *Pſal.* lxxviii. 49. *He caſt upon them the fierceneſs of his anger, wrath and indignation, and trouble, by ſending evil angels among them.* Kept not their firſt eſtate in which they were created. *Jude* 6. *And the angels which kept not their firſt eſtate, but left their own habitation, he hath reſerved in everlaſting chains.* The prince of whom is called the devil. *Matt.* viii. 28. *And when he was come to the other ſide into the country of the* Gergeſenes *there met him two poſſeſſed with devils.* And the great dragon, and the old ſerpent, and ſatan. *Rev.* xii. 9. *And the great dragon was caſt out, that old ſerpent called the devil, and ſatan.* And the accuſer of our brethren, *Rev.* xii. 10. *And I heard a loud voice in heaven, ſaying, now is come ſalvation, for the accuſer of our brethren is caſt down.* And the prince of this world. *John* xiv. 30. *Hereafter I will not talk much with you, for the prince of this world cometh.* And a prince that ruleth in the air. A ſpirit working in the children of diſobedience. *Eph.* ii. 2. *Wherein in times paſt ye walked according to the courſe of this world, according to the prince of the power of the air, the ſpirit that now worketh in the children of diſobedience.* And our adverſary. 1 *Pet.* v. 8. *Be ſober, be vigilant, becauſe your adverſary the devil as a roaring lion walketh about ſeeking whom he may devour.* Whoſe children the wicked are. *Matt.* xiii. 39. John viii. 44. *The tares are the children of the wicked one, the enemy that ſowed them is the devil.* To him we we ought not to give place, *Eph.* iv. 27. Whose power Christ hath overcome for us. *Heb.* ii. 14. *For as much then as the children are partakers of flesh and blood, he also himself likewise took part of the same, that through death he might destroy him that had the power of death, that is the devil.* And for him and his angels everlasting fire is prepared. *Matt.* xxv. 41. *Then shall he say unto them on the left hand, depart from me ye cursed into everlasting fire, prepared for the devil and his angels.*

XXXIX.

THAT it is our assured expectation, grounded upon promises, that the Lord Jesus Christ shall the second time appear without sin unto salvation, unto his people, to raise and change the vile bodies of all his saints, to fashion them like unto his glorious body, and so to reign with him, and judge over all nations on the earth in power and glory. *Phil.* iii. 20, 21. *For our conversation is in heaven, from whence also we look for the Saviour, the Lord Jesus Christ, who shall change our vile body, that it may be fashioned like unto his glorious body, according to the working whereby he is able even to subdue all things unto himself.* Heb. ix. 28. *And unto them that look for him shall he appear the second time without sin unto salvation.* Acts iii. 19, 20, 21. *That your sins may be blotted out, when the time of refreshing shall come from the presence of the Lord. And he shall send Jesus Christ, which before was preached unto you, whom the heaven must receive until the times of restitution of all things, which God hath spoken by the mouth of all his holy prophets since the world began.*

Matt.

Matt. xix. 28. *And Jesus said unto them, verily I say unto you, that ye that have followed me in the regeneration, when the son of man shall sit on the throne of his glory, ye shall also sit on twelve thrones, judging the twelve tribes of* Israel. *Rev.* ii. 26, 27. *And he that overcometh, and keepeth my works unto the end, to him will I give power over the nations, and he shall rule them with a rod of iron, as the vessels of a potter shall they be broken to shivers, even as I received of my Father.* 1 Cor. vi. 2. *Do ye not know that the saints shall judge the world.* Psal. lxxii. 8, 11. *He shall have dominion also from sea to sea, and from the river unto the ends of the earth; yea, all kings shall fall down before him, all nations shall serve him.* Dan. vii. 27. *And the kingdom and dominion, and the greatness of the kingdom under the whole heaven, shall be given to the people of the saints of the most high: Whose kingdom is an everlasting kingdom, and all dominions shall serve and obey him,* Zach. xiv. 9. *And the Lord shall be king over all the earth. In that day shall there be one Lord, and his name one.* Psal. ii. 8, 9. *Ask of me and I will give thee the Heathen for thine inheritance, and the uttermost part of the earth for thy possession; thou shalt break them with a rod of iron; thou shalt dash them in peices like a potters vessel.* Jer. xxiii. 5, 6. *Behold the day is come, saith the Lord, that I will raise unto* David *a righteous branch, and a king shall reign and prosper, and shall execute judgment and justice in the earth. In his days* Judah *shall be saved, and* Israel *shall dwell safely: And this is his name whereby he shall be called, The Lord our righteousness.* Ezek. xxi. 26, 27. *Thus saith the Lord God, remove the diadem and take off*

off the crown, this ſhall not be the ſame; exalt him that is low, and abaſe him that is high; I will overturn, overturn, overturn it, and it ſhall be no more until he come whoſe right it is, and I will give it him. Iſa. xxxii. 1. *Behold a king ſhall reign in righteouſneſs, and princes ſhall rule in judgment.* Rev. xi. 15. *And the ſeventh angel ſounded, and there were great voices in heaven ſaying, the kingdoms of the world are become the kingdoms of our Lord, and of his Chriſt, and he ſhall reign for ever and ever.* Pſal. lxxxii. 8. *Ariſe, O God, judge the earth, for thou ſhalt inherit all nations.* Rev. v. 9, 10. *And they ſung a new ſong, ſaying, thou art worthy to take the book, and to open the ſeals thereof, for thou waſt ſlain, and haſt redeemed us to God by thy blood, out of every kindred and tongue, and people, and nation, and haſt made us unto our God kings and prieſts, and we ſhall reign on the earth.* Rev. xx. 6. *Bleſſed and holy is he that hath part in the firſt reſurrection, on ſuch the ſecond death hath no power, but they ſhall be prieſts of God, and of Chriſt, and ſhall reign with him a thouſand years.*

XL.

THAT there is a day appointed, when the Lord ſhall raiſe the unjuſt as well as the righteous, and judge them all in righteouſneſs. *John* v. 28, 29. *Marvel not at this, for the hour is coming, in the which all that are in the graves ſhall hear his voice, and ſhall come forth, they that have done good, unto the reſurrection of life, and they that have done evil unto the reſurrection of damnation.* Acts xxiv. 15. *And have hope towards God, which they themſelves alſo allow, that there ſhall be a reſurrection of the dead, both of the juſt and unjuſt.*

(But

(But every man in his own order.) 1 *Cor.* xv. 23. 1 *Thes.* iv. 16. Taking vengeance on them that know not God, and obey not the gospel of our Lord Jesus Christ, whose punishment will be everlasting destruction from the presence of the Lord. 2 *Thes.* i. 7, 8, 9, 10. *Jude* 14, 15. *And* Enoch *also, the seventh from* Adam, *prophesied of these, saying, Behold the Lord cometh with ten thousand of his saints, to execute judgment upon all, and to convince all that are ungodly among them, of all their ungodly deeds, which they have ungodly committed, and of all their hard speeches which ungodly sinners have spoken against him.* Rev. xx. 11, 12, 13, 14. *And I saw a great white throne, and him that sat on it, from whose face the earth and the heavens fled away, and there was found no place for them. And I saw the dead small and great stand before God, and the books were opened, and another book was opened which is the book of life, and the dead were judged of those things which were written in the books, according to their works. And the sea gave up the dead which were in it; and death and hell delivered up the dead which were in them, and they were judged every man according to their works, and death and hell were cast into the lake of fire; this is the second death, and whosoever was not found written in the book of life was cast into the lake of fire.*

XLI.

THAT there is a place into which the Lord will gather all his elect, to enjoy him for ever, usually in scripture called heaven. 2 *Cor.* v. 1. *For we know, that if our earthly house of this tabernacle were, dissolved we have a build-*

building of God, an houſe not made with hands, eternal in the heavens. John xiv. 2,3. *In my father's houſe are many manſions; if it were not ſo I would have told you; I go to prepare a place for you, and if I go and prepare a place for you, I will come again, and receive you unto my ſelf, that where I am there ye may be alſo.*

XLII.

THAT there is a place into which the Lord will caſt the devil, his angels and wicked men, to be tormented for ever, from his preſence and the glory of his power, uſually in ſcripture called hell. *Mark* ix. 43, 44, 45. *And if thy hand offend thee cut it off, it is better for thee to enter into life maimed, than having two hands, to go to hell, into the fire that never ſhall be quenched, where their worm dieth not, and the fire is not quenched. And if thy foot offend thee cut it off, it is better for thee to enter halt into life, than having two feet to be caſt into hell, into the fire that ſhall never be quenched.* Pſalm ix. 17. *The wicked ſhall be turned into hell, and all the nations that forget God.* Matt. xxv. 41. *Then ſhall he ſay alſo to them on the left hand, depart from me ye curſed into everlaſting fire, prepared for the devil and his angels.* Matt. x. 28. *And fear not them which kill the body, but are not able to kill the ſoul; but rather fear him, which is able to deſtroy both ſoul and body in hell.* Matt. xxiii. 33. *Ye ſerpents; ye generation of vipers; how can ye eſcape the damnation of hell.* Luke x. 15. *And thou* Capernaum, *which art exalted to heaven, ſhalt be thruſt*

down

down to hell. Luke xvi. 23. *And in hell he lift up his eyes being in torment.*

XLIII.

THAT it is both the duty and privilege of the church of Christ (till his coming again) in their fellowship together in the ordinances of Christ, to enjoy, prize, and press after, fellowship through and in the Spirit with the Lord, and each with other. *Acts* ii. 42. *And they continued stedfastly in the apostles doctrine and fellowship, and in breaking of bread, and in prayers.* 1 Cor. xi. 26. *For as often as ye eat this bread, and drink this cup, ye do shew the Lord's death till he come.* Eph. ii. 21, 22. *In whom all the building fitly framed, groweth unto an holy temple, in whom also ye are builded together for an habitation of God through the Spirit.* Eph. iv. 3, 4, 5, 6. *Endeavouring to keep the unity of the Spirit in the bond of peace. There is one body, and one spirit, even as ye are called in one hope of your calling, one Lord, one faith, and one baptism, one God and father of all, who is above all, and through all, and in you all.* 1 Cor. xii. 13. *For by one spirit are we all baptized into one body, whether we be* Jews *or* Gentiles, *whether we be bond or free; and have been all made to drink into one spirit. Now ye are the body of Christ and members in particular.* Eph. iii. 9. *And to make all men see, what is the fellowship of the mystery, which from the beginning of the world hath been hid in God, who created all things by Jesus Christ.* Col. ii. 2. *That their hearts might be comforted, being knit together in love, and unto the riches of the full assurance of understanding,*

derstanding, to the acknowledgment of the mystery of God, and of the Father, and of Christ. Which we believe to be attained through the exercise of faith, in the death, resurrection, and life of Christ, 2 *Cor.* v. 14, 15, 16. *For the love of Christ constraineth us, because we thus judge, that if one died for all, then were all dead, that they which live should not henceforth live unto themselves, but unto him which died for them, and rose again, wherefore henceforth know we no man after the flesh, yea though we have known Christ after the flesh, yet now henceforth know we him no more.* Col. ii. 12. *Buried with him in baptism, wherein ye also are risen with him through the faith of the operation of God, who hath raised him from the dead.* Phil. iii. 9, 10, 11. *And be found in him, not having mine own righteousness, which is of the law, but that which is through the faith of Christ, the righteousness which is of God by faith, that I may know him and the power of his resurrection, and the fellowship of his sufferings, being made conformable unto his death; if by any means I might attain unto the resurrection of the dead.* 1 Pet. ii. 5. *Ye also as lively stones, are built up a spiritual house, an holy priesthood, to offer up spiritual sacrifice, acceptable to God by Jesus Christ.*

XLIV.

THAT the ministry of civil justice (being for the praise of them that do well, and punishment of evil-doers) is an ordinance of God, and that it is the duty of the saints to be subject thereunto not only for fear, but for conscience sake. *Rom.* xiii. 1, 2, 3, 4, 5. *Let every*

every soul be subject unto the higher powers, for there is no power but of God; the powers that be are ordained of God, whosoever therefore resisteth the power, resisteth the ordinance of God, and they that resist shall receive to themselves damnation, for rulers are not a terror to good works, but to the evil. Wilt thou then not be afraid of the power, do that which is good, and thou shalt have praise of the same; for he is the minister of God to thee for good; but if thou do that which is evil, be afraid, for he beareth not the sword in vain, for he is the minister of God, a revenger to execute wrath upon him that doth evil; wherefore ye must needs be subject, not only for wrath, but also for conscience sake. 1 Pet. ii. 13, 14. *Submit your selves to every ordinance of man for the Lord's sake, whether it be to the king as supreme, or unto governors, as unto them that are sent by him, for the punishment of evil doers, and for the praise of them that do well.* And that for such, prayers and supplications are to be made by the saints. 1 *Tim.* ii. 1, 2. *I exhort therefore, that first of all, supplications, prayers, intercessions, and giving of thanks, be made for all men; for kings, and for all that are in authority, that we may lead a quiet and peaceable life, in all godliness and honesty.*

XLV.

THAT nothing doth come to pass by fortune or chance, but all things are disposed by the hand of God, and all for good to his people. *Gen.* xlv. 5. *Now therefore be not grieved nor angry with your selves, that ye sold me hither, for God did send me before you to preserve Life*, Gen. l. 20. *But as for you, ye thought evil against me; but God meant it unto good, to bring to pass as it is this day, to save much people alive*, Rom. viii. 28. *And we know that all things work together for good to them that love God, to them that are the called, according to his purpose*, Eph. i. 11. *In whom also we have obtained an inheritance, being predestinated according to the purpose of him, who worketh all things after the counsel of his own will*, Job xiv. 5. *Are not his days determined, the number of his months are with thee, thou hast appointed his bounds which he cannot pass*, Isa. iv. 5, 7. *I form the light, and create darkness; I make peace and create evil; I the Lord doth all these things.*

XLVI.

AND that a church so believing, and so walking, though despised, and of low esteem, is no less in the account of her Lord and King, than though

BLACK, yet comely, *Cant.* i. 5.
FAIREST, without spot, *Cant.* iv. 7.
PRECIOUS, *Isa.* xliii. 4.
BEAUTIFUL, *Cant.* vii. 1.
HOLY, without blemish, *Eph.* v. 27.
PLEASANT, *Cant.* i. 15.
WHOSE soul loveth Christ, *Cant.* i. 7.
RUNNERS after Christ, *Cant.* i. 4.
HONOURABLE, *Isa.* xliii. 4.
THE desire of Christ, *Cant.* vii. 10.
COMPLEAT in Christ, *Col.* ii. 10.
LOVERS of the Father, *John* xvi. 27.
THE blessed of the Father, *Matt.* xxv. 34.
KEPT by the Lord, 1 *Pet.* i. 5. *Isa.* xxvii. 3.

GRAVEN on the palms of his hands, *Isa.* xlix. 16.

TENDER to the Lord as the apple of his eye, *Zach.* ii. 8.

TAUGHT of the Lord, *Isa.* liv. 13.

ONE that hath obtained mercy, 1 *Pet.* ii. 10.

ONE that hath a redemption, *Eph.* i. 7.

THE gates of hell shall not prevail against it, *Matt.* xvi. 18.

IN *that church be glory unto God by Jesus Christ, throughout all ages, world without end.* Amen. *Eph.* iii. 21.

NUMB. IV.

Some parts of a CONFESSION *of* FAITH, *published by certain persons, termed Anabaptists, about the Year* 1611.

HOUGH the Confession of Faith published by seven congregations in *London*, in the year 1644. appears to have been the first that has been put forth by the Calvinistical Baptists; yet there were some who, for their rejecting infant-baptism, were called Anabaptists, that, long before this, published, in certain conclusions, the articles of their Faith. They appear to be such as rejected the grosser errors charged on the Anabaptists, but retained some of the *Arminian* Doctrines.

IT

It came out in the reign of King *James* I. about the year 1611; and in 1614 Mr. *Robinson*, pastor of the *English* church at *Leyden*, printed some remarks upon it, and says it was published by the remainder of Mr. *Smith's* company. We have none of its articles but from him: and he has pick'd out all those passages, which to him appeared either dark or erroneous; and says of the rest, he found it agreeable to the scriptures, so that what we have is only the worst parts of it.

Conclusion 7. That to understand and conceive of God in the mind, is not the saving knowledge of God; but to be like to God in his effects and properties, to be made conformable to his divine and heavenly attributes, this is the true saving knowledge of God, whereunto we ought to give all diligence. 2 Cor. iii. 18. Mat. v. 48. 2 Pet. i. 4.

9. That God, before the foundation of the world, did foresee and determine the issue and event of all his works. Acts xv. 8.

10. That God is not the author or worker of sin; though he did foresee and determine what evil the free will of men and angels would do; yet he gives no influence, instinct, motion or inclination to the least sin.

16. That *Adam* died the same day that he sinned; for that the reward of sin is death: and that his death was loss of innocency, peace of conscience, and comfortable presence. Gen. ii. 17. Rom. vi. 13.

17. That *Adam* being fallen, did not lose any natural power or faculty, which God created in his soul; because the work of the Devil, which is sin, cannot abolish God's works Gen. iii. 23, 24.

works and creatures; and therefore being fallen, he ftill retained freedom of will.

Ezek. xviii. 20. Gen. ii. 17. Heb. xii 9.

18. THAT original fin is an idle term; and that there is no fuch thing as men intend by the word, becaufe God threatned death only to *Adam*, not to his pofterity, and becaufe God createth the foul.

Apoc. xiii. 8.

19. THAT if orginal fin might have paffed from *Adam* to his pofterity, yet is the iffue thereof ftayed by Chrift's death, which was effectual, and he the lamb of God flain from the beginning of the world.

Gen. v. 2, & i. 27. 1 Cor. xv. 49. Rom. iv. 15. —— v. 13. Mat. xiii. 9. Neh. viii. 3. 1 Cor. xv. 49.

20. THAT infants are conceived and born in innocency, without fin, and therefore they are all undoubtedly faved: where there is no law there is no tranfgreffion: now the law was not given to infants, but to them that could underftand.

21. THAT all actual finners bear the image of the firft *Adam* in his innocency, fall, and reftitution, in the offer of grace, and fo pafs under this threefold eftate.

Gen. iii. 8, 15. John iii. 16.

22. THAT *Adam* being fallen, God did not hate him, but love ftill, and fought his good; neither doth he hate any man, that falleth with *Adam*; but that he loveth mankind, and from his love fent his only begotten Son to fave that which was loft.

Ifa. v. 4. Ezek. xviii. 23, 32. and xxxiii. 11. Luke xiii. 6, 9.

23. THAT God never forfaketh the creature till there be no remedy; neither doth he caft away his innocent creature from all eternity; but cafteth away men irrecoverable in fin.

Ezek. xxxiii. 11. Gen. i. 21, 15, 49. and v. 3.

24. THAT as there is in all creatures an inclination to their young, to do them good, fo in the Lord towards man infinitely; who therefore doth not create, or predeftinate any

to destruction, no more than a father begets his child to the gallows.

26. That God hath determined before the world, that the way of salvation should be by Christ, and foreseen who would follow it; and also who would follow the way of infidelity and impenitency. Eph. i. 4, 5. 2 Tim. i. 9. Jude 4.

27. That as God created all men according to his image, so hath he redeemed all that fall by actual sin, to the same end; and that God, in his redemption, hath not swerved from his mercy, which he manifested in his creation. John i. 3, 16. 2 Cor. v. 19. 1 Tim. ii. 6. Ezek. iii. 3 John xvi.

28. God, in love to his enemies, gave Christ to die, and so bought them that deny him. Rom. v. 8. 2 Pet. ii. 2.

30. That Christ is become the mediator of the new covenant, and priest of the church, and hath establish'd this new covenant in his blood.

31. That the sacrifice of Christ's body and blood, offer'd unto God his Father upon the cross, though a sacrifice of sweet savour, and that God be well pleased in him, doth not reconcile God unto us, who did never hate us, nor was our enemy, but reconcileth us unto God, and slayeth the enmity and hatred which is in us against God. 2 Cor. v. 19. Eph. ii. 14, 16. Rom. i. 30.

35. That the efficacy of Christ's death is only derived to them, which mortify their sins, believe, *&c.*

56, 57, and 58. are concerning faith, repentance, and regeneration, and are said to contain these erroneous assertions. That the new creature followeth repentance: That repentance goeth before faith: That man hath power to reject or receive the motions of Luke xiii. 6 Mat. xxiii. 37. Acts vii. 51. and vi. 10.

God's Spirit. That the new creature is part of our Justification before God *.

* *This last sentence is not all in Italic, as those are which are their own words.*

James i. 15. 1 Pet. i. 23. 59. THAT God doth not, in our regeneration, use the help of any creature; nor doth it by the doctrine of faith and repentance, but immediately in the soul.

1 Cor. xiii. 10. 1 John ii. 27. 2 Pet. i. 19. 1 Cor. xi. 26. Eph. iv. 12, 13. 60, 61, 62, 63. THAT the new creature, which is begotten of God, needeth not the outward scriptures, creatures, or ordinances of the church to support him, but is above them; seeing he hath in himself three witnesses, the Father, the Word, and the Holy Ghost; which are better than all scriptures or creatures: though such as have not attained the new creature need them for instruction, comfort, and to stir them up.

64. THAT the outward and visible church consists of penitent persons, and believing only; and that such only are to be baptized.

Rev. i. 10, & xxi. 2, 13, 27 65. THE visible church is a figure of the invisible; and the invisible consists only of the spirits of just and perfect men.

67. THAT there is a root of sin yet abiding in us, which we cannot pluck up out of our hearts.

74. THAT the sacraments have the same use that the word hath, and teach to the eye of them that understand, as the word teaches

Prov. ii. 12. the ears of them that have ears to hear; and that therefore they pertain no more to infants than the word doth.

82. THAT there is no succession in that outward church, but that all the succession is from heaven, and that the new creature only hath

Col. ii. 16, 17 the thing signified, and substance; whereof the

the outward church and ordinances are ſhadows.

83. THE office of the magiſtrate is a permiſſive ordinance of God, &c.

85. THAT Chriſt's diſciples muſt love their enemies, and not kill them; pray for them, and not puniſh them, &c. And Chriſt's diſciples muſt, with him, be perſecuted, afflicted, murder'd, &c. and that by the authority of the magiſtrate.

THAT the magiſtrate is not to meddle with religion or matters of conſcience, nor to compel men to this or that form of religion; becauſe Chriſt is the King and Lawgiver of the church and conſcience. James iv. 12

Laſtly, THAT Chriſtians muſt judge all their cauſes of difference among themſelves; and may not go to law before magiſtrates, nor uſe an oath. 1 Cor. vi. 1,7. Mat. v. 34, 27. James v. 12.

NUMB. V.

The ADDRESS *of the* Anabaptists *to King* Charles II. *before his Restauration, with their* Propositions *annexed, and the* Letter *sent along with it to his Majesty, then at* Bruges, *in the year* 1657-8.

Lord Clarendon's *History of the Rebellion, Folio Edit.* 1719. *Vol.* III. *p.* 359.

To his most Excellent Majesty, Charles *the Second, King of* Great-Britain, France *and* Ireland, *and the dominions thereunto belonging.*

The humble ADDRESS *of the Subscribers, in the behalf of themselves, and many thousands more, your Majesty's most humble and faithful subjects.*

May it please your Majesty,

WHEN we sit down and recount the wonderful and unheard of dispensations of God amongst us; when we call to our remembrances the tragical actions and transactions of these late times; when we seriously consider the dark and mysterious effects of providence, the unexpected disappointment of counsels, the strange and strong convulsions of state, the various and violent motions and commotions of the people, the many changes, turnings and overturnings of governors and governments, which, in the revolution of a few years, have been produced in this land of miracles, we cannot but be even

even ſwallowed up in aſtoniſhment, and are conſtrained to command an unwilling ſilence upon our ſometimes mutinous, and over enquiring hearts, reſolving all into the good will and pleaſure of that all diſpoſing one, whoſe wiſdom is unſearchable, and whoſe ways are paſt finding out.

BUT although it is, and we hope ever will be, far from us, either peeviſhly, or preſumptouſly, to kick againſt the irreſiſtible decrees of heaven, or vainly to attempt, by any faint and infirm deſigns of ours, to give an interruption to that over-ruling divine hand, which ſteers and guides, governs and determines the affairs of the whole world; yet we cannot but judge it a duty highly incumbent upon us, to endeavour, as much as in us lies, to repair the breaches of our dear country; and ſince it is our lot (we may ſay our unhappineſs) to be embarked in a ſhipwreck'd common-wealth (which, like a poor weather beaten pinnace, has for ſo long a time, been toſſed upon the waves and billows of faction, ſplit upon the rocks of violence, and is now almoſt quite devoured in the quickſands of ambition) what can we do more worthy of *Engliſh-men*, as we are by nation, or of *Chriſtians*, as we are by profeſſion, than every one of us to put our hand to an oar, and to try if it be the will of our God, that ſuch weak inſtruments as we, may be in any meaſure helpful to bring it at laſt into the ſafe and quiet harbour of juſtice and righteouſneſs.

TO this undertaking, though too great for us, we are apt to think our ſelves ſo much the more ſtrongly engaged, by how much the more

more we are ſenſible, that as our ſins have been the greateſt cauſes, ſo our many follies and imprudences have not been the leaſt means of giving both birth and growth to thoſe many miſeries and calamities, which we, together with three once moſt flouriſhing kingdoms, do at this day ſadly groan under.

IT is not, the Lord knows, it is not pleaſing unto us; nor can we believe it will be grateful to your Majeſty, that we ſhould recur to the beginning, riſe, and root of the late unhappy differences betwixt your royal father and the parliament. In ſuch a diſcourſe as this, we may ſeem, perhaps, rather to go about to make the wounds bleed afreſh, than tò endeavour the curing of them; yet, foraſmuch as we do profeſs that we come not with corroſives, but with balſoms, and that our deſire is not to hurt but heal, not to pour vinegar, but oil into the wounds, we hope your Majeſty will give us leave to open them gently, that we may apply remedies the more aptly, and diſcover our own paſt errors the more clearly.

IN what poſture the affairs of theſe nations ſtood, before the noiſe of drums and trumpets diſturbed the ſweet harmony that was amongſt us, is not unknown to your Majeſty: That we were bleſt with a long peace, and together with it, with riches, wealth, plenty, and abundance of all things, the lovely companions and beautiful products of peace, muſt ever be acknowledged with thankfulneſs to God, the author of it, and with a grateful veneration of the memory of thoſe princes, your father and grandfather, by the propiti-

ous

ous influence of whose care and wisdom we thus flourished. But as it is observed in natural bodies, idleness, and fulness of diet, do, for the most part, lay the foundation of those maladies, and secretly nourish those diseases which can hardly be expelled by the assistance of the most skilful physician, and seldom without the use of the most loathsome medicines; nay, sometimes not without the hazardous trial of the most dangerous experiments; so did we find it by sad experience, to be in this great body politick. It cannot be denied but the whole common-wealth was faint, the whole nation sick, the whole body out of order, every member thereof feeble, and every part thereof languishing. And in this so general and universal a distemper, that there should be no weakness nor infirmity, no unsoundness in the head, cannot well be imagin'd. We are unwilling to enumerate particulars, the mention whereof would but renew old griefs; but, in general, we may say, and we think it will gain the easy assent of all men, that there were many errors, many defects, many excesses, many irregularities, many illegal and excentrical proceedings (some of which were in matters of the highest and greatest concernments) manifestly appearing as blots and stains upon the otherwise good government of the late King. That these proceeded from the pravity of his own disposition, or from principles of tyranny, radicated and implanted in his own nature, we do not see how it can be asserted without apparent injury to the truth; it being confessed, even by his most peevish enemies, that he was a gentleman, as of the most strong

ſtrong and perfect intellectuals, ſo of the beſt and pureſt morals of any prince that ever ſwayed the *Engliſh* ſcepter. This the then parliament being ſenſible of, and deſirous, out of a zeal they had to the honour of their ſovereign, to diſpenſe and diſpel thoſe black clouds that were contracted about him, that he might ſhine the more glorious in the beauty of his own luſtre, thought themſelves engaged in duty to endeavour to redeem, and reſcue him from the violent and ſtrong impulſes of his evil counſellors; who did captivate him at their pleaſures to their own corrupt luſts; and did every day thruſt him into actions prejudicial to himſelf, and deſtructive to the common good and ſafety of the people: Upon this account, and to this, and no other end, were we at firſt invited to take up arms; and though we have too great cauſe to conclude from what we have ſince ſeen acted, that under thoſe plauſible and guilded pretences of liberty and reformation, there were ſecretly managed the helliſh deſigns of wicked, vile and ambitious perſons (whom though then, and for a long time after, concealed, providence, and the ſeries of things, have ſince diſcover'd to us) yet we bleſs God, that we went out in the ſimplicity of our ſouls, aiming at nothing more but what was publickly owned in the face of the ſun; and that we were ſo far from entertaining any thoughts of caſting off our allegiance to his Majeſty, or extirpating his family, that we had not the leaſt intentions of ſo much as abridging him of any of his juſt prerogatives, but only of reſtraining thoſe exceſſes of government, for the future, which were nothing

thing but the excreſcencies of a wanton power, and were more truly to be accounted the burdens than ornaments of his royal diadem.

THESE things, Sir, we are bold to make recital of to your Majeſty; not that we ſuppoſe your Majeſty to be ignorant of them, or that we take delight to derive the pedigree of our own, and the nation's misfortunes; but like poor wilder'd travellers, perceiving that we have loſt our way, we are neceſſitated, though with tired and irkſome ſteps, thus to walk the ſame ground over again, that we may diſcover where it was that we firſt turned aſide, and may inſtitute a more proſperous courſe in the progreſs of our journey. Thus far we can ſay, we have gone right, keeping the road of honeſty and ſincerity; and having yet done nothing, but what we think we are able to juſtify; not by thoſe weak and beggerly arguments, drawn either from ſucceſs, which is the ſame to the juſt and to the unjuſt, or from the ſilence and ſatisfaction of a becalmed conſcience, which is more often the effect of blindneſs than virtue, but from the ſure, ſafe, ſound, and unerring maxims of law, juſtice, reaſon and righteouſneſs.

IN all the reſt of our motions ever ſince, to this very day, we muſt confeſs, we have been wandering, deviating, and roving up and down, this way and that way, through all the dangerous, uncouth, and untrodden paths of Fanatick and Enthuſiaſtick notions; till now, at laſt, but too late, we find our ſelves intricated and involved in ſo many windings, laberinths, and meanders of knavery,

very, that nothing but a divine clew of thread, handed to us from heaven, can be sufficient to extricate us, and restore us. We know not, we know not, whether we have juster matter of shame or sorrow administer'd to us, when we take a reflex view of our past actions, and consider, into the commission of what crimes, impieties, wickednesses, and unheard of villanies, we have been led, cheated, cousen'd, and betrayed by that grand impostor, that loathsome hypocrite, that detestable traitor, that prodigy of nature, that opprobium of mankind, that landskip of iniquity, that sink of sin, and that compendium of baseness, who now calls himself our protector. What have we done, nay, what have we not done, which either hellish policy was able to contrive, or brutish power to execute? We have trampled under foot all authorities; we have laid violent hands upon our own sovereign; we have ravished our parliaments; we have deflower'd the virgin liberty of our nation; we have put a yoke, an heavy yoke of iron, upon the necks of our own countrymen; we have thrown down the walls and bulwarks of the people's safety; we have broken often repeated oaths, vows, engagements, covenants, protestations; we have betrayed our trusts; we have violated our faiths; we have lifted up our hands to heaven deceitfully; and that these our sins might want no aggravation to make them exceeding sinful, we have added hypocrisy to them all; and have not only, like the audacious strumpet, wiped our mouths, and boasted *that we have done no evil:* But in the midst of all our abominations (such as are too bad to be named amongst

amongst the worst of Heathens) we have not wanted impudence enough to say, Let the Lord be glorified: let Jesus Christ be exalted: let his kingdom be advanced: let the gospel be propagated: let the saints be dignified: let righteousness be established: *Pudet hæc opprobia nobis aut dici potuisse, aut non potuisse refelli.*

Will not the holy one of *Israel* visit? will not the righteous one punish? will not he, who is the true and faithful one, be avenged for such things as these? will he not, nay, has he not already come forth as a swift witness against us? has he not whet his sword? has he not bent his bow? has he not prepared his quiver? has he not already begun to shoot his arrows at us? who is so blind as not to see, that the hand of the Almighty is upon us? and that his anger waxes hotter and hotter against us? how have our hopes been blasted? how have our expectations been disappointed? how have our ends been frustrated? All those pleasant goards, under which we were sometimes solacing and caressing our selves, how are they perished in a moment? how are they withered in a night; how are they vanished and come to nothing? Righteous is the Lord, and righteous are all his judgments. We have sown the wind, and we have reaped a whirlwind; we have sown faction, and have reaped confusion; we have sown folly, and we have reaped deceit; when we looked for liberty, behold slavery; when we expected righteousness, behold oppression; when we sought for justice, behold a cry, a great and a lamentable cry, throughout the whole nation.

EVERY

EVERY man's hand is upon his loins, every one complaining, ſighing, mourning, lamenting and ſaying, I am pained, I am pained! pain, and anguiſh, and ſorrow, and perplexity of ſpirit has taken hold upon me, like the pains of a woman in travail; ſurely we may take up the lamentation of the prophet, concerning this the land of our nativity. How does *England* ſit ſolitary? how is ſhe become as a widow? ſhe that was great amongſt the nations, and princeſs among the provinces, how is ſhe now become tributary? ſhe weepeth ſore in the night, her tears are on her cheeks; amongſt all her lovers, ſhe hath none to comfort her; all her friends have dealt treacherouſly with her, they are become her enemies: ſhe lifted up her voice in the ſtreets; ſhe crieth aloud in the gates of the city, in the places of chief concourſe; ſhe ſitteth, and thus we hear her wailing and bemoaning her condition: is it nothing to you all ye that paſs by? Behold and ſee, if there be any ſorrow like unto my ſorrow, which is due unto me, wherewith the Lord hath afflicted me in the day of his fierce anger. The yoke of my tranſgreſſions is bound by his hands; they are wreathed and come up upon my neck: he hath made my ſtrength to fall; the Lord hath delivered me into their hands, from whom I am not able to riſe up. The Lord hath trodden under foot all my mighty men, in the midſt of me: he hath called an aſſembly to cruſh my young men: he hath trodden me as in a wine preſs: all that paſs clap their hands at me; they hiſs and wag their heads at me, ſaying, Is this the nation that men call the perfection of beauty, the joy

joy of the whole earth? All mine enemies have opened their mouths againſt me; they hiſs and gnaſh their teeth; they ſay, we have ſwallowed her up. Certainly this is the day that we looked for, we have found, we have ſeen it.

How are our bowels troubled? How are our hearts ſadned? How are our ſouls afflicted, whilſt we hear the groans, whilſt we ſee the deſolation of our dear country? It pitieth us, it pitieth us, that *Sion* ſhould lie any longer in the duſt. But alas! what ſhall we do for her in this day of her great calamity? We were ſometimes wiſe to pull down, but we now want art to build; we were ingenious to pluck up, but we have no skill to plant; we were ſtrong to deſtroy, but we are weak to reſtore. Whether ſhall we go for help? Or to whom ſhall we addreſs our ſelves for relief? If we ſay, we will have recourſe to parliament, and they ſhall ſave us; behold, they are broken reeds, reeds ſhaken with the wind, they cannot ſave themſelves. If we turn to the army, and ſay, they are bone of our bone, and fleſh of our fleſh, it may be, they will at laſt have pity upon us, and deliver us; behold, they are become as a rod of iron to bruiſe us, rather than a ſtaff of ſtrength to ſupport us. If we go to him, who hath treacherouſly uſurped, and does tyrannically exerciſe an unjuſt power over us, and ſay to him, free us from this yoke, for it oppreſſeth us, and from theſe burthens, for they are heavier than either we are, or our fathers were ever able to bear; behold, in the pride and haughtineſs of his ſpirit, he anſwers us, you are factious, you are factious: If your burthens are heavy, I will make them yet heavier: If I have hitherto chastised you with whips, I will henceforward chastise you with scorpions.

THUS do we fly like partridges hunted from hill to hill, and from mountain to mountain, but can find no rest; we look this way and that way, but there is none to save, none to deliver. At last we begun to whisper, and but to whisper only, among our selves; saying one to another, why should we not return to our first husband? Surely it will be better with us then, than it is now. At the first starting of this question amongst us, many doubts, many fears, many jealousies, many suspicions did arise within us. We were conscious to our selves, that we had dealt unkindly with him; that we had treacherously forsaken him; that we had defiled our selves with other lovers; and that our filthiness was still upon our skirts. Therefore were we apt to conclude, if we do return unto him, how can he receive us? Or if he does receive us, how can he love us? How can he pardon the injuries we have done unto him? How can he forget the unkindness we have shewn unto him in the day of his distress.

WE must confess (for we come not to deceive your Majesty, but to speak the truth in simplicity) that these cowardly apprehensions did for a while make some strong impressions upon us, and had almost frighted us out of our newly conceived thoughts of duty and loyalty. But it was not long before they vanished, and gave place to the more noble and heroic confiderations of common good, publick fafety, the honour, peace, welfare, and profperity of thefe nations; all which we are perfwaded, and do find, though by too late experience, are as infeparably, and as naturally bound up in your Majefty, as heat in fire, or light in the fun. Contemning therefore, and difdaining the mean and low thoughts of our own private fafety (which we have no caufe to defpair of, having to deal with fo good and fo gracious a prince) we durft not allow of any longer debate about matters of perfonal concernments; but did think our felves engaged in duty, honour and confcience, to make this our humble addrefs unto your Majefty, and to leave our felves at the feet of your mercy: Yet, left we fhould feem to be altogether negligent of that firft good, though fince difhonoured caufe, which God has fo eminently owned us in, and to be unmindful of the fecurity of thofe, who, together with our felves, being carried away with the delufive and hypocritical pretence of wicked and ungodly men, have ignorantly, not malicioufly, been drawn into a concurrence with thofe actions which may render them juftly obnoxious to your Majefty's indignation. We have prefumed, in all humility, to offer unto your Majefty thefe few propofitions hereunto annexed; to which, if your Majefty fhall be pleafed gracioufly to condefcend, we do folemnly proteft in the prefence of Almighty God, before whofe tribunal we know we muft one day appear, that we will hazard our lives, and all that is dear unto us, for the reſtoring, and re-eſtabliſhing your Majeſty in the throne of your Father; and that we will never be wanting, in a ready and willing compliance to your Majeſty's commands, to approve our ſelves

Your Majeſty's moſt humble,

moſt faithful, and moſt devoted

Subjects and Servants,

W. Howard,	*John Wildman,*
Ralph Jennings,	*John Aumigeu,*
Edw. Penkaruan,	*Randolph Hedworth,*
John Hedworth,	*Thomas* ——
John Sturgion,	*Richard Reynolds.*

THE earneſt deſires of the ſubſcribers, in all humility preſented to your Majeſty, in theſe following propoſals, in order to an happy, ſpeedy, and well grounded peace in theſe your Majeſty's dominions:

1. FORASMUCH as the parliament, called and convened by the authority of his late Majeſty, your royal Father, in the year 1640. was never legally diſſolved, but did continue their ſitting until the year 1648. at which time, the army violently and treaſonably breaking in upon them, did, and has ever ſince given a continued interruption to their ſeſſion, by taking away the whole houſe of lords, and ſecluding the greateſt part of the houſe of commons; it is therefore humbly deſired, that (to the end we may be eſta-

eſtabliſhed upon the ancient baſis and foundation of law) your Majeſty would be pleaſed, by publick proclamations, as ſoon as it ſhall be judged ſeaſonable, to invite all thoſe perſons, as well lords as commons, who were then ſitting, to return to their places; and that your Majeſty would own them (ſo convened and met together) to be the true and lawful parliament of *England.*

2. THAT your Majeſty would concur with the parliament in the ratification and confirmation of all thoſe things granted, and agreed unto by the late king your father, at the laſt and fatal treaty in the Iſle of *Wight*; as alſo in the making and repealing of all ſuch laws, acts and ſtatutes, as by the parliament ſhall be judged expedient and neceſſary to be made and repealed, for the better ſecuring of the juſt and natural rights and liberties of the people, and for the obviating and preventing all dangerous and deſtructive exceſſes of government for the future.

3. FORASMUCH as it cannot be denied, but that our Lord and Saviour Jeſus Chriſt, by his death and reſurrection, has purchaſed the liberties of his own people; and is thereby become their ſole Lord and King; to whom, and to whom only, they owe obedience in things ſpiritual: We do therefore humbly beſeech your Majeſty, that you would engage your royal word never to erect, nor ſuffer to be erected, any ſuch tyrannical, popiſh, and anti-chriſtian hierarchy (epiſcopal, preſbyterian, or by what name ſoever it be called) as ſhall aſſume a power over, or impoſe a yoke upon the conſciences of others;

 but

but that every one of your Majeſty's ſubjects may hereafter be at liberty to worſhip God in ſuch a way, form and manner, as ſhall appear to them to be agreeable to the mind and will of Chriſt revealed in his word, according to that proportion, or meaſure of faith and knowledge, which they have received.

4. FORASMUCH as the exaction of tithes is a burthen, under which the whole nation groans in general, and the people of God in particular. We would therefore crave leave humbly to offer it to your Majeſty's conſideration, That, if it be poſſible, ſome other way may be found out for the maintenance of that which is called the national miniſtry; and that thoſe of the ſeparated and congregated churches may not (as hitherto they have been, and ſtill are) be compelled to contribute thereunto.

5. FORASMUCH as in theſe times of licence, confuſion and diſorder, many honeſt, godly, and religious perſons, by the crafty devices, and cunning pretences of wicked men, have been ignorantly and blindly led, either into the commiſſion of, or compliance with many vile, illegal, and abominable actions, whereof they are now aſhamed: We do therefore moſt humbly implore your Majeſty, That an act of amneſty and oblivion may be granted for the pardoning, acquitting, and diſcharging all your Majeſty's long deceived and deluded ſubjects, from the guilt and imputation of all crimes, treaſons, and offences whatſoever, committed or done by them, or any of them, either againſt your Ma-

Majeſty's father, or your ſelf, ſince the begining of theſe unhappy wars; excepting only ſuch who do adhere to that ugly tyrant who calls himſelf protector; or who, in juſtification of his, or any other intereſt, ſhall, after the publication of this act of grace, continue and perſevere in their diſloyalty to your Majeſty. The Letter was as followeth:

May it pleaſe your Majeſty,

TIME, the great diſcoverer of all things, has at laſt unmaſked the diſguiſed deſigns of this myſterious age, and made that obvious to the dull ſenſe of fools, which was before viſible enough to the quick-ſighted prudence of wiſe men, *viz.* That liberty, religion, and reformation, the wonted engines of politicians, are but deceitful baits, by which the eaſily deluded multitude are tempted to a greedy purſuit of their own ruin. In the unhappy number of theſe fools, I muſt confeſs my ſelf to have been one; who have nothing more now to boaſt of, but only that, as I was not the firſt was cheated, ſo I was not the laſt was undeceived; having long ſince, by peeping a little (now and then, as I had opportunity) under the vizard of the impoſtor, got ſuch glimpſes, though but imperfect ones, of his ugly face, concealed under the painted pretences of ſanctity, as made me conclude, That the ſeries of affairs, and the revolution of a few years, would convince this blinded generation of their errors; and make them affrightedly to ſtart from him, as a prodigious piece of deformity, whom they adored and reverenced as the beautiful image of a deity.

NOR did this my expectation fail me: God, who glories in no attribute more than to be acknowledged the ſearcher of the inward parts, could no longer endure the bold affronts of this audacious hypocrite; but, to the aſtoniſhment and confuſion of all his idolatrous worſhippers, has, by the unſearchable wiſdom of his deep-laid counſels, lighted ſuch a candle into the dark dungeon of his ſoul, that there is none ſo blind, who does not plainly read treachery, tyranny, perfidiouſneſs, diſſimulation, atheiſm, hypocriſy, and all manner of villany, written in large characters on his heart; nor is there any one remaining, who dares open his mouth in juſtification of him, for fear of incurring the deſerved character of being a profeſſed advocate for all wickedneſs, and a ſworn enemy to all virtue.

THIS was no ſooner brought forth, but preſently I conceived hopes of being able, in a ſhort time, to put in practice thoſe thoughts of loyalty to your Majeſty, which had long had entertainment in my breaſt; but till now were forced to ſeek concealment under a ſeeming conformity to the iniquity of the times. A fit opportunity of giving birth to theſe deſigns, was happily adminiſtred by the following occaſion:

GREAT was the rage, and juſt the indignation of the people, when they firſt found the authority of their parliameut ſwallowed

up

up in the new name of a protector; greater was their fury, and upon better grounds, when they observed, that under the silent, modest, and flattering title of this protector, was secretly assumed a power more absolute, more arbitrary, more unlimited, than ever was pretended to by any king. The pulpits straightway sound with declarations *; the streets are filled with pasquils and libels; every one expresses a detestation of this innovation by publick invectives; and all the nation, with one accord, seems at once to be inspired with one and the same resolution of endeavouring valiantly to redeem that liberty, by arms and force, which was treacherously stolen from them by deceit and fraud.

* *I suppose it should be declamations.*

When they had for a while exercised themselves in tumultuary discourses (the first effects of popular discontents) at length they began to contrive by what means to free themselves from the yoke that is upon them. In order hereunto, several of the chiefest of the male-contents enter into consultations amongst themselves, to which they were pleased to invite and admit me. Being taken into their counsels, and made privy to their debates, I thought it my work to acquaint my self fully with the tempers, inclinations, dispositions, and principles of them; which (though all meeting and concentring in an irreconcileable hatred and animosity against the usurper) I found so various in their ends, and so contrary in the means conducing to those ends, that they do naturally fall under the distinction of different parties.

Some,

Some, drunk with enthuſiaſms, and beſotted with fanatic notions, do allow of none to have a ſhare in government beſides the ſaints; and theſe are called *Chriſtian Royaliſts*, or *Fifth Monarchy-men*. Others, violently oppoſing this, as deſtructive to the liberty of the free-born people, ſtrongly contend to have the nation governed by a continual ſucceſſion of parliaments, conſiſting of equal repreſentatives; and theſe ſtile themſelves *Common Wealth's-men*. A third party there is, who, finding by the obſervation of theſe times, that parliaments are better phyſick than food, ſeem to encline moſt to *Monarchy*, if laid under ſuch reſtrictions as might free the people from the fear of *tyranny*; and theſe are contented to ſuffer under the opprobious name of *Levellers*: To theſe did I particularly apply my ſelf; and after ſome few days conference with them in private by themſelves apart, I was ſo happy in my endeavours as to prevail with ſome of them to lay aſide thoſe vain and idle prejudices, grounded rather upon paſſion than judgment, and return, as their duty engaged them, to their obedience to your Majeſty. Having proceeded thus far, and gained as many of the chief of them, whom I knew to be leaders of the reſt, as could ſafely be intruſted with a buſineſs of this nature (the ſucceſs whereof does principally depend upon the ſecret management of it) I thought I had nothing more now to do, but only to confirm and eſtabliſh them, as well as I could, in their infant allegiance, by engaging them ſo far in an humble addreſs unto your Majeſty,

jeſty, that they might not know how to make either a ſafe, or an honourable retreat.

I MUST leave it to the ingenuity of this worthy Gentleman, by whoſe hands it is conveyed, to make anſwer to any ſuch objections as may perhaps be made by your Majeſty, either as to the matter or manner of it. This only I would put your Majeſty in mind of, That they are but young proſelytes, and are not to be driven *lento pede*, leſt, being urged at firſt too violently, they ſhould reſiſt the more refractorily.

As to the quality of the perſons, I cannot ſay, they are either of great families, or great eſtates. But this I am confident of, that, whether it be by their own virtue, or by the misfortune of the times, I will not determine; they are ſuch who may be more ſerviceable to your Majeſty in this conjuncture, than thoſe whoſe names ſwell much bigger than theirs, with the addition of great titles. I durſt not undertake to perſuade your Majeſty to any thing, being ignorant by what maxims your counſels are governed; but this I ſhall crave leave to ſay, that I have often obſerved, that a deſperate game at cheſs has been recovered after the loſs of the nobility, only by playing the pawns well; and that the ſubſcribers may not be of the ſame uſe to your Majeſty, if well managed, I cannot deſpair; eſpecially at ſuch a time as this, when there is ſcarce any thing but pawns left upon the board; and thoſe few others that are left, may juſtly be complained of in the words of *Tacitus*, *Præſentia*

&

& tuta, quàm vetera & periculoſa malunt omnes.

I HAVE many things more to offer unto your Majeſty, but, fearing I have already given too bold a trouble, I ſhall defer the mention of them at preſent; intending, as ſoon as I hear how your Majeſty reſents this overture, to wait upon your Majeſty in perſon; and then to communicate that *viva voce*, which I cannot bring within the narrow compaſs of an addreſs of this nature. In the mean time, if our ſervices ſhall be judged uſeful to your Majeſty, I ſhall humbly deſire ſome ſpeedy courſe may be taken for the advance of two thouſand pounds; as well for the anſwering the expectation of thoſe whom I have already engaged, as for the defraying of ſeveral other neceſſary expences, which do, and will every day inevitably come upon us in the proſecution of our deſign. What more is expedient to be done by your Majeſty, in order to the encouragement and ſatisfaction of thoſe gentlemen, who already are, or hereafter may be brought over to the aſſiſtance of your Majeſty's cauſe and intereſt, I ſhall commit to the care of this honourable perſon; who, being no ſtranger to the complexion, and conſtitution of thoſe with whom I have to deal, is able ſufficiently to inform your Majeſty by what ways and means they may be laid under the ſtrongeſt obligations to your Majeſty's ſervice.

FOR

For my own part, as I do now aim at nothing more, than only to give your Majesty a full essay of my zeal for, and absolute devotion to your Majesty; so I have nothing more to beg of your Majesty, but that you would be pleased to account me,

May it please your Majesty, &c.

FINIS.

Index
to all 4 Volumes
is in the back of
Volume 4.

www.ingramcontent.com/pod-product-compliance
Lightning Source LLC
Chambersburg PA
CBHW021812300426
44114CB00009BA/136

* 9 7 8 1 5 7 9 7 8 9 0 1 5 *